Praise for *The End of Love*

"Eva Illouz presents a bleak but fascinating analysis of what the modern world has done to love . . . The great French novelist Honoré de Balzac said he wanted to be the historian of the human heart. The Franco-Israeli sociologist Eva Illouz might be called the historian of human heartbreak."

The Irish Times

"Eva Illouz's work combines theoretical sophistication with a sharp eye for what's essential in contemporary culture. This singular blend has made her an intellectual star of the European world. *The End of Love*, the fruit of twenty years of reflection about the ways in which 21st-century emotions are inevitably bound up with consumer capitalism, will show American readers too why Illouz is one of the most important thinkers of her generation."

Susan Neiman, Director of the Einstein Forum

"*The End of Love* is a provocative new installment in Eva Illouz's two-decades-long interrogation of the relations between the modern idea of love and the cultures of capitalism. As contemporary capitalism thrives on dislocation, disruption, casualness, uncertainty, and precarity, Illouz draws attention to a corresponding morphing of sexual relations and inner life. Our contemporary culture, she shows, is suffused with practices of 'unloving', of quickly forming and dissolving intimate ties in a quest for self-empowerment understood as radical autonomy and the exercise of free choice. Written with passion, insight, and breathtaking scope, it is the best sociological examination of the disorganization of emotional life wrought by the capitalist market, consumer culture, and the paradoxes of freedom."

Gil Eyal, Columbia University

T0048604

The End of Love

The End of Love

A Sociology of Negative Relations

EVA ILLOUZ

polity

Originally published in German as *Warum Liebe endet: Eine Soziologie negativer Beziehungen*

© Eva Illouz 2018
© Suhrkamp Verlag Berlin 2018

All rights reserved by and controlled through Suhrkamp Verlag Berlin

First published in the United States of America by Oxford University Press in 2019
English Translation © Oxford University Press 2019

This edition published by Polity Press 2021

6

Polity Press
65 Bridge Street
Cambridge CB2 1UR, UK

Polity Press
101 Station Landing
Suite 300
Medford, MA 02155, USA

ISBN-13: 978-1-5095-5025-8 (pb)

A catalogue record for this book is available from the British Library.

Printed and bound in Great Britain by TJ Books Ltd, Padstow, Cornwall

The publisher has used its best endeavors to ensure that the URLs for external websites referred to in this book are correct and active at the time of going to press. However, the publisher has no responsibility for the websites and can make no guarantee that a site will remain live or that the content is or will remain appropriate.

Every effort has been made to trace all copyright holders, but if any have been overlooked the publisher will be pleased to include any necessary credits in any subsequent reprint or edition.

For further information on Polity, visit our website:
politybooks.com

To my sons, Netanel, Immanuel, and Amitai
To my mother, Alice,
To my brothers and sister, Michael, Marc, Nathalie, and Ari
with whom the suffix "un" never applies.

Contents

I am just a chronicler, I want my work to be about what it means to be a person living now.

—Marc Quinn[1]

Comprendre qu'être subversif, c'est passer de l'individuel au collectif.

—Abd Al Malik, "Césaire (Brazzaville via Oujda)"[2]

I don't ask people about socialism, I ask about love, jealousy, childhood, old age. [...] This is the only way to chase the catastrophe into the framework of the mundane and attempt to tell a story.

—Svetlana Alexievitch, *Secondhand-Time*[3]

Acknowledgments

After a two decades-long inquiry into the topic of love, I became interested in its frequent handmaiden "unloving," which is all at once a process, a feeling, and an event. "Unloving" is not a topic as exhilarating as "love." But, as I found out, it is one that shows even more acutely and incisively the forces of the social in our psychic life. Many people have helped me think about the nature of these forces.

Chronologically the first, Sven Hillerkamp was a wonderful partner for discussion. Sven's notion of negative modernity has not much in common with my own notion of negative relationships, but his cheerful intelligence was the best soundboard for budding ideas. A large number of people made this text better and helped me all along its writing: Daniel Gilon and his indefatigable energy, rigor, responsiveness, and thoroughness brought this book a few notches higher. Ori Schwarz, Shai Dromi, Avital Sikron, and Dana Kaplan read and offered insightful comments and bibliographical references. I want to thank students and teachers at Yale University, Cambridge University, Harvard University, New York University, Princeton University, EHESS, and fellows at the Institute for Advanced Studies. Some critiques were stinging and hostile, some were sympathetic, but all were helpful. They all made me think harder. I want to thank Paris Sciences Lettres, without whose generous grant in the form of a Chair of Excellence I could not have achieved this project.

I thank mostly John Thompson and the entire team of Polity Press who have saved this book from many shipwrecks.

Finally, and perhaps most importantly, I thank the men and women who shared stories—in formal interviews or in informal conversations—and helped me piece together the ordered landscape of disordered lives. All of the above are reminders that academic and intellectual life is deeply collaborative and that the solitary confinement of writing would not be possible without the bonds of confession and conversation. To all I send my deep thanks.

The End of Love

1

Unloving

Introduction to a Sociology of Negative Choice

[T]o see what is in front of one's nose needs a constant struggle.
—George Orwell, "In Front of Your Nose"[1]

Western culture has endlessly represented the ways in which love miraculously erupts in people's lives, the mythical moment in which one knows someone is destined to us; the feverish waiting for a phone call or an email, the thrill that runs our spine at the mere thought of him or her. To be in love is to become an adept of Plato, to see through a person an Idea, perfect and complete.[2] Endless novels, poems, or movies teach us the art of becoming Plato's disciples, loving the perfection manifested by the beloved. Yet, a culture that has so much to say about love is far more silent on the no-less-mysterious moment when we avoid falling in love, where we fall out of love, when the one who kept us awake at night now leaves us indifferent, when we hurry away from those who excited us a few months or even a few hours ago. This silence is all the more puzzling as the number of relationships that dissolve soon after their beginning or at some point down along their emotional line is staggering. Perhaps our culture does not know how to represent or think about this because we live in and through stories and dramas, and "unloving" is not a plot with a clear structure. More often than not it does not start with an inaugural moment, a revelation. On the contrary, some relationships fade or evaporate before or soon after they properly started, while others end with slow and incomprehensible death.[3] And yet, "unloving" means a great deal from a sociological perspective as it is about the unmaking of social bonds, which, since Émile Durkheim's seminal *Suicide*,[4] we have to understand as perhaps *the* central topic of sociological inquiry. But in networked modernity, anomie—the breakdown of social relationships and social solidarity—does not primarily take the form of alienation or loneliness. On the contrary, *the unmaking of* bonds that are close and intimate (in potentiality or in reality) seems to be deeply connected to the increase of social networks, real or virtual, to technology, and to a formidable economic machinery of advice-giving or help-giving. Psychologists of all persuasions— as well as talk-show hosts, pornography and sex toy industries, the self-help industry, shopping and consumer venues—all of these cater to the perpetual process of making and unmaking social bonds. If sociology has tradition- ally framed anomie as the result of isolation and the lack of proper mem- bership to community or religion,[5] it now must account for a more elusive property of social bonds in hyperconnective modernity: their volatility despite and through intense social networks, technology, and consumption. This book inquires into the cultural and social conditions that explain what has become an ordinary feature of sexual and romantic relations: leaving them. "Unloving" is the privileged terrain to understand how the intersection between capitalism, sexuality, gender relations, and technology generates a new form of (non) sociality.

*

Psychologists have been entrusted with the task of repairing, shaping, and guiding our sexual and romantic life. While they have been, on the whole, remarkably successful in convincing us that their verbal and emotional tech- niques can help us live better lives, they have produced little or no under- standing of what plagues our romantic lives collectively. Surely the myriad stories heard in the privacy of psychological consultation have a recurring structure and common themes that transcend the particularity of their tell- ers. It is not even difficult to guess the recurring theme and structure of the complaints voiced in those settings: "Why do I have difficulties forming or maintaining intimate, loving relationships?" "Is this relationship good or bad for me?" "Should I stay in this marriage?" What is common to the ques- tions endlessly reverberated throughout continual all-invasive therapeutic advice in the form of counseling, workshops, or self-help books used to guide our life is a deep, nagging *uncertainty* about emotional life, a difficulty in interpreting our own and others' feelings, knowing how and what to com- promise about, and a difficulty in knowing what we owe others and what they owe us. As psychotherapist Leslie Bell put it: "[I]n interviews and in my psychotherapy practice with young women, I have found them to be more confused than ever about not only *how* to get what they want, but *what* they want."[6] Such confusion, common inside and outside the office of psychologists, is often taken to be the result of the ambivalence of the human psyche, the effect of a delayed entry into adulthood, or of a psychological confusion produced by conflicting cultural messages about femininity. Yet, as I show in this book, emotional uncertainty in the realm of love, romance, and sex is the direct sociological effect of the ways in which the consumer market, therapeutic industry, and the technology of the Internet have been assembled and embedded by the ideology of individual choice that has become the main cultural frame organizing personal freedom. The type of uncertainty that plagues contemporary relationships is a sociological phenomenon: it did not always exist, or at least not to this extent; it was not as widespread, at least not to this extent; it did not have the content it has today for men and women; and it certainly did not command the systematic attention of experts and knowledge systems of all persuasions. The puzzles, difficulties, and elusiveness that are the characteristics of many relationships and the source of psychological gloss are nothing but an expression of what we may call a generalized "uncertainty" in relations. That so many modern lives display the same uncertainty does not point to the universality of a conflicted unconscious but rather to the globalization of the conditions of life.

This book is another installment in a two-decades-long study on the ways in which capitalism and the culture of modernity have transformed our emotional and romantic life. If there is a single tenet that my work on emotions has advocated for the last twenty years it is that the analysis of the disorganization of private, intimate life cannot come from psychology alone. Sociology has an immense contribution to make in its insistence that psychological experiences—needs, compulsions, inner conflicts, desires, or anxiety—play and replay the dramas of collective life, and that our subjective experience reflects and prolongs social structures, *are*, in fact, concrete, embodied, lived structures. A non-psychological analysis of the inner life is all the more urgent because the capitalist market and consumer culture compel actors to make their interiority into the only plane of existence that feels real, with autonomy, freedom, and pleasure in all its forms as guidelines for such interiority.[7] While we may experience our retreat to individuality, emotionality, and interiority *as* sites of self-empowerment, we are in fact ironically implementing and performing the very premises of an economic and capitalist subjectivity, which fragments the social world and makes its objectivity unreal. This is why a sociological critique of sexuality and emotions is crucial to a critique of capitalism itself.

I bring my inquiry into emotional life, capitalism, and modernity to a preliminary conclusion by engaging more forcefully with *the* question that has been put on the table of liberal philosophy since the nineteenth century: does freedom jeopardize the possibility of forming meaningful and binding bonds, more specifically romantic bonds? In its general form, this question has been insistently asked for the last two hundred years, in the context of the demise of community and the rise of market relations,[8] but has been less frequently raised in the emotional realm, and this despite the fact that emotional freedom has entirely redefined the nature of subjectivity and intersubjectivity and is no less central to modernity than other forms of freedom. Nor is it less fraught with ambiguities and aporias.

Love as Freedom

Love—the quintessentially fusional emotion—paradoxically contains a fragment of the vast and complex history of autonomy and freedom, a history that has been told mostly in political terms. To take one example, the genre of the romantic comedy—which emerged with the Greek Menander, continued with the Romans (the plays of Plautus or Terence), and flourished in the Renaissance—expressed the claim to freedom by young people against parents, tutors, and old men. While in India or China love was told in stories shaped by religious values, was part and parcel of the life of gods, and did not as such oppose social authority, in Western (and to a relative but lesser extent Eastern) Europe and in the United States, love progressively detached itself from the religious cosmology and was cultivated by aristocratic elites in search of a life-style.[9] As a result, love, previously destined for God,[10] was the main vector for the formation of emotional individualism,[11] directing emotions to a person whose interiority is perceived as independent from social institutions. Love slowly affirmed itself against rules of endogamy, against patriarchal or Church authority, and against community control. An eighteenth-century bestseller like *Julie ou la Nouvelle Héloïse* (1761) raised the question of the individual's right to his or her sentiments, and thus the right to choose the object of his or her love and to marry according to one's will. Interiority, freedom, emotions, and choice formed a single matrix, which would revolutionize matrimonial practices and the place of marriage. Will, in this new cultural and emotional order, was no longer defined as the capacity to regulate one's desires (as in Christian religiosity), but precisely as the opposite capacity to act according to their injunction, and to choose an object that corresponded to individual emotions as emanating from one's will. In that respect, in the personal realm romantic love and emotions became the ground for moral claims to freedom and autonomy, as powerful as these would be in the public and male realm of politics, with the exception that this revolution did not have its public demonstrations, Parliament bills, and physical struggles. It was led by novelists, proto-feminists, philosophers, and thinkers on sexuality as well as by ordinary men and women. The claim to emotional autonomy contained in love was a powerful agent of social change, altering in fundamental ways the process of pairing up, the vocation of marriage, and the authority of traditional social agencies.[12] And thus, while seemingly private and emotional, romantic love in fact contained a proto-political aspiration. The right to choose one's object of love became slowly the right to make individuals' feelings be their own source of authority,[13] itself an important part of the history of autonomy. The history of love in the West is thus not just a minor theme in the large-scale fresco of the history of modernity but was in fact a principal vector recasting the relationship of individuals to marriage and kinship, with dramatic consequences for the relationship that marriage had hitherto entertained with the economic sphere. Bestowing moral authority to love and sentiments changed marriage, and in changing marriage it changed patterns of reproduction and sexuality, of economic accumulation and exchange.[14]

What we call emotional and personal freedom is a multiform phenomenon that emerged with the consolidation of a private sphere, far away from the long arm of the community and the Church, and slowly became protected by the state and by privacy laws; it fed into the cultural upheavals spearheaded by artistic elites and later by media industries; and finally, it helped formulate women's rights to dispose of their bodies (a woman's body had not belonged to her but more properly to her guardians). Emotional autonomy thus contains claims about the freedom of the interiority of the subject as well as (later) claims to sexual-bodily freedom even if both types of freedoms have different cultural histories: emotional freedom is grounded in the history of freedom of conscience and in the history of privacy, while sexual freedom evolved from the history of women's struggle for emancipation and from new legal conceptions of the body. Women indeed did not properly own their bodies until recently (they could not, for example, refuse the sexual act to their husband). Sexual and emotional freedom became closely intertwined, the two becoming handmaidens of each other under the broad category of libertarian self-ownership: "The libertarian principle of self-ownership says that each person enjoys, over herself and her powers, full and exclusive rights of control and use, and therefore owes no service or product to anyone else that she has not contracted to supply."[15] More concretely, the libertarian principle of self-ownership includes freedom to have and own one's feelings and the freedom to own and control one's body that would later entail the freedom to choose one's sexual partners and to enter and exit relationships at will. In short, self-ownership includes the conduct of one's emotional and sexual life from within the space of one's interiority, without hindrance from the external world, thus letting emotions, desires, or subjectively defined goals determine one's choices and experiences. Emotional freedom is a particular form of self-ownership in which emotions guide and justify the freedom to have physical contact and sexual relations with a person of one's emotional choosing. This form of emotional and bodily self-ownership marks the shift to what I suggest calling "emotional modernity." Emotional modernity was in the making from the eighteenth century onward, but became fully realized after the 1960s in the cultural legitimation of sexual choice based on purely subjective emotional and hedonic grounds and has observed yet a new development with the advent of Internet sexual and romantic apps.

Anthony Giddens was one of the first sociologists to make explicit the nature of emotional modernity, viewing intimacy as the ultimate expression of individuals' freedom, of his or her progressive unmooring from older frames of religion, tradition, and from marriage as a framework for economic survival.[16] For Giddens, individuals have the resources to shape from within themselves the capacity to be autonomous and intimate at once. The price to be paid for this, according to him, is a state of "ontological insecurity," a permanent anxiety. But on the whole his much-discussed concept of "pure relationship" was a descriptive and normative endorsement of modernity, since it suggested that intimacy enacted the core values of the modern liberal subject as being aware of her and his rights, able to implement these rights, most notably in the capacity to enter and exit close relationships at will through an implicit contract. For Giddens the subject entering the pure relationship is free, knowledgeable about his or her needs, and able to negotiate with another on such needs. The pure relationship was the liberal social contract writ large. In a resonant vein, for Axel Honneth (and Hegel before him), freedom comes to its realization through a relationship to another.[17] Freedom is thus the normative ground for love and the family, with the family becoming the very expression of freedom realized in a caring unit. Thus, both Giddens and Honneth complexify the traditional model of liberalism in which the self views the other as an obstacle to one's freedom: for both thinkers the free self comes to its full realization through love and intimate relationships.

But as this book is set to show, this model of freedom raises new questions. Intimacy is no longer—if it ever was—a process of two fully aware subjects entering a contract the terms of which they both know and agree on. Rather, the very possibility of drawing a contract, of knowing its terms, of knowing and agreeing on the procedures to enforce it has become distressingly elusive. For a contract to be entered into, there must be an agreement on its terms; it presupposes a clearly defined will, aware of what it wants; it entails a procedure to enter into an agreement, and a penalty in case one of the two signatories defaults. Finally, by definition, a contract includes clauses against surprises. These conditions for contract-based relationships are hardly present in contemporary relationships.

The institutionalization of sexual freedom via consumer culture and technology has had an opposite effect: it has made the substance, frame, and goal of sexual and emotional contracts fundamentally uncertain, up for grabs, incessantly contested, making the metaphor of contract highly inadequate to grasp what I call the negative structure of contemporary relationships—the fact that actors do not know how to define, evaluate, or conduct the relationship they enter into according to predictable and stable social scripts. Sexual and emotional freedom have made the very possibility of defining the terms of a relationship into an open-ended question and a problem, at once psychological and sociological. Not contractual logic but a generalized, chronic and structural uncertainty now presides over the formation of sexual or romantic relations. While we have commonly assumed that sexual and emotional freedoms mirror each other, that they sustain and reflect each other, this book casts a doubt on this assumption and begs to suggest that emotional and sexual freedom follow different institutional and sociological paths. Sexual freedom is nowadays a realm of interaction where "things run smoothly": actors dispose of a large abundance of technological resources and cultural scripts and images to guide their behavior, to find pleasure in an interaction, and to define the boundaries of the interaction. Emotions, however, have become the plane of social experience that "poses a problem," a realm where confusion, uncertainty, and even chaos reign.

In tackling sexual freedom through the question of the emotional experiences it generates or does not generate, this study hopes to skirt altogether the conservative lament on sexual freedom and the libertarian view that freedom trumps all other values. Instead, it will engage critically with the meaning of emotional and sexual freedom by exploring empirically its impact on social relationships. Whether endorsed or condemned, freedom has an institutional structure, which in turn transforms self-understandings and social relations. This impact must be examined by suspending a priori assumptions about the merits of monogamy, virginity, the nuclear family, of multiple orgasms, and group or casual sex.

The Malaise with a Critique of Freedom

Such inquiry is bound to generate unease or resistance from a number of intellectual quarters. The first comes from sexual libertarians for whom to criticize (sexual) freedom is tantamount to being in a "reactionary phase of hysterical moralism and prudery"—to quote Camille Paglia's stern condemnation.[18] However, this position is itself equivalent to the claim that a critique of economic freedom and deregulation is a return to a hysterical desire to build kolkhozes. The critique of freedom has been the prerogative of conservatives as much as of emancipatory scholars and nothing about it calls for a return to moral prudery, shaming, and double standard. The critical examination of the current state of emotional and sexual freedom is in fact a return to the core questions of classical sociology: What is the fault line between freedom and anomie?[19] When does freedom end and amoral chaos start? In that sense, my inquiry about the social and emotional impact of sexual freedom here marks a return to the core of Durkheim's questions on social order and anomie: I interrogate how the intrusion of capitalism in the private sphere has transformed and disrupted core normative principles of that sphere.

A second objection can come from various academic disciplines such as cultural studies, queer studies, and gender studies that have traditionally been preoccupied with disenfranchisement, thus implicitly or explicitly making freedom the supreme value orienting their scholarship. As Axel Honneth correctly claims: for moderns, freedom trumps most or all values, including equality and justice.[20] All in their different styles, libertarian feminists and gay activists (especially the pro-porn activists and scholars), literary scholars and philosophers, have viewed freedom as the most vulnerable of all goods and have thus been reluctant to focus on its pathologies, except when it takes the form of the tired critique of neo-liberalism or when it refers to "narcissism" or "utilitarian hedonism" fostered by the consumer market. To this reluctance one may offer two different types of responses. The first has been very well formulated by Wendy Brown: "Historically, semiotically, and culturally protean, as well as politically elusive, freedom has shown itself to be easily appropriated in liberal regimes for the most cynical and un-emancipatory political ends."[21] If that is the case, then freedom is a social arrangement we should always be eager *both to preserve and to question.* The second response to the objection follows from the first and is method-ological. Relying on David Bloor's principle of symmetry—examining dif-ferent phenomena in a symmetrical way without presuming to know who is good or bad, victor or loser—we may suggest that freedom should be exam-ined critically in a symmetrical way in both the economic and the interper-sonal realms.[22] If we, critical scholars, analyze the corrosive effects of freedom in the realm of economic action, there is no reason not to inquire about these effects in the personal, emotional, and sexual realms. The neo-con celebration of markets and political freedom and the seemingly progressive celebration of sexual freedom should be equally scrutinized not in the name of neutrality as Richard Posner demands in his study of *Sex and Reason,*[23] but in the name of a more encompassing view of the effects of freedom.[24] The principle of symmetry is relevant in yet another respect: critiques of the current sexualization of culture come from several cultural quarters—from movements for a-sexuality that reject the centrality of sexuality in defini-tions of healthy selves; from feminists and psychologists worried about the effects of the sexualization of culture; and finally from Christian majorities and (mostly Muslim) religious minorities living in Europe and in the United States. All these critiques are uneasy about the intensity of the sexualization of culture. Feminist scholars are the only ones who have paid attention to this unease, and anthropologists like Leila Abu-Lughod and Saba Mahmood have criticized Eurocentric models of sexual emancipation from the stand-point of the subjectivity of Muslim women,[25] inviting us to imagine other forms of sexual and emotional subjectivities. The critical examination of sexuality in this book does not stem from a puritan impulse to control or regulate it (I do not have such program in mind), but rather from a desire to historicize and contextualize our beliefs about sexuality and love, and to understand what in the cultural and political ideals of sexual modernity may have been hijacked or distorted by economic and technological forces that conflict with emotional ideals and norms held as essential for love. If this work is traversed by an implicit norm, it is that love (in all its forms) remains the most meaningful way to form social relationships.

A final possible objection to my query has to do with the looming presence of the work of Michel Foucault in the human and social sciences. His *Discipline and Punish*,[26] has been widely influential, spreading the suspicion that democratic freedom was a ploy to mask the processes of surveillance and disciplining entailed by new forms of knowledge and control of human beings. Sociologists devoted their attention to surveillance and viewed, à la Foucault, freedom as a liberal illusion, undergirded by a powerful system of discipline and control. In that sense, freedom as such was a less interesting object of study than the illusion of subjectivity that freedom creates. Yet, at the end of his life, in his *Cours* at the *Collège de France*, Foucault increasingly paid attention to the relationship between freedom and governmentality, that is, to the ways in which the idea of freedom in the market had redefined, in his words, a field of action.[27] My book subscribes to the late work of Foucault from the standpoint of a cultural sociology of emotions.[28] It views freedom as indeed a restructuring of a field of action, as the most powerful and widespread cultural frame organizing the sense of morality, conception of education and relationships, the fundaments of our law, visions and practices of gender, and, more broadly, the basic definition of selfhood of modern people. For a sociologist of culture, freedom is not a moral and political ideal upheld by courts, but represents an enduring, deep, and widespread cultural frame organizing modern people's self-definition and relationship to others. As a value relentlessly harbored by individuals and institutions, it orients a myriad of cultural practices, the most salient of which is perhaps that of sexual subjectivity defined as "a person's experience of herself as a sexual being, who feels entitled to sexual pleasure and sexual safety, who makes active sexual choices, and who has an identity as a sexual being."[29] Where Foucault debunked sexuality as a modern practice of self-emancipation ironically perpetuating the Christian cultural obsession with sex, I focus on another question: how does sexual freedom, expressed in consumer and technological practices, reshape the perception and practice of romantic relations, at their beginning, in their formation, and during shared domestic life?

The question of freedom has become even more pressing as the public philosophy and legal organization of liberal polities has privileged one specific type of liberty, namely negative liberty—defined as the freedom of actors to do what they please without hindrance from the external world, as long as they do not hurt others or obstruct their freedom. Such freedom is guaranteed by law and cultivated by many institutions supposed to guarantee one's rights and privacy and that contain little or no normative content. It is the "emptiness" of negative freedom that has created a space (the space of "non-hindrance") that could be easily colonized by the values of the capitalist market, consumer culture, and technology, which have become the most powerful institutional and cultural arenas of modern societies. As Karl Marx remarked long ago, freedom contains the risk of letting inequalities flourish unhindered. Catharine MacKinnon drives this point aptly: "[T]o privilege freedom before equality, freedom before justice, will only further liberate the power of the powerful."[30] Freedom then cannot trump equality, because inequality vitiates the possibility of being free. If heterosexuality organizes and naturalizes inequality between the sexes, we can expect freedom to meet, confront, or naturalize such inequality. Only rarely does freedom trump inequality in heterosexual relationships.

What Isaiah Berlin called "negative freedom" has let the language and the practices of the consumer market reshape the vocabulary and grammar of subjectivity. The same language of interests, utilitarianism, instant satisfaction, ego-centered action, accumulation, variety, and diversity of experiences now pervades romantic and sexual bonds and thus demands from us a sobering inquiry into the meaning and impact of freedom, without, however, ever putting into question the moral progress that the struggles of feminist and LGBTQ movements represent. To endorse the historical accomplishments of these movements and to continue their struggle should not prevent us from examining the ways in which the moral ideal of freedom has been deployed historically and empirically in market forms, which also appeal to freedom.[31] In fact, understanding how ideas and values, once institutionalized, have a trajectory that is not always the one intended by their proponents will help reclaim the initial ideal of freedom, which was the impulse behind these movements. Thus if neoliberalism has notoriously entailed a demise of normativity in economic transactions (transforming public institutions into profit-making organizations and turning self-interest into the natural epistemology of the actor), there is no reason not to ask whether sexual freedom does not have similar effects on intimate relationships, that is, whether they do not mark a demise of normativity in naturalizing self-centered pleasure and instituting sexual competition and sexual accumulation, thereby letting relationships go unregulated by moral and ethical codes. In other words, has sexual freedom become the neoliberal philosophy of the private sphere,[32] a discourse and practice that melts away the normativity of relations, naturalizes the consumer ethic and technology as a new form of emotional self-organization, and makes the normative and moral core of intersubjectivity less intelligible? While freedom itself has been a powerful normative claim to oppose the institution of forced or loveless marriages, to assert the right for divorce, to conduct one's sexual and emotional life according to one's inclinations, to grant equality to all sexual minorities, we may wonder if today that same freedom has not unmoored sexual relations from the moral language in which it was initially steeped (for example by disposing of the language of obligation and reciprocity in which all or at least most social interactions had been traditionally organized). In the same way that contemporary monopolistic capitalism contradicts the spirit of free exchange that was at the center of early conceptions of the market and commerce, a sexual subjectivity tightly organized by consumer and technological culture conflicts with the vision of emancipated sexuality, which was at the heart of the sexual revolution, because such sexuality ends up reproducing, compulsively, the very schemes of thought and action that make technology and economy the invisible movers and shapers of our social bonds.

Heterosexuality is a more privileged terrain from which to study this question than homosexuality for a number of reasons. In its present form, heterosexuality is based on gender differences, which more often than not function as gender inequalities; heterosexuality in turn organizes these inequalities in an emotional system that places the burden of success or failure in relationships on people's psyche, mostly women's. Freedom makes emotional inequalities go undetected and unaddressed. Men and women, but mostly women, turn to their psyche in order to manage the symbolic violence and wounds contained in such emotional inequalities: "Why is *he* distant?" "Am I acting too needy?" "What should I do to catch him?" "What mistakes did I do to let him go?" All these questions, asked for women and by women, point to the fact that heterosexual women feel culturally largely responsible for the emotional success and management of relationships. In contrast, homosexuality does not translate gender into difference and difference into inequality, nor is it based on the gender division between biological and economic labor that has characterized the heterosexual family. In that sense, the study of the effect of freedom on heterosexuality is sociologically more urgent: because it interacts with the still-pervasive and powerful structure of gender inequality, sexual freedom makes heterosexuality ridden with contradictions and crisis.[33] Moreover, because heterosexuality was closely regulated and codified by the social system of courtship supposed to lead to marriage, the shift to emotional and sexual freedom enables us to grasp in a crisper way the impact of freedom on sexual practices and the contradiction such freedom may have created with the institution of marriage (or partnership) that remains at the heart of heterosexuality. In contrast, homosexuality was, until recently, a clandestine and oppositional social form. For that reason, it was *ab origine* defined as a practice of freedom, conflicting and opposing the domestic institution of marriage, which used and alienated women and ascribed men to patriarchal roles. This book then is an ethnography of contemporary heterosexuality (although I occasionally interviewed homosexuals as well), which, as a social institution, has been under the push-and-pull of forces at once emancipatory and reactionary, modern and traditional, subjective and reflective of the capitalist, consumerist, and technological forces of our society.

My approach to emotional and sexual freedom contrasts with various forms of libertarianism for which pleasure constitutes a final telos of experience and for which the astounding expansion of sexuality in all walks of consumer culture is the welcome sign that—in Camille Paglia's trenchant words—popular culture (and its sexual content) is "an eruption of the never-defeated paganism of the West."[34] For sexual libertarians, sexuality mediated by consumer market frees sexual desire, energy, and creativity, and calls on feminism (and presumably other social movements) to open themselves up to "art and sex in all their dark, unconsoling mysteries."[35] Such a view is seductive but it rests on the naive assumption that the market forces that drive popular culture in fact channel and coincide with primary creative energy, rather than, for example, spread the economic interests of large corporations seeking to encourage a subjectivity based on the quick satisfaction of needs. I can see no convincing reason to assume that the energies tapped into by the market are more naturally "pagan" than they are, for example, reactionary, conformist, or confused. As a prominent queer theorist put it, Margaret Thatcher and Ronald Reagan, who advocated family values, actually enabled the greatest sexual revolution in their neoliberal policies, which deregulated markets.[36] "Individual freedom cannot stop at the market; if you have an absolute freedom to buy and sell, there seems to be no logic in blocking your sexual partners, your sexual lifestyle, your identity or your fantasies."[37]

Choice

Rather than being the expression of raw pagan energy freed by amoral popular cultures, contemporary sexuality is the vector for a number of social forces, which undermine the values that animated the struggle for sexual emancipation. Sexuality has become the site of psychological human techniques, of technology and the consumer market, which have in common the fact that they both provide a grammar of freedom that organizes and translates *desire* and interpersonal relations into a sheer matter of individual *choice*. Choice—sexual, consumer, or emotional—is the chief trope under which the self and the will in liberal polities are organized. To have a modern or late-modern self is to exercise choice and to increase the subjective experience of choice.

Choice is the trope of selfhood linking freedom to the economic and emotional realms; it is the main modality of subjectivity in the consumer and sexual realms. Choice contains two separate ideas: one refers to the supply of goods, namely that something exists objectively in large supply (as in "this supermarket supplies a large choice of fresh organic vegetables"), while the second touches on a property of subjectivity, as when an individual faced with possibilities makes a decision also called choice (as in "she made the right choice"). Choice then expresses both a certain organization of the world, which presents itself as an assorted set of possibilities encountered by the subject in a direct, unmediated way, and an organization of the will into wants, emotions, and desires. A choosing will is a specific kind of deliberative *will*, facing a world that seems to be structured like a market, that is, as a set of abundant possibilities, which the subject must seize and choose in order to satisfy and maximize his or her well-being, pleasure, or profit. From the standpoint of a sociology of culture, choice represents the best way to understand how the formidable structure of the market translates into cognitive and emotional properties of action. The specific will entailed by a culture of choice has considerably changed under the impact of technology and consumer culture, compelling us to ask sociological questions about the relationship between the economy of desire and traditional social structures.

This book explores then the following line of argument: Under the aegis of sexual freedom, heterosexual relationships have taken the form of a market—the direct encounter of emotional and sexual supply with emotional and sexual demand.[38] Both—supply and demand—are heavily mediated by objects and spaces of consumption and by technology (chapter 2). Sexual encounters organized as a market are experienced both as choice and uncertainty. By letting individuals negotiate themselves the conditions of their encounter with only very few regulations or prohibitions, this market-form creates a widespread and pervasive cognitive and emotional *uncertainty* (chapter 3). The concept of the "market" is not here simply an economic metaphor, but is the social form taken by sexual encounters that are driven by Internet technology and consumer culture. When people meet on an open market, they meet each other directly with no or little human mediators; they do it through technologies that aim at increasing the efficiency of the search for a mate; they do it using scripts of exchange, time efficiency, hedonic calculus, and a comparative mindset, all characteristic of advanced capitalist exchange. A market is open-ended in the sense that it is a social form governed by supply and demand, themselves structured by social networks and social positions of actors. Sexual exchange located on a market leaves women in an ambivalent position: at once empowered and demeaned through their sexuality (see chapter 4), an ambivalence that points to the ways in which consumer capitalism works through empowerment. The nexus of sexual freedom-consumer culture-technology and a still-powerful male domination in the sexual arena undermines the possibility of entering and forming what had been the main social form assumed by the market and marriage, namely the contract (chapter 5). Leaving relationships, being unable or unwilling to enter a relationship, moving from one relationship to another—what I put under the broad term of unloving—are part and parcel of this new market-form taken by sexual relationships. These difficulties and uncertainties carry over to the very institution of marriage (chapter 6). Unloving is the signpost of a new form of subjectivity in which choice is exercised both positively (wanting, desiring something), and negatively (defining oneself by the repeated avoidance or rejection of relationships, being too confused or ambivalent to desire, wanting to accumulate so many experiences that choice loses its emotional and cognitive relevance, leaving and undoing relationships serially as a way to assert the self and its autonomy). Unloving then is at once a form of subjectivity—who we are and how we behave—and a social process that reflects the profound impact of capitalism on social relationships. As sociologists Wolfgang Streeck and Jens Beckert have convincingly argued, capitalism transforms social action, and one may add, social sentiments.[39]

*

In *War and Peace*, the hero, Pierre Bezukhov meets Prince Andrew, who inquires about him. "Well, have you at last decided on anything? Are you going to be a guardsman or a diplomat?" asks Prince Andrew after a momentary silence.[40] Choice, in his formulation, is an alternative between two clear options, known to the person who must make a choice and to the outside observer. It is an act that has unmistakable boundaries: to choose one option is necessarily to exclude the other. Moreover, Prince Andrew's question assumes what many economists and psychologists have claimed, namely that choice is a matter of personal preference and of information. For Pierre to choose his profession, he simply needs to exercise the (universal) capacity to know and hierarchize his own preferences, to figure out if he prefers the art of war or the art of diplomacy, two neat and clearly differentiated options. Since the end of the nineteenth century, sociologists have taken issue with this view of human action, arguing that human beings are creatures of habit and normative compliance rather than of deliberate decision. As James Duesenberry quipped: "Economics is all about how people make choices; sociology is all about how they don't have any choices to make."[41] Yet, sociologists may have missed what economists and psychologists unknowingly grasped: that capitalism has transformed many arenas of social life into markets, and social action into a reflexive choice and decision-making, and that choice has become a new and crucial *social form*, through which and in which modern subjectivity understands and realizes itself in most or all aspects of their life.[42] It would not be an exaggeration to claim that the modern subject grows into adulthood by exercising her capacity to engage in the deliberate act of choosing a large variety of objects: her sartorial or musical tastes, her college degree and profession, her number of sexual partners, the sex of her sexual partners, her own sex itself, her close and distant friends are all "chosen," the result of reflexively monitored acts of deliberate decision. Worried that endorsing the idea of choice would be a naive and voluntarist endorsement of rational action, sociologists dismissed and missed altogether the fact that choice had become not only an aspect of subjectivity but a way to institutionalize action as well. Instead, sociologists persisted in viewing choice as a pillar of the ideology of capitalism, as the false epistemological premise of economics, as the flagship of liberalism, as a biographical illusion produced by the psychological sciences, or as the principal cultural structure of consumer desire. The perspective offered here is different: while sociology has accumulated an indisputable amount of data showing that constraints of class and gender operate and structure choice from within, it remains that whether illusory or not, *choice* is a fundamental mode for modern subjects to relate to their social environment and to their own self. Choice structures modes of social intelligibility. For example, the "mature and healthy self" is one that develops the capacity to make emotionally mature and authentic choices; to flee

compulsive, addictive behaviors; and to transform them into a freely chosen, informed, self-conscious emotionality. Feminism presented itself as a
politics of choice: In her official site, Stephenie Meyer, the author of the
worldwide bestseller series *Twilight*, puts it succinctly, "[T]he foundation of
feminism is this: being able to choose. The core of anti-feminism is, conversely, telling a woman she can't do something solely because she's a
woman—taking any choice away from her specifically because of her gender."[43] "Pro-choice" is even the nickname of one the most important strands
of the feminist movement. Consumer culture—arguably the fulcrum of
modern identity—is based almost axiomatically on the incessant practice of
comparison and choice. Even if choices *are* in practice limited and determined, it remains that a good chunk of modern lives are experienced and
stylized as the result of subjective choice, a fact that changes in a significant
way how people shape and experience their own subjectivity. Choice then is
a major cultural story of modern people. If choice has become the main
vector of subjectivity in the various institutions of marriage, work, consumption, or politics—how people enter and feel as members of these institutions—it must become a category worthy of sociological inquiry in itself,
a form of action in its own right, shot through by cultural frames, the most
prominent of which are "freedom" and "autonomy." Institutionalized freedom produces a quasi-endless set of possibilities in the realm of consumption, ideas, tastes, and relationships, and compels the self to perform and
enact its self-definition through myriad acts of choice that have different
and definite cognitive and emotional styles (e.g., choosing a mate or choosing a career now entail different cognitive strategies). Thus choice is not
only a widespread ideology as Renata Salecl has showed us so well,[44] but a
real concrete effect of the institutionalization of autonomy in most social
institutions (the school, the market, the law, consumer market) and in
political movements (feminism, gay rights, transgender rights). Choice is a
practical relation one has to oneself where one aims to live according to
one's "true" and "ideal" self by transcending and overcoming the determin-
ism of class, age, or gender (by getting a college degree, by undergoing cosmetic surgery, by changing one's sexual assignation).

Under the influence of economic thought, we have been mostly interested
in positive acts of choice—what is called "decision-making"—but we have
let slip from our attention a far more significant aspect of choice, namely
negative choice, the rejection, avoidance, or withdrawal from commitments, entanglements, and relationships in the name of freedom and

self-realization. The intellectual (and cultural) situation was apparently different at the beginning of the twentieth century when famous thinkers like Sigmund Freud and Émile Durkheim had inquired about "negative relations," Freud under the heading of the death instinct and Durkheim under that of anomie. In 1920, in an essay known as "Beyond the Pleasure Principle," Freud confronted the compulsion to repeat and rehearse distressing experiences, a repetition that could lead to the self-destruction of the subject, to the impossibility of he or she fully entering into or maintaining relationships. Earlier, in 1897, Durkheim had published the founding text of sociology, *Suicide*,[45] which may be viewed as an inquiry into negative relations, a sociality in reverse, that is, into the undoing of social membership. Both Freud and Durkheim have seized at once two conflicting principles, sociality and anti-sociality, as coextensive and contiguous. I continue in their footsteps without, however, viewing anti-sociality in essentialist terms. Instead, I explore negative sociality as an expression of contemporary ideologies of freedom, of technologies of choice, and of advanced consumer capitalism, in fact as part and parcel of the symbolic imaginary deployed by capitalism. In neo-liberal sexual subjectivity, negative sociability is not experienced as a negative mental state (made of fear, or thoughts of death or isolation), but rather as what Günther Anders called "self-assertive freedom," a freedom in which the self affirms itself by negating or ignoring others.[46] Self-assertive freedom is perhaps the most prevalent form of freedom in personal relationships and, as I show, presents all the moral ambiguities of freedom in the institution of heterosexuality.

Negative Choice

Sociologists of modernity have viewed the period ranging from the sixteenth to the twentieth centuries as one that saw the generalization to all social groups of the cultivation of new forms of relationships—the love marriage, the disinterested friendship, the compassionate relationship to the stranger, and national solidarity, to name a few. All of these can be said to be novel social relations, novel institutions, and novel emotions all in one, and they are all resting on choice. Early emotional modernity was thus a modernity in which freedom (to choose) was institutionalized and individuals experienced their freedom in the refinement of the practice of choice, experienced through emotions. Bonds of "friendship," "romantic love," "marriage," or "divorce" were self-contained, bounded social forms, containing clear emotions and names for these emotions, studied by sociology as definable and relatively stable empirical and phenomenological relationships. In contrast, our contemporary hyperconnective modernity seems to be marked by the formation of quasi-proxy or negative bonds: the one-night stand, the zipless fuck, the hookup, the fling, the fuck buddy, the friends with benefits, casual sex, casual dating, cybersex, are only some of the names of relationships defined as short-lived, with no or little involvement of the self, often devoid of emotions, containing a form of autotelic hedonism, with the sexual act as its main and only goal. In such networked modernity, the non-formation of bonds becomes a sociological phenomenon in itself, a social and epistemic category in its own right.[47] If early and high modernity were marked by the struggle for certain forms of sociability where love, friendship, sexuality would be free of moral and social strictures, in networked modernity emotional experience seems to evade the names of emotions and relations inherited from eras where relationships were more stable. Contemporary relationships end, break, fade, evaporate, and follow a dynamic of positive and negative choice, which intertwine bonds and non-bonds.

It is this dynamic I want to elucidate in this book, thereby continuing my previous preoccupation with the interaction between love, choice, and the culture of capitalism.[48] But while in my previous study, I shed light on the changes in the very notion and structure of choice of a mate, here I focus on another and new category of choice: the choice to "unchoose"—a form of choice that comes after the various struggles for freedom we saw during the last two hundred years. If during the formation of modernity actors fought for their right to have a sexuality unhindered by community or social constraints, in contemporary modernity they take for granted that sexuality is a choice and a right, unquestioned and unquestionable (with the exception perhaps of gay marriage, which has been the latest frontier of the old struggle). One's freedom is incessantly exercised by the right to not engage in or disengage from relations, a process that we may call the "choice to unchoose": to opt out of relationships at any stage.

Although I am not suggesting a straightforward, direct causality, the analogy between the history of capitalism and that of romantic forms is striking. In its modern period, capitalism took such economic forms as the corporation, the limited liability company, the international financial markets, and the commercial contract. In these economic forms, hierarchy, control, and contract are central. These were reflected in the view of love as a contractual relationship, freely entered, bound by ethical rules of commitment, yielding obvious returns and demanding long-term emotional strategies and investment. Insurance companies were crucial institutions to minimize risks, acting as third parties between two contractors, thus increasing the reliability of the commercial contract. This social organization of capitalism evolved and morphed into a ramified global network, with scattered ownership and control. It now practices new forms of non-commitment through flextime or outsourcing labor, providing little social safety nets, and breaking bonds of loyalty between workers and workplaces in legislation and practices that decreased dramatically corporations' commitment to workers. Contemporary capitalism has also developed instruments to exploit uncertainty—for example, derivatives—and even makes the value of certain goods uncertain creating "spot markets," offering prices that are incessantly adjusted to demand, thus simultaneously creating and exploiting uncertainty. Practices of non-commitment and non-choice enable a corporation's quick withdrawal from a transaction and the quick realignment of prices, practices that enable corporations to quickly form and break loyalties, and the swift renewal and changing of lines of production and the unhindered firing of the workforce. All of these are practices of non-choice. Choice, which was the early motto of "solid capitalism," then has morphed into non-choice, the practice of perpetually adjusting one's preferences "on the go," not to engage in, pursue, or commit to relationships in general, whether economic or romantic. These practices of non-choice are somehow combined with intensive calculative strategies of risk assessment.

Traditionally, sociology—symbolic interactionism in particular—has almost axiomatically focused on the micro-formation of social bonds, and has by definition been unable to grasp the more elusive mechanism of how relationships end, collapse, evaporate, or fade. In networked modernity, the proper object of study becomes the ways in which bonds dissolve where this dissolution is taken to be a social form. This dissolution of relationships occurs not through a direct breakdown of relationships—alienation, reification, instrumentalization, exploitation—but through the moral injunctions that constitute the imaginary core of the capitalist subjectivity, such as the injunction to be free and autonomous; to change, optimize the self and realize one's hidden potential; to maximize pleasure, health, and productivity. It is the positive injunction to both produce and maximize the self that shapes "negative choice." I will show that the choice to unchoose is now a crucial modality of subjectivity, made possible by a variety of institutional changes: the no-fault divorce (which made it easier for people to opt out of marriage for their own subjective emotional reasons); the contraceptive pill, which made it easier to have sexual relationships without the institutional stakes of marriage and thus without emotional commitment; the consumer market of leisure, which provides a large number of venues to meet and an ongoing supply of sexual partners; the technology afforded by the Internet, especially by dating sites such as Tinder or Match.com, which turn the subject into a consumer of sex and emotions, entitled to the right to use or dispose of the commodity at will; and finally the worldwide success of platforms like Facebook, which both multiply relationships and which enable the quick "unfriending" as a technical feature of a software. These and many other less visible cultural features documented in this book make the choice to unchoose into a dominant modality of subjectivity in networked modernity and societies characterized by advanced processes of commodification, the multiplication of sexual choice, and the penetration of economic rationality to all domains of society.[49] The question of how and why actors will break, disengage from, ignore, or neglect their relationships is all the more interesting because there is powerful empirical evidence that actors in general are "loss averse," meaning[50] they will go through great efforts not to lose something they already have or can have. In fact, as chapters 2 and 3 show, in hyperconnective polities actors easily and regularly overcome loss aversion through the convergence of market, technology, and consumer forces. "Negative choice" is as powerful and present in the lives of people in hyperconnective modernity as was the positive choice to form bonds and relations with others in the formation of modernity.

The social effects of negative choice are apparent in many significant ways. One is the fact that many countries cannot maintain their populations in terms of their birth rates. Young Japanese, for example, have tremendous difficulties "in pairing up," with the result that "the fertility rate has plunged. The number of children a Japanese woman can expect to have in her lifetime is now 1.42, down from 2.13 in 1970."[51] Negative population growth rates are observed in Eastern and much of Western Europe as well, and they are threatening not only demography but economy as well. The shrinkage of the population has powerful rippling political and economic effects, from immigration flows to the difficulty of guaranteeing pension funds or supporting aging populations. If the expansion of capitalism was predicated on population growth and on the family as the structure mediating between economy and society, that connection is increasingly being undone by the new forms of capitalism themselves. Capitalism is a formidable machine to produce goods but is no longer capable of ensuring the social need for reproduction, what philosopher Nancy Fraser has called capitalism "crisis of care."[52] Negative relations are apparent in the conscious decision or non-conscious practices by many men and women not to enter stable bonds or have children and in the fact that single households have considerably increased in the last two decades.[53] A second way in which negative choice is made apparent is by the development of divorce rates. In the United States, for example, the rate more than doubled between 1960 and 1980.[54] In 2014 it was more than 45 percent for people who married in the 1970s or in the 1980s,[55] making divorce a likely occurrence in a large portion of the population. Third, more people live in multiple relationships (of the polyamorous or other types), putting into question the centrality of monogamy and attendant values as loyalty and long-term commitment. An increasing number of people leave and enter, enter and leave a larger number of relationships in a fluid way throughout their lives. A fourth, seemingly opposite, manifestation of non-choice is sologamy, the puzzling phenomenon of (mostly) women who choose to marry themselves,[56] thereby declaring their self-love and affirming the worth of singlehood. Finally, negative choice is somehow implicated in what a commentator has called the "loneliness epidemic": "An estimated 42.6 million Americans over the age of 45 suffer from chronic loneliness, which significantly raises their risk for premature death, according to a study by AARP (American Association of Retired Persons).[57] One researcher called[58] the loneliness epidemic[59] "a greater health threat than obesity."[60] The loneliness epidemic has another form. As Jean Twenge (a psychology professor at San Diego State University) has suggested, members of the *iGen* generation (the generation after the millennials) have fewer sex partners than members of the two preceding generations, making the lack of sexuality a new social phenomenon, explained I would argue, by the cultural shift to negative choice, to the quick withdrawal from relationships or to the fact that relationships themselves never get formed.[61]

In the realm of intimate relationships, choice is exerted in a context that is very different from the one of Pierre Bezukhov, in which choice often took place between two clear alternative paths. Under the massive influence of new technological platforms, freedom creates now such a large number of possibilities that the emotional and cognitive conditions for romantic choice have been radically transformed. Whence the question addressed here: what are the cultural and emotional mechanisms, voluntary and involuntary, that make people revise, undo, reject, and avoid relationships? What is the emotional dynamic by which a preference changes (leaving a relationship one was engaged in)? Although many or most live in some satisfactory form of couplehood (or temporary sexual and emotional arrangement), this book is about the arduous *path* of many to reach that point as well as with the fact that many, by choice or non-choice, do not live in a stable relationship. This book is not an indictment of the ideal of couplehood or a plea to return to more secure ways of forming it, but rather a description of the ways in which capitalism has hijacked sexual freedom and is implicated in the reasons why sexual and romantic relationships have become puzzlingly volatile.

Much of sociology has been about the study of the regular, routine structures of daily life and has developed to that effect an impressive array of methods. But the contemporary era commands perhaps another type of sociology, which I would tentatively call the study of crisis and uncertainty. The orderliness and predictability of modern institutions have been disrupted for large swaths of the population; routine and bureaucratic structures coexist with a pervasive and nagging sense of uncertainty and insecurity. If we can no longer count on lifelong employment, on the returns of increasingly volatile markets, on the stability of marriage, on geographical stability, then many traditional sociological concepts have served their time. It is high time that we listen to the practitioners of the new culture of unloving, and therefore I conducted interviews with ninety-two people in France, England, Germany, Israel, and the United States from the age of nineteen to the age of seventy-two.[62] Their stories form the empirical backbone of the book—and they all bear the traces of what Lauren Berlant calls the "crisis of ordinariness," that is, the low-key ways in which actors, located in different cultural contexts and socioeconomic positions, struggle with the minute dramas of precariousness and uncertainty,[63] with the properties of what I call negative relationships. Negative relationships obviously take different forms in different social classes and different national frameworks, but they contain a few recurring elements: they enact economic and technological features; they do not gel in a stable social form but *are valued* as ephemeral and transitory; and they are practiced even when that entails loss and pain. Whether these two processes produce pleasure or pain, they constitute, as we will see, *unloving*, whereby the prefix "un-" expresses both the willful undoing of something established (as in "untying" the knot), and the inability to achieve something (as in "unable"). One form of unloving necessarily precedes loving (e.g., the one-night stand) and another follows it (the divorce). Both cases enable us to understand the conditions of emotions and relationships in the era of radical personal freedom. It is this condition I decipher in this book.

2

Pre-Modern Courtship, Social Certainty, and the Rise of Negative Relationships

> After all, if my generation of writers represents anything, if there's anything we've fought for, it's a sexual revolution.
>
> —Norman Mailer[1]

Anthony Trollope's 1884 novel *An Old Man's Love* offers a powerful literary illustration of the ways in which in the nineteenth century, emotions were aligned with the social norm of matrimony. The author tells the story of the young Mary Lawrie, an orphan who has been taken to live in the household of old Mr. Whittlestaff. Because Mr. Whittlestaff has never been married, Mary anticipates the decision she will have to make when he proposes. She muses about her decision in the following way:

> She told herself that he personally was full of good gifts. How different might it have been with her had some elderly men "wanted her," such as she had seen about in the world! How much was there in this man that she knew that she could learn to love? And he was one of whom she need in no wise be ashamed. He was a gentleman, pleasant to look at, sweet in manner, comely and clean in appearance. Would not the world say of her how lucky she had been should it come to pass that she should become Mrs Whittlestaff? [...] After an hour's deliberation, she thought that she would marry Mr Whittlestaff.[2]

These reflections are not formulated as an interrogation about her or Mr. Whittlestaff's feelings. In fact, she *knows* he will propose although nothing explicit has been said. Her decision to such presumed proposal is also clear. In a matter of one hour, Mary has settled with herself her matrimonial future by invoking and rehearsing mentally a set of arguments for accepting Whittlestaff's proposal, and these arguments have much to do with his virtues and what she imagines "the world would say" should she become his wife. She sees in him the same virtues that the world will see in him, thus suggesting an overlap between private and collective judgement. In conformity with sociological theories of the "looking glass self,"[3] Mary's decision incorporates the opinion of the world on her choice. Her own and the world's evaluation of Whittlestaff are shaped by known social scripts of the good man, by norms of matrimony, and by conventions of the proper role of a woman, as her evaluation of him and affection for him are grounded in common standards. When she makes up her mind she participates in this known and common world. Her feelings and her decision incorporate all in one her sentiments, the economic advantage of a marriage, and the social expectations of a woman in her situation. Feelings and norms form a single cultural matrix and shape directly her decision-making.

Mary's decision and later promise to marry the old man morphs into a dilemma when the reader is informed that three years earlier, she had given her hand to John Gordon. The two young people had a few brief encounters, enough to promise to marry each other after his return from South Africa where he went to look for a fortune. Without any news from him for three years, Mary Lawrie releases herself from her pledge and accepts Mr. Whittlestaff's proposal and the drama of the novel starts when John Gordon reappears, thus making Mary face a second and much more dramatic act of choice, this time between two people and two different sentiments. She in particular must choose between breaking a promise to an "old man" she has affectionate fondness for and acting upon the emotional pledge made to a young man she was in love with three years beforehand. Because promise-keeping was a fundamental value to the nineteenth-century English gentry and middle class, she makes the honorable decision, and does not desist from her promise.

It would be tempting to view the dilemma constructed by this novel as one opposing an emotional to a reasonable decision; social duty to individual passion. But this would be merely confusing psychology and sociology. In fact, each of Mary's two choices is emotional—affection or love—and each is congruent with the norms of her environment. In both cases, Mary's sentiments are closely aligned with a normative order. To marry a man she has met three times without sexual contact is socially as respectable as marrying the "old" Whittlestaff. These two different emotional options lead to the same moral and social pathway of matrimony. In both cases, Mary's emotions move in a hierarchized moral cosmos. In fact, it is through her emotions that she is made to immerse herself in the normative cosmology of matrimony in the nineteenth century.

Sociologically, rather than psychologically, Mary's reasoned affection to Whittlestaff and her impetuous love for Gordon, her personal feelings and social conventions, form a single matrix. Moreover, however confused Mary and other characters may be, they all know the terms of one another's hesitation. This is a world where everybody shares the same normative information about how the personal and the normative should be ordered. In fact, it is precisely because Whittlestaff knows the normative constraints under which Mary operates that he ultimately releases her of her promise. Promise-keeping and the institution of matrimony are normative orders that pervade desire and love and organize them from within.

*

Émile Durkheim may be credited for being the first to have grasped what the collapse of such emotional, normative, and institutional order was about.[4] Infrequently noticed by sociologists is the extent to which Durkheim's notion of *anomie* in his much-famed and now canonical sociological study on suicide referred to sexual and matrimonial desire. In extraordinarily prescient words, Durkheim described the emotional structure of a new social type that had appeared in French society—the single man:[5]

> Though his [the married man's] enjoyment is restricted, it is assured and this certainty forms his mental foundation. The lot of the unmarried man is different. As he has the right to form attachment wherever inclination leads him, he aspires to everything and is satisfied with nothing. This morbid desire for the infinite which everywhere accompanies anomy may as readily assail this as any other part of our consciousness; it very often assumes a sexual form which was described by Musset. When one is no longer checked, one becomes unable to check one's self. Beyond experienced pleasures one senses and desires others; if one happens almost to have exhausted the range of what is possible, one dreams of the impossible; one thirsts for the non-existent. How can the feelings not be exacerbated by such unending pursuit? For them to reach that state, one need not even have infinitely multiplied the experiences of love and lived the life of a Don Juan. The humdrum existence of the ordinary bachelor suffices. New hopes constantly awake, only to be deceived, leaving a trail of weariness and disillusionment behind them. How can desire, then, become fixed, being uncertain that it can retain what it attracts; for the

anomy is twofold. Just as the person makes no definitive gift of himself, he has definitive title to nothing. The uncertainty of the future plus his own indeterminateness therefore condemn him to constant change. The result of it all is a state of disturbance, agitation and discontent which inevitably increases the possibilities of suicide.[6]

Durkheim here offers an extraordinary program for what we may call a sociology of desire and of emotional decision-making: some desires translate into direct decision-making and some don't. The single man's desire is anomic because it undermines the capacity to will an object with a definite purpose. Anomic desire is neither depressive nor apathetic. It is, on the contrary, restless, hyper-active, in perpetual quest of something, a state Durkheim goes as far as calling "morbid." It is a desire that cannot enter marriage because it cannot create the psychic conditions to *want* a single object. It is a desire that properly lacks an object, and that, in lacking an object, is insatiable. This creates a particular form of action, one that is at once in perpetual motion (moves from one object to the other) and lacks an overarching purpose.

According to Durkheim then, anomic desire has a number of characteristics: (1) It has no teleology, that is, it does not have a purpose. It is free-floating, free-circulating, and nomadic. (2) It does not have a teleology because it is devoid of an internal normative peg around which one could build an overarching narrative structure. (3) For the single man, the future is uncertain and cannot provide guidance for the present. The married man on the other hand has a known and certain future based on normative knowledge and participation: He knows which pleasures are waiting for him, and, through the very institution of marriage, is assured of their continued possession. In contrast, the single man cannot imagine the future and is locked in a present that contains only hopefulness—*espérance*—a far more vague and amorphous sentiment than one's projection in the future. Through *espérance* one contemplates the potentiality of a new pleasure likely to be short-lived. This type of desire displays the properties of *anomie*: it lacks integration (it does not emanate from social norms) and one does not aim to participate in a social unit. (4) Finally, in anomic desire the subject's inner life—what Durkheim calls his "mental plate"—becomes indeterminate, moving from one object to the next, and thus acts in a state of uncertainty, unable to make a decision because of an inability to fixate desire on a person and an institution. The married man is the one who has by definition made a decision, while the single man can only accumulate, indefinitely, experiences, desires, and partners, without being able to bring the perpetual motion of his desire to an emotional and narrative closure or decision. Uncertainty, accumulation, motion, inability (or unwillingness) to imagine the future—all of these constitute the essence of what Durkheim views as anomic desire, unable to appropriate social norms or to identify with institutions. Anomic desires exist on a plane of horizontal equivalence. They are not organized by a hierarchized normative and teleological cosmos, as in Trollope's story.

Sexual anomie is thus many things at once: an excess of desire, a form of desire that originates in the self unmoored from social norms and, precisely because of that, something indecisive, unable to fixate on an object. Here a self-centered subjectivity does not have the trenchant clarity of needs and desires, but on the contrary, is diffuse, vague, ambivalent, and purposeless. Because such subjectivity is unable to feel clear emotions, it cannot propel itself forward along a narrative and normative path. Let me say this differently: The Durkheimian single man is unable to reach a decision because his "mental plate" is not organized around certainty. For Durkheim then, emotions can be a source of certainty and decision-making only if they are grounded in a clear normative structure.

Durkheim offers here the grounds for a sociology of desire and emotional decision-making and helps articulate two grammars of social bonds and of emotional choice: one in which desire is free-floating, lacking in finality and originating in subjectivity; and one in which desire is organized through things external to the self, such as economic interests, norms of matrimony, and gender roles. These two grammars help formulate the paradox that is at the heart of sexual liberation: desire liberated from normative constraints and from ritual structure obstructs emotional choice. The remainder of this chapter is devoted to exploring these grammars.

Courtship as a Sociological Structure

It has not sufficiently been noticed that the passage from traditional romance to the sexual order that followed the 1970s was the shift from courtship as the prevailing mode of interaction between men and women to an order in which rules of engagement changed entirely, becoming fuzzy and uncertain and, at the same time, closely regulated by an ethics of consent. The disappearance of courtship is a rather striking feature of modern romantic practices and marks a stark difference between traditional and contemporary romantic practices. Therefore it deserves a more insistent scrutiny than has been provided so far by sociologists of sexuality and marriage. By examining traditional courtship, I want to draw a comparison between the two grammars of social bonds and desire, and thus will simplify a great deal the description of the actual pre-modern practices of courtship by drawing a too-sharp contrast between the traditional and the contemporary (sexual anomy existed prior to modernity; and courtship here and there survived its demise in modern society). Thus my strategy has its limitations: it does not capture the range of behaviors that make the past similar to the present, and it fails to grasp the ways in which the past still lives in and structures the present. Being aware of these limitations, I am nonetheless confident that it will adequately account for the nature of the *shift* undergone by courtship practices, that is, the changes in the rules and modes of engagement of emotional subjects entering social interactions. Courtship practices in Christian Europe cannot be understood without reference to the regulation of sexuality. In fact, the regulation of sexuality shaped the structure and content of courtship.

Pre-Modern Regulation of Sexuality

To understand the specificity of sexuality in the Christian world, we may briefly contrast it to the ancient Greek world, in which sex was not construed in relational terms, or as "a shared experience reflecting emotional intimacy, but as something—penetration—done to someone else."[7] Sex reflected and performed relations of power and male status. Sex, for a young or older man, like behavior in a battlefield, could be "honorable" or "dishonorable." In that sense, sexuality was organized by the political and social codes of masculinity and was a direct continuation of one's public and political status. It was Christianity that slowly made sexuality into a heterosexual and relational bond, expressing and regulating the interiority of the subject, connecting it to the spiritual conduct of the soul. Augustine formulated for generations to follow the doctrine of original sin according to which lust was a reminder of our finitude, a trace of the original sin that stamped human beings with a permanent shame.[8] In transferring sex to the problematic of temptation, to sin committed in the heart, it transferred sex to the inner realms of thoughts, intentions, and private desires. Sexuality came to mark the content and boundaries of one's virtuous (or depraved) "soul," thus becoming the centerpiece of the realm of an inner life, that was incessantly scrutinized and monitored to satisfy the spiritual requirements of a religion that now staked salvation on sexual purity. In Christianity then, sexuality was at once deeply moral—the site of sin and salvation—and emotionalized, the site of intentions, emotions, and desires. Love and pleasure were, on the whole, hindrances to the good soul.[9] Realizing it could not demand from everyone abstinence and purity,[10] the Church came to view marriage as a compromise with its own ascetic ideal and increasingly defined the legitimate boundaries of sexuality as those drawn by marriage.[11] If legitimate sex could happen only between married people, adultery and premarital sex were unavoidably illicit. Most European societies contained "an elaborate system of jurisdictions to police adulterers, fornicators, prostitutes, and bastard-bearers. Statutes, common law, manorial and borough customs, and the courts of the Church—all actively upheld the rule that illicit sex was a public offence which could not be safely tolerated."[12] Transgressions of sexual norms were relatively common, but were viewed as threatening the entire community. With the grip of Christianity on sexual practices, sex came to reflect and contain deeply religious meanings. Such concepts as "fornication" contained beliefs about the nature of the human soul, and implicitly referred to such lofty topics as the origin of the world and the damnation or salvation of the soul, both of the individual and of the community that allowed transgressive behavior. As historian Richard Godbeer put it: "Early Americans worried about sex because they believed that it embodied, quite literally, their identity and worth, individually and collectively."[13] Theological concerns played out the political struggles of the Church of England and sexuality was the terrain for it to affirm its authority.[14] In early America, the political disorder of the incipient nation was fought through attempts to control sexual behavior. Sexuality was thus key to the entire moral and metaphysical world inhabited by a Christian as it connected the self to grand narratives of salvation, redemption, the Fall, Original Sin, and spirituality. Such a vision of sexuality was imbued and fundamentally constrained by theological beliefs, such as the sacraments of the matrimonial union. These grand narratives in turn translated themselves into key emotions as shame, guilt, temptation, and self-control.

This state of affairs started changing at the end of the eighteenth century, with a rise of sexual permissiveness and secularism, which marked a "decisive break" with the past.[15] The Enlightenment ideas, as in other realms, brought important changes, although they did not fundamentally challenge the view that sexuality and the body ought to be regulated (with the exception of libertine elites who indeed challenged it). David Hume and Immanuel Kant, who were otherwise opposed to each other on their views about the foundation of morality, spoke strongly against a relaxation of sexual mores.[16] Kant went as far as viewing sex as antinomic with morality, because sex provided pleasure thereby tainting relationships with instrumentalism. "Sexual love makes the loved person an Object of appetite; as soon as that appetite has been stilled the person is Cast aside as one casts away a lemon which has been sucked dry."[17] For Kant, sexual love is "nothing more than appetite" and "taken by itself, it is a degradation of human nature."[18] The great novelty however was that for Kant sex was an offense to another human being rather than to God, thus shifting sexuality from theology to the realm of human morality. In the nineteenth century, libertine elites and utopian socialists' advocacy of free love as well as early feminists' critics of matrimony[19] further questioned the stronghold of the Church on sexuality. However, despite the fact that claims to sexual permissiveness were increasingly voiced, premarital sex remained regulated until well into the twentieth century (until the 1960s, a woman who had been "compromised" could expect a man to "assume his responsibilities"). In such closely regulated normative order, sexuality tended to follow the clear moral and social grammar of courtship, which was a platform for young people to engage in romantic interactions.

Courtship as a Pre-Modern Mode of Emotional Decision-Making

Courtship is a formal social interaction, organized around the sexual restrictions imposed by families and the clergy. In its French, medieval version, it was the formal and ritualized behavior of a knight (often a vassal to a lord) to a lady (sometimes the very wife of the lord). It mixed masculine rhetoric of valor and courage and religious motives of devotion and fervor[20] (some forms of love were extended forms of courtship to dead women as was the case with Petrarch and Laura or Dante and Beatrice).[21] With the formation of courts in Europe, courtship came to mean the behavior of the courtier in court[22] and later took on the more general meaning of engaging in a ritual interaction with a woman with sexual and/or romantic intent.[23]

Reflecting this process, from the Renaissance onward, but more especially in the seventeenth and eighteenth centuries, a social system of gallantry developed in the French court. As defined by Niklas Luhmann, gallantry is a "socially binding style both for deceptive and seductive behavior as well as for truly loving courtship."[24] Gallantry could be a pure surface of sociality, an aesthetics of heterosexual interactions, which had its own codes, rules, and etiquette. It occasionally circumvented the premium on virginity. As an aestheticized interaction, gallantry was not necessarily geared to marriage but rather reflected the complicated rules of etiquette of aristocrats and sometimes even morphed into libertinage.

In Protestant countries where the bourgeoisie held greater sway over definitions of morality, the regulation of sexuality was more crucial to marriage and to the perception of the social order.[25] In Protestant countries, courtship was not gallantry and was more explicitly geared to marriage. Thus in courtship, men and women displayed the moral and religious codes of sexuality intertwined with class-based linguistic and behavioral modes of expression.[26]

In the eighteenth and nineteenth centuries in Europe and the United States courtship reflected changes that Lawrence Stone has characterized as the rise of affective individualism among the middle classes and aristocrats.[27] Courtship could be conducted after the couple had obtained the approval of the female's parents, and thus was the public expression of the family principled assent to marriage and to the young people's exploration of their feelings; with increasing individualization, it became a framework geared to ascertain and explore emotions and to make (or not) the decision to marry. Courtship was a social framework for the organized, ritualized circulation of feelings according to rules of expression, reciprocation, and exchange usually known to the two parties involved. The outcome was a clear yes or no, but quite often the simple fact of starting a courtship signaled that each was interested in matrimony and induced young people to move toward that goal. In that sense, courtship was a framework for decision-making or for confirming what was an early decision to explore marriage-oriented feelings.

I would thus define courtship as a structured social framework for decision-making, where the decision was either emotional ("Do I love him?"), practical ("Do I want to marry him?"), or both. It has a beginning, a set of ritualized rules that organize its progression, and a formal end (usually moving to a marriage proposal, but occasionally ending the connection).

Courtship is thus a cultural technique to make a decision by providing procedures in which the interiority fixated itself and gelled around known rules. Another way to say this is to suggest that courtship was a social structure in which actors could make a risky decision (marriage) under social conditions that increased certainty (as well as what Anthony Giddens would dub ontological security).[28]

As a social form, pre-modern courtship produced certainty not in the sense that it guaranteed the outcome (although it did help secure it) but in the double sense that, on the one hand, it did not make the future into a problem (because its purpose was known and accepted by all parties) and in that, on the other hand, it relied on a clear set of rules that organized emotions and interactions into known cultural pathways. Emotional certainty—deciphering one's own and another's feelings and following a set of predictable sequences as a result—was made possible by the fact courtship was teleologically organized around the goal of marriage.

Certainty as a Sociological Structure

German sociologist Niklas Luhmann made "certainty" into a central feature of social interactions. In his view, the reduction of complexity and uncertainty are fundamental components of social processes.[29] Love—along with truth, money, or power—is a medium of communication, helping create expectations, select one decision among many, connect motivation to action, and create certainty and predictability in relationships. Such media of communication create roles that in turn generate expected outcomes (to use Luhmann's example, a wife will not be rejected if she asks her husband "why are you home so late today?").[30] Predictability is a fundamental dimension of social interactions, to be found, for example, in rituals. When interactions are ritualized, they generate certainty about the actors' definition of a relationship, of their position in such relationship, and of the rules to conduct such relation. Certainty can be described as "refer[ring] to a person's ability to describe, predict, and explain behavior within social situations."[31] Or, conversely, as defined by *The Blackwell Encyclopedia of Sociology* uncertainty is "unclear, ambiguous, or contradictory cognitive constructions, which cause feelings of uncertainty."[32] Not only ritual but also normative clarity (knowing what the norm, the rule, and the role are) generate certainty—about definitions of situations and of one's position in a given situation. Certainty is a psychic attribute of persons but it is also an attribute of interactions. What are the components of such interaction?

Normative Certainty

Normative certainty pertains to the perceived clarity of norms and values present in an interaction. The easier it is to identify (consciously or not) the norms present in an interaction, the more forceful the norms are and the more predictable that interaction is (e.g., going out fully clad is far more predictable than buying flowers on a third date).

The protection of women's virginity remained one of the most fundamental norms at the center of traditional courtship until well into the twentieth century. Women had to protect their sexual purity and men were held responsible for deviations from sexual codes of conduct.[33] For example, when the open-minded Adele Schopenhauer, the devoted sister of Arthur, the philosopher, found out that her brother had impregnated their housekeeper, she wrote: "I find it disgusting." Arthur ran away but the codes and conventions of the period obliged him to "take care" of the situation, which he (indecorously) asked his sister to do for him by financially supporting the mother of the child.[34]

Women of lower condition were often the victims of unpunished sexual predations of men of higher social class (for example in the houses in which they worked as maids), but because norms of sexual conduct appeared as moral codes, men had to give the appearances of respecting this code, which meant that a great deal of sexual behavior was hidden or needed to be subsumed under the prospect or appearance of matrimony. In seventeenth-century early modern England, for example, "[w]idespread premarital intercourse did not represent a wanton rejection of moral propriety by ordinary people. Instead, it arose from a common belief that the boundary between illicit and licit sex was crossed once a couple became committed to each other."[35] In the same way one displayed one's adequate grooming through one's ability to play the piano, ride a horse, or write letters, one also expressed one's grooming by displaying the appropriate respect for the rules of courtship, sexual retine, and respect for the proper norms of conduct. Examples of how the awareness of the proper norms of conduct inhered in courtship are numerous.

During their long courtship in the nineteenth century, Rev. John Miller and Sally MacDowell had to overcome many obstacles. At the beginning of their correspondence, in a letter written in September 1854, he was exploring his feelings: "In treading in the sanctuary of your private history even with the lightest & most hasty step, I *am cruelly afraid of acting in some way indelicately* (...) I am under *such painful motives to be honorable*, & you have been *so good to me in imagining that I intend to be correct*, that I am perhaps beyond your suspicion of intentional indelicacy.

"And I do beg that this may be the case, & that you will attribute to want of sense what you might otherwise attribute to a careless indiscretion."[36] "Painful motives to be honorable" suggests clearly that this man prefers to be thought of as an idiot ("want of sense") than to be thought of as indelicate, lacking the appropriate manners and codes in honoring a woman. The capacity to show respect for social norms was thus crucial to one's sense of self in a romantic interaction. Conforming to certain codes of behavior, which are based both in class and morality, meant that one deserved to love and be loved in return. Love was entirely steeped in normativity.

To take another example: George Herbert Palmer courted Alice Freeman,[37] who felt unsure about the appropriateness of their courtship. Addressing her concerns, he wrote in 1887: "When Robert Browning married Elizabeth Barrett, all the world saw the fitness and consequent wealth of the new life, and was glad. To one another we each bring a life no less suitable and supplemental. It will be felt so. The pride we feel will be felt by the world as approval. I have too much confidence in the generosity of people, and *in their ability to see what is fitting, to believe that we should be thought censurable*."[38] Referring to the famous story of the two poets who transgressed against Elizabeth's father's prohibition for his daughter to wed her suitor by eloping, Palmer reassured Alice about the future normative approval of their courtship by "the world." Such reassurances suggest how deeply aware each one of them was of the judgment of others and that they sought the world's approval. Sentiments were experienced through the interiorization of outside, normative social judgment (exactly as Mary Lawrie did). That she should be worried of their society's approval does not make him doubt her love for him. On the contrary, her worries and his reassurances suggest they are both trying to anchor their sentiments in known norms that constitute the legitimate pathways to organize feelings.

Existential Certainty

Normative certainty yields what I could call existential certainty, that is, the perceived fit between one's subjective and objective (social) experience. Existential certainty enables one to answer easily the questions, Who am I in this situation? Who is the other to me? As a result it is also easy to respond to the question, What do I owe this person in this situation? Gender division and distinction were crucial aspects of that system in the predictability of the courtship system. Courtship was geared to an object—a woman—who had to decide to reciprocate an emotion or an action initiated by a man and in that respect was structured by a clear division of gender roles. As Jane Austen put it in *Northanger Abbey* (1818) through the mouth of Henry Tilney: "[M]an has the advantage of choice, woman only the power of refusal."[39] Once a man selected an object of courtship, it was incumbent on the woman to accept or refuse, and the courtship then proceeded according to a path that structured the exchange, the experience, and the communication of emotions. The fact that women were the object of men's desire rather than subjects of their own desire was based on a dichotomous gender division that in turn made possible the formalization of courtship. Existential certainty derives from the fact that we identify the frame of meaning of an interaction and know our place and role in it. It accrues to interactions in which class and gender boundaries are clear and relatively nonnegotiable, thus creating a "sense of place."

Consider the example of how a rural Texas couple courted. In 1892 David Fain addressed Jessie Bledsoe, whom he had just met, as follows:

> Dear Miss I hope you will pardon me for the liberty I have taken in writing you this short letter I thought that I would have an opportunity of meeting you again before leaving Shepherd and having a talk with you. The subject of which I wish to talk to you about is a very serious one and one that is to be well considered and that is the subject of matrimony.[40]

Fain had barely met Bledsoe but he could broach the topic of matrimony so quickly because he could enact his male role (the man was the one who could propose). In this case to offer her matrimony was also to offer her to care for his children (from a deceased wife). In other words a marriage proposal amounted to offer a clear role to the woman. This is the reason why raising the question of marriage so quickly did not pose a threat to his masculinity or his good name.

Ontological Certainty

The third mechanism creating certainty in courtship lay in the objectivation of feelings through the material world of tokens and gifts. Despite their legendary force, emotions are plagued by the fact that they are shifting and volatile. In pre-modern courtship, the exchange of gifts and tokens (of various value) marked and sealed the intention of each of the partners. Gifts mattered not as expressions of interiority, but for their capacity to bind one's intention and feelings. As historian John Gillis remarks: "The intention of the giver [of a gift] had much to do with whether a gift had binding powers."[41] Objects played an important role in objectifying relations, that is, in marking their progression and pacing them, and indicating their beginning, their progression, and their commitment. For example, there was a custom in Britain to break a three-penny coin in two and each to keep each part as a token of commitment. If the courtship was interrupted, each had to bring back the piece.[42] In other words, feelings were organized in the tangible and material framework of gift-giving; they acquired an ontological objectivity that derived from the fact the relationship was translated into objects, making sentiments tangible and objective, outside the subject. In another novel by Anthony Trollope, *Can You Forgive Her?* (1864–1865), the heroine Alice Vavasor is engaged to her cousin George, but fails to show him signs of love and care. In a state of rage at her seeming indifference, he looks for an object in her room, and takes it, as if the object were a substitute for the emotions she refuses to show and as if to seal further her engagement to him. "[G]ifts were believed to have a magic power, so that to deliver a lock of hair, articles of clothing, even a kiss was to place oneself in another's possession."[43] As John Gillis further suggests, in order to determine if someone was a casual seducer or a serious suitor, there was extensive use of intermediaries, as witnesses to the words and actions of another[44]—a system of fixation and inscription of promises, intentions, words, and feelings in objects and witnesses that took sentiments out of the interiority of subjects and placed them in a public and visible world. Consent given in public transformed friends into lovers and lovers into prospective spouses, thus suggesting that an objectified system of gift exchange and witnesses established the relationship performatively rather than through the subjective intro-spection and emotional expression. If one desisted from marriage, one frequently gave back or brought back the gifts one had received, thus illus-trating that the economy of exchange of objects was a binding one because it was inscribed in an external world that made emotions tangible entities that could not be made easily volatile.

Evaluative Certainty

Evaluative certainty is the capacity to gather reliable information about oth-ers or to know how to evaluate them according to established standards and criteria of evaluation, or both. In pre-modern courtship this task was achieved by the fact that prospective partners belonged to close social net-works. "Partners either came from the same village or town or knew each other through the sharing of a common residence during employment. Most couples knew each other very well before marriage through religious and community group affiliations and many marriages occurred among servants and apprentices of the same household."[45] Most people knew quite well the person they married from the village or the town or knew of them by reput-ation. That mode of information gathering made evaluation both personal and collective, with reputation playing an important role in mate selection. This mode of information gathering was not, of course, more reliable than the more individualized modern one. This state of affairs continued until quite late in the twentieth century.

In 1932, a large study of residential propinquity in marriage selection found something astonishing: In a population of ten thousand people who registered for marriage, more than six thousand lived twenty blocks or less from their partner, with more than half of this number living actually less than five blocks from the other.[46] And as late as the late 1960s, spatial homogamy was still the dominant predictor of choice of a mate—and a tool to gather information about others since it was likely to have entailed homo-philic social networks. In other words, even when the family did not exert a direct control over the choice of a mate, spatial homogamy ensured that that choice of a mate was traceable to known social networks. This reduced eval-uative as well as normative uncertainty. Even when individual taste played a role in the choice of a mate—and of course, it did—that taste relied on close social networks, which helped in turn consolidate evaluative certainty.

Procedural Certainty

Procedural certainty pertains to the rules with which one is able to carry forward an intention and an interaction. Rules differ from norms in that they pertain to the sequential order in which things are done and to the capacity to carry forward an interaction. For example, in middle-class homes, the widespread nineteenth-century practice of "calling" observed a protocol whereby a suitor would submit his desire to court a woman for her parents' approval and would subsequently be admitted. We can appreciate the role that rules played in courtship with a literary example of Gustave Flaubert's realistic rendering of the provincial mores of nineteenth-century France in *Madame Bovary* (1856). In the following excerpt we still know nothing of the fate of Emma Rouault and Charles Bovary. We know only that Charles is timid and awkward and that he has set his sights on Emma. Charles's timidity is a good way to appreciate the role of social rules in making actors declare their sentiments and see these sentiments be translated into decisions. Flaubert describes the thoughts of Monsieur Rouault—Emma's father—regarding the relationship:

> So, noticing that Charles went red in the face when he was near his daughter, which meant that one of these days he would ask for her hand, he [Monsieur Rouault] pondered the whole matter in advance. It was true he thought him a bit of a loser, and not what he'd have chosen as a son in-law; but people said he was a steady young man, careful with his money, and very learned; and probably he wouldn't haggle too much over the dowry. Now, as Monsieur Rouault was going to have to sell twenty-two acres of "his place," and he owed a lot to the mason, a lot to the harness-maker, and the shaft of the cider-press needed replacing, he said to himself: "If he asks me for her, I'll let him have her."[47]

The time had come.

> Charles gave himself as far as the corner of the hedge, and finally, when they had passed it: "Maitre Rouault," he murmured, "There's something I want to tell you." They stopped. Charles said nothing. "Well come on, out with it! As if I didn't know what's on your mind!" old Rouault replied with a soft chuckle. "Père Rouault [...] Père Rouault," stammered Charles. "There's nothing I'd like better," continued the farmer. "I'm sure me little

girl feels the same, but still, I'd better ask her…" Next morning he [Charles Bovary] was at the farm by nine. Emma blushed when he came in, although she tried to cover her embarrassment with a little laugh. Père Rouault embraced his future son-in-law. They put off any discussion of money matters, there was plenty of time for that.[48]

In these short passages, someone as emotionally awkward as Charles is immediately understood by Emma's father, who can convey his formal offer to Emma, thus initiating the process of courtship, which is enabled again by the fact this is a world whose rules were very clear to all parties involved. In this vignette, there is a subtle and intricate mix of individual sentiments and public conventions, the protagonists' retinue is combined with their ability to decipher the shades and nuances of others' concealed emotions and to carry the intentions of the protagonists forward through well-known scripts and rules. Social rules and social conventions are doing the work of realizing Charles's will and intentions, not his sentiments. In such a world, there is very little need to introspect about one's feelings. From his silent blush to her embarrassed laughter, everything has been settled because this is a world in which social rules carry forward social interactions and feelings. Social rules and procedures rather than subjective emotions do the work of bringing people together.

Rules and procedures moved along with the fact that the courtship had a narrative structure. Courtship was an experience of going through different stages or sequences. This is why the emotional exchange was likely to follow a narrative progression. One moved step by step, with a sense of "direction," and the "direction" of the interaction gave certainty to its meaning and to the part each one was supposed to play. "There existed a well-established sequence of events leading up to marriage, including the announcement of banns to solicit community comment and input."[49] The narrativity or sequentiality of courtship was made possible by the fact that social interactions and emotions were enmeshed with religious cultural cosmologies, which consecrated the emotion of love and sexuality in the sacraments of marriage.

Emotional Certainty

The last dimension of certainty conveyed by traditional forms of courtship pertains to the fact that actors acted as if they knew the nature and intensity of their own emotions, and could easily ascertain those of others. Emotional certainty is tightly connected to the capacity to translate emotions into sequences, narratives, goals, and objectified signs, which express and performatively induce emotions. Emotions were built up through the interaction and were the catalyst for it. The mere fact of starting a courtship often engaged the totality of one's emotions. For example, in 1836, Theodore Dwight Weld, one of the architects of the American abolitionist movement, had met the Grimké sisters—Sarah and Angelina—who fought against the brutality of men against their gender. After a few meetings, in February 1838, Weld wrote a carefully worded letter in which he confessed his love for Angelina Grimké. He wrote: "For a long time, *you have had my whole heart*."[50] A short few weeks later, when she had agreed to be courted, he wrote he felt himself "reaching out in very agony after you, and cleaving to you, feeling that we are no more twain but one flesh."[51] Love is here conceived and practiced as an emotion that can be known quickly and that thus only needs to be "confessed," most often by a man to a woman. This confession constituted the beginning rather than the endpoint of courtship and women were often courted after the man's sentiments had been established. Writing to Angelina after he met her briefly in March the same Weld confessed that his feelings "were all rushing as by rapid instantaneous *absorption into yours*."[52] Weld and Angelina committed themselves to each other for life in a matter of weeks, in the name of a spiritual, equal conception of marriage. In another example, Sally McDowell wrote to John Miller on October 13, 1854:

> They [your sentiments] had clustered thick about me whilst as yet I was wholly unconscious of their existence. That I should have awakened them was a wonder to me then, is a mystery to me still. But, when they were *revealed*, I endeavored to treat them with every kindness. For the first time, in many years I have listened to proposals such as yours. Heretofore, for reasons my previous letters have given, I turned from them with a kind of horror. But in your case (I speak too frankly to be misconceived) I paused, not that my resolution wavered, but because my regard for you indicated a different & a kinder course. I thought you too precipitate. *I did not know how you could learn to love me in so short a time. You seemed overtaken & overcome by a feeling that might exhaust itself in the first outbreak.* Yet you were painfully in earnest & I shrank from any semblance of severity in dealing the blow I was forced to give.[53]

Emotions are "declared" at the very beginning and once declared, they follow a course known in advance by all parties, a fact that made the "declaration" of feelings into a crucial moment. Calvin Lindley Rhone courted an
African American school teacher in Brenham, Texas, named Lucia J. Knotts.
His courtship took the same form of revelation as the one described above.
On May 31, 1886, Calvin wrote to Lucia a letter that would start a nineteen-
month-long courtship and decision to marry. His letter stated: "Do you ever
think of me? Miss Lucia, it is unnecessary to say, I love you with all my
heart."[54] In many cases of nineteenth-century courtship, love was declared
at the outset and was the starting rather than end point of the interaction.
Declaring love at the beginning of courtship thus neutralized emotional
uncertainty. More, emotional certainty was often the condition under which
a woman interacted with a man. By declaring himself, the man increased
his chances to win the heart of the beloved. Anthony Trollope, a very useful
source of information about courtship in the English middle class of the
nineteenth century, presents the moment called the "declaration " in his
1867 novel *The Claverings*. Mr. Saul declares to Fanny Clavering who has
been unsuspecting of his intentions:

> Yes, Miss Clavering, I must go on now; but not on that account would I
> press you to give me an answer to-day. I have learned to love you, and if
> you can love me in return, I will take you by the hand, and you shall be my
> wife. I have found that in you which I have been unable not to love,—not
> to covet that I may bind it to myself as my own forever. Will you think of
> this, and give me an answer when you have considered it fully?[55]

Here the declaration of love is, as it was often the case, immediately accompanied with a marriage proposal, which she must agree to or reject.

The many forms of certainty described above derive from a crucial sociological characteristic of courtship, namely the fact it had the structure of
ritual. Rituals are not about cognitions or representations. Rather, they create a dynamic field of energy that binds actors together through the enact-
ment of shared rules and through the shared participation in a hot symbolic
reality.[56] Rituals, like norms, define the intensity, boundaries, and object of
emotions. This is because, as Durkheim made clear, rituals reduce uncertainty and ambiguity.[57] Social reality always threatens to lose its order, to let
chaos and unpredictability enter our consciousness. Rituals are precisely
the device to offset the threat of chaos. As Joel Robbins insightfully puts it

(in reference to Roy Rappaport's massive work on rituals), rituals bring "clarity, certainty, trustworthiness, and orthodoxy on the information [they convey]."[58] Rituals bring people together through predictable and shared rules that intensify and sharpen emotions, reduce self-awareness, and increase the capacity to believe in the reality of the situation. Because ritual is a structured behavior, it directs attention to the object of the interaction rather than to the inner self. This is the reason why Douglas Marshall suggests that actors who engage in rituals experience their own will: When attention is focused on some external object, it is the emotional relation to the object that occupies the center of consciousness. Introspective focus on the rules of expression of sentiments would by contrast make the interaction more uncertain, and will make it the object of a negotiation rather than the result of well-known paths.[59] Moreover, the courtship ritual has a deeply narrative and sequentialized structure, itself the result of its strong normativity. Even when the tone was practical and matter-of-fact, a courtship had a telos, making the interaction highly purposive and based on progressive sequences.

To sum up: Pre-modern courtship was organized within a semiotic, social, normative framework that created cultural pathways for emotions to be organized teleologically and narratively through shared norms and rules. These pathways, to be sure, were based on gender inequality, on the equation of sexuality with sinfulness, on heteronormativity enshrined in law, and on the centrality of marriage for economic status and moral reputation. This form of certainty cannot be separated from religious patriarchy, gender inequalities, and the equation of sex with sinfulness. Even if it was increasingly contested, this moral and cultural frame was prevalent until the 1960s. For example, reminiscing about his life in a conversation with Harry Kreisler, the American philosopher Michael Walzer recalls that in 1957 he was about to leave for England to study at the University of Cambridge. His then-girlfriend, Judy, wanted to join him, but could do so only after he married her, to overcome her parents' opposition.[60]

For Niklas Luhmann, love consists in the creation of a shared world of two subjectivities, and moves within fixed and known meanings.[61] But probably because Luhmann did not pay much attention to sentiments, he missed altogether the distinction between the sentiment of love and the rituals that enable the unfolding of such sentiment. Love produces certainty when it is organized in social forms that make the future plausibly embedded in the interaction.[62] In the absence of a social structure that produces certainty, love in itself cannot generate certainty. Moreover, the demise of courtship—and of its attendant cultural and emotional structures—was caused by what has been conventionally dubbed sexual freedom, which unfolded through a complex institutional apparatus. The next section examines the collapse of certainty and the shift to uncertainty through the moral and institutional prevalence of freedom.

Sexual Freedom as Consumer Freedom

In her book *Sexuality: A Short Introduction*, sociologist Véronique Mottier asks: "How have we come to believe that sex is so important to who we are?"[63] I believe the answer to this question boils down to this: our sexuality is lived as the value and practice of freedom, a freedom that is all the more powerful and pervasive that it has been institutionalized in multiple arenas.

As I indicated in chapter 1, in evoking freedom in general and emotional and sexual freedom in particular, I do not refer to the glorious moral ideal that has guided democratic revolutions.[64] Following Foucault's thrust,[65] I view freedom as an institutionalized practice that reorganizes the relationship between constraint and choice, as a productive field of practices, as the source of new and multiple economic, technological, medical, symbolic practices. Moreover, freedom does not remain static; it evolves and changes its form and meaning because it operates differently in social contexts of disenfranchisement and in social contexts where freedom and autonomy are already guaranteed, morally and legally. The freedom in the name of which women and homosexuals fought and continue to fight against patriarchy is different from the freedom to engage in live sex in webcam rooms (the latter does not have a political or moral intent, but rather a specular one).

How Sexuality Became Free

What may look like a progressive liberation from religion was the result of powerful economic and cultural forces, which slowly and invisibly transformed the meaning of sexuality. The first social force operating on its redefinition took place in courtrooms. By the middle of the nineteenth century, the idea that sexuality was a private matter and should not be the object of public scrutiny and punishment took hold.[66] The "right to be let alone" expressed such widely held theory. It was penned in a very influential article with the title "The Right to Privacy" by famous American lawyers Samuel Warren and Louis Brandeis and stated: "The general object in view is to protect the privacy of private life."[67] This was an important precedent used to draw the boundaries of a private life in which sexuality could be practiced far away from the scrutiny and supervision of community. The "right to be let alone" has been interpreted to mean the right of a person to remove herself from the attention of others and to be immune from scrutiny in a private setting. This early legal concept—freedom from scrutiny— paved the way for subsequent legal views that guaranteed sexual freedom and for the cultural view that sexuality is the prerogative of the individual's private choice and thus freedom.

Another important change in the history of modern sexuality was the emergence of sexual science at the end of the nineteenth century. Beforehand, women's bodies had been thought to be imperfect imitations of males' bodies—a simple variation of a generically male body whose sexual organs were turned inside. But sexual science made men and women into sharply and ontologically distinct sexual and biological creatures.[68] Differences between men and women became biological, inscribed and visible in the materiality of their sexed bodies. This entailed the view that the sexes were not only different but also opposite. "Now men and women were distinctly different, with complementary strengths and weaknesses."[69]

If sexuality was a biological drive, this meant it was natural and as such it was not stained with sin.[70] If it was not sinful, it was easy to conceive of the sexual body as a hedonic entity, the site of pleasure and satisfaction. The Freudian revolution contributed to enshrine such view of sexuality as a pleasure principle that, albeit repressed by society, always simmered under the surface of consciousness, thus sending psychoanalytical subjects on a quest for the liberation of such pleasure. The biological hedonic body became the main object and target of a third massive cultural force, namely the consumer leisure sphere.[71] Under the influence of urbanization and the rise of a consumer leisure sphere, sexuality became recreational, for fun rather than for reproduction, the site for the exploration and realization of the "un-repressed" self in a variety of consumer venues.[72]

Thus, sexuality underwent major cultural shifts, which fed into one another: Through the legal sphere it was privatized and made into the prerogative of the individual. It was scientized through biological views of the body and thus snatched away from religious morality. Finally, the sexual body was converted into a hedonic unit both through Freudianism and consumer culture. Sexuality became a central topic of popular commercial and visual culture, of the scientific study of man (and woman), of art and literature;[73] it redefined the meaning of the good life and became an essential attribute of the healthy self, to be liberated from the oppressive yoke of social norms.[74] These various changes took place throughout the nineteenth and the twentieth centuries. They quickly spread in society because they were, if not endorsed, at least practiced by a variety of social and cultural elites, even before the 1960s, including celebrities who lived "scandalous lives": actors (Ingrid Bergman, who divorced), intellectuals (Simone de Beauvoir and Jean-Paul Sartre), writers (D. H. Lawrence; F. Scott Fitzgerald, Henry Miller, Vladimir Nabokov, Anaïs Nin, etc.), artists and avant-garde figures,[75] and scientists (Sigmund Freud, Alfred Kinsey, William Masters and Virginia Johnson, Margaret Mead). They all redefined a free sexuality as quintessentially modern, a free rather than sinful biological impulse, as a glamorous attribute of an elite lifestyle. Mostly, this new model of sexuality was promoted by movie actors, fashion models and artists, people working in public relations and in the "beauty industry," as they cultivated at once sexual attractiveness, beauty, and an erotic-romantic life located in the leisure sphere.[76] By cultivating their bodily appearance and "look," they were setting up and diffusing new sexual norms that incorporated at once fashion attires, sexuality, and leisure goods.

Throughout the twentieth century, it became increasingly clear that it was now up to the individual to fashion his or her sexuality in order to achieve glamour, attractiveness, well-being, and intimacy. Consumer culture provided the main cultural resource for that project. It did so in a number of ways.

Consumption as the Unconscious of Sexuality

From the beginning of the twentieth century, visual industries (cinema and advertising) became purveyors of images of beautiful sexual bodies, which elicited the viewer's desire. Through visual culture, sexuality became a visible feature of selfhood. Sexuality was no longer a secret part of one's interiority or a shameful identity to be liberated in the privacy of the psychoanalyst's office, but became a visual performance, located in visible consumer objects rather than in (sinful) thoughts and desires.[77] Such sexuality was mediated by consumer items (e.g., fashion clothing or cosmetics) and was put on display through the consumption of stories and images (e.g., in the cinema). Sexuality took on the form of a scopic regime of action, consumed through a variety of images of sexually attractive bodies displayed in public through a variety of consumer objects (see chapter 4). Sexual attractiveness mixed the sexual and the consumer in one. The visual consumer sphere, which emerged at the end of the nineteenth century, gained in extraordinary cultural and economic strength throughout the twentieth century because it made sexual identity into a visual performance mediated by consumer items[78] and sexual liberation into a cultural practice marked by a set of visual signifiers, codes, and style. Furthermore, sexual encounters increasingly took place in leisure venues and became the oblique commodity consumed through an array of direct consumer practices (bars, dance halls, clubs, restaurants, cafes, tourist resorts, beaches).

Sexuality was also made into an element of consumer culture in a third way: unmoored from religious prescriptions, sexuality meant that a market for sexual guidance could flourish. Such market came to be roughly divided within four major types of industries: the first was the industry of therapeutic-pharmacological services (provided in therapy, sexology, and pharmaceutical aids); the second was the industry of sex toys supposed to help and to improve sexual performances; the third was the advertising and film industrial complex, which provided guidelines for sexual demeanor, allure, behaviors, and interactions. The fourth industry is pornography, which uses men's and women's naked sexual bodies in the most obvious way. All of these simultaneously "liberated," shaped, and provided new visual guidelines for sexuality. For therapists, a free sexuality became an attribute of identity and mental health, to be painstakingly fashioned by scrutinizing one's psyche. For people working in the visual industrial complex, a liberated sexuality helped create new visual contents, enriching the cinematic plots and narratives by intertwining soft eroticism with the spectacle of attractive consumer goods.[79] For the sex toys industry, improving sexuality was a matter of using objects or technological devices to enhance sexual pleasure and performance. Finally, in pornography it is sexual excitation itself that is a commodity. In these markets, sexuality became a commodity to be consumed in order to achieve and realize well-being and pleasure.

Sexuality and consumer culture were made into seamless, coterminous practices through cultural objects that started playing an important role in inducing sexual moods. John Gagnon (unknowingly) describes this in his study of the transformation of sexual desire in the aftermath of World War I:

> These decades were also a period in which new social forms for desire were being created, especially for the young. The independent girl with her bare legs and short hair, young people dancing first to jazz and then to swing, double-dating in cars while listening to the sounds of Glenn Miller and Guy Lombardo, and the exquisite pleasures and anxieties of truly forbidden and dangerous unbuttonings and touchings were all inventions of this period.[80]

Gagnon refers to sexuality, sexual desire, and sexual liberation as induced, intertwined with, and elicited by consumer objects (bare legs, short hair, jazz singers, radio, cars are all consumer objects around which circulates an erotic atmosphere). The Woodstock music festival, held in 1969 in the aftermath of the 1968 revolts, was an example of the ways in which "cool" and emancipated cultural commodities came to be associated with sexuality.

The role of objects in constructing erotic atmospheres became all the more accentuated after 1960s capitalism faced the need to expand its own boundaries as markets became saturated with "solid" and standardized goods. It expanded by tapping into the self itself, into intimate life, and into sentiments, all of which started being heavily commercialized.[81] As Wolfgang Streeck puts it:

> The commercialization of social life [...] aimed to save capitalism from the specter of saturated markets after the watershed years. [...] The 1970s and 1980s were also a time when traditional families and communities were rapidly losing authority, offering markets the opportunity to fill a fast-growing social vacuum, which contemporary liberation theorists had mistaken for the beginning of a new age of autonomy and emancipation.[82]

Emancipated sexuality spread to most social classes through the slow shift from Fordist consumer economy to a post-Fordist one, using images and ideals of authenticity, fun, coolness, and pleasure. Sexuality was the key cultural value and practice bridging between "authentic" liberation projects and the commercialization of social life.[83] "Liberation" became a consumer niche and a consumer style. For example, the American feminist activist Susie Bright wrote a sexual memoir about her sexual awakening in the aftermath of the 1960s. Referring to the 1990s she writes: "At the boardwalk last summer, the fashion was to wear tight white pants, big hair—or no hair—and tattoos that disappeared down the cleavage. Not everyone was 'pretty,' but almost everyone was sexy. I could feel the fuck-me in the air."[84] Sexiness was universal where beauty was not because it was a matter of clothing style and marks on the body while beauty was in-born. Under the powerful influence of media and advertising culture, fashion, and cosmetics industries, consumer desire circulated through sexual desire and vice versa, sexual desire fixated on objects (see chapter 4). As Susie Bright again puts it in her sexual manifesto:

> Those top-forty hits I heard on the radio were more sexy than a hundred nudist diagrams. *Rock 'n' roll was sex,* and so were all those novels and movies I thrilled to—because those things actually possessed sexual creativity, and the people who composed them were probably as inspired as I was when they first came up with their ideas.[85]

Jeans, music, and media images sexualized women and men; all of these objects exist in a state of synergy in an atmosphere of liberation and freedom. Objects were eroticized and eroticism circulated through consumer objects. Bright here illustrates the tight intertwining of cultural and consumer artifacts with sex and sexiness, producing new sexual and cultural atmospheres.

Sexuality provided capitalism with extraordinary opportunity to expand because it required incessant self-fashioning and provided endless opportunities to create sexy atmospheres. Sexuality was the cultural platform to consume solid and standardized goods (e.g., bras, underwear, Viagra, or Botox), experiential goods (e.g., cafes, "singles" bars, or nudist camps), more intangible goods as therapeutic advice to improve sexual experience and competence, visual commodities (e.g., women's magazines or pornography), and what I would call atmospherical goods supposed to induce a sexy atmosphere. Sexuality thus became a manifold consumer object saturating consumer culture and private identity at once: it was an image of a beautiful self widely circulating in media industries; a form of competence in need of toys, expert advice, or medicine; a practice displayed in consumer venues; and a form of self-fashioning relying on vast variety of consumer objects. In short, sexuality was a consumer project, aiming to achieve one's deepest self and life's projects through a variety of consumer practices.

Interestingly then, it is not sexuality that is the unconscious of consumer culture, but consumer culture that has become the unconscious drive structuring sexuality.

Sexuality as Morality, Liberation as Power

Veronique Mottier points out:

> [T]he call for sexual liberation from capitalist and patriarchal repression by the Freudian Left was to have a deep influence on the leftist and feminist movements that emerged in the 1960s and 1970s, as well as on various new types of sex therapy which promoted the release of sexual energy. It reproduced a biological understanding of sexuality as a natural force, repressed by bourgeois society.[86]

This revolutionary understanding of sexuality had a deep and wide-ranging influence on society, significant for the economy and for the organization of the family. The goal of sexual revolution, as viewed by some of its proponents, was "to free women from the tyranny of biology, end the nuclear family, return to poly-morphously perverse sexuality, and allow women and children to do whatever they wished sexually."[87] The heterosexual family—with the man in control and the woman in the kitchen and at the cradle—was viewed as a source of oppression and false consciousness for women.[88] Feminist activists, who were at the forefront of the sexual struggle, demanded "sexual freedom, lesbian rights, reproductive control, abortion on demand, and freedom from sexual fear."[89]

Throughout the twentieth century, the demand for sexual freedom was forcefully affirmed by a variety of social actors: sexologists, psychoanalysts, the fashion industries, and the visual media, actors, and artists. But it could penetrate consumer practices because it became a key aspect of morality when feminists, sexual libertarians, and gay minorities demanded sexual equality and freedom, the two key values of modern morality. Sexuality thus became a political and moral project. It became a key motif of self-identity, at once moral and consumer. A contemporary proponent of sexual freedom, the German sexologist and sociologist Kurt Starke, provides an apt example of the ways in which sexual freedom writ large came to occupy the center stage of selfhood.

The human being does not need any prohibitions and also no injunctions. He needs nothing but free spaces. That is actually also what I fight for in my research. In my findings, I sense what incredible yearnings human beings have; how much they want not to put a brake on their feelings, but rather develop them; how they want to make themselves vulnerable, because it is a beautiful thing to be vulnerable, and not be wounded; because it is completely wonderful if one is allowed to have feelings that are chaotic; when one is permitted to be weak; when the tender one has more chances than the brutal one. And societies have to be organized so that human beings are protected, so that they can live all this out.[90]

Starke illustrates the ways in which free sexuality entirely reshaped conceptions of self and social relations. Because it concerned so many aspects of society, the effects of the sexual freedom did not take long to be felt:

In 1963, 65% of respondents identify a campus sexual normative pattern limited to "necking" as appropriate, expected behavior for casual daters. An additional 23% felt that no form of sexual behavior was expected. By 1971, although a majority of respondents continue to identify necking as the appropriate normative standard, a substantial minority chose the next highest category, light to moderate petting. By 1978, the selection of necking had diminished to a third of all responses, and the category of light to moderate petting was now the most frequently selected option.[91]

The baby boomer generation changed patterns of premarital sex with their tendencies to actively engage in premarital sex having grown throughout the years since the 1970s.[92] Active premarital sex became an ordinary feature of the lives of young men and women and even adolescents.

The moral and political sexual revolution made sexuality into a prime terrain for feminist struggles, dividing feminists into sexual libertarians (wanting to multiply and affirm sexual pleasure in all its forms) or sexual skeptics, those for whom sexuality remained a terrain for male domination. But whatever the content of these debates, mass media seized on the image of the liberated and powerful woman and recycled a key feminist message: an emancipated, strong, and positive woman was comfortable in her body and sexuality, themselves mediated by consumer items. During the 1980s and most definitely in the 1990s advertising (e.g., Victoria's Secret),[93] TV (e.g., Sex and the City), and movies (see among endless cinema examples, the 1983 *The Hunger* featuring Susan Sarandon and Catherine Deneuve in a lesbian sex scene) presented sexuality as a site for the display of "girls' power," equating power with sexuality. Advertising and popular music increasingly used the spectacle of quasi-naked bodies to advertise for a variety of products from music clips to lingerie, tourist sites or cars.[94] Media industries thus played a crucial role in endorsing sexuality by recycling a partial and distorted version of feminism, whereby sexual equality and freedom were equivalent to buying power and sexuality on display.[95] Women's bodies were no longer the site of direct male discipline and control but the site for the experience and exercise of their agency through consumer freedom. The famous American TV series *Sex and the City* (which ran from 1998 to 2004) exemplified such post-feminist equation of girl's power through a free sexuality mediated by the market. The series offered to the world the spectacle of women's increased economic power, of sexual adventurousness, and of their deep embeddedness in the industries of beauty, fashion, cosmetics, thinness, sports and leisure. *Sex and the City* reflected the fact that women were espousing sexual and consumer freedom in a single embrace. The series also reflected the fact that sexual encounters had become increasingly structured *like* a market, a social arena governed by competition in which value is established by supply and demand.[96] In that market, men of middle and high social status were becoming subtly in control of the sexual field *through* sexual freedom and not through a direct control of women's bodies. As the following three chapters will show, patriarchy intersected with capitalism and exercised its grip through the intense sexualization of women, through the generalization of casual sex, through beauty myths, through increasingly forceful norms of female sexual attractiveness,[97] and through the different positions of men and women in the romantic and sexual field, all of which are elements of scopic capitalism. This scopic capitalism is defined by the extraction of surplus value from the spectacle and visual display of bodies. Scopic capitalism is key to understanding how sexual changes went hand in hand with new instruments of cultural power deployed by capitalist entreprises.

A New Social and Sexual Grammar

Sexual liberation was accompanied by legal changes that granted greater rights to women and greater autonomy and agency to their bodies.[98] This legal and political revolution was undergirded, as we saw above, by an economic one[99] in which the consumer market penetrated and reorganized a large segment of identity and selfhood.[100] Inasmuch as sexual freedom was mostly and chiefly reorganized in a series of landmark judicial cases under the umbrella of negative freedom—letting people do what they want in their bedroom—it became a vector for negative freedom (doing what one wants without hurting others). The consumer market (later aided by technology) and therapy could colonize the empty space opened by negative freedom through what Axel Honneth dubs "reflexive freedom."[101] Reflexive freedom requires actors to think about what they want and makes them scrutinize their will. It is about self-determination and self-realization of desires and subjectivity. According to Honneth, reflexive freedom is of two kinds: Kantian-rational (it asks itself if it conforms to rational ends and strives for autonomy) and Hegelian-romantic (it asks itself if it expresses the true self). Sociologically, the romantic character of reflexive freedom has been vigorously organized in the consumer market and its technological avatars (enabling the endless expression of authentic wants, desires, pulsions, needs). Its rational character has been expressed in therapy, which constitutes a vast institution to organize and scrutinize the will guided by the ideal of autonomy. The combination of the consumer market and psychology has had a power parallel to the one that Peter Brown ascribed to Christianity, which, in his words made "the will [win] over the cosmos."[102] Psychology and the consumer market replaced the "will" with "(individual) desire," making sexual desire the root model for other forms of desire, making sexuality itself moral, and offering techniques and practices to free and implement sexual desires. Sexuality, which was one of the chief political terrains of feminists and homosexuals, became a politically muddled terrain, at once the site for uprooting the source of patriarchy and the revolving platform for a wide array of consumer practices. These different social forces changed the place of sexuality in kinship, marriage, and broader conceptions of the self.

The first significant impact of the sexual revolution and what made it properly modern in the philosophical sense of the word was its radical shift to immanence. The sexual revolution disentangled sexuality from the kinship system and from the cosmology that had tied sexuality to religion. Kinship rules define lineage, one's ancestors, heirs, and kin. But more crucially, they bind sexuality to culture, with biology playing a secondary role in determining relationships of proximity (as when in certain tribes a

mother's brother is viewed as the mother of a child).[103] As defined by
Marshall Sahlins, kinship is "'mutuality of being': people who are intrinsic to
one another's existence."[104] In that sense, sexuality regulated by kinship
rules was organized within and by a system of mutuality. More than that: as
Enric Porqueres and Jérôme Wilgaux suggest, "Christians, through the
Epistles of Saint Paul, but also the Talmud of the same period, take seriously
the idea that through sex husband and wife become '*one flesh*,'"[105] where the
fusion is here to be taken both metaphorically and literally as the joining of
two bodies.[106] The pre-modern Christian view of sexuality consecrated the
conjoining of souls and bodies. Sacramental sexuality expresses the participation of persons in a cultural cosmos that binds them.

In disentangling sexuality from kinship system, that is, from most rules
of endogamy, from the cosmological vision in which men, women, sexuality, and the cosmos form one single entity, and from the view of married
bodies forming a single flesh, "free" or "emancipated" sexuality created a
new plane of immanence in which the sexual body became its own self-
referential point, disconnected from other bodies and persons. If sexuality
was a "natural instinct," the sexual body could become pure physiology,
governed by hormones and neural endings. It underwent the same process
as nature under the rational gaze of science: it became emptied of meanings
that connected personhood to larger cosmological or moral conceptions of
self, with the body becoming a materiality, a matter endowed with an
agency of its own, aiming at its own pleasure now conceived as a biological
force (or as a drive) and as property of a separate individual. More exactly,
such a self-referential sexual body searched for meaning in the authenticity,
pleasure, and self-affirmation provided by the consumer market and
therapy.

The second transformation entailed by the sexual revolution is that the
number of partners in a lifetime has significantly changed, with sexual
experience and exploration becoming a significant and independent aspect
of many or most people from different socioeconomic groups. As historian
Barry Reay describes it:

[I]t is essential to note that morality and practice changed over time. [...]
Martin King Whyte's 1984 Detroit Area Study found that the cohort of
women married between 1925–44 said that (on average) they had dated
4–7 males, the baby boomers married from 1945–64 had dated 10–14
males, and the youngest cohort of 1965–84 estimated 12–15 potential

premarital sexual partners. Those who were calculated to have had sex before marriage ranged across the cohorts from 24 percent (1925–44) to 72 percent (1965–84). But if finer divisions are made in the last cohort, it goes to 56 percent (1965–9), 67 percent (1970–4), 85 percent (1975–9), and 88 percent (1980–4).[107]

In other words, premarital sex increasingly became legitimized and the longer the time span between the first partner and the choice of a stable regular mate, the more likely people tended to accumulate sexual experiences.[108] This implies that sexuality is now conceived as the experience of accumulating encounters and meeting a large amount of partners. Against this backdrop, sexuality also became a new form of status and competence. While the ideal of virginity had been previously indexed on social reputation and value, and was equalitarian (in the sense that a virgin was equivalent to any other virgin in her virginity), "sexiness" and "sexual performance" became signals of one's position in sexual fields with unequally distributed forms of ranks and status.

The third impact of the sexual revolution is to have splintered romantic encounters from within, between three different cultural logics, institutions, and discourses: marriage markets, emotional experiences, and sexual practices. Three cultural structures—the emotional, the matrimonial, and the sexual—exist on different social planes, each having different, and even conflicting, phenomenological and normative structures. In the sexual market, for example, one has sexual relations without feeling morally obligated to maintain contact, whereas in the emotional or marriage market one is more likely to be accountable for one's behavior.[109] The autonomization of these three paths—emotional, matrimonial, sexual—means that sexuality has become a sphere of action in its own right, independent from emotional exchange or from shared domesticity and that each of these spheres of conduct, albeit connected, now follows a cultural logic of its own; it forms "a regime of action," as French sociologists Luc Boltanski and Laurent Thévenot called it.[110] This splintering of the emotional and sexual encounter into different regimes of action is a chief effect of sexual freedom and has had tremendous consequences in making men's and women's interactions far more uncertain (as I will explore in chapter 3). While both men and women have embraced the sexual revolution, it has thrown them on distinct sociological paths to navigate differently emotions, matrimony, and sexuality (see chapters 4 and 5). As has often been argued, men tend to separate sexuality from emotions far more easily than women, while women tend to view themselves as emotionally far more competent than men (see chapters 5 and 6).

Finally, sexual freedom presupposes a free will that can enact contractual definitions of social relationship, and redefines the content of sexual morality. For sexual libertarian Gayle Rubin, the greatest moral evil in sexuality is inequality and the double standard. Rubin compares traditional sexual morality to an ideology of racism in that it enables one group to claim sexual virtue and to relegate the sexually non-virtuous to an inferior, morally dangerous status. Rubin offers a substitute sexual ethics:

> A democratic morality should judge sexual acts by the way partners treat one another, the level of mutual consideration, the presence or absence of coercion, and quantity and quality of the pleasures they provide. Whether sex acts are gay or straight, coupled or in groups, naked or in underwear, commercial or free, with or without video, should not be ethical concerns.[111]

This redefinition of sexual morality, which reflects well the historical shift observed by sexuality after the 1970s, has had an overwhelming effect: to free the sexual and romantic terrain from what might be called thick normativity by introducing a thin, procedural one. Thick normativity contains elaborate stories and prescriptions that define actions in terms of good and bad, immoral and moral, pure and impure, shameful and commendable, virtuous and vile, and thus connects human behavior to cultural cosmologies, large collective stories (such as that of the original sin or purity) that contain definite conceptions of the good and the bad, the moral and the immoral. Thin, procedural morality on the other hand gives individuals the right to decide about the moral content of their preferences and focuses on the rules and procedures to secure respect for the psychic and bodily autonomy of the individual. It is thus relatively silent on the moral valence of actions, and evaluates them in reference to the degree to which they respect the subject's autonomy and capacity to experience pleasure. While sexuality has obviously remained the object of intense moral, political, and social struggles, their center of gravity has shifted: It is no longer questions of purity or sinfulness that preoccupy contemporaries, but rather issues that touch upon sexual equality and consent, with rape, abortion, pornography, sexual harassment, or teen pregnancies becoming the focus of social and public debates. Questions about the regulation of the image of women's bodies in the above-mentioned key industries, sexual harassment, or date rape are all, deep down, questions about consent (Can/Should women consent to participate in industries and practice that demean and commodify them? How explicit should one be in asking permission to engage in intercourse?) Consent derives from an epistemology based on the body (since bodies are separate and cannot be violated) and views the relationship as a series of encounters since it is, in principle, to be secured at each encounter. Making consent into the chief ethical discourse implies a deep transformation of the moral and ethical discourses regulating sexual intersubjectivity and has a deep impact on the entry in relationships, which become based on the subjective will and desire (see chapter 5).

These four transformations of sexuality in the process of sexual liberation— the immanence of the sexual body recuperated by the consumer market and by Internet technology, the formation of a category of experience based on the accumulation of sexual experiences, the splintering of the heterosexual encounter in possible different paths, and the shift to a procedural ethics based on consent—constitute the new terrain for the formation of heterosexual relations. All the transformations described above made sexuality highly permeable to the values, vocabulary, and grammar of the market, into a realm of self-affirmation of the self and into a terrain of struggle between men and women.

All these characteristics and changes of sexuality have disposed the ritual character of sexual interactions and have made sexual relationships riddled with uncertainty and negative sociality, that is, a sociality in which men and women frequently and quickly withdraw from relationships. In the next chapters, I turn to a closer analysis of the mechanisms through which sexual social relations become what I call "negative."

3

Confusing Sex

He changed women often because he concluded that only the first encounter was worth anything: he was an expert at the essentially modern art of dropping women.

—Irène Némirovsky[1]

Few cultural projects have been as total as the project of sexual freedom: it disentangled sex from sin and shame, and, with psychologists aiding, made sexuality a synonym of emotional health and well-being. It was also a project that aimed at making women and men, heterosexuals and homosexuals, into equals.[2] It was thus a fundamentally political project. Sexual freedom also legitimized sexual pleasure for its own sake[3] and thus instilled hedonic rights, a diffuse cultural sense that individuals are entitled to sexual pleasure in order to achieve the good life. Finally, sexual freedom was part and parcel of the culture of authenticity, as well as a practice of authentication of the self: sexuality revealed and enacted one's true self.[4] But what made sexual freedom into the pervasive cultural structure it has become was the fact that it was appropriated by and enacted in the economic sphere. Sexuality became performatively achieved through the economy and vice versa, and economic practices converged in sexualized selves and performances.

Industrial capitalism was based on the factory and the family, as the two central pillars organizing economic and biological reproduction.[5] The courtship system described in the previous chapter was part of the broader socialization *to* the bourgeois family that emerged as the hidden pillar of industrial capitalism. The family trains and prepares the individual for the psychic renunciation, self-discipline, and cooperation required by the capitalist workplace. After World War II, and most decisively after the 1960s, an important aspect of the culture of capitalism shifted: as Gilles Deleuze suggests, capitalism "was no longer for production but for the product, which is to say, for being sold or marketed."[6] As Deleuze further argues, this new form of capitalism was essentially dispersive: the family stopped being the social pillar of economic production. Instead, it was individuals—as creative laborers and authentic consumers—who replaced the factory worker and, one may add, the family itself as the privileged center for the formation of the self.[7] This form of dispersive capitalism did not need the traditional social agencies that had regulated sexual encounters and channeled them to the formation of families. Sexuality was not only what one did in one's bedroom, but a myriad of consumer practices reorganizing the body, its appearance, one's *rapport a soi*, one's desires, presentation of self, and social relationships in general. In fact, sexuality became so intrinsic to the economy that we may speak properly of the emergence of a new form of action: *sexual action*, where one's body, cultural strategies, values, goals, and sense of self are ordered from within a core that perceives itself at once as sexual, psychological, and economic.[8] The social form that captures best this major transformation of sexuality in capitalism is "casual sex," understood here as a form of sexuality for its own sake, legitimately and even commendably distinct from sex in stable relationships.

Casual Sexuality and Its Elusive Effects

In itself, there is nothing historically new about casual sexuality.[9] But in its modern form, it emerged as the political and moral demand to free sexuality from religious taboos and economic exchange; it was, at least in principle, gender-blind; it became associated with broader practices of self-affirmation, authenticity, and autonomy. Casual sex took place in modern spatial venues, cities or university campuses for example, thus enabling men and women from varied geographical, ethnic, and social locations to interact with one another, far away from the social control exerted formally or informally by one's primary and secondary groups. In that sense, casual sex was a striking expression of the democratic lifting of social, ethnic, and religious boundaries that had hitherto separated social groups. Casual sex thus at once contained new moral norms and made abundant use of the commercialized leisure sphere. Both aspects became fused in a single matrix: casual sex was an expression of individual freedom.

That casual sex was the ultimate mark of freedom was aptly captured in Erica Jong's memorable expression "the zipless fuck"—defined as a guilt- and shame-free sexual interaction, with no ulterior motive beyond its own experience, that is, without any goal beyond the sexual interaction itself.[10] Casual sex did not remain a static form. It evolved and became a distinct social form known under various names as "hookup," "friends with bene-fits," or "fuck buddy."[11] In French, it is known as "*plan cul*," literally "pussy plan" (an expression that suggests an obvious male bias in casual sex). In the words of historian of sexuality Barry Reay, casual sex is "ephemeral, transi-tory, outside or supplemental to the context of a longer-term sexual rela-tionship."[12] Because casual sex is transient and relatively well structured in time, it can take a commodity form and be highly suitable to the high veloc-ity of consumption of consumer spaces, adventures, and experiences. The elective affinity between casual sex and consumption became obvious with the technology of the Internet, which accelerated and sharpened the organ-ization of sexual encounters as a market (people meeting each other follow-ing the attribution of value) and made the encounter into a commodity purchased and disposed of, most glaringly in the wide gamut of available Internet sites and apps such as Tinder. To quote a *Vanity Fair* article about the Tinder app:

> Mobile dating went mainstream about five years ago; by 2012 it was over-taking online dating. In February, one study reported there were nearly 100 million people—perhaps 50 million on Tinder alone—using their phones as a sort of all-day, every-day, handheld singles club, where they might find a sex partner as easily as they'd find a cheap flight to Florida. "It's like ordering Seamless," says Dan, the investment banker, referring to the online food-delivery service. "But you're ordering a person. [...] Dating apps are the free-market economy come to sex."[13]

I would like to interrogate the features of casual sex from within the tradi-tion of symbolic interactionism and phenomenology:[14] How have casual sex and the generalized sexualization of relationships transformed the for-mation of relationships? As I will show, heterosexual casual sex generates a profound uncertainty that is driven at once by the high volume of interac-tions afforded by technology, by consumer culture that defines interactions as hedonist and short-lived ones, and by gender asymmetries that remain highly operative in the competitive organization of capitalism.

According to therapist and sociologist Leslie Bell, "[T]he current average age of first sexual intercourse for girls is seventeen, leaving ten years of sex-ual and relationship activity before the current average age of marriage at twenty-seven. These women don't think twice about cohabiting with a partner, or about delaying marriage until their own careers are on track."[15] In this view, sexual activity simply delays marriage, that is, creates a longer buffer period during which sexuality is explored. This perspective implicitly suggests that free sexuality does not fundamentally alter the traditional structure of relationships and marriage, but only changes their onset. Yet, Leslie Bell is perplexed by the current malaise her clients manifest. As I show now, increased sexual activity and the prevalence of casual sex do not simply create a buffer period: they have effects on the formation of relationships that are as powerful as they are elusive. Free sexuality framed by consumer culture and technology reverberates on the structure of relationships and creates forms of uncertainty that in turn are at the heart of negative relations.

Endless accounts of casual sex stress the fact that people can engage in sex without knowing their partner's name, suggesting anonymity is an attribute of casual sex.[16] As Lisa Wade reports in her analysis of sex on American campuses, men at parties typically signal their sexual intentions by sticking their genitals in the back of a woman. "Because men generally come up to women from behind, sometimes the identity of the man whose penis abuts their backside is a mystery."[17] As a social form, casual sex is characterized by symbolic strategies to de-singularize the sexual partner (approaching someone from behind obliterates the face and thus de-singularizes the other person). Names on the other hand both identify and singularize a person. In its pure form, people engaging in casual sex *must* remain strangers to each other. In that sense, casual sex mimics the anonymity and transience of interactions in the consumer sphere and mixes features located at two opposite poles: distance and strangeness on the one hand (as is the case of interactions where one does not know another's name), and closeness on the other (cultural signs of closeness include showing oneself naked, sharing one's bedroom or bed, sharing sexual pleasure). It disconnects between body and selfhood since it views the body as an autonomous source of pleasure and thus as a pure materiality. Finally, casual sex actively demands that partners cut themselves off from any projection in the future. Casual sex makes interactions legitimately short-lived, pleasure-centered, and self-referential, pursued for their own sake. As a result, like all anonymous relationships, casual sex has one key characteristic: it weakens rules of reciprocity.[18] This is strikingly illustrated by classicist scholar Daniel Mendelsohn's memoir *Elusive Embrace*:

[W]e have all done what he does: the thrill of seduction, the absolute pleasure, brief of course but heady, of knowing *they want you*. [...] I would have to make a count of the boys whom I myself have fled once I've had them; the gentle and hopeful Southern neighbor whose breath was sweet with Jack Daniel's when we finally kissed and whose calls I stopped returning the next day, and who wrote me an angry note that I pretended to find amusing but then shoved to the bottom of the trash can, as if it might physically hurt me, the tall and beautifully muscled copper-haired man from the gym who, over dinner, after I'd found him in the locker room, turned out to be surprisingly shy and wanted to talk about writers and writing, and I condescended to do so only because I wanted to make sure he'd come back to my apartment even though I knew, because he's told me, that he didn't like one night stands, and when I finally got him back to Twenty-fifth Street and started unbuttoning his shirt he pulled back but finally gave in, and two weeks later left his last unanswered phone message on my machine, as I sat there listening, too panicked to pick up the phone, or the others, the men you meet-on-line, the men whose numbers you get in restaurants and bars, the men whose notice is so precious to you at the moment you perceive it that you do anything and tell them anything just to get them, to have them, and once you do, you need to have another, someone else, someone different, and you must fill off the earlier boy, the one you'd been so desperate to get the other night, you must make him disappear because if you see him again he will become a particular boy and not just Boy, not just the thing that keeps you out all night or up all night or on-line all night in the hopes that he, like so many others, will pass your small apartment where desire is something about *you*, something you can control, something, finally, that has nothing to do with the other person who happens to be in the room.[19]

In this account, casual sex is exhilarating, as it affirms the subject's freedom and the ongoing renewal of a steady supply of desires, but it obliterates the possibility of reciprocity, attachment, and bonding. In fact, one of the pleasures of such interactions probably resides in the fact they do not implicate the self and do not entail reciprocity. A *New York Times* article on hookup culture drives this point. Introducing a prototypical young male, Duvan Giraldo, the article suggests that casual sex is not based on reciprocity. Claiming that the satisfaction of his partner "is always his mission," the young Giraldo added that "[in casual sex] I'm not going to try as hard as when I'm with someone I really care about." This is because it can be awkward to talk about sexual needs with women he's just met. "You're practically just strangers at that point," he said."[20] In fact, as Lisa Wade put it: "Men have more orgasms than women in hookup culture, then, because the culture doesn't promote reciprocity. It's specifically designed for men's orgasm."[21]

As sociologist Steven Seidman has suggested, casual sex is "pleasure-centered," act-based, interchangeable, and "any expectations of intimacy, commitment and responsibility are restricted to the encounter."[22] In that sense, casual sex is a social form that encapsulates the multiplicity of relationships with strangers that characterize modern urban consumer venues, with anonymity often playing a significant role in them. Precisely because the core of the encounter is the maximization of bodily pleasure, it is devoid of telos (much like Durkheim's single man discussed in the previous chapter).

As a social form, casual sex has considerably evolved from Erica Jong's "zipless fuck." On a site called Quora—whose purpose is "to give the best answer to any question"—we may find the following example of contemporary casual sex (as an answer to the question if...):

Yes. In college. Met a girl at the club. We were both on extasy [sic]. We didn't even flirt or talk more than a few words. She was a friend of my female friend from the dorms (Abbie, who was a stunner). There were 3 females and myself in the group.

When the extasy really started to hit, the girls started touching each other (not groping, just lightly brushing a shoulder or running fingers through their hair), then lightly kissing. I was just sitting there in awe enjoying it. The three of them were on a couch and I was on another. The two couches were facing each other.

At one point, my friend Abbie and one of the other two girls started really making out. The other sat there on the side a bit just rubbing the other girls, but apparently felt left out eventually and she came and sat down by me. We started kissing, and it almost immediately turned from light kisses to deep passionate ones. Next thing I know she reached down and grabbed my erection and caressed it through my pants.

After about 10 minutes of doing this, I grabbed her by the hand and led her to the hallway leading to the bathrooms. The hallway led past the two bathrooms, then turned a corner where there were two locked doors for staff or storage, then downstairs to a fire exit. I had explored the area before and knew it was there. I led her around the corner and down the stairs. She clearly knew what I had in mind...why else would I have been leading her to an extremely private part of the club.

Once there we started making out some more. I was running my hands all over her, but wasn't going under her clothes just yet. She started working at my belt, but was having a hard time because it wasn't a typical style. I started to help and she knelt down. Once we had my pants open she began to give me a blowjob. She was good, and I couldn't let her continue for too long or else the little rendezvous would have been far shorter than I would have liked.

I grabbed her arms and pulled her back into a kiss and then started working at her pants. I got her pants and panties completely off of her and she slung a leg over my shoulder so I could eat her out. She was partially shaven, and that allowed me to really get enthusiastic while doing this. (Its hard to be enthusiastic when you are trying to avoid getting hair in your mouth.) She came a few times while I was eating her out before she pulled me back up for more kissing.

After that, she instructed me to "lose my pants" and lay on the concrete. She then straddled me and sat down on top of me, riding me cowgirl style. This was the only time in my life I didn't use a condom when not in a monogamous committed relationship. But being on extasy and having this beauty sitting on top of me, and riding me bareback was one of the peak sexual experiences of my life. She didn't get too vigorous, mostly she just rocked her hips while on top of me, or slight thrusting on my part while she quickly fucked me from the top.

We did this for probably close to an hour (amazing we weren't caught) when my friend Abbie came to the top of the stairs and called down to us. She couldn't see us completely, but she could tell what we were doing. The other girl Abbie had been making out with had to go home, so she was by herself. She kept talking to us. Normally this probably would have been very weird, but maybe because of the extasy, it felt completely natural. Abbie asked if she could come down and I said yes before her friend could respond. But the girl just smiled, so I figured she was fine with it. Abbie came down the stairs and just leaned against the wall watching with her hand in her pants.

After a bit, Abbie stopped watching, and just leaned her head back with her eyes closed. She said she loved hearing us fuck. We were being pretty quiet, but that was what turned her on, the soft little moans and the slight sound of pounding flesh. She just kept talking to us. She admitted she had taken another hit of extasy and was rolling really hard. I just alternated between looking at the girl on top of me, and then Abbie. I don't know what caught my attention more, this girl riding on top of me, or Abbie standing there with her hands in her pants.

I told Abbie she should take her pants off while she masturbated. She asked why? I said that with it would be far more stimulating seeing a pussy while one was actually making use of my cock. At that she locked her eyes on mine and gave me this terrible look. I thought she was pissed at me, and could tell immediately that I was beginning to lose my erection over this. I decided to play it cool though and gave her my best seductive smile. She then gave me a slight smile and started taking her pants off. At this, my erection was harder than it had been the whole night. She got her shoes and pants off and then leaned back and put her hand in her panties. Of course, I couldn't see her pussy with her panties still on, but I decided not to press my luck.

Her friend was now watching her as earnestly as I was, while still grinding her hips on top of me. Her friend then said "panties too Abbie!" and they looked at each other for a moment, before Abbie complied and took them off. Then to my shock and awe, Abbie walked over to the other side of the large landing we were on and found a place to lift her leg and rest it while leaning back against the wall again. Her upper back was against the wall, but her leg was at least a foot out from the wall. This gave us a great view of her pussy and she seemed to enjoy showing us. Instead of one hand, this time she used both. She spread the outer lips to give us a great view as she rubbed her clit and thrust a finger, then two, then three in and out.

After about ten minutes of this, her friend asked her to come over and she grabbed Abbie's now thoroughly wet hand and sucked and licked it clean. Abbie had now started using her other hand to rub her pussy. I then grabbed Abbie's ankle and directed her legs to either side of my head and told her to sit down.

I proceeded to eat Abbie's pussy while I could hear her and her friend kissing passionately. Amazingly enough, they then decided to switch positions and the friend sat on my face while Abbie impaled herself on my cock. After a short period of time, it got pretty frenzied, and the girl on my face came, then Abbie and I came together, while the girl on my face followed us with one more orgasm.

I just lay there while these two kissed each other softly. They eventually stood up and switched again. This time to clean me up. Abbie kissed me tasting her friend's juices, while her friend sucked on my receding erection, tasting my juices combined with Abbie's. Once she had finished with my cock, she pulled Abby up leaned her against the wall and cleaned Abby up as well, even inserting her tongue and slurping at the deposit I had made.

At this point, I was rock solid again and ready to go for more, but Abbie's friend had to go…we had been at this for well over two hours. I am still amazed we never got caught.

About a month later, Abbie and I went and both got tested for STD's together. We were clean, so she didn't bother asking her friend to do so as well.

Abbie and I dated for a little while, and even included her friend on our lovemaking on occasion. Our relationship didn't last through till summer break though, and she moved away when she graduated and pursued her graduate degree.[23]

This long vignette contains many sociologically interesting elements. First is the obvious sexual competence of each of the actors involved, as each seems to be fluent in a grammar of social bonds based on the production of their own and of others' sexual pleasure. We cannot distinguish passive and active actors, competent or incompetent, inhibited or liberated. As suggested in the previous chapter, sexual competence is a relatively recent form of social competence, formalized and codified by sexologists, by therapeutic advice, by soft and hard pornographic images, and by various "sexual pleasure activists" (various segments of feminist or sex workers advocacy).[24] Moreover, the type of interaction described above requires a complex orchestration of different bodies into a concerted situation whose purpose is to satisfy and be satisfied by many partners at once. The vignette displays then a high degree of coordination and tacit understanding between actors who are mere acquaintances to one another. This occurs precisely because these participants have a high degree of sexual competence. They act as if they are rehearsing a pornographic scene known to all parties, that is, a scene in which all participants display sexual fluency and scriptedness (probably learned from the widespread availability of pornography)[25] and from a scopic *mise-en-scene* where others perform a culturally scripted sexual fantasy and a pornographic cliché (two women have sex with a single man, pleasuring themselves and the man). The high scriptedness of this scene is visual rather than narrative or normative. Its sexuality is public (in a club), unplanned and spontaneous, and beyond conventional sexual binary classifications (intimacy vs. publicness; homosexual vs. heterosexual, monogamy vs. polyamory). The scene is also relatively egalitarian: It does not privilege one's gender pleasure. Each participants' orgasm is the implicit norm moving the interaction forward. The sexual fluidity of all participants derives less from a political ideology than from the fact that the sexualized body searches for its pleasure in a way that transcends binary classifications. Any body, male or female, can be a source or object of pleasure, because bodies are viewed in their materiality, as functional sources of orgasmic pleasure, beyond gender differences (although the vignette corresponds to a traditional male fantasy). The plurality of participants in this scene points to a diffusion of sexual pleasure in both meanings of the word *diffusion*: sex spreads itself, becomes inclusive rather than exclusive, is not concentrated on a single person, and it also becomes a diffuse and genderless quality of an atmosphere, rather than a privileged exchange between two people. Furthermore, the scene is a public performance rather than a private encounter and this in many ways: it is done in public (a club's stairs and back rooms); it is a performance executed for the eyes of a group that extends the traditional dyad; and it is later transformed in a story told on Quora, the site for "the best answer to any question." In that sense, it resonates with the increasingly public character of sexuality through the Internet. Finally, and this is important, the encounter is not the departure point of a life story. It is told as a single episode, which repeats itself as a series of discreet episodes, but does not start a story, affair, or relationship. Casual sex obliterates narrative linearity that inhered in traditional heterosexual relationships. It is lived as a punctual episode, not intended to a specific particular person or individual, but rather to a general attractive sexed body. In that sense, casual sex is an abstract social form that is not geared at particularity. More than that, casual sex strips others of their singularity and neutralizes what Luc Boltanski has called the process of singularization, which, according to him, is an essential aspect of sociality.[26] Sexual pleasure, sexual choice, the accumulation of sexual experience through multiple partners, fundamentally transformed the formation of heterosexual encounters, altering the ways in which stable emotional and cultural frames are formed and maintained.

Because traditional heteronormative sex was sex with a purpose (whether this purpose was marriage, love, shared life, or a child),[27] casual sex subverts the narrative telos of heteronormativity.[28] Instead, it aims at the accumulation of pleasurable experiences, which in turn becomes a status signal, a sign of having a body marked by others as attractive. For example, in her memoirs *Not That Kind of Girl*, the celebrated author of *Girls*, Lena Dunham, recounts her adolescence and entry into adulthood following a narrative of anxiety about her sexual competence.[29] Her entry into adulthood is described as a long, repeated attempt to overcome her virginity (with the clear implication of virginity as a source of shame). For boys and girls, loss of virginity marks the possibility to enter and join the social class of sexually desirable people. In that sense, casual sex is part of the emergence of new forms of social capital, in which sex, sexual activity, and sexual competence form new marks of status and criteria of worth. To summarize: The hookup, the one-night stand, the sex party, the zipless fuck are defined as relationships *without expectations*, in which each actor is legitimately involved in the pursuit of his/her own self-interested pleasure, with no expectations of emotional mutuality, relationality, or projection in the future. Each encounter is supposed to provide pleasure and the accumulation of such encounters in turn bestows status on their actors.

It is thus unsurprising that for some sexual libertarians, prostitution is the paradigm for liberated and pleasurable sex. In the words of Margo St. James, founder of the sex workers' organization COYOTE (*Call Off Your Old Tired Ethics*): "I've always thought that whores were the only emancipated women. We are the only ones who have the absolute right to fuck as many men as men fuck women."[30] In this view, liberated sexuality and gender equality are established in the capacity to "fuck" a high number of sexual partners and in the capacity to detach sexual activity from emotions, moral sentiments, and social norms.[31] As a social performance, a casual sexual encounter is successful if it does not generate any expectations, if no one projects oneself in the future, if it allows partners to experience unhindered physical pleasure and to be equal in their mutual detachment. Casual sex thus defined is akin to a service transaction, based on performing well in a transient and anonymous way, on the de-singularization of others, and on the lack of mutual commitment. In that sense, casual sex has an abstract form, much like money for Karl Marx and Georg Simmel. Money is abstract because it makes commodities interchangeable in subsuming them under their exchange (monetary) value. In casual sex, people, like commodities, become equivalent and subsumed under orgasmic pleasure as a currency. In other words, casual sex subsumes people under their orgasmic value and makes them interchangeable and therefore abstract as mere pleasure functions.

Egalitarian politics was the source of casual sex as a new social form, legitimate for both genders. Yet, it has been frequently associated with a masculine form of sexuality both in scholarly literature and in popular stereotypes.[32] This is for a number of reasons. The first is that men have always enjoyed more sexual freedom than women and can thus roam the sexual field with little normative constraint. Sexual promiscuity is a mark of sexual power for men, while for women it is either ambiguous or a sign of a morally inferior status. Second is the fact that men have not been compelled to use sexuality as a leverage to receive social and economic resources and thus have no reason to implicate their whole self in sexuality. Women's approach to sexuality on the other hand is more emotional *because* it is more economic, that is, used as a resource exchanged for other, material or social resources. Sexuality for women has higher stakes and thus implicates the self. The third reason why casual sex seems to characterize men's sexuality is that masculinity is almost tautologically defined by the capacity to have and display many sexual partners. As scholar of masculinity Robert Connell puts it, for many men, "to be masculine is to fuck women,"[33] a claim largely confirmed by Rachel O'Neill's study of men attending "seduction workshops"[34] (to learn how to have as much sex as possible). Finally, casual sex entails detachment, which in turn provides power and as such is a trope of masculinity. In the same way that a masculinist reason has advocated a separation of emotions and reason in all domains of economy, politics, and law, hegemonic masculinity tends to separate emotions from sexuality.[35] Classical hegemonic masculinity is defined by the capacity to both accumulate sexual casual encounters and dispose of women (Donald Trump is the ideal-type of such masculinity, see next chapter). For example, Ambroise, a forty-nine-year-old finance professor in Paris defines the ideal woman as follows:

[A]fter you have had sex with a woman, she never leaves in the middle of the night; forget it. That would be too good; no, she will stay till the morning, she wants to cuddle, have breakfast. Gosh. The ideal woman is the one who leaves in the middle of the night. She leaves on the table a goodbye note, saying it was great, without her phone number. That's the ideal woman.

Ironically, perhaps, casual sex has been a marker of a feminist politics precisely because it signals autonomy, pleasure, power, and detachment.

A woman accounts for her pleasure in casual sex in the popular lifestyle site Refinery29:

> I've had lots of one night stands and lots of long-term relationships. They're both part of life if that's what you like. It's a choice issue. My one night stands made me feel empowered and beautiful as all I wanted was sex, I got it and I left with no expectations and (in my mind) all of the power. However, I did get tripped up by my last one night stand! He demanded my number, I said we didn't have to pretend it was more than a one night stand and that he'd forgotten my name.[36]

Clearly what is performed here is a ritual of emotional detachment and lack of expectations that provide this woman with a sense of power and autonomy reminiscent of men's approach to sexuality. One may further surmise that for this woman casual sex is pleasurable because it bestows equality found in a symmetrical detachment and lack of expectations. From a historical standpoint, given that men have privileged casual sexuality, achieving equality has demanded from women the same assertion of detachment.

Another confirmation of the hypothesis that casual sex is a (culturally defined) male form of sex can be (obliquely) found in the important study on women and casual sex undertaken by Laura Hamilton and Elizabeth A. Armstrong. Studying female college student's sexuality, the researchers have found that casual sex is in fact a way for women to put aside the ideal of matrimony and to devote themselves to building up a career.[37] The college students who are not necessarily interested in pursuing relationships are looking for jobs, with casual sex being a strategy to maximize the conditions of the search. Casual sexuality is a route to get ahead faster, concentrate on studies, and achieve career goals. What the authors call the "self-development imperative" makes less likely and more difficult the time-consuming and greedy committed relationships before establishing one's career. Thus casual sex is implicitly commended by Hamilton and Armstrong because it functions as a gender equalizer (a woman who would fall in love is more likely to marry, have a child, and be excluded early on from the path to a career). This also suggests that casual sex is a script for a non-relation.[38] If casual sex has been a mark of feminist politics,[39] it is because it mimics male power, as it is a trope of autonomy and signals the capacity to detach, to look solely for one's pleasure, to obliterate care and reciprocity (the traditional signposts of feminine identity), and to pursue market subjectivity.

Casual sex for women is a marker of equality in the mutuality of detachment.

But far from being a self-enclosed social form, casual sex reverberates on the entire structure of relationality (heterosexuality in particular), changing the formation, content, and duration of relationships. In other words, the practice of casual sex must be understood in a broader social ecology of social bonds, as it transforms significantly what I have called the architecture and ecology of choice, the grammar of sexual and romantic choice, the ways in which people engage and disengage from relationships, choose or un-choose each other.[40] To analyze such sexuality only for the pleasures it enables would be equivalent to analyzing Walmart Corporation for the pleasures it gives people looking for cheap bargains. People may enjoy buying cheap goods, yet the analysis of shoppers' pleasure would yield no insight whatsoever on the corporate field in which Walmart operates and on which it in turn impacts. In the same way, the undeniable and varied pleasures that casual sex gives to men and women cannot give us an insight on the overall structure of relationships casual sex hampers or sustains. Casual sex then must be understood in the context of a broader social ecology of heterosexual relations defined by the freedom to be entered into and disengaged from. This freedom, as I am set to show, has introduced a fundamental uncertainty in the process of entering a relationship and choosing a partner because in a situation of freedom, men exert an indirect and subtle power when entering the sexual exchange.

Casualness and Uncertainty

Uncertainty is not ambiguity that inheres in the capacity of words to mean more than one thing, and in the fact that actors' intentions are not always transparent. The first can be enjoyable, while the second does not usually elicit anxiety. Uncertainty pertains to the fact that "the grounds of an interaction cannot be taken for granted,"[41] that the definition of a situation is up for grabs, that the rules to conduct an interaction are unclear, while actors aim for clarity. Uncertainty has thus a direct psychological impact that can range from shame, discomfort, and embarrassment to anxiety and insecurity. Indeed, uncertainty usually generates anxiety and only rarely is addressed in a playful way. In the introduction to the book *Ethnographies of Uncertainty from Africa*, the editors Elizabeth Cooper and David Pratten emphasize such emotional content of uncertainty as they view it as a "struc-ture of feeling [...] the lived experience of a pervasive sense of vulnerability, anxiety, hope and possibility mediated through the material assemblages that underpin, saturate, and sustain everyday life."[42] Below the surface of pleasurable multiple orgasmic experiences simmer contradictory, perplex-ing social experiences that are fundamentally structured by the manage-ment of uncertainty. Some actors are skillful at managing uncertainty, others learn to manage uncertainty through the maze of self-help advice, and still others retreat in self-defeat.

Uncertain Frames

According to Erving Goffman, all interactions between human beings are organized within frames, where frames are conceived as a cognitive, percep-tual, and social process that allows actors to pick up the cues, the schemas, or the patterns of an interaction in order to label that interaction, and orient themselves in it.[43] As observed in the previous chapter, the main result of the autonomization of sexuality as a sphere of action is that modern heterosexual relationships have no built-in teleology and their course is splintered. Here is a facetious but telling example of the way in which the splintering of encoun-ters in three possible and separate regimes of action—emotional, sexual, matrimonial—introduces an uncertainty about the very frame and defini-tion of the interaction. In a video posted on the website of the American magazine *The New Yorker*, the following comic exchange takes place among five young women. The first woman addresses her group of friends and entrusts them with the urgent mission of deciphering a perplexing situation:

YOUNG WOMAN 1—Ladies, thank you for being here today. We have a vital situation on our hands and I appreciate your judgment, expertise and discretion. I'll brief you quickly. I first met Kevin Harper one week ago today at my weird friends' birthday drinks. We talked briefly, he did not ask for my number. Three days later he Facebooked friend requested me, and asked me to get a drink later that week. When I show up, he's there with his friends. One of them is a girl, she's prettier than me but not by much. His friends leave, we have another drink just the two of us. We do not kiss. The question that faces us today [*music stops*], was it like a date, or what?

YOUNG WOMAN 2—Did he invite you back to his place?

YW 1—No, but only because he is unemployed and living with his aunt right now.

YW 3—Did you touch each other at all?

YW 1—His hand grazed my boob during drink three. It could've been an accident.

YW 4—Was the vibe flirty?

YW 1—I think so.

YW 2—Did he buy you drinks?

YW 1—No, but that might just be because he's poor, right?

YW 5—Let's hope so. Did he mention any other girls?

YW 1—No.

YW 3—Is he...gay?

YW 5—No, I found evidence of at least two prior ex-girlfriends on his Facebook and Instagram feeds.

YW 3—I don't know girls, no kiss not a good indicator.

YW 4—But that doesn't mean anything. He could've just been nervous.

YW 2—No way. This is Matt Wiseman in '09 all over again. Three dates, no kiss, we can not have a repeat of that.

YW 3—We all remember Matt Wiseman, okay? He didn't deserve her. Why'd you even bring it up?

YW 2—The warning signs here are all exactly the same.

YW 3—Oh, the warning signs! Eeverybody knows you have it out for me. [overlapping arguing]

YW 5—Ladies. Please, let's not lose our heads here, okay? This is too important.

YW 3—Have you established contact yet, this morning?

YW 1—Yeah, I texted him, "Hey, that was fun last night. 'Winky face.'" He wrote back "Yeah."

YW 4—Emoji?

YW 1—No.

YW 2—In his initial Facebook message, did he ask you to get a drink, get drinks, or grab drinks?

YW 1—Hang out....What?

YW 4—Everybody knows what hang out means. What time did you get to the bar?

YW 5—Was it raining?

YW 3—Where were you in your cycle?

YW 1—10:15, yes, one week past ovulation.

YW 2 [*calculating*]—It's too close to call. [*phone dings*]

YW 1—It's him. "Hey, can you not tell anyone about last night, don't want my GF to find out, lol."

YW 5—He doesn't want his girlfriend to find out?

YW 4—That means it was definitely a date.

YW 3—[*Girls exclaim excitedly*].[44]

This vignette is humorous only because it describes a prototypical situation, highly resonant with ordinary experiences of contemporary women. The female friends of a woman engage with her in a highly elaborate hermeneutic exercise to help her decipher an encounter whose frame is uncertain and whose meaning is ultimately controlled by the man. Because of the splintering of the structure of heterosexuality in sexual, emotional, and matrimonial fields, the very frame of the interaction is uncertain. To provide another example taken from a popular romance novel, *The Big Love*, in which the heroine Alison has two prolonged sexual encounters with her boss Henry (neither the female nor the male protagonist seem to view sex with one's boss as problematic). After these encounters, Alison enters Henry's office and makes the following inquiry:

"I was wondering if we could talk about our relationship [...]."
"Relationship?" Henry said, still busy with the papers. "What relationship?"
"You know," I said. "*This*."
Henry looked up from his papers.
"What?" I said.
"I just, I didn't know we were involved in a relationship," said Henry.
"Well, what would you call it?"

"I don't know. I hadn't thought about it. I didn't know it needed a name."

"We slept together four times," I said.

[....]

"Fine. Okay. I have my answer," I said. I headed for the door.

"What answer is that?" said Henry.

"This is just a fuck. Which is perfectly fine. I just wanted to know."

"I wouldn't call it that," Henry said.

"Then what would you call it?"

[...])"It's a bit of fun. That's somewhere between 'just a fuck' and a relationship."[45]

The dialogue is about finding a name for their relationship, located betwixt and between casual sex and a relationship in which the future is plausible. This relationship does not have a name because it is structured by the woman's uncertainty about the man's intentions and emotions, the only elements that would help this woman orient herself in this interaction. The man himself does not know his own intentions, and is therefore unable to label the interaction. The very multiplication of names of casual relationships—hookups, one-night stands, friends with benefits, and so on—suggests the difficulty of naming and characterizing casual relationships, knowing what they are about, that is, their "*aboutness*," a relatively basic and taken-for-granted feature of all social interactions. Moreover, in the two vignettes above, casual sexuality not only creates confusion but also lacks symmetry. In both examples, it is the man who holds the key to the frame.

In her study *Hooking Up*, Kathryn Bogle shows a striking confusion about the purpose of casual encounters, in which women (and men) frequently state that relationships can go in many different directions they have no a priori knowledge of. In hooking up, there seems to be a complete uncertainty as to the very goal of the interaction, and its overall frame. There is even disagreement on the definition of it as some define hooking up as only kissing, whereas others would view it as having oral sex that excludes intercourse, while still others define it as a way to browse for relationships. Most women interviewed by Bogle had the sense they could not predict the outcome of hookup: "Hook up is a roll of the dice."[46] This uncertainty is significantly magnified and accentuated by the invention of new apps such as Tinder. A popular Internet dating site called AskMen comments on the Tinder revolution as follows:

Tinder has become a one-stop shop for young people who are looking to date, hook-up, or simply check out who else lives in their area, and online dating sites are starting to pale in comparison to the popularity of apps like Tinder, which people see as a more efficient way to meet potential partners. There are an estimated 50 million people using Tinder today, and Tinder has boasted that it has made over 8 billion "connections" since it launched in 2012—although it's not clear whether "connections" means matches, IRL meetings, a combination of the two, or something else altogether. Tinder now constitutes such a large part of the dating world that, for many young people, it *is* the dating world: an always-available, *pocket-sized method for finding the person of your dreams—or, at the very least, a regret-free hook up.*[47]

Tinder can offer just quick, disposable sex or the possibility to meet a "dream woman," thus suggesting a multiform and undefined range of possibilities between these two extremes. This in turn suggests what I would dub "frame confusion" and "frame uncertainty," the difficulty one has knowing which frame one is operating under and thus predicting a likely course of action and using an adequate tool kit to follow a course of action. While traditional courtship and dating were highly scripted, both cognitively and practically (a boy picks up a girl at her home, goes out with her dancing or to a movie, brings her back home, gives her a kiss, followed by necking), modern casual sex un-scripts romantic relationship since sex—which was the end of what was previously a narrative of courtship—is now at the beginning of the story, thus rendering the goal of the relationship uncertain. In other words, the sexualization of relationships means that their entry point is a sexual one, which may or may not be their end as well. In sexualized cultures, sexuality becomes the prima facie terrain for engaging in interactions: men and women are approached as a priori sexualized actors, especially when men view women as objects of sexual satisfaction.

Lana is a thirty-nine-year-old Israeli secretary and high school dropout. She was married for eight years, has two children, and has been divorced five years prior to the interview. She has all the attributes of an attractive woman. This is how she views the ways in which men approach her:

LANA: I was controlled by my father and my husband, now I feel no one can control me. My husband used to tell me how I should dress, have my hair cut, who I could speak to. No one can do that anymore. Also when you grow up in a house where the father was very dominant, macho, he controlled everything, I grew up being beaten. I ran away into my marriage to run away from home, but my husband was worse than my father.

INTERVIEWER: Can you give me examples of men you had relationships with recently?

LANA: I had a relationship with Jackie, it did not work because he did not speak nicely to me, he would threaten me. Now I am with Kai, I liked him a lot, he was tender and sweet, but I met him through Tinder, it is a site for sex, you know? So it was only for sex. I did not know it is a site for sex by the way, I was interested in more than sex, but for him it was only sex. I think it was only sex for him and he could not make it something else. I felt embarrassed when I found out it is a site for sex only. Like he would think I was in it only for the sex. That I was that kind of woman. Anyway, he disappeared. Never called back. Now I have a relationship to someone I was introduced to by a common friend.

[...]

INTERVIEWER: What is the biggest problem you see in your past relationships with men?

LANA: They approach women as sexual objects. It is very different from asking yourself if this person suits me. For example, this new guy I am dating now took me to his parents. He signaled that he is serious, that I am not only a sexual object, but most men view women only as sexual objects and treat them like that. And you never know where you stand with them. What they want from you. If they want anything from you. Sometimes, they just want to be able to have sex. But you know it is not only that. I project an image of me as a very strong woman, like I am the master of myself, I am very independent. I am scared of being controlled by any man. I know that in a relationship you have to make compromises, give up on certain things, make sacrifices. But I have this fear of being dependent. So I project an image of strength and am very self-defensive, I make sure to convey that I am strong, that I have no problem being alone, that whoever wants me must take me as I am. I always tell a guy: if you don't take me as I am, if you want to change me, your loss. Not mine. I tell them that if they don't want me, it will be their loss, not mine. I never convey to them that they are this great thing which I would be devastated to lose.

[Silence]

When I was younger I always felt less attractive than others; my workplace changed me a lot. I work as a senior secretary in a university. I met a friend here, Hannah, who taught me to love myself and to know what I am worth. I know now I had very low self-esteem. I went with her to a course on positive thinking and it changed me completely. After that, I had the strength to divorce. Before that, I could not do it. I was afraid of being alone. I was afraid of the criticism of my family, of my friends. At work, I got a lot of support, I was told in the workplace how good I was, how beautiful and attractive I was, so I got a lot of my strength there. It brought me to the situation where I don't care today what people say or think about me. I went through a process of self-empowerment. My boyfriend now tells me: "You always need to be the stronger one." It is true. I always need to feel the stronger one."

Some themes are striking here. To this woman, relationships seem highly unpredictable as she has difficulties understanding under which frame she operates. What makes them uncertain is their sexualization, that is, the fact that the entry point of relationships is sexual, which for her means that the man is likely to be in this for the "sex only," which this woman perceives as exploitative, that is, oblivious to "who she is." This is the reason why sexualization is frequently approached by women with a Kantian suspicion: it is viewed as containing the possibility of treating another instrumentally, without a full recognition of their entire personhood. This in turn indicates that for at least some women a "sex-only" relationship is perceived as serving men's interests and as a threat to their sense of worth (which Lana here alleviates through her friendships with women). Let's hear what Virginie, a fifty-seven-year-old French woman living in Israel has to say. She was divorced twelve years previous to the interview and is in search of a stable partner, but:

VIRGINIE: Men and women just don't want the same thing. Maybe at some point they do. But when you start a relationship you have the feeling they want different things.

INTERVIEWER: What for example?

VIRGINIE: OK. Let me give you an example. I started a new class in creative writing. And there is this young guy taking the class with me. Young, I mean, really young, twenty-three years old. So last week, after the class, we stayed together, we talked a bit, and at some point he told me: "Look,

I would like to have sex with you." I responded that I liked him as a person but that I was not sure I wanted to have sex and that I needed to know him more. After I said this, he stood up, paid for his coffee, and left, just like that. As soon as I said I wanted to figure things out. He said, OK, have a good night, and he left, like I was a tissue he was throwing on the floor, a useless piece of junk.

As soon as this woman redefined the frame of reference, the man left, thus suggesting that the entry point of sexual relationships is a highly contested one because women experience casual sexuality sometimes as pleasurable and as a source of agency and sometimes as a dismissal of their selves ("a tissue dropped on the floor").

For many of the women I spoke with, sexuality is construed as undermining the possibility of being recognized as a person. Casual sex sometimes transforms the encounter in a zero sum game: her (potential) partner's pursuit of his sexual pleasure against her sense of self-worth, where self-worth is based on reciprocity and recognition. While in patriarchal traditional societies, a woman's worth is indexed on her class and sexual virtue, in a regime of sexual freedom where the the double standard is still prevalent, the locus of the woman's worth becomes fuzzy and uncertain. The autonomization of sexuality creates a built-in uncertainty about the very locus of worth, about the possibility of an emotional interaction, about the very definition of the relationship, about its telos and sequentiality, and about the very status of emotional, nonsexual selves. This is why women are by and large culturally more ambivalent toward casual sex than men.

Indeed, as research shows, casual sex is a predictor of sexual regret among female college students, especially if intercourse took place less than twenty-four hours after meeting the man and if there was no follow-up.[48] Based on a review of relevant studies,[49] Elaine Eshbaugh and Gary Gute argue that women were more likely to experience "sexual regret" than men (who were more likely to regret *not* having had the hookup) and that "female participants were more likely than men to feel 'regretful or disappointed'; they were also more likely to ruminate about a hookup and feel greater shame and self-doubt following the experience. In contrast, men were more likely to feel 'satisfied.'"[50] These findings seem to confirm yet one more time that casual sex is more congruent with a masculine form of sexuality. Gender differences are also found among lesbians and gay men,[51] with lesbian women being more oriented to relationality than gay men. In a longitudinal study of women who never had sex ("virgins") and who transitioned to sex, C. M. Grello et al. found that when examining and comparing adolescents who had transitioned to romantic sex with those who transitioned to casual sex, the latter were far more likely to suffer from symptoms of depression, to be the object of violence, or to commit crime themselves.[52] In a chapter on depression and adolescent romantic relationships the authors write: "Young adolescent females who engaged in sexual intercourse in both casual and dating relationships showed the highest levels of depressive symptoms both before and after becoming sexually active."[53] Other researchers have found that female college students with a history of casual sex had lower levels of self-esteem than women who had been involved in romantic sexual rela- tionships or, even more surprising, who had no sexual experiences at all.[54] Moreover, for women who experienced guilt when having casual sex, the authors hypothesized that guilt may in turn lead to feeling uncomfortable or confused, which may be related to low self-esteem.[55] More surprising perhaps is the fact that contrary to the authors' prediction that the sexual double standard would make women feel less self-esteem after a hookup, the authors found that both men and women had a diminished level of self- esteem. In many studies, the correlation between low self-esteem and casual sex is a robust one,[56] and while scholars quibble about the directionality of this correlation, it may be said that whatever the direction of the correla- tion, for women (and sometimes men) casual sex does *not* enhance self- worth, despite the fact that sexuality has become a new form of capital for both sexes, something they pursue for pleasure and for status. The sexuality of women remains "embedded" in social relationships, while male sexuality is more frequently and more likely to be disembedded, even morphing in what we may call "meaningless sex." In Hamilton's and Armstrong's felici- tous formula, women's sexuality is shaped by "the relational imperative."[57] (a view they, however, reject, both because they view it as empirically incor- rect and normatively undesirable).

Many have interpreted the presence of women's negative emotions in casual sex as an indication of the still-powerful shame culture around sex and of the looming presence of the double standard—men can engage in casual sex without incurring symbolic penalty. This interpretation has the main merit of reminding us that the power of patriarchy still looms large, that men and women are subject to different sexual norms, that men have more sexual freedom, and that women's sexuality is constrained by normative and sexist pressures. But this explanation has also the flaw of implicitly taking men's sexuality as the reference point by which sexuality should be evaluated. Indeed, as argued above casual sexuality has been modeled on a masculinist view of sexuality. To claim that only detached sex is liberated sex implicitly endorses the equivalence between free sexuality and detached sexuality and between male sexuality and free sexuality. "Embedded sexuality" is more likely to reflect the woman's position in the sexual field not only because traditionally women implicated their selves more fully—they exchanged sexuality for something meaningful, such as economic resources and social status—but also because men and women have very different positions in the social production of care. Because men's identity is not geared to childbirth or care-giving, because the social organization of patriarchy makes men the object of women's care rather than providers of care, because marriage and motherhood remain for many women crucial to their identity and socioeconomic status,[58] the sexuality of women is far more likely to be relational than men's. For women, care and relationality are at one and the same time a social role (e.g., mothers), an economic position (e.g., nurses or baby sitters), and an emotional-cultural identity. To this extent, relationality remains central in women's sexuality because it reflects the fact that women bear the lion's share in the economic, cultural, and social production of care.[59] This is the reason why men and women are likely to have different attitudes and positions in the experience of casual sex, with women more likely to experience it as an experience conflicting with the cultivation of relationships and emotions.

The tension between the detached and relational modes is illustrated by Claire, a fifty-two-year-old CEO of a powerful French firm. She has no children and has had two stable relationships that both ended, the first after nineteen years, and the second after three years. She claims to have had many sexual relationships with men.

CLAIRE: At this point of my life, you know, I am looking only for a man to sleep with. Not even very frequently. Once a week would be very satisfying.

INTERVIEWER: You want a sexual relationship with a man once a week?

CLAIRE: No, of course that's not what I want. I would prefer to have the whole package, the whole thing, love, living together, but it seems so difficult that I am willing to settle for the weekly sex.

INTERVIEWER: So if what you want is the whole package as you put it, why you would want something else actually?

CLAIRE: I do need the sex. I thought it would be easier to find a real full relationship, but if I can't, then I will settle for the sex [laughs]. It's important to have someone hug your body once a week. [*Silence*] And also, if you don't put pressure on them [men], if you don't project this "I want the whole thing" maybe they are more likely to want to settle for a no-strings-attached relationship. A relationship with no expectation is lighter, much easier to manage. Men can't stand women who have expectations. That's when things become complicated. When you have expectations you become more easily hurt and disappointed. You have to start negotiating. Two people never have the same image of how to do things. So maybe sex with no expectations is the safest way of having a relationship. A sexual relation is just pleasure. Without the hassle of dealing with another person's emotional baggage.

This quote indicates a few interesting elements. Sexuality is viewed as a terrain in which it is easier to meet men, with emotions appearing as volatile and uncertain, eliciting expectations and disappointment. Emotions, rather than sexuality, now produce anxiety because they are perceived to threaten actors' (especially men's) claim to autonomy.[60] While the rules for a sexual relationship seem clear and simple, the rules for an emotional relationship seem elusive and difficult. It is interesting to observe that this otherwise extremely articulate and attractive woman has willingly subsumed her expectations of a relationship under a sex-only bond because sexuality does not threaten men's claim to autonomy. She is willing to settle for what she perceives an emotionless relationship, as long as it regularly satisfies her sexual needs, suggesting that sexuality is both an interactional terrain easier to negotiate and that it has an ontological reality more powerful than the emotional one. Sexuality does not elicit uncertainty, while the traditional "stuff" of consciousness—intentions, expectations, emotions—does. Sexuality replaces emotionality as a source of relationality. As a widely quoted article in *Vanity Fair* put it:

People used to meet their partners through proximity, through family and friends, but now Internet meeting is surpassing every other form. [...] [T]he lengthy, heartfelt e-mails exchanged by the main characters in [the movie] *You've Got Mail* (1998) seem positively Victorian in comparison to the messages sent on the average dating app today. "I'll get a text that says, 'Wanna fuck?'" says Jennifer, 22, a senior at Indiana University Southeast, in New Albany. "They'll tell you, 'Come over and sit on my face,'" says her friend, Ashley, 19.[61]

Given that sexualization relies on an epistemology of relationships based on the body, it is the body that provides a reliable source of knowledge about the interaction and becomes the anchor to initiate the interaction.

Casual sex thus reflects a widespread sexualization defined by scholars as containing any one of the following four components:[62] (1) sexual appeal is the sole determinant of a person's value; (2) sexual appeal is based on physical attractiveness, narrowly defined; (3) one partner at least is sexually objectified (objectification); or (4) sexuality is so pervasive that it can be forced on people.[63] Sexualization then is the fact that sexuality imbues and pervades many or most interactions and many or most social groups. The American Psychological Association Task Force views sexualization as opposite to healthy sexuality, which implies mutuality. But my point about sexualization is different. In my view, the major problem with and effect of sexualization is that in making the body the prime terrain of interaction, it also makes emotional expression and exchange illegitimate and uncertain and foregrounds the body as a source of interpersonal knowledge. It thus renders processes of social recognition contradictory, located sometimes in the body and sometimes in the self, where these two modes of self-knowledge do not always overlap.

Because bodies are viewed as separate and autonomous,[64] an epistemology of relations that relies on the body is not easily reconciled with sociality based on reciprocity.[65] Pierre Bourdieu showed, for example, that temporality and expectations of future returns structure the exchange of the gift, thus making reciprocal sociability steeped in time.[66] Temporality and the future are inherent to reciprocity. Yet, since in casual sexuality pleasure is more or less instantaneous (two bodies have pleasure at the same time or at a short interval), this disconnects the social exchange from the future. Casual sex thus differs from traditional sociability, conventionally based on mutuality, narrativity, expectations, and projections in the future (the counter-gift is always in the future). It also differs from interactions with strangers where non-mutuality is scripted, expected, and nonnegotiable. Casual sex is an uncertain form of interaction because it admits a wide spectrum of possibilities. For sociologists and economists, uncertainty is precisely about expectations and more exactly about the very difficulty in producing, imagining, and negotiating expectations.

[Uncertainty] refers to the future and to whether our expectations will be met and also to the present and our capacity to produce expectations. Typically, norms and institutions structure our expectations. They support clear and unambiguous notions and expectations even though they are always—to a certain degree—uncertain.[67]

Casual sex creates uncertainty because it has no clear internal normative core, because its underlying institutional structure is located in a dispersed consumer market, based on transience and obsolescence, and because it is based on different and divergent gender scripts of relationality. While in pre-modern relationships gender roles were ultimately subsumed under the definition of marriage and morality, the entanglement of sex in the consumer market plays out gender differences and identities. Casual sex is a social script in reverse: a script for a non-relationship.

To recap: Sexual freedom for men has been practiced on the mode of autonomy, detachment, and accumulation, while for women sexual freedom has been more ambivalent; it is lived alternatively on the mode of autonomy and on the mode of relationality, trying to accomplish with others some common emotional goal. For women casual sex creates a conflict between relationality and the autonomization of the body, while for men casual sex is the opportunity to accumulate sexual capital and status. Women's social being remains largely relational because women still provide the overwhelming bulk of care work in society,[68] while for men casual sexuality is a way to perform the main tropes of masculinity: power, detachment, autonomy, instrumentality geared to the satisfaction of one's pleasure. In that sense, sexualization of relationships conflicts with the relational imperative and places men and women in different positions in the sexual field and in the social structure of intimate relations.[69]

The Uncertain Territorial Geography of Relationships

Sexualization creates confusion in yet another way. In enabling and even encouraging the accumulation of sexual experiences, it blurs the very boundaries between relationships. Modernist ways of forging relationships were based on the capacity to draw boundaries between them, that is, to define the protocols of how and where different relationships start and end. But the accumulation of relationships makes it far more difficult to hold on to clear emotional and conceptual categories in order to be able to draw boundaries between relationships, as for example when we distinguish sharply between friends and lovers.

Arnaud is a sixty-three-year-old French high official in a powerful position in a French ministry. He has been divorced for eleven years, has two sons, and uses Internet dating sites:

ARNAUD: I have had many relationships since my divorce, some of them were actually long, but they all ended, at some point or another.

INTERVIEWER: Do you know why?

ARNAUD: Sure I know why. Because after five minutes, well you know what I mean, not literally five minutes, but quickly, the woman wanted to move in, to think about the future, to take the relationship seriously and I could not do that. I felt good with them, I liked them, sometimes loved them, but I could not sacrifice my freedom. My freedom was always more important to me.

INTERVIEWER: So when you meet a woman, you prefer sex to be casual?

ARNAUD: Not at all! I hate casual sex, I hate one-night stands. I love relationships, but I do not want all the trappings of relationships, I want to live in the present, I do not want to know what my partner is doing in her free time when she is not with me, and I do not want her to know what I am doing. Our sex lives should be free. Separate.

INTERVIEWER: So you do not want a regular committed monogamous relationship, do I understand you correctly?

ARNAUD: Yes, exactly. Why do you need to define relationships? Why do women have this need to know "where they are going"? [*he does the air quotes with his hands*]. I don't need to know anything about the direction of a relationship. We should keep each other free.

INTERVIEWER: So for you a relationship is open-ended, does not need to have a clear goal.

ARNAUD: Exactly! I see you understand me very well [*laughter*]. Yeah, a relationship is for the pleasure of the moment [*le plaisir de l'instant*]. It does not have to go beyond that. *Que sera sera.* No future. No definition. From one pleasurable moment to another. Which is why the idea of a woman owning my body seems so ridiculous to me.

INTERVIEWER: So love, in the sense of great love, with monogamy, is an inadequate concept according to you?

ARNAUD: Love always ends. I don't know anyone for whom it has lasted. It always ends. There are always new desires. New bodies to discover. So I have drawn my lessons; I don't have any more expectations. I have what I call "arrangements."

INTERVIEWER: Can you explain?

ARNAUD: I told you before [before the interview], I have several relationships with several women at once. Each one of them knows that she can't
have me for her alone or live with me. I say it at the beginning so no one
is lied to. I find it much more comfortable this way. I like each one of
them but I do not feel tied to one in particular.

INTERVIEWER: Each one of them?

ARNAUD: Yes. I don't privilege one in particular. Each gives me something
different. It is a very comfortable way of having relationships. My philosophy is to give and take pleasure when we can. It is a much more
simple and relaxing way to live.

Reciting the gospel of "negative freedom" Arnaud continues and says: "I
have only one rule, not to hurt anyone; other than that, it is very important
for me to keep my freedom."

Arnaud illustrates clearly that casual sex spills over and redefines long-
term relationships themselves. Casual sex rejects the distinctive mark of
heteronormativity in which sexuality is subordinate to a telos, marriage,
monogamy, and domesticity.

This is further illustrated by another example in an Internet site called
LoveShack where the writer tells the following story, suggesting yet other
ways in which casual sexuality transforms the ecology of romantic relations:

I broke things off with a guy a week ago after dating for four months and
him deciding that he should *continue to keep his options open*. The kicker
was meeting his family twice over the weekend and then *finding him on
match.com all day long on Sunday*. This was the typical hot and cold I
had been getting from him since the beginning of Feb. We would take a
big step towards a relationship and he would backtrack completely after
that step went well. We had a heated exhange [*sic*] via text *where he basically told me he had dated another girl* (I didn't know)—who called
things off because she felt he was looking for a relationship. He told me
I was well off the mark in saying he wasn't looking for a relationship
because the other girl obviously felt he was...he told me he was giving
us a chance "to grow" into something and that he did care and like me but
he wasn't sure.[70]

This story conveys well the emotional confusion and uncertainty that pervades the protagonist's difficulty in knowing her own and her boyfriend's

feelings. If traditional cultural sociology is based on the assumption that actors have strategies of action,[71] these examples suggest that what is precisely difficult for actors is to develop a strategy of action for their relationships. It is not clear who this woman's boyfriend is dating, neither to her nor to him; it is not clear what he feels for her and for the other woman he dates; nor is it clear to this woman what he wants or for that matter what she herself wants. This describes a state of relationships that have no clear boundaries around them, are fluid in Zygmunt Bauman's terminology,[72] and whose telos seems uncertain to the protagonists themselves. The open-endedness of relationships unsettles both the expressive and instrumental dimensions of action, making actors confused about the proper regime of action they are engaged in. Because sexuality is lived in a situation of seriality and open-endedness, the sociological boundaries of relationships are transformed; they become contiguous and continuous with each other, with overlapping frames and fuzzy goals. Such subjectivity is less able to singularize others and to feel singularized by them.

This is the account of another relationship by Venn on an Internet forum used to discuss broken or difficult relationships.

2009–2010 (Me at age 19 and my second year college and she is age 15 and her third year high school.) At this point we were in an open relationship. I really didn't do much effort in our relationship and she had confused feelings about me. It's like I did something very wrong in this...she always goes on and off about the relationship and then I still always fight for her like I'm forcing her to be in a relationship with me because I was seriously in love with her. At one point when we broke up with our open relationship, she entertained some suitors and her crushes but due to me being so fierce on wanting to come back with her rejected most of them...either probably touched by how I keep on fighting for her or she is forced on coming back with me. But when we do get back together in our open relationship, I don't even do much effort in it....It is always her that does the efforts in the relationship...I actually do some effort but not that much. Just me loving her always and not doing much action. She's the one that comes to our house, wants to go on dates and always tells me to go to prayer meetings at church and I still decline about the dating thing....

I took her for granted because I was comfortable with the relationship
and think that she will never leave me. What I didn't know is that her love for me at this point is kind of slowly declining to a point where she just doesn't love me anymore...because I was too busy with my games

and other stuff....Still even if we are like this, we act like a real couple. We kiss, we hold hands, and we do stuff almost going to the point where I almost have sex with her and we do it almost every so often when we are alone....The thing is, I never am interested in sexual intercourse...that's why I never had sex with her this 6 years.

Then comes a guy that courted her and is as forceful as me on having a relationship with her...actually she fell in love with somebody else in her class and its [sic] a friend of the guy that is courting her. She told me about it and then I just told her to not entertain him because we are the ones who are in an open relationship and that time will come that we will be officially together. Little did I know that she kept on entertaining him because...this guy is more caring than me, texts more than me, always calls her. Now when we were already having a date, kissing and holding hands, by the next day she accepted the guy to be her boyfriend...so it's some sort of cheating that she has already done by this point, I still didn't know about it and only knew it after only 3 weeks...I begged for her to come back but she says that she is already satisfied with her relationship right now.[73]

The post of this man is titled "on the verge of killing myself" and is a rambling and complicated account of the ways in which his relationship with this woman kept fading in and out, for many years, changing its status from open to steady, from steady to open, from committed to uncommitted and back to committed. In other words, the very capacity to keep the frame of the relationship in focus seems here jeopardized by sexual multiplicity and openness. The relationship here does not follow a clear cultural script, but seems to have been random. Interestingly enough, in his account, his girlfriend left him precisely because her new boyfriend was able to provide her with a clear frame.

While sexual exclusivity remains for most heterosexuals the sign of a committed relationship, the technology available makes it far more difficult to hold on to a script of sexual exclusivity, and to know the rules about its applicability. As Robert, a thirty-two-year-old French man, who is single and a self-defined musician put it:

ROBERT: I am always in several "deals" at once ["*sur plusieurs coups a la fois*"]. Most don't work out anyway; so you might as well not wait to start something new again. I always have at least three, four things going on at the same time.

INTERVIEWER: Do they know?

ROBERT: Of course not. Why should they? That's my life. I don't know what they do when they're not with me. I don't ask and I expect the same from them.

Here sexual multiplicity is taken for granted because it is viewed as a prerogative of one's private life and because "most relationships don't work anyway." Casual sex thus introduces an uncertainty not only about the frame and goal of the interaction but also about its boundaries (how and where one's sexual and emotional relationship ends, and where another starts).

Sexuality as a Source of Certainty

Paradoxically, the autonomization of the body means that bodily experiences are a source of certainty (one knows what a sexual body or experience is) and that emotions attached to such experiences either become uncertain or must follow bodily experiences. Because sexualization centers personhood on the body, defined as a biological entity and a physiological source of pleasure, it makes emotions less relevant to the entry in relationships. The body henceforth becomes the only or at least the more reliable source of knowledge. As Lena, a fifty-six-year-old feminist lesbian Israeli artist, put it:

LENA: After I meet a woman, if I am attracted to her, I have to go to bed with her. It is the first thing I do, not the restaurants, drinks, and movies bullshit. I don't ask myself if I want a relationship with her before I sleep with her. I have to sleep with her first to know if I even want a relationship. Without sex, I wouldn't know.

This is echoed by Aviva, thirty-four-year-old heterosexual Israeli woman, who is a medical doctor:

AVIVA: The first test a man has to pass is the one in bed. I want to know if we are compatible sexually, if he knows how to touch me, if yes, we can check the relationship, if not, then I don't pursue it.

INTERVIEWER: You don't pursue it even if, say, everything else works well?

AVIVA: Right. I don't pursue it. Sexual life is too important.

These quotes indicate an entirely new way of approaching and getting to know others, where sexuality plays a role of epistemology, a way to know a person and establish the truth of a relationship. In that sense, we may say that the sexualization of relationships entails a paradox: the body and sexuality become a source of certainty (how we get to know the deep self of our potential or real partner), but the overall frame of relationships is uncertain. Uncertainty is not only about the frame, the goal, and the boundaries of interaction but also about the role that sexual attractiveness and sexuality should play when approaching a person. Because the body and sexuality have become the repositories of the new relational epistemology, they function as the truth of a relationship, yet they are unable solely to generate emotional strategies of action.

While pre-modern courtship started with emotions and ended with sex that could produce guilt and anxiety, contemporary relationships start with (pleasurable) sex and must grapple with the anxious task of generating emotions. The body has become the site for the expression of emotions (see the cliché that "a good relationship is expressed in good sex"), and emotions become extraneous to sexual interactions.

Uncertainty and Negative Sociality

I dub these relations "negative." My use of the term "negative" is neither the one it has in common parlance ("deleterious," "harmful") nor is it the same as the meaning it has in the philosophical tradition. For Theodor W. Adorno, negative thinking was a feature of non-identity thinking, the kind of thinking that could help us grasp particulars and does not fall prey to abstract and instrumental rationality.[74] My use of "negative" is also quite different from the one that has been popularized by Alexandre Kojève's interpretation of Hegel's *Phenomenology of Spirit*.[75] Commenting on Hegel, Kojève asserted:

> For Self-Consciousness, and hence philosophy, to exist, there must be in Man not only positive, passive contemplation which merely reveals being, but also negating Desire, and hence Action that transforms the given being. The human I must be an I of Desire—that is, an active I, a negating I, an I that transforms Being and creates a new being by destroying the given being. Now, what is the I of Desire—the I of a hungry man, for example—but an emptiness greedy for content; an emptiness that wants to

be filled by what is full, to be filled by emptying this fullness, to put itself—once it is filled—in the place of this fullness to occupy with its fullness the emptiness caused by overcoming the fullness that was not its own?[76]

This meaning of negativity—the self as an emptiness that longs for fullness—was further popularized by Jacques Lacan for a whole school of thought, and came to practically define desire itself.[77] It is the mark of a subjectivity that is in quest of the recognition by another, of another's desire, and yet that can never settle with the appropriation of the other's recognition or desire. One finds oneself desiring an object one can never grasp or possess, or must become confronted with the void and emptiness that the appropriation of such object would entail. Such negativity is a positive movement of the self, in the sense that it unfolds through the projection of oneself onto the desire of another that it wants to absorb or struggle with, and to that extent, it is generative both of identity (or the search for it) and of social bonds.

I call here "negative bonds" something else altogether (a non-Hegelian meaning): "negative" here means that the subject does not want relationships or is unable to form them because of the structure of his or her desire. In a "negative bond," the self evades the mechanism of desire and recognition altogether. It is a bond in which there is no attempt to find, know, appropriate, and conquer the subjectivity of another. In negative bonds, others are means for self-expression and for the assertion of one's autonomy—and not the object of recognition. Jean-Paul Sartre's notion of "nothingness" (although intending to describe a different set of problems) is actually useful here. Sarah Bakewell, the author of a popular yet comprehensive history of the existentialist movement, summarizes "nothingness" as follows:

> Let's imagine, [Sartre] suggests, that I have made an appointment to meet my friend Pierre at a certain café at four o'clock. I arrive fifteen minutes late and look around anxiously. Is Pierre still here? I perceive lots of other things: customers, tables, mirrors and lights, the café's smoky atmosphere, the sound of rattling crockery and a general murmuring hubbub.[78]

This vignette is meant to illustrate something about consciousness itself, the fact that it is indeterminate, that it apprehends itself like an absent Pierre. A negative relationship is like looking for someone in an ensemble of people, artifacts, spaces, and not finding him or her; it is feeling this absence and the indeterminateness of one's intentions and desires. A negative relationship is thus not a voluntary renunciation to sex or love because of a higher injunction (monasticism for example); nor is it the void inscribed inside the act of desiring (Kojève and Lacan), but rather it is the perception of an absent other in the midst of the ongoing humming of the presence of many others and the perception of the indeterminateness of my own intentions.

An additional meaning of "negative" remains in the same philosophical tradition and derives from Martin Heidegger (Sartre had read closely *Being and Time*[79] and was deeply influenced by it). To speak about the unproblematic relationship of human beings with the world, Heidegger uses the metaphor of a hammer. I am hammering, being barely aware of the hammer and of my project of hammering this piece of wood. But if something goes wrong and the hammer or the nail breaks, I will suddenly start paying attention to what I do and will look at myself in a new way. "What had been ready-to-hand flips into being present-at-hand: an inert object to be glared at," explains Bakewell.[80] In this new sense of negative, relationships that are established do not work the way they should, they thus force and compel my attention, they become "an object to be glared at," discussed, puzzled over. Here the relationship becomes the departure point of a reflexive detachment from a routine way of doing and feeling.

"Negative bonds" are negative in one of these two meanings: they point to an absent object I cannot seize because the situation is indeterminate; or they reveal that something is not quite working as it should when the relationship is here. Negative relationships have fuzzy, unclear, undefined, or contested purposes; they have no scripted rules of engagement and disengagement, and carry no or little penalty for being undone. The first form of negative bonds disappears quickly not because it is contractually defined as transient (as, for example, the relationship of a bank teller to a customer) but because of their relative normlessness, their lack of scripted rules and lack of shared frame of meaning. The second form of negative bonds has to do with the fact something in them does not quite work properly.

It should be clear that "positive" and "negative" have no moral implications; these terms refer only to the ways in which social bonds are generated, whether by being clearly formulated in cultural scripts (e.g., being a teacher, a parent, or a husband) or by being (relatively) unscripted and normatively fuzzy[81] (e.g., casual sex). A negative social relationship is one that is driven by uncertainty, while a positive relationship is relatively structured and organized around clear norms. The "fuzziness" of negative relationships has the meaning it has in "fuzzy logic" and expresses the fact that normativity is not defined by a "normative-deviant" binary opposition, but rather contains unclear and contested rules. For example, in Jewish religion, a woman's adultery is normatively defined in an unmistakable manner: it is always prohibited and always harshly punished (by lapidation for example). Man's adultery, on the other hand, is normatively fuzzy; it is prohibited, but only sometimes, when the married man commits adultery with a married woman; while not being recommended, adultery with a single woman does not incur severe punishment, and does not threaten the normative core of Jewish law and family. Men's adultery is thus located on what I would call a fuzzy normative scale, while a married woman's is always prohibited and punished.

I would thus venture the following hypothesis: in the realm of love and sexuality, we have moved from a modality of cultural action in which culture described the world thickly in symbols and moral narratives, prescribed and guided behavior through hot meanings or well-laid-out plans of action (courtship being an example of such well-laid-out plan of action), to a modality of culture in which autonomy and freedom produce relatively weakly scripted, fuzzy rules of interactions with unpredictable outcomes, that is, relatively normless interactions, at least in the private and intimate domain (the work-sphere on the contrary has become highly scripted). By normlessness I mean not only that behavior is improvised and that its rules are up for grabs[82] but also the less playful meaning that the norms governing the conduct of sexual bonds are unclear, that they do not follow a moral script, and that little social punishment is incurred for breaking rules of reciprocity. Normless interactions do not sharply differentiate adequate from inadequate behavior, because few punishments come attached to inadequate behavior. This lack of thick normativity derives from the very practice of freedom, and its associated positive injunctions such as self-reliance, autonomy, and hedonism, all dominant vocabularies of selfhood.[83] These positive injunctions generate negative bonds, bonds that are normatively fuzzy, chaotic, have multiple definitions and purposes, and are the site for the expression of one's autonomy through withdrawal or unchoice. If for Ulrich Beck and Elisabeth Gernsheim-Beck the "normal chaos of love" was a source of positive sociality, that is, a source for improvisation and productive relationality, chaos here is a source of negative sociality, of a reordering of the formation and management of relationships through uncertainty.

This also entails a rethinking of the notion of culture. In traditional anthropology and sociology, culture shapes social bonds through roles, norms, rituals, and social scripts, that is, through positive injunctions to belong, identify, execute, or even improvise. In contrast, in negative relations actors grapple with the elusiveness and meaning of their own actions. If culture is increasingly taking the form of advice or self-help culture, it is done precisely because in the realms of love, parenting, and sexuality, few cultural schemas guide action in a binding way and compel men and women to align themselves around agreed-upon rules and norms. Self-help culture and psychological advice contain and emit scripts for relationality[84] but it does not do this from within a set of ordered and sacred symbols, but from a sociality ridden with uncertainty. Psychological self-management is nothing but the management of a pervasive uncertainty in interpersonal relationships where sexual freedom and pleasure, both organized in the grammar and semantics of the market, have been traded for psychological certainty.

*

In his analysis of what he thought would be the crisis to come, the historian Ken Jowitt uses a sexual metaphor to make sense of a new social order. He thinks the world of the post-cold war would resemble a bar for singles:

> It's a bunch of people who don't know each other, who, in the lingo, hook up, go home, have sex, don't see each other again, can't remember each other's names, go back to the bar and meet somebody else. So it's a world that's made up of disconnections.

This brave new world is made up of people who do not know each other, go to sleep with each other, leave each other without knowing each other's name, and return the week after to look for new people.[85] This world, Jowitt suggests, is connected and disintegrated at the same time.[86] Sexuality serves here as an organizing metaphor for the political and social order—it reflects organization and disorganization at once. More exactly, casual sexuality has become the paradigm for negative sociality. Where "classical choice" was about selecting, ordering, excluding, and singularizing an object, sexual non-choice is achieved through accumulation as a hoarding practice (partners coexist with each other; relationships overlap with each other), or through the disposal of a sexual object after enjoying it. Abundance and interchangeability of partners are the two operative modes of a free sexuality governed by non-choice and negative sexuality.

For Freud pleasure derives from mastery of stimuli, and pain erupts when the ego cannot master an outside occurrence, when the stimuli threaten to disorganize the self. Casual sex is a pleasurable experience as long as it affords a sense of mastery, autonomy, and control for both parties. But often, it generates the opposite experience of disorganization of the self and uncertainty in at least one side of the pair interacting. This experience of frame uncertainty is redoubled by what I dub ontological uncertainty, explored in the next chapter.

4

Scopic Capitalism and the Rise of Ontological Uncertainty

J'écris de chez les moches, pour les moches, les frigides, les mal bai-
sées, les imbaisables, toutes les exclues du grand marché à la bonne
meuf, aussi bien que pour les hommes qui n'ont pas envie d'être
protecteurs, ceux qui voudraient l'être mais ne savent pas s'y pren-
dre, ceux qui ne sont pas ambitieux, ni compétitifs, ni bien
membrés.

—Virginie Despentes, *King Kong Theorie*

I write as an ugly woman, for the ugly ones, for the frigid, for those
who are badly fucked, for the unfuckable, all the excluded from the
big market of the hot chick, I write as well for the men who do not
want to be protectors, those who would like to be but do not know
how to do it, those who are not ambitious, competitive or well
hung.

—Author's translation

In the meantime I was able to observe you some, though it did not
matter to me in the least what you looked like—your words were all
I cared about [...]so great was the power of your words over me,
that from then on I liked what you were wearing very much.

—Franz Kafka[1]

The problem is no longer how to do what you want, but to know
what would satisfy you.

—Stanley Cavell[2]

The Harvey Weinstein scandal will remain one of the watershed moments of
2017. The Hollywood mogul was accused of harassing or raping over one
hundred women with the complicit knowledge of his colleagues, assistants,

and employees for more than two decades.[3] The worldwide reaction to the Weinstein scandal—with millions of women on social media telling their own stories of sexual abuse, harassment, and rape under the hashtag #MeToo—exposed to the public eye one of the central questions of feminism: Why is it that despite modest but meaningful inroads toward equality, the sexual domination of men over women remains deep and widespread?[4] Sexual domination is manifest through male violence, of course, but it is also manifest in more diffuse, elusive, and vague processes of devaluation of women. Building on the previous chapters in this book, this chapter aims to understand the economic, social, and cultural mechanisms explaining how women are devalued through sexuality, and rendered disposable through mechanisms that remain to be clarified.

Whether sexuality is the authentic part of ourselves repressed by a too-long religious and patriarchal history, or a psychic truth that we are compelled to reveal under the watchful eye of experts, an indisputable fact remains: sexuality has become the conveyor belt of consumer and technological practices. "Sexual practices and interactions are subsumed under the economy."[5] The sexual subject who was conceptualized by Sigmund Freud as a bundle of unconscious drives later turned these drives into the truth of desires[6] to be realized in the images, values, stories, and ideals of the good life promoted by the consumer market[7] and, for the last decade, by a wide array of technological devices. In the process of being recruited by the consumer market and technology, the sexual body has become the producer of an economic surplus value that is as formidable as it is inadequately conceptualized.

The economic-sexual subject is *the* proper subject of modernity. It enacts its individuality through wants and desires, through choices and, increasingly, through non-choices that all take place in a consumer sphere saturated with intimacy[8] and in a private sphere that is commodified.[9] It is virtually impossible to separate sexuality and love from the consumer and technological arenas in which they are deployed. Sexual desire produces economic value, while commodities are interwoven in the production of sexual desire. When combined, sexual and economic forms of action create what I call a hyper-subject, a subject defined by the activity of having needs and desires and by practices to satisfy such needs and desires. Hyper-subjectivity, however, rests on a paradox: it activates *ontological uncertainty*, an uncertainty about the very nature of the self. Ontological uncertainty is shaped by three processes—valuation, evaluation, and devaluation—all three determined by the still-powerful economic and symbolic domination of men over women. These three processes are at once economic, cognitive, and cultural; they mark a new stage in the history of capitalism and intimate relationships.

Value does not inhere in objects but is the result of a social relationship.[10] Valuation is the process of generating worth through economic or symbolic mechanisms (for example, exhibiting one's works in a national museum increases the economic worth of one's art). Evaluation is the activity of appraising, comparing, and measuring the worth of an object.[11] Evaluation and valuation are concomitant social processes (the art collector or a credit rating agency engage at once in evaluation and valuation). Devaluation is then the process of lowering worth, through symbolic mechanisms as speech acts by powerful actors[12] or through economic mechanisms as overproduction, when a commodity is in higher supply than demand. Evaluation, valuation, and devaluation are tightly connected to the intensification and dissolution of subjectivity in capitalist culture.[13] These processes are mediated by the consumer market, by Internet technology, and by media industries, and reciprocally shape one another.

The Value of the Body

As social psychologist Roy Baumeister and feminist scholar Paola Tabet have argued, in all societies where women lack social and economic power, they trade their sexuality with men's power.[14] This is what Tabet calls the economico-sexual exchange. In such societies, women exchange sexual services with the men who control them for different prices, usually a long courtship and marriage, but also for gifts as found in dating or for money as found in prostitution.[15] After the 1970s and in the consumer economy afterward, two important changes took place. Thanks to the contraceptive pill, sexual access to women became practically unrestricted, demanding very low costs from men, neither marriage, courtship, or even dating;[16] second, the sexualization of women's bodies undertaken by the media and fashion industries generated a formidable economic value that benefited mostly (albeit not exclusively) men. As Carole Pateman put it: "[T]here is a huge, multimillion dollar trade in women's bodies."[17] (It is in fact more likely to be a multi*billion*-dollar trade.)

While the early liberation movements had imagined a free sexuality as an essentially non-commercial, non-monetized aspect of the self, sexuality became both a remunerated and non-remunerated source of surplus value for a consequential number of industries controlled by men.

The economic valuation of the female body was made possible by the fact that it was transformed into a tradable visual unit. New norms of attractiveness started being diffused through a vast network of industries. From the beginning of the twentieth century onward, mass media and the fashion-cosmetics industrial complex propagated images of beautiful and fashionable women on an unprecedented scale.[18] These images created new norms of attractiveness that transcended class-based sartorial codes and had a cross-class appeal through what sociologist Ashley Mears calls "the look,"[19] a mixture of clothing styles, allure, and bodily shape. A "look" is a tradable asset that circulates in an economy of images. The individual body thus became a legitimately tradable commodity through a process of spectacularization; it became an image that imitated and reflected public images of bodies.

Procedures of self-production and self-presentation always reflect the dominant economic and cultural interests of the time.[20] Sexual attractiveness constitutes a new way for the body to stage itself, through media visual symbols and consumer items. The sexy body is in turn at the heart of the "widespread fascination with sex and the sexually explicit in print and broadcast media."[21] This is aptly captured by Ambroise, the same man quoted in the previous chapter:

AMBROISE: My buddies and I we call each other very often and we say to each other: "It's impossible, there are so many gorgeous-looking girls in the street, incredible asses, women who have an incredible body, with tightly fit dresses, or jeans, incredible breasts, so shapely, and they know how to show it," and this I call, the street frustration, you know, it has become ordinary, you come home in the evening, and you feel that is not possible, that's impossible, all these sexual temptations.... All these gorgeous women. Just impossible.

Walter Benjamin's *flâneur* strolled in a street that was becoming a spectacle through new architectural design and window display but also through the sexualization of objects:

The masses first made it possible for the sexual object to be reflected simultaneously in a hundred different forms of allurement-forms which the object itself produced. Beyond this, salability itself can become a sexual stimulus; and this attraction increases wherever an abundant supply of women underscores their character as commodity. With the exhibition of girls in rigidly uniform dress at a later period, the music hall review explicitly introduced the mass-produced article into the libidinal life of the big-city dweller.[22]

As Benjamin incisively remarks here, the sexual object circulates in many reverberated versions of itself in consumer culture, which eroticizes the promotion and sale of goods. The modern *flâneur* like Ambroise is a sexual spectator, who consumes women's bodies as a commodity-spectacle of sexuality and consumer objects.[23] This spectator attends to the body as a visual surface containing signs of sexuality and experiences the consumer sphere as an ongoing low-key flow of sexual desire, organized in urban public spaces.[24]

"Sexiness" is the result of new ideologies of sexuality as a commodity form and of the self as an image. Sexiness relies on consumer items for revealing, displaying, and emphasizing the sexual body. It points to the (desirable) naked body, with consumer attires doing the work of signaling and evoking the naked body. Being sexy becomes a matter of wearing certain types of clothes (jeans, for example) worn in a certain way (tightly fit on the body, for example). Sexiness was more democratic than beauty in that it could be achieved by a much larger pool of people, the handsome and the comely, the physically lucky and the unlucky; because it is the result of self-fashioning rather than of in-born beauty, it makes consumption an ongoing and permanent feature of the experience of the self. Sexual attractiveness is performatively established through consumer items and practices and is thus an economic performance: through sports, fashion, cosmetics, medical and pharmaceutical goods, it makes the body a visual surface destined to be visually consumed as an object defined by its capacity to elicit sexual desire. While the notion of *hexis* as it was reformulated by Pierre Bourdieu[25] suggested that one's class position was encoded in the body, the scopic industrial complex (constituted by the symbiosis of the beauty-fashion-sports-media industries) generated relatively classless models of attractiveness and sexiness, diffused through new social groups associated with those industries. Fashion designers of all walks, stylists, models, actors, photographers, women's magazine editors, cosmeticians, hairdressers, movie makers, and much more—all promote visual appearance as a tradable commodity.

The sexual gaze seizes objects and persons as a single unit and creates a seamless continuity between the two through the cultural category of the sexy attractive body in which sexuality and consumption reciprocally perform each other for the gaze. This is illustrated by Uri, a twenty-eight-year-old Israeli man, speaking about the type of woman he finds attractive:

> URI: I don't like too much the "fem" style; polished nails, high heels, make-up, like very careful dressing, I don't find it attractive. It's like an image for me. I like women who look more casual, when they wear jeans for example. Tight jeans and tight T-shirts. And boots. I find it sexy.

Notice how the sexual category this man is attracted to (or not) is a construct of consumer objects and images (or a departure from them). Here, a sexual type is in fact equated with a consumer type ("fem" types are consumer types; or as another example, in gay male culture, "leather culture" marks a sexual and consumer type). What is marked as femininity or masculinity is thus a consumer substyle, which follows a visual logic of consumer recognition. As Guy Debord put it, the society of spectacle is not a mere collection of images, but rather *is* a social relationship mediated by images.[26] This is nowhere more true than in the sexual encounter, which is indeed a performance of the social bond through images of personhood that themselves point to and are performed by consumer objects. Sexual identity is inscribed in the aesthetization of everyday experience through consumer objects[27] with the body becoming a visual and aesthetic commodity.[28] As Nicolas Mirzoeff put it, the visual subject is at once the agent of sight, the person who looks, and the object of others' gaze. The visual sexual agent is an expert in his skillful capacity to relate to others as visual surfaces (assessing quickly thinness, breast size, or muscle tone), and is aware that she or he is the object of others' visual evaluation.[29] What Hegel called recognition,[30] the intersubjective process of two subjectivities meeting and acknowledging each other, has moved here to a visual and sexual plane, in which one is simultaneously audience and performer. This self-awareness of others' gaze is distinct from traditional symbolic processes of recognition: it is grounded in the media-market-technology nexus; it concerns the bodily surface and its "hotness" (sexiness); and it is a process more or less controlled by men who have the symbolic and economic power to define women's worth and attractiveness.[31]

This is well expressed by a self-defined "sugar baby" blogger who, referring to the attention she pays to her body in order to catch the attention of a rich man, speaks for many women:

> Could I really be happy with a man old enough to be my father? Yes, yes and yes! You see, by being meticulously preened and fabulous at all times I give up nothing. I love coordinating my outfits, getting manicures/pedicures and especially shopping. I love all these things with or without the benefit of meeting rich men (preferably with). Looking my best gives me a high because I am a perfectionist to the core and nothing less will do. Besides, if I was married to a rich man I would be carrying on the same. [...]The woman you see walking down the street is a piece of art. A lot of maintenance—manicures, pedicures, hair cuts, waxing, bleaching, plucking and SHOPPING—goes into that piece of art. Art reflects your lifestyle and status. If a trophy is what you want, then you must be prepared to pay.[32]

Beauty and sexual attractiveness are here predicated on the male gaze, and in turn require a preliminary intensive work of self-fashioning grounded in the consumer sphere, to be recycled and circulated as an image of themselves, consumed by men who detain economic power. This sugar baby suggests that she is at once a sexual and economic agent, a consumer and producer of her own value.

Producing Symbolic and Economic Value

Consumer culture has transformed the ontology of sexuality into a theater of the self,[33] a visible, public performance mediated by consumer objects. While bourgeois sexuality was the prerogative of the secrecy of bedrooms, it is now a visible feature of the self, regulated by a scopic regime of consumption. As Daniel Mendelsohn put it: "My gay friends and I are inhabitants of a culture in which libido is [...] a product to be consumed."[34] Similarly, femininity is visual performance situated in a market controlled by men, destined to the male gaze and consumed by men. If traditional women's sexuality was exchanged for men's money and power,[35] modern women's sexuality is now located in a market where women's sexualized body is end-lessly and continuously appropriated through male gaze. Yet, it is through the exercise of their freedom that women are enjoined to display their sexu-ality. It is as an act of power that they are called to turn the sexual value of their body into an aesthetic, symbolic, and economic performance. Hence, if women's bodies have been sexualized and commodified so widely, it is because sexualization is an economic and symbolic value at once: The attractive body is the cornerstone of consumer culture, can be processed in return by the sphere of production, thus generating capital.

One form of such capital is to be found in the plethora of services offered by industries that require a "pleasant" and attractive appearance: restaurant hosts, flight attendants, public relations representatives, and the like—all must have an attractive appearance, or what Catherine Hakim has contro-versially called "erotic capital."[36] In that sense, sexuality belongs to the sphere of immaterial labor,[37] the set of intangible skills and competences actors bring to the workplace and that in some cases even define the work position. As Ashley Mears points out: "Increasingly, companies are seeking employees who embody the right look."[38] The importance of attractiveness for the workplace produces a management of the self akin to forms of self-branding (that is, to self-consciously present oneself as endowed with a unique set of skills and attractiveness). Indeed, "[s]elf-branding may be considered a form of affective, immaterial labor that is purposefully under-taken by individuals in order to garner attention, reputation and potentially, profit."[39]

A second way in which sexual selves produce value is through the visual (media) industries in which sex and sexuality are consumed as an image, in the advertising, film, or TV industry down to the industry of pornography. While until the 1950s, cinema ostentatiously displayed women's bodies through fashionable clothes that revealed and concealed sexual parts, after the 1960s, nakedness and sexuality became ordinary features of cinema and, later, of television. Women have been consistently shown dispropor-tionately more in revealing clothes than men. "By 1999, over two thirds of evening TV shows contained sexual content, an increase of 12 percent over the previous year. If sex had a defining feature in the 1990s, it was ubiquity."[40]

We may thus say that the consumption of the image of the attractive and sexual body has considerably expanded throughout the twentieth century, increasing the revenues of a variety of visual industries exposing women but overwhelmingly owned and managed by men.[41] As *New York Times* columnist Maureen Dowd puts it:

> Even though women are half of ticket buyers, only 4 percent of the 100 top-grossing films over the last decade were directed by women. Women make up 11 percent of writers, 3 percent of cinematographers, 19 percent of producers and 14 percent of editors.[42]

Pornography, the most blatantly commodified industry of women's bodies, is predominantly male both on the production and consumption side.[43] As Heather Rupp and Kim Wallen state: "Pornographic magazines and videos directed at men are a multi-billion dollar industry while similar products directed towards women are difficult to find. It is estimated that of the 40 million adults who visit pornography websites annually, 72% are male while only 28% are female."[44] The porn industry only amplifies what is present, directly or obliquely in other fields, namely the sexual female body as a visual commodity for the consumption of the male gaze (many sex acts consist in making erotic violence toward women).

Once the body is made into a visual unit ready for sexual consumption, it can also be converted into a third form of economic value generated by the valuation of the sexual body for its performance and competence. This competence—"how to achieve orgasm," "how to find her secret erogenous zones," "how to perform fellatio"—is widely promoted and sold by a variety of economic segments: self-help literature, counseling and therapy, the pharmaceutical industry,[45] sex toy industry, prostitution, and escort services (in which women of different social classes increasingly participate). All of these combined account for the production and circulation of hundreds of billions of dollars.[46]

A fourth form of valuation of the body through its sexualization occurs through the economy of reputation created by Internet platforms and social media relayed by cell phone technology that circulate widely photos of attractive bodies, both clad and naked. This circulation of photographs is inscribed in a symbolic economy of reputation,[47] which can be capitalized in Internet platforms through the sponsoring of corporations or advertising.[48] For example, beauty vlogs developed by women who do not work in the beauty industry can be used as platforms for large companies such as L'Oreal to reach women through ordinary actors perceived not to be a part of the industry.[49] A top model posing on Instagram or other platforms can be paid several tens of thousands of dollars for a single post.[50]

Finally, the visualization of sexual personhood can be converted into capital in the increasingly expanding market of short-term or long-term sexual transactions, a market that also has intensified and become formalized with Internet technologies (see for example "sugar-daddies" sites that promote a soft middle-class form of prostitution under the guise of "gifts" or "common leisure"). The sexual, romantic, and matrimonial market blurs the distinction between the monetary and the non-monetary and takes multiple forms: casual sex, hookups, short-term or long-term dating, living together, or marriage. The cultivation of sexual attractiveness constitutes a form of self-branding traded on markets that are at once economic and sexual. Internet dating sites brokering between "sugar daddies" and "sugar babies" offer a powerful illustration of the ways in which the market form increasingly imposes itself on sexual encounters, putting women and men in situations where direct visual display and competition are regulated by mechanisms of supply and demand. As described by a site: "Sugar Daddy for Me was launched in 2004. They promote the usual sugar daddy stuff: young, beautiful, ambitious women willing to please; affluent, caring, generous mentors, who want to pamper and spoil someone special."[51] Women expose their faces and bodies on an organized market of profiles visible to the public, and thus convert their bodies into images that themselves become commodities to be traded and even auctioned.[52] Both the producers of value (women) and the consumers of value (men) meet in a social field that takes the form of the market. Donald Trump's reported affairs with a porn star and his marriage to a former model are both glaring examples of the ways in which erotic capital becomes a fungible commodity in different social arenas, in two different visual markets (pornography and modeling) as well as in the sexual and matrimonial market.

To recap: Women's bodily attractiveness and sexuality are fungible commodities. Women's bodies consume an abundant panoply of consumer goods destined to improve and shape appearance that are in turn "invested" in multiple markets to produce capital. The circulation of money in these markets is sustained by a symbolic economy that makes sexuality and sexual attractiveness into an attribute of femininity as a real commodity produced for the gaze. A YouTube beauty vlog, a pornographic movie, a job as a company representative, a rich husband, a sugar daddy who pays for entertainment, a casual boyfriend who will pay for outings—all of these are examples of the ways in which sexuality as an image becomes a tradable commodity. We may thus suggest that the image of the sexual body has been intrinsic to the emergence of what I call scopic capitalism, a capitalism that creates a formidable economic value through the spectacularization of bodies and sexuality, their transformation into images that circulate in different markets. Visuality makes the body into a site for consumption, shaped by consumer objects; it is converted into an asset in the productive sphere of labor as an image to be sold in various visual industries; it posits sexuality as a form of competence that demands the consumption of expert advice; it can circulate in media technologies through an economy of reputation; and finally, it can provide actors with a high position in the sexual field. In scopic (or visual) capitalism, the "look" is a form of self-investment that circulates along networks of money and sexuality. In this consumer and sexual chain, the economic and the sexual seamlessly constitute each other and sexuality is a point of incessant circulation of money. We can literally speak of a criss-crossed network of different markets intersecting in the sexual body and in sexual exchange. This intersection produces *scopic markets* where value is created through the valuation of images of sexual bodies destined to be consumed by the gaze in economic and sexual markets. A continuous chain converting visual icons of beauty and consumer objects into sexually attractive bodies is incessantly fueled and refueled in the economy by making the attractive body into a source of value. The gaze is an essential instrument for the extraction of this sexual and aesthetic surplus value. The scopic regime has been magnified and intensified by the advent of Internet dating sites and social media that place agents in the position of presenting an idealized and attractive self, which circulates widely in a variety of visual platforms. These platforms formalize the marketization of bodies and sexual encounters.

Feminist theory has crucially illuminated the non-paid work of women in the formation and maintenance of the capitalist engine inside the family.[53] Consumer capitalism uses women differently, through the performative work of producing a sexually attractive body. In the civil society of industrial capitalism, men demanded that women's bodies be for sale "only" through marriage or prostitution.[54] Consumer capitalism has changed this. The social and economic structure organizing sexuality is one where the female body is no longer regulated by the family and has undergone a *generalized* process of commodification that make it circulate in markets that are at once economic and sexual, sexual and matrimonial. This appropriation of the female sexualized body constitutes an expropriation of value in Marx's meaning: one class (men) extracts value from the body of another class (women). This in turn explains a paradoxical feature of contemporary women's social existence: while feminism has gained in strength and legitimacy, women have been reassigned to relations of economic domination through the sexual body.

Evaluation

As Axel Honneth argues, recognition has two aspects: a perceptual one (seeing someone; registering the presence of someone) and a symbolic one (doing the necessary work to acknowledge the social status and value of someone else).[55] For Honneth, the first precedes the second and is even its precondition. However, perceptual recognition is not just a perceptual act. To register the presence of others depends on historically variable moral and cognitive tools. The visualization of personhood and social relationships entails indeed new modes of apprehension and perception, which in turn profoundly affect recognition. Evaluation is one such mode of apprehension that affects the perceptual act of recognition.

Evaluation has been increasingly thought of as a crucial cognitive and social feature of modern interactions, primarily in the educational system and in corporations through formalized tests.[56] Evaluation is a feature of bureaucratic organizations concerned with assessment, performance, and productivity. But it has become a generalized social activity extended to the media—in reality shows for example—and to social networks through "like" and "share" buttons. We can in fact hardly think of social media without thinking about the crucial role of evaluation as a social and technological activity, built-in on Internet platforms but practiced in corporations and schools as well. Evaluation has become an ordinary feature of the cognitive orientation of actors, geared to the identification of worth, with actors being simultaneously evaluators and evaluated in the same way that they are consumers of images and turn themselves into images for the gaze of others. The sexualization of personhood turns encounters into visual evaluative performances. Because visual evaluation has a number of key cognitive features, it has consequences for the ways in which relationships are formed and unformed.

Visualization mobilizes snap, instantaneous evaluations; objects are typically apprehended and evaluated visually in a matter of milliseconds.[57] As cognitive psychologists found out, a visual evaluation is a type of cognition that is "fast and frugal," it relies on and needs little information to form a preference toward an object.[58] Because of the speed of visual evaluation, actors will tend to look for and privilege conventional features of attractiveness, which have been codified in media images and fashion industries (cleavage, narrow waist, long legs, blond hair, fair and smooth skin, thinness, etc). Visual evaluation tends thus to privilege those closest to standard models and codes of attractiveness and to dismiss those who don't, thus creating vast pools of unattractive people.

The speed of visual evaluation also makes sexual evaluation a relatively non-interactional and one-sided feature of social interactions. Contrary to recognition that demands a symbolic and social exchange, visual evaluation can in principle take place without any significant interaction and be one-sided. It is mediated by the gaze of the evaluator who decides on his own who is attractive and who is not.

A third feature of visual evaluation, connected again to its speed, is that it transforms the attribution of worth into a binary process: a person is either hot or not, attractive or unattractive. As Dan, a forty-one-year-old Israeli male journalist put it: " When I meet a woman, I know immediately if this is someone I would want to kiss or not." This binary classification is again based on a form of evaluation induced by conventional media images that have codified femininity and more marginally masculinity as sexual attractiveness and sexiness.

These three attributes of visual evaluation—speed, one-sidedness, and binary character—have become further formalized and institutionalized by apps like Tinder, turning persons into consumed images and profiles. Indeed, Tinder's main technological innovation consisted precisely in enabling speed and binarity (the famous "swipe right or left"). This entailed the capacity to enact a fourth attribute of visual evaluation as formalized by Internet technologies, namely the fact that its speed enabled a much higher volume of interactions. Swiping right or left demands a quick form of evaluation that is purely based on visuality, enabling fast selection and fast interaction, more efficiently geared to sexually desirable partners. Tinder deepens the snap character of visual evaluation, executed through the recognition of well-codified traits, and has a discrete outcome (either "hot" or not). Persons become bodies, moving and speaking bodies become still images or snapshots, and evaluation itself becomes a quasi-instantaneous act of evaluating a still shot, making attraction into a punctual, quick, and discrete yes or no, thus creating a seamless harmony between the visualization of sexual personhood and technology.

Vanessa is an Austrian-born creative writer for marketing companies. She resides in London and is thirty-two years old. She offers an example of the ways in which the visualization of sexual personhood is particularly well suited to Internet technology:

VANESSA: My friends in Berlin never used to use Tinder, but now they all use it.

INTERVIEWER: Do you use Tinder?

VANESSA: Oh sure.

INTERVIEWER: Can you describe to me how a typical interaction on Tinder would go?

VANESSA: So you go through the profiles. Most of them, you don't like their face. It's actually fun to swipe left. It's very nice to do that to the faces of men who look machos, arrogant, or dumb.

INTERVIEWER: But some you like?

VANESSA: Sure.

INTERVIEWER: What happens then?

VANESSA: You swipe right, and if they've swiped right as well, we start chatting, exchanging text. Usually the conversation gets quickly sexual.

INTERVIEWER: How for example? Do you feel comfortable telling me?

VANESSA: Oh sure! It goes like this: "Hi. Do you want to meet?" "Yes. I'd like that." "Tell me what you're thinking about?" You would typically answer something sexual. "I am getting hot here. I can meet you in ten minutes at [name of a bar]. I am getting really hot here." You can also add, if you want to really turn them on: "I think I'm gonna suck you hard."

INTERVIEWER: You say this is a normal, regular way of interacting before meeting?

VANESSA: Yes. Totally normal. No one thinks there is anything unusual about it. I mean, that's why you got in touch with him in the first place.

Tinder posits the sexual subject as an image and bases the interaction on a binary visual evaluation—choice or non-choice, swiping right or left. The sexual image circulates in multiple technological platforms and social media in order to be evaluated.[59] For example, the practice of "sexting"— sending a sexual image of oneself with a text (flashing one's breasts during a chat or sending a shot of one's genitalia)—has become a very widespread way of communicating, suggesting the interplay of sexuality, visuality, technology, and evaluation (more on this below).

The generalization of visual evaluation creates a process of benchmarking that is reminiscent of the practice of corporations.

> Benchmarking is a technique employed by managers to improve the operations of their own department or organization. [...] The technique consists of two components: measurement of the performance and efficiency of the organization's key operations, followed by comparison with the best performance of other organizations in order to target areas for improvement.[60]

Benchmarking requires a conscious and unconscious reference to standards (of performance or of beauty, etc.) and a comparative mindset (comparing the object of evaluation to others, while expecting greater optimization). Sexual benchmarking is also amplified and institutionalized by Internet culture as is evidenced by the efforts users put in their (professional or personal) profile and self-presentation to increase their attractiveness. Tinder further institutionalizes this by using algorithms to pair users through attractiveness metrics, thereby submitting the visual marketplace of attractive bodies to a form of benchmarking refined by algorithmic calculation.[61] As the primary mode of self-presentation on social networks, the visual self that circulates in social media has become, in the words of a *New Yorker* commentator, a "punishingly idealized form."[62] This is, I believe, one of the causes for the widespread practice of sexting, which can be viewed as a practice to evaluate a sexual body and be evaluated accordingly.

The Encounter as an Evaluative Interview

Visual evaluation pervades the romantic encounter and is a prerequisite for it. But given that selves meet as branded selves—trying to put forward their best appearance—non-visual evaluation of personality attributes also pervades encounters, especially when their aim is to establish compatibility of tastes, lifestyles, and psychological traits. Through the influence of Internet dating sites, such evaluation increasingly takes the form of an interview. Like its visual counterpart, the "interview" increasingly becomes a binary form of evaluation.

Katya is a sixty-one-year-old French woman, divorced for nine years at the time of the interview, who muses on the pressure put on people when they meet:

KATYA: When I go out on dates, it feels really high pressured, because you meet, and you are constantly asking yourself: "Is it him or not?" and you use anything to decide that he is not. Any small mistake would disqualify him.

INTERVIEWER: Like what kind of mistake?

KATYA: There are so many ways. Like he speaks about himself all evening and barely asks me questions about me. Or he would boast about something: "I was the first to do this." Or "I am the best at this." I find them ridiculous when they boast or play the macho guy. Or he drinks too much alcohol. Complaining about the food or expressing dislike for something that matters to me, like opera. In such situations you are looking at people and you give them a pass or fail grade. That puts a lot of pressure. [...] It was not this way in the past. Say you know someone through work or friends, you would have many opportunities to give them a second or third look. I remember when I was young, I met guys mostly in the settings I was involved in, at the university or at work. I remember this man, Philippe, at first I did not notice him at all. He was a bit effaced, average looking, he was not the kind of guy you notice. Then one day, after we knew each other for a few months, we were having dinner with friends, and he started making the funniest jokes, and suddenly I saw this guy differently, I thought wow, this guy can be funny, so I became interested. We dated for two years. Did you see *Bridget Jones*? Did you see that movie?

INTERVIEWER: Yes. I read the book too.

KATYA: I didn't read the book but even though these are obviously not artsy masterpieces, I loved the movies actually, three movies. They don't like each other at first, but they keep bumping into each other for twenty years, or maybe ten years, then they take a second and third look, and somehow what did not work the first time works the second time. So they give each other plenty of second chances. They belong to the same circles; they blunder, then correct the blunder; they make mistakes about each other but then they see something they did not see before. They kind of get each other, slowly. Not in this kind of "Bang! You have to decide in an instant."

Katya expresses very aptly a transformation of modes of evaluation that operate negatively, that is, in reference to an implicit and highly scripted model of the right partner and whose outcome, as in the work sphere, is statistically more often a no than a yes. The interview form so prevalent in corporations has thus penetrated the romantic encounter: its purpose becomes filtering out and disqualifying unsuitable candidates. An additional example can be found in Ralph, a forty-four-year-old manager working for an investment firm in London and Zurich. From a discussion we had prior to the interview, I found he has been looking for a woman to settle with for a decade, without success. He says:

RALPH: I have been dating for, what, more than twenty years, and I can tell you something has changed since I started looking for a girl, in my mid-twenties. I can see it very clearly. I am not that old, but I can see a change.

INTERVIEWER: How would you describe this change?

RALPH: It's like it is very difficult to simply get the attention of a woman. They seem absorbed by their cell phone, their FB page, Instagram, what people are saying about them. They are constantly checking their mail. When I was twenty and on the dating scene, I never felt that way. Today I feel very much that their attention is somewhere else. Not in the meeting. They have difficulties just focusing on you. Maybe it is a self-selected sample and those that stay on the market are like that. But I don't think so. I think it is more general.

[*later in the interview*]

I met this woman last time and she did not know where Miami was. She thought Los Angeles was closer to Europe than Miami. I found it embarrassing. I have no time for this kind of person. Out. In a second. I have no patience. Hundreds of others are waiting for me on Tinder.

An open sexuality organized on an open market through technologies of encounters generates the problem of evaluating people. The abundance of potential partners afforded by the technology makes evaluation take on a formal character, akin to an "interview" that must efficiently sort out suitable from unsuitable candidates. Because potential partners are decontextualized, that is, disembedded from their social frameworks, agents become purely selecting and evaluative agents, trying to understand the worth of a person in an abstract context that has itself an abstract commodity form (in the same way that corporations are abstract spaces, cafés, bars, or restaurants are standardized abstract consumer spaces). Moreover, the questions often take the form of a standard test. For Katya and Ralph the encounter is an interview equivalent to a situation of pass/fail examination. While the "interviewers" do not always have a clear idea of their preferences, they do have a clear idea of what they do not want, and thus use these meetings as occasions to exercise a "fail" verdict, expressing their personal matrix of tastes and judgments through non-choices that are similar to the left swipe of the Tinder app.

Consumer Evaluation

Sexual and romantic transactions not only presuppose prior consumer acts, and are located in consumer settings, but partners are also evaluated as consumers. One of the deepest and most significant sociological changes in twentieth-century formation of romantic sentiments and attachments is to be found in the inextricable dependency of romantic interactions in consumer tastes. At the beginning of the twentieth century, traditional companionate marriage was replaced by a view of marriage as the sharing of consumer leisure.[63] Dating itself became structured in and by the consumer sphere, with restaurants, bars, movie theaters, touristic locales, and discotheques becoming the main venues to meet and interact.[64] A *New Yorker* column that comments ironically on the contemporary situation of dating and love illustrates nicely the connection of love, the leisure sphere, and consumer taste:

> For a while, you met up at restaurants and bars, but tonight you decided to stay in and cook together. People say that the secret ingredient to a homemade meal is love. That's true. Other important ingredients include a small panic attack and buying *your mozzarella from the store that alludes to Impressionist painters in its cheese descriptions*.[65]

This example is facetious only because it captures a fundamental element of modern dating: dating takes place in commercial leisure venues and consists in the identification of similar consumer tastes, based in the senses (the right cheese) and in cultural competence (the Impressionist painters). In a famous column from the *New York Times* describing the many ways in which people fall in love, a writer asked the question, How do you know you have fallen in love? Here is one answer:

> When you feel like you met someone from your dreams. As a teenager growing up in Le Mars, Iowa, Paul Rust, thirty-six, a writer, director, and

producer with the Netflix series *Love*, dreamed of meeting someone who liked *underground punk rock* as much as he did, someone with the "spirit of an artist." [...] Years later, while hiding in the kitchen during an intimidating birthday party in Los Angeles, he locked eyes with Lesley Arfin, thirty-eight, a writer for the HBO series *Girls*, who was visiting from New York. They struck up a conversation. She liked *punk rock*. She was a writer. She was incredibly smart and beautiful.[66]

Note here the importance of punk rock, that is, a musical taste as the defining characteristic of the person he dreamed about and identified among many. Falling in love here takes place through consumer evaluation. Starting in the first decades of the twentieth century, but more decisively after the 1970s, the capacity to share in common leisure activities and cultural tastes is at the core of the ways in which people pair up, thus consolidating consumer subjectivity through the experience of intimacy. Consumer tastes and evaluation then structure from within the pairing process and desire itself. They deepen one's sense of unique subjectivity. Here is one example that illustrates *a contrario* how a consumer evaluation can affect a bond. Tina, a fifty-year-old German lesbian woman recounts her last relationship:

TINA: I have Celiac disease. You know what it is?
INTERVIEWER: It's an autoimmune disorder that makes you severely allergic to gluten.
TINA: Exactly. So I cannot eat gluten of any kind. Not even traces. And one of the things that bugged her [her previous girlfriend] was that I could not taste some of the food she ate. She whined that I could not taste some of the things she loved. That I could not share her love of food with her.

This woman's former partner could continue her own dining practices but deplored the fact that her partner could not share her sensorial love for food, suggesting the role of consumer objects and practices in structuring intimacy. The sharing of consumer tastes functions as an emotional and sensorial platform to forge intimacy. It is around common hobbies, food or wine tasting, travel, sports, and cultural consumption that attachment is now organized, making consumers' habits the object of evaluation. A difficulty in engaging together in the leisure sphere, to appropriate the same objects, entails a difficulty in organizing intimacy and hence desire. Commodities here function as transitional objects for the formation and consolidation of bonds, as well as for their devaluation and undoing. They are transitional objects in the sense given to this word by psychoanalyst Donald W. Winnicott:[67] They organize the boundaries between external world and inner self, and negotiate autonomy and attachment being at once an expression of one's individuality and the ground for engaging in a process of attachment to others. Body, personality, and tastes are the object of constant evaluation and the transitional points for the making and unmaking of bonds.

Sexual Devaluation

According to feminist scholar Alice Echols, second-wave feminism's main goal was to offer strategies to counter the "cultural valuation of the male and devaluation of the female."[68] Yet, while women have made some (still modest) inroads in the economic and political spheres, they seem to have undergone a serious process of devaluation in the sexual-romantic sphere.[69] Such devaluation has been analyzed by many feminists and scholars in sexual economics, for whom sex has been "cheapened,"[70] literally due to the fact that men do not need to pay for sex anymore. For Mark Regnerus, sex for free is the result of three distinctive technological achievements: "(1) the wide uptake of the Pill as well as a mentality stemming from it that sex is 'naturally' infertile (2) mass-produced high-quality pornography, and (3) the advent and evolution of online dating/meeting services." He euphemistically calls all three "price supressors," that is, factors that lower the costs and value of dating, of sex, and, one presumes (although he doesn't say it), of women.[71]

Yet, this explanation conveniently ignores the fact that men can value many activities they do not pay for (going to church, volunteering, walking on the beach, etc.) and therefore leaves unexplained the reason why sex with women (and by extension women themselves) has no or little value once men do not have to "pay" for it anymore. The very fact that unpaid sex entails the devaluation of women must be explained.

A psychologist advertising what she calls her "dating rehab" program describes—without naming it properly—the devaluation of women I have in mind here:

Dating today is broken, and the proof is in the symptoms. See if you've experienced any of these:

You meet someone who seems very interested, but then his ardor for you rapidly vanishes—and he exits your life as quickly as he entered. You fear getting your hopes up because you don't want to be let down yet again. You'll click with someone at a party and you can feel that there's chemistry, but then he never makes a move. You're left wondering if you misread his signals—or maybe later you find out that he's actually seeing someone. Why, then, was he flirting with you—and how can you trust anyone—let alone your instincts? You have intense exchanges with someone you "met" online, and you are bursting with excitement on the way to your first date. But reality is far different—this person is nothing like they said they were, and the apparent connection just isn't there. You got your hopes up for nothing. You actually start seeing someone exclusively, but then as soon as the first argument hits or you make any mention of commitment, a chilling distance enters the relationship. You start regretting the things you said and wonder if you've completely blown it—yet again.

These scenarios, although they may feel unique when they happen to you, are extremely common. *Seemingly intense connections that suddenly fizzle with little to no warning have become the NORM.* I've seen this happen with such alarming frequency in my single clients, that I knew dating today wasn't working—it had devolved into a haphazard "system" that was woefully inept at creating CONNECTION.[72]

Making demeaning jokes about a woman's body, disdaining overweight women, denigrating women of one's own age or older than one, privileging young women over women of one's age, ranking a woman's physical appearance, date rape, parceling a woman's body, seeking status through the undifferentiated accumulation of sexual partners, creating hierarchies of worth according to beauty and thinness—all of these constitute very widespread and routine strategies of devaluation of women's bodies and selves. Yet they are often viewed as the benign and unavoidable hazards of dating, with women bearing the main psychological burden of coping with them by using, for example, self-help literature or seeking psychological advice. Sexual encounters can generate harrowing experiences of diminished value, and the fact that some or most people end their search happily does not invalidate the fact that devaluation seems to have become intrinsic to sexual life.

In critical feminist theory, the notions of "objectification" and "sexualiza-tion" have done most of the heavy work of explaining the lessening of woman's worth. As stated by Linda Smolak and Sarah Murnen:

> As a pervasive influence, sexualization exists in multiple forms and is directed at rewards for being sexy. Furthermore, there are punishments, or at least fewer opportunities, for not following the sexy norms.[73]

This definition misses the fact that objectification provides a sense of pleas-ure, empowerment, and subjectivity because it enables women to generate economic and symbolic value from their bodies. In ignoring the economic underpinnings of sexualization, the notion of self-objectification ultimately reduces women's voluntary participation to their self-objectification to false consciousness and omits to account for the mechanisms of (symbolic and economic) valuation contained in it. Moreover, it does not differentiate enough between different processes at work in the devaluation of women by men, some voluntary and connected to the ways in which men build their status by denigrating women, some involuntary, stemming from the cogni-tive difficulty of attributing value in the face of large sexual markets. There is nothing intrinsic about sexuality or even sexualization that is demeaning. Rather, it is the fact that sexuality is located in a market controlled by men that makes sexualization into the experience of domination for one and humiliation for the other. Despite the sense of empowerment and pleasure they offer, I am critical of the commodification of sexuality and the pornifi-cation of culture[74] because these constitute mechanisms to control women through the seemingly invisible male hand of the (sexual) market.

Men's control of sexual markets is apparent (and hidden) in more than one way. First, as we have seen above, men control the bulk of visual-sexual industries and thus control the definition of what matters in women. Controlling the gaze has enormous economic and ideological consequences and more especially for what men value in women and what women value in themselves. To give one example: As Harvard economist Sendhil Mullainathan suggests: "One study found that men are less likely to want a date with a woman who is more intelligent or ambitious than they are."[75] One should add to his remark that the same men would hardly mind a date with a woman who is sexually more attractive than they are. This is because defining women's worth through her sexual attractiveness is indeed a way of indirectly diminishing women's talents and intellect, keeping their social place inferior to that of men and affirming men's economic and social domination. Second, men control the definition of the criteria that constitute women's attractiveness as illustrated by the premium put by men on woman's youth, while youth is not a distinctive or necessary trait of male attractiveness. This is because women do not control the ideological-visual-economic apparatus that shapes standards of attractiveness and beauty. By contrast, men's attractiveness reflects their position in the social field: it is mostly established through their social status and assets.[76] The fact that men with higher incomes and education command a higher position in the sexual field gives them three outstanding advantages: their sexual power is not as obsolescent as women's and even increases with time. Men's attractiveness has more lasting power than that of women, making age a resource and form of capital in the sexual field.[77] Moreover, they have access to larger samples of potential partners because they have access to women of their own age and much younger.[78] Finally, there is an overlap and even tight fit between men's sexual and socioeconomic goals. Men's sexual power is not distinct or opposite to their social power and each reinforces the other. Conversely, women's sexual and social positions are far more likely to conflict with each other.

Beauty as Obsolescence

Objectification contains different meanings. To objectify another is to make the person the object of my power and control by defining its worth in ways that depend on my gaze and approval. If sexualization entails the power of one side to define the worth of the other side, then it follows that the sexualized object is in fact in an inferior relationship.

> Sexualization facilitates women's development of the belief that a sexy appearance is important not only to appeal to men but also to be successful in all areas of life. This belief is key to internalizing the sexual gaze, that is, self-objectification.[79]

Most moral philosophers view self-objectification as a reduction of the moral value of the self. For philosophers Avishai Margalit and Martha Nussbaum, objectification means relating to others in a way that diminishes their value, either on the basis of their appearance, or by treating them as inferiors (as animals for example), or by focusing only on (parts of) the body, primarily in sexual terms.[80] The second sense of objectification is adjacent to and derives from the commodification of selfhood. It implies not only that we evaluate others and ourselves in terms of bodily and visual appearance but also that we treat our body as a commodity situated in a market of similar and competing commodities. The body becomes an object of measurement, ranking, and commensuration. Finally, some feminist critics have been mostly worried about the fact that internalization of the objectifying male gaze separates the body from holistic notions of personhood.[81]

These views omit what I take to be an even more important aspect of self-objectification: it creates forms of uncertainty about one's value and thus creates diminished experiences of self. This is because for most women, the production of their sexual value remains actually unrealized. In Marxist sociology, the value of a commodity is fully produced when it is realized in a concrete social interaction, for example purchase or barter. But the value women produce is often prevented from being fully realized in the sexual or economic market,[82] as when, for example, women are deemed "too old" to be hired for a specific position or sought after for a relationship. For women, sexual valuation often functions as a uselessly produced capital, as a value that generates uncertain or weak returns. This is in contrast to men's attractiveness, which has a much longer shelf life and coincides with their social value, thus creating more stable forms of selfhood, where the sexual and the social coincide.

Moreover, ontological uncertainty arises because visual evaluation is typically unreliable. As research has shown, the opinion that is formed on the basis of visual attractiveness or visual cues can easily change when there is a prolonged attention to the object. People wearing glasses, for example, are deemed more intelligent than those who are not when they are looked at for fifteen seconds. But when they are looked at for a longer time, the difference disappears.[83] Contained in visual evaluation is the fact that it is intrinsically unreliable. Ambroise muses about his failed marriage in this way:

INTERVIEWER: Why do you think you got divorced?

AMBROISE: That's because I love beautiful women.

INTERVIEWER: You love beautiful women. I am not sure I understand. Do you mean that you had many affairs?

AMBROISE: No. Not at all. I mean that I married my wife because she was gorgeous, drop-dead gorgeous. I enjoyed so much going out with her, looking at the eyes of others when they saw me with this gorgeous woman. But you know, we have no formula to turn beauty into a good character. She had a shitty character. So no matter how much I loved her figure and face, in the end, I had to deal with a person. I think I am much less prone today to make the mistake I made, to think that beauty and good personality go together. Still, I find it hard to resist beautiful women.

Because male symbolic sexual capital consists in the capacity to exhibit the possession of a sexually attractive woman, a man's initial choice is quickly confronted to other modes of evaluation (about her "character"), which make his choice based on beauty ultimately unreliable.

Moreover, visual evaluation is constructed as binary ("attractive" vs. "unattractive") and thus encourages a quick appraisal and dismissal of others. For example, in the New York Times bestseller, The Love Affairs of Nathaniel P., the hero, shortly after having met the woman he will have a significant relationship with during most of the novel, muses about her:

> If Hannah had been *more obviously hot, he was pretty sure that he would have given her more thought before the other night,* when she had been the only woman present who was at all a viable candidate for his interest.[84]

Hannah, the novel shows, turns out to be a supremely intelligent, generous, tactful, poised woman, but lacking "obvious hotness"—the conventional, media-induced signs of sexiness—Nathaniel could easily dismiss her. This binarity is intrinsic to visuality and has become encoded in the technology. We may say then that in visual capitalism, sexual worth is also a highly visible affair,[85] following a binary logic of "hot"/"not-hot," which in turn implies the frequent experience of being rejected and the acquisition of a social skill of rejecting others, often based on minor details of self-presentation. In other words, scopic capitalism creates mechanisms to quickly dismiss and dispose of others. Dismissal and obsolescence are also at work in the fact that sexiness implicitly privileges consumer objects for the evaluation of others. For example, Berenice, a thirty-seven-year-old divorced French woman, who is a theater stage decorator, muses:

BERENICE: Since my divorce, I have dated a few men but I find it surprisingly difficult. Not so much because of the men but because of me.

INTERVIEWER: What's difficult about it?

BERENICE: Details can throw me off.

INTERVIEWER: Like what?

BERENICE: I was on a third date with a guy, I liked him on the first two dates, and then he shows up with this silly, low-class, embarrassing shirt, not a stylish working-class shirt, but a shirt his grandfather probably bought in the 1940s in a thrift shop. I thought to myself either he lacks basic taste or he really doesn't care about me or he belongs to a different world than mine, like this guy doesn't know the world. And just like that because of his shirt, I could not feel attracted to him. I mean, not exactly like that, but I felt it distracted me, I struggled to recover the feelings of attraction. It's embarrassing to say but the shirt was a big turnoff.

Here sexual attractiveness is induced by consumer items and is easily shaken by the wrong "look" or appearance, as sexual attraction now heavily depends on the alignment of real persons with media-induced icons, images, and commodities. Visual evaluation stitches together personhood and commodity and is the affirmation of a consumer taste and an emotional liking all in one. Consumer objects thus are the points generating dismissal.

In another example, a strikingly attractive forty-eight-year-old French woman, Claudine, recounts a relationship with her previous boyfriend:

CLAUDINE: One day, he came to visit me early on a Sunday morning, he was coming back from a trip, he rang at my door, and I had not yet brushed my teeth, or put clothes on. I was wearing my night gown, I had no make-up, my hair was not especially arranged. He came in and I saw the look on his face. He said to me: "What happened? Are you sick? Are you ok? You look so different from usual."

INTERVIEWER: What did you answer?

CLAUDINE: I hugged him, I thought he would kiss me but he didn't. It made me think whether this guy would love me when I am old and wrinkled.

As both examples suggest, attraction to someone can be easily put into question when the visual set-up, the spectacle that made it possible in the first place, disappears. If consumer objects have become the implicit background of attractiveness, they become also equated with personhood, and create a seamless equivalence between objects and persons, thus suggesting that persons are (d)evaluated as objects.

Finally, the entire economy of visual attractiveness relies on the constant renewal of looks through the equation of attractiveness with fashion and youth (whence the extraordinary flourishing of the anti-aging industry, whether by chemicals or by surgery).[86] Because young women are at the top of the hierarchy of sexual capital, they command the highest position in the sexual field, especially with men in possession of the highest economic capital (Donald Trump is again a paradigmatic example of this market logic).[87] But, contrary to other forms of social assets, youth contains by definition a built-in mechanism of obsolescence: In the fashion industry, a twenty-three-year-old model is deemed old.[88] This means that the field of sexuality is structured by obsolescence (and the anxiety attendant to it), a key component of the capitalist economy, because it fuels the constant renewal and improvement of looks through consumer goods geared to maintain youth and attractiveness (defined as youth).[89] Here is a striking example of the built-in obsolescence entailed by visual evaluation: Terry is a thirty-four-year-old French woman, a high school dropout who drives a taxi, and has no children:

INTERVIEWER: Do you have a boyfriend?

TERRY: You see my hair? What color is it?

INTERVIEWER: It is red.

TERRY: Yes, it is red. Not because I am red. I dye it. You know why I dye it?

INTERVIEWER: No.

TERRY: Because my hair turned gray overnight when my boyfriend left me. He took my money, and left me, like that, overnight. It was a year and half ago and I am not over it. I can't stand it. I cry all the time. I can't stand it.

INTERVIEWER: What can't you stand?

TERRY: I feel like I should have done certain things that I did not do.

INTERVIEWER: Like what? What is it you should have done? Would you mind telling?

TERRY: I think I do not pamper my body enough; I did not pamper my body enough for him. I didn't do my nails, like other women; I wore sneakers; I wore jeans. I work, I like to work, and I think he thought I behaved like a boy, that I was not feminine enough. That I should wear dresses, that I should put [on] makeup, go to the hairdresser, you know what I mean right?

INTERVIEWER: I know what you mean. But I am sure many men find you very pretty all the same.

TERRY: You say this just to be nice. [*Bursts into tears*] I don't think I am pretty. Even though I loved him like mad, and gave him all my money, and now they came to take my furniture, because I got into debts because of him. But I still feel it is my fault.

INTERVIEWER: I am sorry you feel this way. Why do you feel it is still your fault?

TERRY: Because maybe it was easy to fix. Maybe it was easy for me to give him what he wanted. It was easy to be the kind of woman he wanted and I didn't do it.

This woman's self-accusation for not having turned herself into a standard feminine icon of attractiveness—all the while her boyfriend "took her money"—is a testimony to the internalization of a male gaze that evaluated her negatively, using aesthetic benchmarking. Iconic evaluations, as Terry also suggests, remain a permanent feature of the romantic relationship, where (especially female) partners continue to be judged for their sexual appearance. A sixty-seven-year-old Austrian woman, married for thirty-eight years, similarly recounts (in response to my question why she fought with her husband):

JULIA: He criticizes me for not being careful enough with my weight. We often have fights about it but the bottom line is that I have been dieting all my life. George really does not like even slightly overweight women. So I have had to watch my body my entire life. But I like it. In the end, even though I did it for him, and we fought about it, I also enjoyed it. It kept me attractive.

Even married women feel the looming dread and threat of devaluation because sexual benchmarking is an ongoing attribute of heterosexual relationships. Abundant research has showed the following paradox: The more preoccupied with her sexual attractiveness a woman is, the less likely she is to be satisfied with her body and herself in general.[90] Sexual benchmarking is exercised toward others and oneself because of a comparative self-evaluation vis-à-vis standards of beauty. This in turn suggests that in sexual markets value and valuation are difficult to create or maintain, or both, for most women. It is this difficulty to create value that creates uncertainty vis-à-vis one's self-concept.[91] As a commentator put it: "Women's hatred of their bodies is such an everyday phenomenon that we pay no heed to just how deeply it cuts into our sense of self."[92] The sexualized body has become the

site and the source of self-harm through the anticipation of others' evaluations, their reference to ideals of bodily and psychic perfection, and to the
threat of devaluation.[93]

Men evaluate women and their physical appearance because men are
located in a competitive sexual field where they are evaluated by other men.
This is illustrated by Adam, a forty-seven-year-old French head of a research
team of a large pharmaceutical industry. He has been in a relationship with
a woman for three years. But as he tells me during the conversation, despite
the fact he is faithful to his girlfriend, he has been reluctant to introduce her
to his two children from a former marriage and to his friends:

INTERVIEWER: Why haven't you shown her?
ADAM: I am sure you are going to be shocked by my response.
INTERVIEWER: Try me. I am not easily shocked.
ADAM: We met on OK Cupid. I was on this site but I was totally uncon-
    vinced. But I saw her picture and she looked really, really beautiful. The
    mulatto, exotic style, with beautiful face, thin body, artist, educated,
    funny. We met and when I met her, she looked quite different, a bit
    chubby, pretty but not gorgeous. I wanted to pay and leave immediately
    but out of politeness, I did not want to hurt her feelings, I spoke to her
    and to my surprise I actually enjoyed talking to her a lot. She is smart
    and funny and it feels easy to talk to her. I felt good with her. I saw her a
    second time and then a third time, and before I knew it we were in a
    relationship. We actually have great sex too. But I could not bring myself
    to show her to my friends. I just couldn't.
INTERVIEWER: Can you say why?
ADAM: I have always had pretty girlfriends. I think how others look at me,
    would judge me through the person I am with, is important. Coming
    with a girlfriend that was chubby, even though she is pretty, would have
    been difficult for me. It would be as if I acknowledged I had failed in
    some way.

Like Ambroise, Adam displays the ways in which women's sexual attractiveness is used as a form of social and symbolic capital by men who feel evaluated by other men in a competitive field of struggle over attractive women.
Men gaze at women under the gaze of other men, as sexuality has now
become an index of (men's) social value. The role of men's gaze and evaluation is all the more striking in that Adam senses emotional well-being and

has "great sex" with her, thus suggesting that the marketplace of visual evaluation carries a great deal of symbolic power and even overrides other forms of evaluation. The devaluation of women's bodies here occurs because bodies are located in a male competitive arena where men are evaluated by other men through the women they possess sexually.

Devaluation through Parceling

Another mechanism of visual devaluation is found in parcelization. By definition, visual sexualization entails the capacity to detach sexuality from selfhood as a center to organize values, emotions, and goals and to focus on erotic organs. The parcelization of the self into sexual organs makes these acquire an agency of their own, which in turn generates new ways of perceiving sexual actors.

In fascinating cognitive experiments, researchers were able to build on a body of evidence showing that when people attend to an object in a holistic way, they are less able to recognize and memorize it when that object is inverted. Conversely, when objects are approached analytically, that is, as a patch of different elements, they are equally well recognized and memorized regardless of whether they are displayed upright or inverted. Based on this body of work, researchers were able to show that it does not matter how women are displayed—upright or inverted—whereas men are less well processed and recalled when displayed inverted. This suggests in turn that women are approached a priori as a disparate set of body parts while men are approached holistically.[94] This is a powerful empirical confirmation of the effects of sexualization, which tends to focus on sexual organs and thus to parcel out women's bodies. Parcelization is prevalent in the ways in which men gaze at women, and engage in a relationship with them (viewing them as "breasts" or "butts" or "a pair of legs"), but is also becoming a generalized feature of the circulation of images in technological culture at large. Parcelization is a key cognitive mechanism to ignore women's self.

Angie is a twenty-six-year-old British woman, who works as a movie assistant and creative writer living in Berlin:

INTERVIEWER: Do you have a boyfriend?

ANGIE: I just broke up with one. I guess it's going to stay that way for a while because I can't bring myself to go back to Tinder and to look for one.

INTERVIEWER: Why?

ANGIE: As soon as I reconnect, I will start getting dick pics. I just don't have the stomach for it.

INTERVIEWER: You will receive what?

ANGIE: Dick pics. You don't know what it is?

INTERVIEWER: Not sure what you mean.

ANGIE: [*Laughing*] They send you an image of their dicks.

INTERVIEWER: You mean the men you get in touch with send you photos of their penises without their faces, I mean after you've seen their face?

ANGIE: Right. Just the dick. That this is just the way people date today.

INTERVIEWER: That is the way people date today?

ANGIE: Absolutely. Welcome to the Tinder era.

INTERVIEWER: And you do not like it?

ANGIE: No. Not at all.

INTERVIEWER: Can you say why?

ANGIE: Maybe it's uncool to say this, but I just find it gross to pick someone by the size of their dick. It's like we're not anything beyond our sexual organs. I find it demeaning. Even though I am supposed to be the one who is picking them, I feel demeaned by the guy when I choose him by the size or the shape of his penis. I know that as a feminist I am supposed to not care about this, but the truth is that I do. I find it demeaning. Not sure why.

Sexting breaks down the body into sexual organs, isolating organs not only from personhood but from a holistic view of the body itself. Visualization and sexualization of the body thus dissociate the body from the self, make it the object of a quick, snap gaze, with an organ becoming the object of the interaction. The men Angie refers to parcel themselves as a way to signal that they approach the woman as a set of fragmented organs. Angie hesitates in interpreting her own response: "feminism" tells her to be cool (that is, detached), yet such injunction to coolness collides with her sense that the display of sexual organs is "gross." Such self-sexualization, as Rosalind Gill insightfully put it, differs from former and earlier forms of sexual objectification because it is a *response* to feminism, a seemingly *knowing* and *playful* one, from women who feel empowered to play with masculinist codes and serve them back to the men.[95] Finally and maybe most interestingly, we do not know exactly who is a subject and who is an object in this interaction. Is the man and his dick an autonomous subject or are they detached from personhood in a way that makes them the object of appropriation by the woman? Is the dick objectified or objectifying? It is difficult to say as it does both at the same time. The man's self-presentation through his penis is a mirror image of the ways in which he himself posits his potential partners, as a set of sexual organs. The dick pick invites women to a type of interaction in which men have power because they have a greater capacity for detachment. But it invites women to the same detachment.

The visualization of the self and the new scopic regime it entails are processes of reification since they entail the possibility of detaching the self into pieces and to place such "pieces" in a market where high-speed forms of evaluation are at work to sort out an abundance of competing commodified sexual organs. Given that sexualization parcels out the body in sexual organs, it tends to separate the body from other sources of social identity, reflecting and magnifying the duality and separation between body and self. This process is at the heart of the increasingly widespread practice of sexting. Kathy Martinez-Prather and Donna Vandiver studied university college freshmen at a midsize southern university in the United States and have found that "approximately one-third of the participants reported sending a sexting image of himself or herself in high school to someone else using a cell phone."[96] Lee Murray et al. studied young people (ages eighteen through twenty) from different educational institutions in Sydney and found that 47 percent of young people surveyed reported engaging in sexting.[97] Such practices intermix sexuality, visuality, and technology, and parcel out the body into organs.

Parceling enables devaluation because organs are by definition less particular or unique than whole bodies or whole persons. This is precisely why legal scholar Richard Posner can advocate a market for organs (kidneys) but not a market for bodies.[98] Organs, in fact, are more like commodities than persons, because they can be dissociated from the perception of whole emotional or psychological selves behind a body, because they are more abundant and more easily fungible. Organs differ from bodies because as feminist scholar Carole Pateman put it: "There is an integral relationship between the body and the self. The body and the self are not identical, but selves are inseparable from bodies."[99]

Hans Jonas distinguishes between pre-modern and modern technology.[100] Part of what characterizes modern technology, he suggests, is that the relationship of means and ends is no longer linear but circular, so that "new technologies may suggest, create, even impose new ends, never before conceived, simply by offering their feasibility. [...] Technology thus adds to the very objectives of human desires, including objectives for technology itself."[101] We may say then that technology indeed has added new sexual ends, amplifying the commodification, process of parcelization, and circulation of sexual organs.

All of the above suggests that sexualization and recognition are at opposite ends of the moral spectrum. Recognition entails the capacity to acknowledge properly a whole person, her goals and values, and to engage in a relationship of mutuality.[102] Evaluation approaches another in order to evaluate her or his worth through pre-established grids. Evaluation and recognition are two different cognitive postures and the increasing prevalence of the former over the latter explains the prevalence of the sociological event I call "non-choice," since evaluation more often than not entails dismissal.

In his Tanner Lectures, Axel Honneth claims that reification is a complex interplay between recognition and cognition[103] and insightfully suggests that reification entails a forgetting of recognition and asks how cognition can lead antecedent recognition to be forgotten, that is, how what we perceive and how we perceive do not enable us to register properly the presence or humanity of another. Sexual markets offer a powerful example of such forgetting. Honneth evokes the role of attentiveness and especially of low attentiveness as an explanation for how this act of recognition comes to be forgotten. I would further suggest that attention regulated by visuality generates low attentiveness, especially when visual objects take a commodity form, that is, exist in abundance, compete with one another, are on view, and become easily interchangeable. Quoting Honneth, we may speak here of a perceptual reification: "[O]ur social surroundings appear here, very much as in the autistic child's world of perception, as a totality of merely observable objects lacking all psychic impulse or emotion."[104] Visual evaluation in a large market of bodies as images entails devaluation through low attentiveness.

Devaluation through Refinement of Taste

Much of the sociology of taste inspired by Pierre Bourdieu and his many followers is based on the assumption that tastes are not only stable, but form the deepest core of the self, the matrix organizing one's choices, social trajectory, and identity.[105] Tastes are ingrained through one's class position and through the systemic application of dispositions that are acquired throughout one's life (the habitus). In this way, taste is deep, long-lasting, and structures one's identity. It manifests itself chiefly through choice and evaluation, which Bourdieu viewed as the natural outcome of taste.[106] According to this view, a relationship based on the common cultivation of tastes is bound to be strong precisely in that it finds an anchor in the powerful determinants of class habitus. Yet, this conception of taste is inadequate to capture the fact that consumer and sexual culture is as much about choice as it is about non-choice, that is, about disposing of what one had previously chosen. This form of non-choice is contained and implied in what I call the refinement of tastes.

As I elaborated elsewhere, the refinement of tastes undermines the stability of habitus and makes the dynamic of choice fundamentally unstable. Contrary to needs, which are fixed, refinement is inherently unstable because a taste already contains its own surpassing.[107] In that sense, refining one's taste undermines the stability of the habitus. While the latter presupposes a subjectivity shaped by fixed social determinants, refinement entails an instability in the formation of preferences, making one's previous choice unsatisfactory. This same dynamic is at work in relationships, either because sexual actors view their partners as consumer objects in need of refinement or because their own refinement of consumer tastes makes them dispose of someone whose tastes did not change.

Alexander is a fifty-two-year-old Jewish English senior accountant, divorced at age twenty-seven, who never remarried:

ALEXANDER: The only thing I regret very much is not to have married a woman I knew twenty years ago.
INTERVIEWER: What do you regret?
ALEXANDER: She was not religious and I was becoming more religious. At the time I did not realize it is not that important because [I was] totally absorbed in this new lifestyle. I thought it would be very important for me. I thought we would not have the same lifestyle, that we would fight about it. So I decided not to marry her, like that, because I thought it would not work. But it was a mistake. Today I wouldn't care but I did not know that then.

This man operated a subtle translation from the realm of consumption to the realm of emotions, equating lifestyle with emotional intimacy, making the choice of a partner grounded in the epistemology of consumer choice—an element of the cultivation of tastes and subjectivity. At the time, this man was in the process of refining his taste, changing who he was, and thus thought someone inappropriate to this new lifestyle would be an inappropriate emotional choice. His decision illustrates quite aptly Adam Phillips and Leo Bersani's provocative claim that "knowing what one wants is an incitement to violence."[108] Because the epistemology of relationships is organized around consciously cultivated tastes, hobbies, and consumer practices, a relationship becomes evaluated as a lifestyle choice, as a consumer act of preference. Lifestyles, hobbies, and tastes activate then-evaluative schemes that, more often than not, entail devaluation and non-choice of persons all the more easily disposed of as they do not insert themselves in a matrix of tastes ("not my taste"). Discarding persons is thus intrinsic to the continuous exercise of taste—where taste concerns both consumer goods and the choice of a partner.

Shifting the Reference Point of Evaluation

The process of pairing through visual, personality, and consumer evaluation is located in a competitive market of many others and must thus implicitly use comparative cognitions. Comparison has become one of the main cognitions, if not the main cognition, entailed in the search process. Comparison and choice are affected by the reference point of one's judgment, which in turn has a deep impact on the evaluation of another's worth.

To be realized in a market, the value of a commodity must be attributed symbolic worth that itself depends on the ways in which this commodity is situated vis-à-vis other commodities. "Valuing something presupposes measuring and comparing it according to a scale," say sociologists Jens Beckert and Patrik Aspers.[109] Research in cognitive psychology shows that the evaluation of an object—judging how much something is worth—will change significantly if the reference point changes. Christopher K. Hsee and Jiao Zhang, two psychologists at the University of Chicago, study the process of evaluation and its relationship to decision-making. They show that the process of evaluation changes depending on whether one considers different options or whether one is immersed in a single experience. The first they call the joint evaluation mode, whereas the other they call the single evaluation mode. In the joint evaluation mode, people compare the attributes and pay attention to differences between various objects; in the single evaluation mode, on the other hand, people evaluate by referring to what they like or think is beautiful, and are able to commit to an object, as is the case for a purchase in an auction house.[110] In the joint evaluation mode, people think about trade-offs, what they stand to lose or to gain if they make a specific choice, while in the single evaluation mode, people commit to an object in a non-calculative way. To put it succinctly: We evaluate the worth of an object differently in a supermarket and in an auction house, attributing greater value to the object in the auction house and far lesser value to the object in the supermarket, depending on whether the evaluation sets off a cognitive process of comparison. This in turn means that when objects are compared with one another, the attribution of worth becomes more difficult. Or more exactly, these objects lose their worth. A facetious but autobiographical real-life example told by a man using the Internet illustrates this tellingly:

[…] [T]here was:
The JAMAICAN WOMAN who was getting her PhD in literature at Stanford. Dates: 1 (coffee shop). Problem: She was way too smart for my B-lifetime-average ass.
A VIETNAMESE LADY who was in dental school. Dates: 2 (coffee shop, dinner at crepe restaurant). Problem: While attractive, I couldn't get over the fact that she had an affair with a married man. Gag me with a toothbrush.
A CAUCASIAN GAL, student, who had a thing for Asian guys. Dates: 1 (coffee shop). Problem: She was bisexual. Hmmm, come to think of it, that was a problem?
And an AFRICAN AMERICAN woman who was studying psychiatry. She had dazzling eyes and a cute figure. Dates: 2 (coffee shop, video at my place). Problem: Quiet people make me nervous, and especially quiet psychiatry students. Was she analyzing me? What did she see? I didn't want to know.[111]

This vignette illustrates the difficulty in finding a "fit" because with each encounter, his point of reference and evaluation shifts, making it difficult to attribute worth, ultimately diminishing each one's worth. This in turn means that we simply do not really know how to evaluate the worth of an object when we are in a market situation of comparing one object to others of similar value. Moreover, as sociologist Ashley Mears insightfully put it with regard to the modeling industry, in many cultural areas, the price or worth of a model, work of art, or actor is unclear. "The problem of pricing exemplifies a larger quandary faced by cultural producers, and, for that matter, people in any market of intangibles. It is the problem of uncertainty, the inability to state in advance what one wants."[112]

Pre-modern romantic evaluators chose as if they were in an auction house because they operated in conditions of scarcity. Modern sexual and romantic evaluators choose as if they are in the supermarket and lack a clear reference point of their choice, not knowing what they want. The insertion of romantic and sexual practices in the consumer market leads then to a deflation of worth. Because sexual actors meet in a market situation, these actors face what we may call emotional deflation, much like economic mechanisms of deflation, the fact that the overall price or worth of goods falls either because competition brings down prices or because greater efficiency diminishes the costs of production. Sexual freedom, the contraceptive pill, the transformation of women's bodies into sexual images, the Internet technology, can be all said to be mechanisms that have increased sexual abundance and competition, have made men's access to female sexual partners more efficient, have lowered the costs of sexual interactions for men, have generated tremendous economic surplus value for male-controlled visual industries, and have legitimized the bestowal of status to men through serial sexuality. This has the consequence of either diminishing the value of a woman's body or making it worthless in sexual markets, literally an object to which it is difficult to attribute worth. Thus the fact that sexual encounters have now a market form and are shaped by economic scopic markets creates a difficulty either to establish worth or to keep stable one's worth and value, or both.

We may make this point differently, by stressing the role of scarcity in valuation processes. An experiment conducted by Sheena Iyengar and Mark Lepper reveals this process (although this was not the purpose of the experiment).[113] In this experiment, participants must conduct evaluation of different types of chocolate and are divided in two groups: one in which participants are asked to evaluate many types of chocolate; and another group in which there is little variety to choose from and evaluate. At the end of the experiment, participants were offered two types of possible payments: either money ($5) or chocolate (worth $5). The results are striking. Those who were given very few types of chocolate to evaluate were far more likely to choose the chocolate for compensation, rather than the money. This clearly suggests that diminished choice is conducive to a process of valuation; or to put it differently, abundance triggers devaluation because in a situation of abundance, objects and persons become more likely to be interchangeable. In conformity with what Marx would have predicted about the increasing importance of exchange value over use value, when there are many types of chocolates, they become interchangeable and thus reducible to their abstract monetary value. Essential then to sexual abundance is the problem of establishing the value of the sexual object and its subsequent devaluation. Thus, while capitalist producers create a value that is socially realized,[114] the sexual self-value created and produced by women through consumer culture is more often than not only partially completed or even not completed at all, since commodification of bodies multiplies the abundance of sexual choice, thereby devaluing bodies, either because they can be easily replaced or because their value becomes quickly obsolete. Female sexual capital confronts the problem of maintaining its social value in a far greater way than men's sexual capital. Because men's worth is located in more durable assets, their worth does not change for the worse and even increases with time. In other words, the entire sexual and consumer system is based on women's difficulty in keeping stable their symbolic and economic value, while men's value is stable or increases with time.

According to Marx, the falling rate of profits will make the value of work diminish.[115] In the same way, we may say that the worth and value of a female body goes down with age. The female sexualized body produces itself as a commodity, is the object of evaluation, and risks devaluation. As David Harvey put it insightfully: "[M]ass devaluation of commodities, of hitherto productive plant and equipment, of money and of labor" are endemic to capitalism.[116] Devaluation is intrinsic to capitalism because it enables the creation of new value, needed for the replenishing of consumer markets. Given that sexual bodies and tastes circulate widely in the consumer economy, they must be quickly outdated and updated in order to remain economically productive. Sexual and romantic encounters are not only mediated by the consumer market but have taken on characteristics of markets. Sexual bodies are shaped to generate value and therefore demand a constant management, self-branding, and attempts to establish and maintain their worth because they are in a state of permanent competition with other bodies; they engage in evaluation and benchmarking and must constantly face risk and uncertainty about worth. If sexuality and consumer tastes generate value—both economic and symbolic—this value constantly threatens to dissolve under evaluation, comparison, benchmarking, and devaluation.

According to Adam Arvidsson, the wide availability of knowledge and information changes what matters in economic exchange. The production of goods has become "commons," a shared resource;[117] thus the problem for capitalists is not to produce goods anymore, but to find a singularity in them ("innovation" and "branding" are forms of singularization of commodities). In the same way, because sexuality has become widely available, the problem is now to find (or invent) a singularity, which in turn translates in what we call "falling in love" or "loving." It's all about finding the singularity one would want to get attached to. The sexualization of relations creates an abundance of sexual choice and shifting reference points, and thus diminishes the capacity of the self to attribute worth, to latch on a single subject, to singularize him or her, and to engage with another in a trajectory that derives from the capacity to be cognitively and emotionally focused— to perceive the other in a situation of scarcity. And the analogy with the state of contemporary capitalism goes even deeper. Economic markets contain an inherent uncertainty about the *real* price of a commodity. Theorists of neo-liberal persuasion have addressed the problem of uncertainty of price by arguing that only unhindered markets can let supply and demand dictate the real prices of goods.[118] But, as the example of sexual market suggests, the market form *increases* uncertainty about the nature and the stability of one's worth. The abundance of sexual choice activates evaluation processes that short-circuit recognition, namely the capacity to singularize others[119] as whole selves. The difficulty in engaging in recognition provokes ontological uncertainty, which is an uncertainty about the worth, the value, and ultimately the nature of the self engaged in an interaction.

The Confused Status of the Subject

Positive views of sexualization refuse the diagnostic of objectification and would view all the processes described above—devaluation and uncertainty—as the unhappy but necessary price to pay for greater freedom. Commenting on the negative view of sexualization issued by the American Psychological Association's report,[120] one author avers that "[t]here is no consideration whatsoever if or how sex, sexualization, or even objectification can be self-controlled, intrinsically positive, empowering, or lust enhancing."[121]

This debate among feminist scholars in itself is a cogent illustration of the deeply confusing status of the sexualized subject. Is the (female) sexual agent an object or a subject? This is, in fact, one of the main questions dividing critics and advocates of sexual freedom. I would argue that the reason why it has proven extremely difficult to respond to this question in a clear way has to do with the fact that objectification itself has changed. It has taken the form of subjectification, or of what I dubbed early in this chapter hyper-subjectivity.[122] This hyper-subjectivity is paradoxically based on a fundamental uncertainty about the status of the subject.

Marie, twenty-six, is a French art student, studying in an art academy in Italy for a few months:

INTERVIEWER: Do you have a boyfriend?

MARIE: Good question! I have, I had a boyfriend in Paris. But when I came here [to Italy], I felt, "far from the eyes, far from the heart." I connected to Tinder, which I always have on my phone, and in...three weeks I think, found a boyfriend. He is from Canada. He is also on some exchange program. So I broke up with my French boyfriend, although I probably could have carried on, but he was going to visit me here, and it was getting complicated.

INTERVIEWER: You always have Tinder?

MARIE: Oh, yes. I don't like to be alone. Wherever I am, I can meet people. I find it difficult to be alone. No. Let me put it differently. It is much nicer to be with someone.

INTERVIEWER: Was your French boyfriend surprised that you broke up?

MARIE: No. I don't think so. I think he would have done the same. There was a kind of understanding where it was obvious that each one of us would do it with the right opportunity. Just the kind of things you know without ever spelling it out. Anyway when we were together it's not like we had decided to live together or that we felt this was a great love. Actually I was relieved to break up with him. When I was with him I felt like a piece of meat or something like that.

INTERVIEWER: What do you mean "a piece of meat"?

MARIE: He was not very affectionate. It was obvious he just wanted the sex. So even though I would have preferred it otherwise, I learned too to be in it just for the sex. I wasn't sure myself what I wanted. I guess

I wanted sex also. I wanted the sex but I felt a piece of meat. Because that was the way to have a relationship and regular sex. But I felt often like a piece of meat. No feelings. Just sex.

INTERVIEWER: And with your new boyfriend, it is different.

MARIE: Yeah I feel it is different. We talk [*laughs*]. I mean he has issues with his former girlfriend. He still feels very connected to her and that bugs me and puts a distance sometimes. They broke up because they were fighting but he still feels very connected to her. But I don't feel like a piece of meat with him. We actually talk and we do things together, and we are interested in each other. But it feels like when I will leave this place, then it will be over. Both of us know that. We are together because we are both lonely in a place we do not know. Tinder was there to connect us! [*Laughter and music of a jingle.*]

INTERVIEWER: You know that because you said so to each other?

MARIE: No, no. It's like with my previous boyfriend. You don't need to say things to know that this is what will happen. We both know that this is something for here; not to be in need of sex [*en manqué*].

This young woman has a clear idea of what an emotional relationship is like, but accepted to be "a piece of meat" because of her own privileging of sexuality as the prime terrain of engagement with men. She enters relationality on bodily terms, according to an epistemology in which the body is equivalent to its sexual function and has no intrinsic moral or emotional meaning. In doing so, she experiences herself as a free subject. But this freedom is peculiar as sexualization renders emotional demands illegitimate, and compels this woman to redefine her own wishes and desires, to align them along the man's sexualization of their relationship, and thus to treat herself as an object, a sexual body devoid of intentionality—a piece of meat. As a subject this woman has thus a confused status: She denies to herself her own emotional goals, and accepts being treated as "a piece of meat"; she feels objectified, but in turn objectifies her boyfriend, uses him for her own sexual needs, which in turn empowers her. It is thus the same emotional and moral vector that enables devaluation and empowerment through the mutual instrumentalization of the other for one's sexual needs.[123] Everything happens as if when another is devalued or treated instrumentally, one regains a sense of power. Sexual objectification is thus the not-so-hidden logic of sexual culture, but it provides men and women with a sense of power derived from the fact that it instrumentalizes others and seems to play into a zero-sum game. If the capacity to objectify others, men and women, is widely commercialized by a vast industry of sex and is somewhat endorsed by many strands of feminism, it is because it is recoded as subjectification found in pleasure, empowerment, and detachment.[124] As Stephane, a fifty-two-year-old French strategic consultant for an investment firm put it [about his use of Tinder]:

> [T]here is something exhilarating about swiping right and left. It gives a feeling of power. I think the designers of Tinder work on this feeling. You have a feeling of omnipotence on your romantic destiny. It is a feeling we don't have in daily life, obviously.

Subjectivity thus seems to be intensified through the capacity to objectify others in an emotionally detached stance, to choose and unchoose as a consumer. Through choice and non-choice the sexual sphere has become regulated by instrumental rationality writ large.[125] That self-objectification based on sexualization that dissociates the self from the body and creates an uncertainty not only about one's value but also about one's own desire can be illustrated with the help of Steve McQueen's 2011 movie *Shame*, which is a dark and stylized discussion of the splitting of the self into two paths, sexual and emotional.

The hero, Brandon, is a sex addict. He is a heavy consumer of pornography, frequently hires sex workers, and engages in quick hookups. He likes a co-worker, and the movie makes it clear that this is an opportunity for him to have a deeper and more meaningful relationship. Yet, when they get together to have sex, he is unable to get an erection. After she leaves the room, he has frantic sex with a sex worker, thus suggesting to the viewer the poignant way in which sexuality and emotionality follow independent routes that can no longer connect. Brandon belongs to a new sexual regime, in which technology, visuality (a stream of pornographic images accessed through the Internet), and rapid turnover of anonymous partners render the body the sole source of agency, actively disconnected from what we traditionally recognized as desire, self, and emotion. In this story, it is difficult to say whether Brandon remains a "subject" since his body seems to have acquired an autonomy that escapes his own emotional volition. Moreover, given that he is unable to meet other subjects—he can interact with women only as sexual objects and not as subjects—it is also unclear how much he is himself a subject. We may say that Brandon, like a typical

modern subject, experiences his intense scopic regime of sexual consumption as an addictive form of self-affirmation, of hyper-subjectivity. This
addictive self-affirmation is also a repeated experience of non-choice, which
has a wide variety of institutional supports: technological, visual, and
human in the form of cheap sex work. Emotions, on the other hand, have
little or no outside institutional anchor that would organize them into what
Ann Swidler called a plan of action.[126] A technology-based consumer sexuality is thus now a highly institutionalized realm of action, especially for
men who are the heavy consumers of pornography and sex work, creating
splintered forms of selfhood. The sexual self, the technological self, and the
consumer self are aligned in a single powerful matrix, relatively dissociated
from the emotional self. The selfhood at the center of these processes is at
once objectified and objectifying.

Women's sexual experience is no less confused and splintered. Given that
sexuality has become the arena to display "girl power," women have experienced sexuality as a source of autonomy and enjoy feeling their sexual
power over men; yet, sexual encounters remain replete with threats to the
self-worth of women. It is virtually impossible to disentangle objectification
from recognition since so much of a woman's worth is defined by her sexual
appeal and sexual competence. Hyper-subjectivity is thus concomitant with
processes of objectification (of oneself and others) and both entail what I
would call a fundamental ontological uncertainty about the status of the
subject: Who and what is a sexual subject? Does she or he desire subjects or
objects? It is difficult to say.

Ontological uncertainty is overdetermined by a number of factors: the
fragmentation of desire in multiple sites, in sexuality, emotions, and consumer lifestyle; making and approaching personhood as a visual performance; evaluating through benchmarked standards of beauty; meeting
others through a visualized sexual marketplace driven by competition; and
the parceling of bodies (which isolates sexual interaction both from whole
bodies and from selfhood)—all of these constitute difficulties for women to
form a stable sense of self-worth.

Ontological uncertainty about one's value and about the nature of desire
itself creates a deep analogy between our relationship to nature and our
relationship to other (sexualized) human beings, what Heidegger calls "the
standing-reserve" in "The Question Concerning Technology."[127] The idea of
a standing reserve designates a fundamental attitude to the world, by which
we place others and nature on call to make available to our needs. We can

bring a feminist twist to Heidegger's idea of the standing reserve: the contraceptive pill, the institutionalization of sexuality in consumer culture, and the high velocity of Internet technology all place human beings, and especially women, in a state of permanent availability to other people's sexual needs, men's in particular. Such availability, Heidegger claimed, threatens essentially both the object and the subject. The object loses its capacity to be an object, that resists our aims. An objectless world—one in which the object does not resist our desires anymore—threatens the very structure of our subjectivity. We may wonder if the generalized sexualization of relationships does not make human beings, women in particular, standing-reserves.[128] It is this structure of the object–subject relationship that changes altogether the nature of subjectivity and makes ontological uncertainty its core, especially for women. Ontological uncertainty stems from the difficulty in holding onto a sense of worth and identity that "resists" one's availability to the gaze and to the sexual appropriation of others, and to instrumentalization through sex.

*

Valuation—as the process of creating subjective and economic value in economic and sexual markets produced for the scopic evaluation of others—paradoxically explains the process of devaluation of women through mechanisms of evaluation. We may clarify this by way of contrast by invoking an alternative mode of sexual evaluation. Vita Sackville-West, the aristocrat who passionately fell in love with Virginia Woolf, described the famous writer upon meeting her as follows:

> She is utterly unaffected: there are no outward adornments—she dresses quite atrociously. At first you think she is plain, then a sort of spiritual beauty imposes itself on you, and you find a fascination in watching her.[129]

Vita's visual evaluation does not take place in a market of many possible others; it is non-binary, it sees what is "atrocious" and what is compelling in a single gaze. Consumer objects play no role in determining how attractive Virginia is, indeed she dresses atrociously. The evaluation is not a snap judgment and does not proceed from benchmarking; it evolves with time and in fact it morphs into a process of recognition (what Vita calls Virginia's "spiritual beauty"). It does not gaze at a body situated in a market of competing attractive bodies, but rather identifies a singularity. It creates value effortlessly.

Contemporary visual markets contain intensified mechanisms of evaluation and devaluation, perhaps most visible in the margins of the heterosexual market. Two examples will suffice: The first is by the famous French
writer Virginie Despentes, who became lesbian and views heterosexuality
as follows:

> My vision of love has not changed, but my vision of the world, yes, has
> changed. It is very pleasant to be lesbian. I am less preoccupied with femi-
> ninity; with men's approval, by all those things we impose on ourselves in
> order to please them. And I also feel less preoccupied with my age: it is
> much harder to become older when you are heterosexual. Seduction
> between girls exists but it is much cooler; you are not deposed and fallen
> after 40.[130]

Despentes's explanation for her shift from heterosexuality to homosexuality
is clearly about feeling less objectified, of depending less on men's gaze and
approval, and of thus being free of the powerful grip of the consumer market. Or, listen to an Islamic blogger who rejects Western sexuality for very
similar reasons:

> When I wear Western clothes, men stare at me, objectify me, or I am
> always measuring myself up against the standards of models in magazines,
> which are hard to live up to—and even harder as you get older, not to
> mention how tiring it can be to be on display all the time. When I wear my
> headscarf or chador, people relate to me as an individual, not an object;
> I feel respected.—Veiled.[131]

I am not suggesting that either lesbian or an Islamic sexuality is the only
solution to heteronormative oppression; rather I use these testimonies of
women who have left heteronormativity to highlight the link between male
domination and consumer objectification both feeding each other in creating new forms of classification, social worth, and symbolic domination.

Sexual objectification has been hotly debated by feminists as an expression and practice of power. But the problem with objectification is located
somewhere else. Because sexualization is lived as empowerment *and* objectification, it creates a deep ontological uncertainty about one's self and its
value. It empowers because it puts into motion mechanisms of valuation.
And it creates ontological uncertainty because subjectification and

objectification become difficult to disentangle. Selfhood becomes splintered and fragmented between the body, its organs, the consumer objects used to produce it, and the consumer activities and contexts that create sexual interactions. Given that visual evaluation is unstable, that consumer tastes change, that capitalist commodities and the attractive body are based on a structural obsolescence, that the self is incessantly evaluated, and that the value of self and other is uncertain, it is not surprising that heterosexual markets are experienced by many women as harrowing. The 2017 #MeToo movement erupted on the world scene with astonishing force because women are not only the object of violence but also the more elusive object of an invisible and widespread form of devaluation. Although the #Metoo movement was confused in its one-size-fits-all denunciation of the trivial, the offensive, and the criminal, it powerfully resonated with the myriad ways in which women are habitually and routinely devalued in the sexual realm. These forms of patriarchal symbolic violence are highly resilient because they are grounded in the far-reaching economic and cultural structures of what I have dubbed throughout scopic capitalism.

5

A Freedom with Many Limits

I am afraid of offending any one whom I love, and especially any one to whom I owe any duty.

—Anthony Trollope[1]

They loved each other, but neither
Would admit to the other they could:
As enemies, they saw each other,
And almost died of their love.
In the end they parted and only
Saw each other sometimes in dreams:
It was long ago they had died,
But they scarcely knew it, it seems.

—Heinrich Heine[2]

The famous musician Robert Schumann had long known the Friedrich Wieck household. He fell in love with Clara Wieck and asked Clara's father for permission to marry her. When her father refused, Robert and Clara petitioned the court to overrule that refusal. After a difficult one-year battle in court, a judge ruled in favor of the couple on August 1, 1840. They were married on September 12, 1840.[3] The father's refusal was not unusual for the times and suggests that the freedom to act upon one's sentiment was neither natural nor self-evident. G. W. F. Hegel was a staunch proponent of emotional freedom that for him was to be secured in the right to marry someone according to one's heart (probably a derivative from the freedom to act upon one's conscience). An ethically valid marriage was to be based on the will and freedom of two people who mutually surrender their personality to each other.[4] Yet, despite Hegel's exhortations to freedom, fathers, families, courts, and communities continued to overrule one's personal choice of a mate. Long after Hegel's death, the right to marry according to one's sentiments remained bitterly contested. Such freedom to marry was to civil society and private life what freedom of speech was to the political sphere.

Axel Honneth has pursued the Hegelian understanding of freedom as a total phenomenon equally relevant to the private and public spheres; for him, an institution or practice is legitimate in terms of how they each actualize freedom in better or worse fashion,[5] marriage, the family, and love being no less privileged terrains for the realization of freedom than the political realm. Two types of freedom—which Honneth dubs negative and reflexive freedom[6]—enable individuals to focus on private identities and aims and to enact their preferences for which they are not accountable, as long as they do not harm others. Social freedom, on the other hand, throws individuals squarely back into the social arena, in the sphere of communicative action.[7] In social freedom, we encounter each other in mutual recognition, intersubjectively rather than as monads. Social freedom thus surmounts the dilemma of liberal thought that had the problem of reconciling individual autonomy with mutuality. Love is such a realm for the exercise of social freedom, a view that resonates with the normative claims of many cultural quarters of our culture. As an Internet site with the name "Loving in Freedom" puts it: "Ideally our love should be a completely free choice from both sides, a voluntary commitment, renewable as often as we please."[8]

Such conception of freedom rests on one of the main moral principles of liberalism in the political and economic sphere, namely contractualism. Through contracts, agents respect others' freedom and enter relationships by posing and affirming their own ends. Contracts have not been the only form assumed by social freedom but it has been the dominant one. As Carole Pateman put it in her classic *The Sexual Contract*: "Contract theory was the emancipatory doctrine par excellence, promising that universal freedom was the principle of the modern era."[9]

However, when taken to the realm of empirical scrutiny, we may wonder if negative and reflexive freedom have not, in fact, become powerful cultural forces interfering with social freedom, that is, with the possibility of forming intersubjective bonds through contracts. Reflexive freedom privileges the subject's scrutiny of her or his own will, making such preferences the anchor of relationality and legitimizing relationships according to utilitarian principles of needs satisfaction. Negative freedom, on the other hand, respects others' freedom but does not specify procedures to engage in social relationships, nor mutual obligations to one another. As I argue throughout, negative and reflexive freedom does not really enable one to form contracts that are at once emotional and sexual.

As a social philosophy and as an economic practice, contractualism presupposes a free will to enter (or not) into an interaction based on one's goal and

preferences. This doctrine has pervaded civil society as well as private relationships. As Carole Pateman puts it again (precisely in reference to Hegel):
"[S]ocial life and relationships not only originate from a social contract but,
properly, are seen as an endless series of discrete contracts."[10] In this vein, intimate relationships came to be viewed as a contract passed between two wills, a
view that became supported by legislation that increasingly made individuals'
free consent the legitimating core of interpersonal action and transactions.[11]

Contractualism has become the dominant social philosophy regulating
marriage and intimacy. Until the 1960s most countries in the world recognized only the "at-fault divorce," where divorce could be agreed to by the
courts only if one of the partners could prove that the partner had committed acts "incompatible with marriage." In the 1970s, many countries started
adopting the no-fault divorce: the simple act of declaring that one was not
willing to continue the marriage was enough to dissolve it.[12] This change
reflected the legal and moral importance of "consent," of the active will of
each partner in the marital union. In parallel to these changes, legislation
made "consent" a new and necessary moral and legal requirement of
sexual interactions. Contract—as a relationship based on the free will of two
parties—became the master metaphor for thinking about intimate relationships.
Love, marriage, and sex were legitimate as long as they were consented to
by two parties and were entered into as if in a contract.

Anthony Giddens has famously theorized this state of affairs in defining
modern intimacy as a contract. The pure relationship as he puts it "is entered
into for its own sake, for what can be derived by each person from a sustained association with another; and it is continued only insofar as it is
thought by both parties to deliver enough satisfactions for each individual
to stay."[13] For Giddens, contractualism augurs greater democratization of
the social bond at large, even if it comes at the price of ontological insecurity, which Giddens recognizes as a threat looming over the "pure relationship" governed by two free wills. But as showed in previous chapters, Giddens
dismissed too easily and offhandedly the effects of ontological insecurity generated by contractualism and did not ask the more fundamental question of
whether a juridical language of rights can be transferred to the intimate sphere
without deeply transforming its meaning. Commitments in pure relationships,
as Neil Gross and Solon Simmons put it, are "contingent." The sexual and
emotional contract will continue to be upheld as long as the other satisfies
one's needs, knowing full well that these needs can change at any time. "[I]f
the values, interests, and identities of the partners begin to diverge in

non-complementary ways, the relationship loses its reason for being and becomes subject to dissolution."[14] The fundamental question at the heart of a liberal and modern model of intimacy is then this one: can the contract—as a social form institutionalized and perfected in the legal and economic realms—be indeed transferred to interpersonal relationships without threatening the nature of intimacy and intersubjectivity? As Pateman has cogently argued, the social and the sexual contract profoundly differ.[15] While the first granted to men accession to freedom, the second entailed the continued subjection of women. Giddens ignored entirely the different positions of men and women in the very formation of the sexual contract and simply assumed they were equal signatories. Moreover, his theory was written before the prevalence of technologies of instant and virtual communication, which are dissolving the very notion of contract because they undermine or bypass the traditional cultural signposts of the stable will presupposed by contracts. Finally, the theory was also written before it became clear that the advent of neoliberal policies foregrounded a very specific type of entrepreneurial will,[16] which must provide and secure alone the grounds of its own worth, in the workplace and in interactions, a process that turns out to undermine the possibility of forming and maintaining contracts (see infra). The self trying to enter a sexual-emotional contract is busy assessing the other's intentions and calculating risks.

Consent to What?

The contract is a metaphor to describe the freedom actors have to enter or exit a relationship. But the metaphor runs so deep that it has extended to the emotional realm: partners explicitly stipulate the terms of their contract, occasionally even signing an actual piece of paper. For example, in the widely popular *New York Times* advice column "Modern Love," this is how the model of a new relationship is defined:

> A few months ago my boyfriend and I poured ourselves two beers and opened our laptops. It was time to review the terms of our relationship contract.
>   Did we want to make changes? As Mark and I went through each category, we agreed to two minor swaps: my Tuesday dog walk for his Saturday one, and having me clean the kitchen counters and him take over the bathtub.

The latest version of "Mark and Mandy's Relationship Contract," a four-page, single-spaced document that we sign and date, will last for exactly 12 months, after which we have the option to revise and renew it, as we've done twice before. The contract spells out everything from sex to chores to finances to our expectations for the future. And I love it.

Writing a relationship contract may sound calculating or unromantic, but *every relationship is contractual; we're just making the terms more explicit*. It reminds us that love isn't something that happens to us—it's something we're making together. After all, this approach brought us together in the first place.[17]

This testimony presents contractualism as an ideal way of organizing life—as a practical solution to define roles, duties, and privileges. Contracts are egalitarian, premised on the freedom of each contractant to enter and to formulate conditions to exit. They are also utilitarian insofar as they transform relationships into a set of utilities, exited when they stop satisfying the subject.

However, heterosexual contracts contain, known or unbeknown to their "signatories," different forms of consent. The notion of contract hides the fact that the two wills trying to enter a contract may profoundly differ. As Pateman suggests, in the sexual contract the woman remains subjugated to the male.[18] This subjugation occurs precisely through the different ways in which men and women form their attachment and desire in the process of entering a sexual-emotional contract. One box-office hit and one bestseller both express this asymmetry cogently. In the 2011 romantic comedy *Friends with Benefits*, the male hero Dylan Harper (Justin Timberlake) and a female heroine Jamie Rellis (Mila Kunis) meet after having each experienced acrimonious breakups. They start a friendship that morphs into a contract of casual sex; its terms stipulate that they are to have sex without feelings or attachment. The complication of the plot revolves around the fact that Jamie starts developing feelings for Dylan while he resists her attempts to draw him to her emotional terrain. Whereas initially both feel equally comfortable in a no-strings-attached sexual relationship, the woman's emotions break the sex-only contract. Echoing a widespread stereotype held up by social reality, the male character fears commitment, while the female character is unable or unwilling to draw a distinction between her sexuality and her emotions. This romantic comedy presents the contract as a key motif of contemporary sexual and romantic relationships and resonates with a worldwide bestseller, *Fifty Shades of Grey*, published the same year *Friends with Benefits* came out. The first volume of the trilogy revolves around the sexual contract that Christian

Grey—the powerful, handsome man—offers to Anastasia Steele, the young, virgin college girl. This sexual contract formulates the terms of a sadomasochistic relationship. Ultimately Anastasia rejects the contract and the reader is amply informed that she is in love with him while Christian's feelings remain unknown. Only his sexual will is known. In both cases of *Friends with Benefits* and *Fifty Shades of Grey*, the contract posits a clear distinction between casual sex and feelings and is ultimately not respected by the woman who wants a sexual-emotional rather than purely sexual relationship.

The impossibility of properly contractualizing emotions explains why the sexual-emotional contract is inherently fraught with aporias and uncertainties. In the pure relationship, a bond can be exited at will, and this in contradistinction with economic/legal contracts, which are binding because breach of contract usually incurs penalties. While economic/legal contracts are based on the implicit premise and promise that they will be fulfilled, this is not the case of sexual contracts. The freedom to enter and exit relationships at will creates conditions of uncertainty, which in turn explain how and why people withdraw quickly from relationships. Ultimately, the metaphor of the contract is inadequate to grasp the form that relationships take in a free, open-ended sexual market, devoid of regulations, limitations, or penalties. To use Clifford Geertz's famous expression, the metaphor of contract that has become dominant to form and maps intimate bonds is a very poor model of and for relationships. It does not describe how relationships are formed and it does not provide a good prescriptive model for how such relationships should be shaped.[19]

Muddled Wills

The sexualization of relations is by definition a relationship between bodies. It should be no surprise then that the epistemology of sexual encounters somewhat entertains an affinity with another ethics that also regulates the body, namely medical ethics, which, like sexual ethics, has put consent at the center of the interaction between two parties, the patient and the doctor. Both sexual and medical ethics have increasingly viewed the body as an entity that cannot be appropriated, infringed upon, invaded, used by someone else, and which thereby requires the explicit knowledge and consent of the body's owner. Consent is the philosophical and legal premise of medical and sexual contracts. It is not the contract proper, but its precondition.

Consent is conditional on the premise that the subject can and must understand the meaning and implications of her decision to let another appropriate her body, to make that body feel either pleasure or pain. But sexual and medical ethics differ in an important way: while the doctor and the patient presumably want the same thing—the patient's health—in the realm of sexuality, two bodies have two distinct wills that may or may not converge. I may agree to be kissed, but not to have intercourse. Or I may agree to have intercourse if I presume it is the beginning of a relationship, but not if it is a one-night stand. It is precisely the fact that the wills can diverge at any point of a sexual interaction that makes the idea of consent in sexual relationships different from patient consent and far thinner than in most areas where consent is required. In an article on gray rape, well-known author Laura Sessions Stepp provides a telling example:

> Alicia had asked another student, Kevin, to be her "platonic date" at a college sorority formal. The two of them went out for dinner first with friends and then to the dance. She remembers that they got drunk but not what she would call sloppy wasted. After the dance, they went to Kevin's room and, eventually, started making out. She told him flat out that she didn't want it to proceed to sex, and he said okay. But in a few minutes, he had pushed her down on the couch and positioned himself on top of her. "No. Stop," she said softly—too softly, she later told herself. When he ignored her and entered her anyway, she tensed up and tried to go numb until it was over. He fell asleep afterward, and she left for her dorm, "having this dirty feeling of not knowing what to do or who to *tell or whether it was my fault.*" While it felt like rape to her—she had not wanted to have sex with Kevin—*she was not sure if that's what anyone else would call it.*[20]

I have emphasized "if that's what anyone else would call it" because it suggests clearly that this woman, who was de facto raped, has difficulties evaluating in normative terms the man's violence because she isn't sure if she articulated her lack of consent clearly enough. This difficulty derives from the fact that sexualization presupposes axiomatically a sexual will and renders more confused the possibility of formulating to oneself (and to another) a non-sexual will. While law enforcement and general awareness against rape have increased, a culture of sexualization defines people in terms of their readiness to have sex, making sexiness and sexual performance into criteria of worth, rendering a non-sexual will less legitimate and less intelligible to oneself and to others. That this woman would have difficulties evaluating the violation of her own consent suggests that her will is confused and muddled by the competing norm of sexualization and by the naturalness of male sexual power in the form of his sexual desire. Consent presupposes a will that is not susceptible to pressure. Yet the pervasive pressure exerted by a culture that defines worth in sexual terms and male sexual power renders illegitimate or unattractive a non-sexual will (this is true for women and for men). If sex is the telos of encounters, if sex has no (or little) emotional meaning, if it is detached from broader conceptions of personhood, if it has no built-in structure of reciprocity, consent becomes "casual," presumed rather requested, viewed as an act that does not have a deep connection to the core self. The very cultural definition of casual sex—cool, easy, emotionally detached, with no clear frame of definition, stressing sexual prowess and performance—makes consent "casual," that is, presumed rather than secured. It also makes women's will muddled to themselves, because in order to follow norms of sexualization, women are supposed to always be available for sex. Sexual freedom was fought for, and has in turn become a pressuring norm.

Moreover, because sexual consent is anchored in the body, it bypasses the emotional content of relationships. The question of what exactly we consent to in an emotional relationship is far less clear than in a sexual one. It is clear what a masochist in a sexual relationship consents to, but it is far less clear what exactly a dissatisfied or abused woman agrees to, if she agrees at all. Because men and women have a different position in the sexual field, they enter sexual and emotional contracts differently. Here is a cogent example. Caroline is a twenty-eight-year-old Dutch student studying architecture who lives in Paris:

INTERVIEWER: Do you have a boyfriend?
CAROLINE: I had, what should I call it, a semi-boyfriend, till two months ago.
INTERVIEWER: [laughs] Why do you call him a semi-boyfriend? He was living far away?
CAROLINE: It's like you're together and you're not together at the same time.
INTERVIEWER: What do you mean?
CAROLINE: I liked him, I liked him a lot actually. But nothing happened between us for a long time. We'd hang out together. But nothing happened. And one night it happened; I went up to his place after a party, we were both drunk, and we did it, I had wanted it for a long time, but I think for him, he did it mechanically, like I was there, late at night, so

hey, of course, he was going to sleep with me. I guess a man can't pass up an opportunity to sleep with a woman. Whereas for me, I had wanted it for a long time. We slept together a few times and at some point, I think maybe one or two months in our relationship, he told me: "Look, I am not sure about this. I mean. I am not sure I want something beyond sex." He also said, "So I don't want to use you or anything." I told him that it was all right, that it suited me, I made jokes that it was me who was using him for the sex. I wanted to look cool. Like not the kind of girl who would be *expecting something*. I really liked him, it was important for me to look like we were symmetrical, but I think I was hoping...I don't know what, that with time he would change, that the sex would be so good that he would not want to leave. It kept going on like this; we fucked; we saw each other for three months maybe, and at some point, he organized a warming-up party for his new apartment and he did not invite me. I found out afterward through some FB post that he was having a warming-up party. People took pictures and posted them. I was so hurt. Devastated actually. When I told him about it, he was surprised; he said it was just a small party for his close friends. That this is not what our relationship was about, that he had always been very clear about it, that there was nothing in his behavior that had been misleading, that I had agreed to be in it just for the sex, that I was guilt-tripping him. I was very confused at first, I thought maybe he was right, maybe I should not have expected it, that I had agreed to sex only, but after a while I stopped seeing him. It took me some time to become angry. Because I felt I had agreed to his fucked-up contract but still I felt used, even though he was always clear. So in hindsight, it was all in my head alone. Our relationship was only about fucking.

INTERVIEWER: Why do you think you felt used?

CAROLINE: Because something in me kept hoping he would fall in love with me. I mean you see someone regularly, you have sex with them, you cook food together, you wake up in the morning together, you make jokes, wouldn't you feel some kind of closeness after a while to that person?

This story reveals some profound features about the ways in which consent and contract regulate intimate relationships. Here, both the man and the woman seemingly consent to a sex-only relationship and view it as an inferior form of relationship; yet, both consent to the relationship in different ways. The woman agrees to a sexual relationship, but only because she hopes sex is a preamble to love. Being "cool" and "detached" is a strategic expression of her attempt to reconcile her emotional goal and the man's restrictions. For the man, stipulating the limitedness of his intentions—sex only—is enough to legitimize his lack of emotional involvement.

Thus, as soon as we leave a narrow patch of sheer physical contact, the category of consent hides the fact that the most crucial aspect of relationships cannot be contractualized. This example illustrates that consent is a thin category with regard to emotions, as actors cannot properly contractualize their own emotions. The ethics of consent stresses and even demands an attention to one's will but it ignores the ways in which under certain conditions the will can be (or can become) volatile, confused, subject to pressure, internally conflicted.

The difficulty to contractualize emotionally a relationship gives rise to new forms of relationships that express the refusal or difficulty to properly contractualize emotions, similar to the one described by Caroline. In the United States, these relationships have become known under the popular notion of "situationship."[21] An Internet advice column on "9 Signs You're in a Situationship" defines such relationships:

> You don't even know what to call them when confronted with situations of introduction or mere mention. You may not even be sure if you can call them a friend. As a result you frequently find yourself fumbling to find words to describe their status or gazing off into space as you try to find the words to delineate your relationship. "I mean we're not really...I mean not really friends, but it's not like we're just f&#K buddies either....I mean we definitely care for each other and there's a mutual respect....We're kinda just taking it slow you know." Eventually one of you will grow weary of the ambiguity and ask, "so where is this going?" To which you would both pretend to be on the same page, whatever page that may be.[22]

Situationships are relationships in which participants implicitly or explicitly agree that they are to be non-relationships. These situationships have no or little projected future, no publicness, no commitment, and are lived for the present and usually (not always) satisfy the sexual purposes of one or two parties. Unbeknown to her but known to her partner, a situationship was the relationship Caroline was engaged in. Situationships are extensions of sexual "casualness" to which they give an elongated form. They are non-relationships because at least one of the two sides either lacks an emotional goal or refuses to imagine the future, or both. Such relationships are maintained "until further notice." Situationships are "going nowhere" and have little or no narrativity. Their contractual character consists precisely in agreeing that this is not a relationship. "Situationship" is in my terminology a non-relationship, a negative bond, one in which one party inscribes its end in it. In other words, situationships are examples of emotional contracts that are based on conflicted or muddled wills or even on wills that the relationship would not exist. They are consensual ways of having non-relationships or at least relationships located in the uncertain twilight zone of positive and negative relationships.

Volatility as an Emotional Condition

Emotional and sexual markets are open to any member of any social class, ethnicity, religion, or race. They mingle the socially powerful and the weak, the beautiful and the unattractive, the educated and the uneducated, the rich and the poor. Sexual markets are competitive and open to everyone and thus entail a profound uncertainty about the value of the self, who knows it competes with others who are ranked "higher" on scales of attractiveness or social status. In Rachel O'Neill's *Seduction*, the men she interviewed clearly show an awareness of the possible misfit between their worth and the worth of certain type of women they find very attractive, whence their conscious distinction between two strategies: sleeping with women one can get, and longing for women out of one's reach, a strategy very usefully called by O'Neill *aspirational*, which consists in aiming for less attainable but more desired objects.[23] This distinction is not lost on sexual and emotional actors who know that others have *aspirations* to which they themselves may or may not correspond. Aspirations then become, as in the economic realm, an imaginary core dislocating the sense of one's place in a relationship, making actors aspire for worthy partners, and more crucially making sexual actors aware that they themselves may not correspond to their partners' aspirations. In contrast, a contractual will—a will capable of forming a contract—presupposes the capacity to align one's emotions and one's aspirations. As a user quoted by the eHarmony Internet dating site puts it:

> "He's a really nice guy," Vanessa said, "but I just don't know if Ben and I are meant to be together. I'm thinking about breaking up with him, but I'm not sure. How do I decide?" *It's a question that plagues many singles: should*

*I break up with my partner or stick it out a while longer? The issue is usually
not cut-and-dried, and you have to wrestle with it for a long time before the
answer becomes clear.* However, the following are sure signals that the long-
range forecast for a relationship is worrisome.[24]

Vanessa's question displays emotional confusion and unclarity or difficulty
in aligning her aspirations with her emotions, an uncertainty about the very
nature of her own emotions. Emotional unclarity entails a double uncertainty:
Given the highly interactive and reciprocal nature of emotions—people respond
to others' expressed feelings—a difficulty in interpreting someone's feelings feeds
back on the process of forming stable feelings. Elsa is a French-Israeli fifty-
nine-year-old divorced woman living in Israel and captures aptly this double uncertainty.

ELSA: I divorced five years ago and after twenty-four years of marriage. I
   didn't know the whole dating scene had changed so much. It is really
   difficult to have a relationship with someone these days.
INTERVIEWER: Can you say why? What has changed?
ELSA: I think it is mostly because you never know what they want or what
   even you want. Things could be great, and then all of the sudden for
   something small, everything collapses; I had this great thing going on
   with this guy, he was courting me exactly according to the rules, it was
   very nice and sweet, and one day we spoke about politics, and *pfft*, the
   guy did not like my opinions, I was too left-wing for him. It made him
   mad because he was a businessman who was very proud of what he had
   accomplished, and when he heard I was for redistribution of wealth and
   higher taxes for the rich, he evaporated, disappeared. Just like that. No
   warning. Then this other guy, at first he was crazy about me, wrote to me
   crazy emails, bought me the most extravagant gifts, but one day, he pulled
   away. I found courage to ask him why and he said he didn't like that I
   was critical about his way of dressing. He dressed in an awful, conservative way and I was trying to make him look more jazzy. I said something
   like: "Wouldn't this jacket look great on you? I think it's much nicer than
   the one you have." And that was enough to make him feel I was criticiz-
   ing him. You scratch their ego a bit, and they collapse. Then there is also
   me: a guy would do something inappropriate, fail to acknowledge me, or
   fail to be reliable in some way, I withdraw into my shell, convince myself
   the guy is not worth my time. After the beginning period is over, you

know when you're not in that period where you have stars in your eyes and knots in your stomach, after that period, when you start seeing the real person, I find it hard to know what I feel and what I want.

INTERVIEWER: What do you mean?

ELSA: It is just very chaotic. Sometimes I like the guy, sometimes I don't. I like him when he does what I expect from him. I don't like him when he doesn't. I feel the same from them. I become insecure, and I really don't like that insecurity, I eat much more. But if they are nice to me, I like them. I have no idea how to have stable feelings.

INTERVIEWER: How do you know if a man likes you or not?

ELSA: That's the thing, I don't know. Sometimes I think he likes me, sometimes I think he doesn't. I think they go back and forth. Just like me. These are the moments when I miss being married. The clarity of it. You may be miserably married but at least you know what you have.

INTERVIEWER: Why? Why don't you know? What is it you don't know?

ELSA: Because you never know what things mean to others and even what they mean to you. The guy I mentioned before, the businessman, he would come every evening and take me out to a drink, bought me dinner, or drinks, was really after me and then, with no warning sign, he disappeared. He seemed, he was in love, and then because of a political disagreement, he decided I was not for him, can you believe it? Obviously, it meant very little to him. Or maybe it meant something at some time, and then it didn't. Now I am seeing this guy and he often cancels meetings, arrives later, does not call when he should call, but still he sticks around, we have had a few rows, but he seems very hung up on me, and so I don't know anymore what counts or doesn't, whether he is into me or not. You just have the feeling that there is no rule. It is very difficult to know what works or not, and what is the meaning of what a guy does or doesn't do. Maybe he is not calling because he is busy? Maybe because he just does not like to get intense? Maybe because he doesn't like me? Hey, it could be anything. So I never get to the point where I have the sense that I *know* what this is about, how you are supposed to do it.

The story here refers to the difficulty in entering a contract because people are constantly negotiating the rules to enter relationships and the meaning of these rules for their own sense of worth. If "uncertainty refers to a person's ability to describe, predict, and explain behavior within social situations,"[25] clearly this actor is faced with a great deal of uncertainty, her own and that of others. The lack of ritual structure and normative anchors leaves the subject struggling on her own to decipher another's intentions, to devise a course of action, to create strategic responses to uncertainty, and to form clear and steady feelings. In other words, uncertainty creates meta-emotions, emotions about emotions that make the process of meeting some-one both confusing and highly reflexive, with subjects attempting to control the process by consciously monitoring the flow and intensity of their feel-ings. This reflexivity characterizes the entry of relationships, precisely when the intentions of actors are both unclear and difficult to decipher. These two layers—emotions and meta-emotions—render the process of entering a rela-tionship cumbersome. Here is another example of this.

Tamar is an thirty-two-year-old Israeli student in the humanities who also works in a high-tech company:

TAMAR: A friend of mine called me and said: "I met a guy and he was great; friends introduced me; but he did not SMS in two days. On the other hand, he said he would be very busy, so what do you think? I think he should be the one to do a step because he should court me. My gut feeling is that he should do it, but I am not sure." My answer to my friend was: "If you do not want to remain up in the air, you should ask him. Ask him out. Send him a nonchalant SMS. For me, I hate to be up in the air." She said: "I hate this thing of sending something 'nonchalant' like I am cool, when behind it I am the least nonchalant in the world. If he had wanted to say 'let's talk' he would already have written." But me? I hate to be up in the air. I need to know. I write. I don't care to be the first to write. I need to know. Then my friend says: "Ouf!!! I am fed up. He must free me. Yes, yes. No, no. I need to free myself from him. He must write to me." [Tamar again speaking in her own name]: I lack patience for the whole "will he SMS me or not, I need to know. [...] I go on many dates but you know sometimes I doubt myself, I am not even sure I know any-more when the date was good or not. Sometimes you think the date was good, but you come home and you ask yourself, "Was this good?" Many of [my] friends are also full of doubts. I am very instinctual, but I have doubts. I live in Tel Aviv where everybody looks, everybody wants one-night stands. In Tel Aviv everybody is looking. It makes the whole thing very cheap. You feel like one among one thousand. You really feel like that. You can send text messages for hours and then find out they only want one-night stands. I talked with men, and the feeling is that they have a lot of choice, that they can find another beautiful and smart woman very quickly. I have all the time the feeling that there are always more girls, which is why I feel the whole thing is cheap.

INTERVIEWER: Suppose you meet someone you like.

TAMAR: How?

INTERVIEWER: However you want.

TAMAR: Through friends it is easier.

INTERVIEWER: Can you describe to me what would be complicated?

TAMAR: Except for the excess of choice, the fact there is much so choice, I think there is no commitment when you meet through dates, the feeling is "I can do whatever I want." If it comes through friends, he is more committed. He has to be more careful. But if it does not come through friends the feeling is that they can do whatever they want.

Despite the generational gap, Tamar and her friend resonate with Elsa, as all describe a state where the rules of engagement are unclear, where the intentions of actors are up for grabs and demand a reflexive verbalization and monitoring, and where the expression of desire is highly constrained by the perception that men have the power to decide how to engage in the relationship that they can and do leave very easily. Moreover, what fuels the exchange between Tamar and her friend is the question of whether "calling first" diminishes their worth, suggesting that the sexual field is saturated with power struggles. Uncertainty plagues these initial interactions because expressing too much or too little interest can equally doom a relationship, the first because it signals one's weakness, and the second because doing so makes one unable to engage in a meaningful intimate interaction. "Not knowing what to do"—to call or not to call, to show interest or not—is the result of the sociological constraint that actors manage the conflicting desires and imperatives circulating in the interaction: the desire not to appear too eager to want a relationship, and yet desiring it eagerly; the desire to have another affirm one's worth, and the self-imposed limits on one's own emotional expressiveness. Not projecting "neediness" has become a key motif of relationships, especially at their entry, making it difficult to form the will to enter an emotional contract or to perform the necessary symbolic work to show either interest or commitment, or both. The sexual-romantic interaction thus contains the following paradox: in order to form a bond, one must signal a certain detachment because it signals autonomy and thus worth. Yet detachment often intimates the other's self-protective strategy. This conundrum is aptly illustrated by fifty-nine-year-old Jean-Pierre, who, after he discussed his own difficulties finding a partner, referred to his two daughters, twenty-five and thirty years old, respectively.

JEAN-PIERRE: None of them [his daughters] has a boyfriend; nothing holds; they see people once or twice, sometimes more, they see someone for a few weeks, but nothing holds. Both of them tell me the same thing: it is very complicated. They find there is no rule. They want the guy to be the one who starts and takes the initiative. They will not initiate. But if the guy sends more than three messages, he is out. One message is good; a second message is tolerable but barely; but a third means the guy is needy, and that is a disaster; he is out. So it's not only the guys who are complicated. They are themselves complicated. They try to find guidelines in feminism to get a sense of what to do in this mess.

INTERVIEWER: How so?

JEAN-PIERRE: They are quick to interpret a man's behavior as a display of power. They are very vigilant not to feel powerless or controlled. But you see, they also wait for him to do the first step. So there is a contradiction there. They are aware of it, but they will not change it. They say that acting otherwise would ruin any chance of relationship with a man. That the key is not acting needy.

Despite the still-pervasive patriarchal modes of domination, feminism, in all its versions and nuances, has had a profound impact on heterosexual relationships, on men's and women's perceptions of themselves and each other, contributing to the formation of psychological mechanisms of nonchoice. As discussed previously, feminism has been, by and large, an ideal of autonomy and equality and in that respect encourages women to be, as this man reports, "vigilant" about marks of power, which in turn makes them scrutinize men's behavior for the signs of power and devaluation of their worth this behavior may contain. Such signs can be found in a lack of reciprocity (not cooking for a woman, calling her less often than she calls him), in sexual aggressiveness (forcing oneself on a woman), in emotional distance (being emotionally less expressive, not calling back quickly enough), or in a lesser willingness to sacrifice personal interests to a relationship. To the extent that feminism aims to equalize gender roles and scrutinizes men's behavior for its hidden signs of domination, it also increases women's dignity and the threshold for the preservation of their sense of self-worth. As we have also seen above, in a market situation worth is fundamentally uncertain and must thus be defended. However, as this man indicates, his daughters will dismiss any man who pays a too-insistent attention to them as they will translate his pursuit into a form of "neediness," the ultimate derogatory view of another in a culture dominated by the ideal of autonomy. This is made more complex by the fact that the line between autonomy and emotional distance is very tenuous indeed, thus creating confusion about others' (even one's own) emotions and intentions. As Jean-Pierre indicates, key psychosocial processes at work in the formation of relationships are of two kinds: evaluating someone's psychological, sexual, and social worth (whether someone acts "needy" or not, whether someone acts in a way that "shows interest or not"); and protecting the self to ensure its integrity and worth are not hurt or diminished. Both processes must navigate conflicting imperatives, between the imperative of autonomy (one's own and another's) and the expression of attachment. The result is that sexual actors self-monitor their feelings: for example, respondents speak about mechanisms as "closing up," "defending oneself," "protecting oneself," "making sure one feels on safe ground," or "moving away from pain." These mechanisms point to the capacity of actors to control the flow of feelings in order to maintain self-worth and autonomy through avoidance of emotional pain. Actors thus develop psychological strategies of risk assessment, trying to evaluate and calculate how much risk they are taking in showing their sentiments and "opening themselves up" when entering a relationship.

Vigilance about others' mark of (dis)interest is accompanied by a sustained attention to one's self-worth where feeling self-value becomes the reliable sign of a good relationship. For example, the influential *Psychology Today* lists the signs of bad or toxic relationships. At the top of the list are the following signs: "Your partner *doesn't make you feel good* about your body; they point out your thinning hair or saggy underarm skin." Or "You feel *worse about yourself* as a person than when you started the relationship— you're less *confident* and can see fewer positive qualities about yourself."[26] At the same time that the structure of relationships becomes uncertain and that women are made to be hyper-vigilant about men's display of power, the self turns to its own feelings and to its sense of self-worth. In doing so, the self develops new forms of hyper-attentiveness to signs of lack of interest or emotional distance, as well as cultural and psychological skills to withdraw from a relationship that threatens the self. In a situation of uncertainty, men and women learn to monitor the flow of their emotional expressiveness to avoid an asymmetrical relationship.

In the face of the uncertainty produced by others' behavior, the emotional semiotics of interactions—deciphering the emotional signs produced by others—can become agonistic; another's intentions may make me vulnerable to loss or harm. While emotions toward another might be uncertain, actors turn to their self-feelings to gain a sense of certainty. The self learns to decipher another's behavior through one's own subjectivity: "How am I made to feel?" becomes the key to the sequential progress and performative accomplishment of emotions. Such attention to one's self-worth in turn increases the risks of an agonistic relationship, based on conflict. Here are two examples of such finely tuned mechanisms of self-defense that rely on the ways in which one is made to feel rather than one how one is attracted to another.

Raphael is an Israeli twenty-four-year-old philosophy student with a part-time job:

INTERVIEWER: Do you have a girlfriend?

RAPHAEL: Actually, I just broke up with a girl.

INTERVIEWER: Do you feel comfortable saying why?

RAPHAEL: I was having a very bad day; I had a fight with my boss at work and I was stressed out from it. In the evening I spoke with her, as we usually did, and I told her I had a hard day. Then she also told me her day. But I think I was not paying as close attention as I usually did. We spoke and we hung up. And half an hour later she calls back, and she says she was bothered by the ways in which I had not listened to her. I should say that she studies to be a clinical psychologist. She is very much into this stuff. And I could imagine how after we talked she told herself [*mimicking a girly voice*]: "Oh my God, he did not listen to me properly" [*tone of mocking irony*]. And you know what? I thought, "Who the fuck are you to tell me after two dates and after I was having a bad day that I was not listening to you carefully enough?" I thought this is hugely inappropriate. After two dates, she can't do something like this. I stopped it right there.

This man and the woman he dated reacted to two different threats: she responded to her perception she was not cared for enough, while he was trying to defend himself from the perceived threat to his autonomy. Both affirm their self and each views the other's assertion of their self as a threat to his or her own self. Self-affirmation and the protection of one's self-worth become a zero-sum game, a struggle between two selves who perceive one's worth as being at the expense of another's.

In another example, Daniella is a thirty-seven-year-old Israeli computer graphics designer in a high-tech firm.

INTERVIEWER: When you are going through the profiles, trying to decide whether to meet someone from the sites you use, how do you do this?

DANIELLA: Well, first of all the looks, of course. He has to have good looks, no, not necessarily good, but something I find attractive. The level of education, also maybe how funny the profile is. Then when we correspond, it would be things like, if he responds quickly enough, if he writes meaningful things, if there is a general niceness about his tone. Like this guy I was talking to yesterday, after we corresponded on an Internet dating site, he looked great, had a very pleasant voice, sounded smart, but something about the tone of his voice did not make me feel good. After ten minutes, he said, "Sorry I must go, please send me your picture (because I did not put my picture on the site). Write to me." But I didn't. Even though all the ingredients were there, I didn't, because he was not nice enough. If I come out of a conversation not feeling good, that's it. I don't pursue it. A man must make me feel good. Without that, I find it difficult to feel free. I mean, no, sometimes I would pursue it, but if I do, I will be on my guard.

INTERVIEWER: Does it mean then that if you do not feel good in a relationship, you leave or break the relationship?

DANIELLA: Obviously not as, uhhm, mechanically as you put it. I mean, one needs to check what the person was thinking about, maybe I misinterpreted something, but on the whole if, especially at the beginning, there are many things that do not make me feel great about myself, if the man acts ambivalent or aloof, or even just not feeling like I am a special person, that he is happy to have met me, then I would view this as a reason not to pursue it. How a guy makes me feel about myself is really important to whether I give a chance to a relationship. Which is why, maybe, when you come to think of it [laughter], I am still alone and single.

As is clear in this example, a threat to one's sense of self-worth ("feeling good") leads to exit. The self in a romantic-sexual interaction negotiates (or not) about the other's capacity to maintain or even enhance his or her self-worth. Strategies of protection of self-worth entail non-choice, withdrawing from a (potential) relationship in which the self fears not to be valued enough. In other words, exiting is a performative act through which actors affirm their worth and offset possible devaluation. In an advice column, the relationships expert Rori Raye lays out the following ground rule for women:

> When a man says he's not sure he's "into you," or "not feeling it for you," *run*. Saying he loves you but isn't ready yet for a serious relationship is way different than saying he's "not sure of his feelings." If he says he's "not sure of his feelings," that would be the cue to get out of there.[27]

The volatility of relationship is thus the result of reactions and counter-reactions to perceived symbolic threats to the self. The therapeutic discourse that is conveyed both through the therapeutic practice and through popular culture reinforces flight mechanisms because a large bulk of psychotherapy in all its forms is used to strengthen self-worth. Listen to the same Elsa quoted above:

> I was dating a man I liked, I had not liked a man like this in a long time, and I even started to think this may be it. But after three to four months, I don't know why, I could feel him become slightly less, what's the word, maybe less enthusiastic, not as careful to please me. He would arrive late, did not always call when he said he would, seemed to want to be more on his own to write. I made remarks about it. I guess I was feeling a bit insecure. And instead of being cool about it, he resented it, and I resented his resentment. So I did everything pop psych books tell you to do, I said straightforwardly that it made me feel bad, that I needed him to behave differently. But it made him more defensive. He resented that I made demands, or criticized his behavior. But you know if a relationship makes me defensive and anxious, then I think that however great the guy may be, I won't pursue it. This is something I learned to do with my therapy. I used to be in relationships where I felt bad, felt insecure in some way, I used to think it would eventually go away. But usually it doesn't go away. Since my therapy, I don't do that anymore. I don't stay in relationships where I don't feel good.

Elsa's story resonates with the other stories: the man unpredictability threatens her capacity to decipher his intentions. This creates uncertainty, a difficulty in interpreting another's behavior and intentions. What actors experience as "insecurity," in turn generates defensive and counter-defensive strategies, each actor trying to protect an essential aspect of his or her self. This is accentuated by the process of undergoing a therapy whose chief purpose is to enhance self-valuation and its proxies (self-esteem, self-love, self-acceptance). We may thus say that it in fact subtly encourages defensive strategies to secure a sense of worth. When one's own or another's desire seems muddled, conflicted, or ambivalent, one plausible strategy is to leave. In other words, emotional confusion and lack of rules of engagement lead to exit, many steps before forming a contract. Mechanisms of non-choice help the self to safeguard its value by un-choosing a relationship that threatens the self. The defense of self-worth thus generates an agonistic logic and makes "exit" the most expedient way to ascertain or preserve such self-worth.

All the examples above illustrate the same point. Actors are caught between two conflicting emotional logics: preserving their self-worth by not engaging in actions that may not be reciprocated and that they perceive as making them vulnerable; and establishing a relationship with another in which the disclosure of emotions is a crucial performative act to bring the relationship into being. Uncertainty is the result of the difficulty in organizing these two logics into what Ann Swidler calls a coherent strategy of action.[28]

The psychological resources actors must develop in sexual-romantic relationships are reminiscent of the economic actor who tries to assess risks and returns on invested value in an uncertain financial environment. While classical capitalism was defined by the direct exchange of money (trading commodities for money or producing known commodities for money), under the impetus of financialization of the economy, value and return have become increasingly uncertain. Economic actors develop mathematical tools to assess the risk of their present investment in the future. As Karin Knorr Cetina put it, such form of thinking is based on the evaluation of hopes and promises.[29] Speculation and assessment of risk have become a critical activity of economics[30] and it is the same mindset that guides people entering relationships. In the same way that the risk management has become central to the economic financial sphere, risk has also become central to the entry in relationships. We may say that some relationships are like direct forms of money exchange—they are structured around established rules of reciprocity as in traditional courtship—whereas other relationships are about evaluating one's strategies in the face of uncertain prospects.

Actors struggling to enter and establish a relationship try to assess risks but, in fact, are often directed by what cognitive psychologists call non-conscious goal conflict, that is, situations where actors are faced with incompatible goals, which demand incompatible strategies, and which do not come to their full awareness, given the limited nature of cognitive capacities. Conscious or non-conscious goal conflicts make decisions or choices prone to "difficulty and unease," and give rise to "inconsistent behavioral intentions and inconsistent affective tendencies."[31] In other words, embedded in contemporary relationships are conflictual goals, such as preserving autonomy and securing self-worth on the one hand and striving to attachment on the other. As cognitive psychologists Tali Kleiman and Ran Hassin put it:

> When two (or more) goals are in active conflict they often create close-call decisions, i.e.,—decisions in which the alternatives seem to have very similar utilities. Metaphorically, then, the "decision scales" are more or less balanced. It is exactly in these cases where minor (and possibly irrelevant) cues in the environment have the potential of tipping the scales.[32]

When faced with multiple choices and conflicting goals, actors are more likely to use irrelevant, arbitrary, or minor details to make a decision, for example between engaging in a relationship or withdrawing. I suggest that in cases of goal conflict, actors are more likely to withdraw, because withdrawal seems to offer the simplest solution to the conflict between self-worth, autonomy, and attachment. This is an example where autonomy conflicts with attachment and generates an exit strategy based on apparently minor detail, exactly what the cognitive psychologists would predict.

See what a man who calls himself goal12 has to say:

> Me and my ex GF broke up 2 months ago was my fault *she loved me so much*. didn't cheat or anything, just broke up with her *out of know where* [sic] *was having a bad day*. I rang her next day and said sorry for doing that but she was after [sic] going out and kissed someone so that kind shook me up but i respected her for being honest.[33]

In this example, the woman's love posed a threat to his autonomy and conflicted with his need for attachment. Unconscious of the goal conflict and unable to regulate it, he broke up with her without understanding why. "Breaking up out of having a bad day" may be seen as an example of what cognitive psychologists would predict would happen to someone caught in non-conscious conflict goals, as a strategy to withdraw from complexity and conflict. Exit and breakup are thus the solution to non-conscious goal conflict and to the need for the preservation of autonomy and self-worth.

Exiting without a Voice

The freedom to enter relationships is concomitant to the freedom to exit them. In fact, exit is a prerogative of the contractual freedom of relationships. As the East German dissident Wolf Biermann wrote in 1965: "I can only love what I am free to leave."[34] Such definition of freedom is certainly different from the one Hegel, the great proponent of freedom in love and marriage, offered. Indeed, the philosopher looked sternly on the individual's prerogative to leave a marriage unhindered. For Hegel, only higher ethical institutions such as the Church or the court of law could dissolve a marriage (see chapter 6 on divorce). In this sense, the cultural ideas of freedom, contract, marriage, and love have considerably evolved: from the freedom to enter them it has morphed into the essential freedom to leave them. Exiting relationships, and repeatedly so, is embedded in the sexual contract. But if exit is embedded in the contract, this is bound to transform the perception of relationships both before and during their occurrence and to undermine the very possibility of forming them.

Breaking relationships at some point along their line has become one of their routine aspects, so much so that many or most relationships contain an intrinsic anticipation of their end. This is, as should be clear by now, particularly true of the brave new world of Internet dating where people routinely do not return a phone call, do not show up at meetings, interrupt a correspondence without explanation, leave a date abruptly, and end a relationship with or without explanation. For many of my interviewees, especially but not only the female ones, this seems to have become the normal fare of relationships. Ross, a forty-one-year-old Englishman employed as a teacher, offers the following example:

> Last week I was on the phone with a woman with a nice profile. We started talking and we were having a nice conversation. She told me she bikes everyday thirty miles inside and outside the city [London]. She also said she did not wear a helmet. So I told her she should wear a helmet. And the third time I brought up an argument to convince her to wear a helmet, all in good spirit I think, she said to me: "Sorry I've got to go." And she added, I think by SMS: "I don't think we are compatible."

Modern actors cultivate their selfhood both through consumer tastes and through psychological self-fashioning and thus become finely attuned to minute differences of style, in turn conducive to quick dismissal. With very few exceptions, most people, married and unmarried, in established or in budding relationships, are likely to experience in their lifetime a breakup or rejection, whether minor—as in Ross's case—or significant, either one-sidedly abrupt or consensual. Interestingly enough, while in economic or other transactions, exiting entails a breach of contract and sometimes even a penalty, in either already-engaged sexual or romantic relationships, or both, exit occurs without any symbolic cost or stigma for the person exiting. Emotional and sexual contracts are unique in that they are practically devoid of penalties for exiting them. This is exemplified in the practice of "ghosting," widely discussed in popular culture. To quote a newspaper article:

What's Ghosting?

Ghost, a word more commonly associated with Cole, the boy who saw dead people, and a 1990 movie starring Demi Moore and Patrick Swayze, has also come to be used as a verb that refers to ending a romantic relationship by cutting off all contact and ignoring the former partner's attempts to reach out.

Who's Doing It?

The term has already entered the polling lexicon: In October 2014, a YouGov/Huffington Post poll of 1,000 adults showed that 11 percent of Americans had "ghosted" someone. A more informal survey from *Elle* magazine that polled 185 people found that about 16.7 percent of men and 24.2 percent of women had been ghosts at some point in their lives. Whether this behavior has become more predominant with the advent of technology is debatable, but perhaps now it stings more, since there are so many ways to see your beloved interacting with other people while ignoring you. The rise of apps like Tinder and Grindr, and the impression they give that there is always someone else—literally —around the corner, is certainly empowering to ghosts.[35]

Ghosting is a prerogative of the freedom to exit sexual-romantic contracts at any point. As a specific form of exit, it does not require explanations or saving face. Ghosting is, in fact, an expression both of the fact that exiting relationships is fairly routine and standard practice and that people feel increasingly unobligated to provide explanations for it. Sarah, a fifty-two-year-old Israeli woman expresses in powerful terms how her sense of self was diminished by having been ghosted by her girlfriend.

We had a relationship for a year, no, a year and half actually, and then she sent me an SMS telling me it was over, that she was ending our relationship.

She did that with an SMS. I tried to call. But she did not respond. I can't get over the humiliation of someone breaking up with me in this way. She did not even bother to speak to me. I tried to call her many times but of course she did not pick up any of my calls, even when I tried from a number she didn't know. I can't get over the hurt and humiliation. Then I found out through a common friend that she had met someone. She didn't even have the decency to tell me.

Other interviewees had also been ghosted. (In my sample only women had been, but this is undoubtedly non-gendered.)

Because the ethics of consent is the main and almost exclusive moral discourse regulating love and relationships, consent makes it legitimate to withdraw from a relationship at any point, as soon as one's emotions change. "To feel less attracted" or "to meet someone else" bestows the right to exit a relationship at will, often without engaging in a "justification." In fact, if there is a single striking characteristic of emotional contractual freedom it is that exiting relationships can be devoid of any regime of justification.[36] People can sometimes give explanations, of course, but they feel increasingly unobligated to do so.

Exiting is so widespread that it creates ripple effects on the entire way of forming and conceiving relationships. Tara, a forty-eight-year-old Scandinavian woman, who is a professor of chemistry, reached out to me through email to share some reflections about her dating experiences through the Internet. In striking metaphors, this is how she describes her experiences:

Just a reflection:

In the novel *Flight Behavior* by Barbara Kingsolver, there is a scene with the main character and her husband shopping in a one-dollar-shop. Everything is cheap and mass-produced in far-away places. The customers pick up things and throw them back on the shelves with disinterest or dismay. They want *something*, the desire is part of the rationale, they just don't know what, and don't really need anything that they see, but still they shop, because it's cheap.

This scene made me think of the dating-dropping-behaviour. […] Finding partners has turned into an entirely personal endeavour of choice, needs and enhancement of one's own identity, a little like buying new clothes.

I suspect on-line dating is to blame for this "fast romance" (like fast food, fast fashion) phenomenon. It's the ultimate alienation: The "goods"

[are] plentiful and easily accessible, but you don't put much emotional investment in it. This take on things [has] spread to other relations as well, so if you meet someone in real life, you can "try them on" for a while, and then put them back on the shelf without explanation. This makes it extra hurtful and confusing. Before, it was common courtesy to end things explicitly. You were supposed to give an explanation to why your interest or feelings ended, or why you'd decided it wasn't right. With the fast love, the dropping seems to be taken for granted, an easy option out, no matter how intense or intimate the romance had been. Many people are "dating" and "shopping," picky consumers on a cheap global market of possible romantic or sexual relations. It's the ultimate commodification.

This woman expresses in a painfully articulate way the fact that relationships are exited at will, easily and with no serious symbolic or moral cost for the person exiting. This is precisely why she feels like a disposable commodity, tried on and thrown away, or, using her metaphor, "put back on the shelf." Breakups constitute an assault on the self and its sense of worth.

German sexologist and physician Volkmar Sigusch has argued that sexual freedom has diluted the sentiment of obligation,[37] a fact nowhere clearer than in the realm of breaking up. The generalization of the culture of breaking up marks a weakening of moral obligation, a weakening that is nowhere as pronounced as it is in the sexual realm. In her *Missing Love Manual that Makes Your Relationship Last*, marriage expert and matchmaker Hellen Chen claims that 85 percent of relationships will end in breakups.[38] While the statistics provided by a non-academic cannot be entirely reliable, it remains that she points to what has undoubtedly become a widespread and structural part of the pairing process. Most contemporary adults, even at a young age, have repeated experience of romantic breakups, either as initiators or as objects of breakups.

In his book *Exit, Voice and Loyalty*[39] Albert O. Hirschman explores two options for customers to express their dissatisfaction with a firm's product: one is exit, to refrain from buying the product; the other is voice, expressing through verbal or other means one's dissatisfaction. But in intimate relationships as well as in economic exchange, exit seems to be the increasingly preferred option. Why is it indeed the case? I would argue that exit is preferred to voice because it incurs no normative penalty, because there is a perception of alternatives (plenty of other stores or other partners), and because voice is perceived as a threat to one's autonomy or self-worth. In the process of forming a bond, exit is often preferred to voice because voice expresses dependence and vulnerability, while exit is a performative expression of the self's assertiveness. Exit is an assertive form of non-choice, that is, of choice to withdraw from and end a relationship that threatens the self's security. This exit is sometimes the result of a conscious decision and sometimes the result of semi-conscious processes, as when someone is caught in goal-conflict, in the course of his defense of his autonomy or self-worth.

We have come to view breakups as such a fundamental prerogative of the late modern subject's freedom to enter and leave relationships that we have barely paused to consider the effects that repeated breakups and disappointed expectations may have on the self and on the possibility of forming relationships. Two aspects about breakups are striking. The first is that they lack moral accountability and are thus relatively normless. The second is that they entail a form of harm we may dub emotional harm. Breakups are relatively costless for the ones breaking up, and potentially harmful for the objects of breakups. Because the ideal of sexual freedom has focused on sexual repression and domination, it has omitted to ponder about the negative effects on cultures dominated by the freedom to exit. We have failed to inquire about the extent to which the repeated or frequent experience of breakup may harm the possibility of holding on to a secure sense of self and of forming durable and meaningful relationships. As research suggests, the effects of breakups do not resemble the frequent casualness with which they are practiced.

> [T]he dissolution of romantic relationships has been empirically associated with a variety of negative physical and emotional responses, ranging from anxiety, depression, psychopathology, loneliness, immune suppression, fatal and nonfatal physical illness or accidents, and decreased longevity to immediate death through suicide or homicide.[40]

Words commonly used by psychologists of breakups are *anger, rage, anxiety, depression, despair, sadness, disorganization,* and *fear of abandonment.* Breakups have been found to increase risks of suicide, which are indeed much higher among divorced rather than married persons:

> Divorced and separated persons were over twice as likely to commit suicide as married persons (RR=2.08, 95% confidence intervals (95% CI) 1.58, 2.72). Being single or widowed had no significant effect on suicide risk. When data

were stratified by sex, it was observed that the risk of suicide among divorced men was over twice that of married men (RR=2.38, CI 1.77, 3.20). Among women, however, there were no statistically significant differentials in the risk of suicide by marital status[41] (probably because women take for granted that relations are uncertain and that they can end).

Another study suggests that for both males and females, separation created a risk of suicide at least four times higher than any other marital status.[42] Still other researchers suggest that the main effect of a breakup is a loss in self-concept clarity, that is, a less-well-defined sense of who one is.[43] Whatever the actual statistics and effects of breakups, the fact remains: a breakup is often a severe psychological experience that has come to be taken for granted in highly sexualized and emotionally volatile cultures. If they increase chances of suicide, affect the desire to create new relationships, generate short-term or long-term depression, affect one's self-concept and self-worth more or less durably, breakups should raise questions about the limits of consent as the implicit philosophy guiding relationships. As legal scholar Robin West put it eloquently: "That non-consensual transactions—rape, theft, slavery—are bad because non-consensual, does not imply the value, worth, or goodness of their consensual counterparts—sex, property, or work. [Consensual relationships] surely may be bad for some other reason."[44]

The expectation and routinization of breakups has also the result of rendering confused and uncertain the moral criteria to evaluate them. Precisely because of the freedom to exit, actors do not know which moral repertoire to draw on after a breakup. Here is an example of the ways in which breakups are plagued by the difficulty to put them in a moral language.

> I'm still learning how to get over it [the breakup]. It's hard. He was my first. He still wants to hang out with me secretly on weekends but otherwise he is HORRIBLY mean to me. He says terrible things to me to put me down. He still wants to control me even though he is talking to this girl. I have to see them together at school and have to deal with the fact it's not me that he spends his time with anymore. Sometimes I think I should let go and move on but then I'm scared I'll regret it if it could have been saved. I figure I'll start letting go and if he really wants things to get better, he won't let me go.[45]

This young person lacks any sense of normative clarity that can guide her: although her boyfriend behaved "horribly," she is uncertain about the moral meaning of his actions, which are translated in an emotional rather than moral language. In fact, the subjectivation of experience entails both a deep uncertainty about one's feelings and about the moral meaning of others' emotions and actions. Should she feel regret? Determination? Determination to fight for her love? Condemnation of her boyfriend? These questions are for individuals to grapple with on their own with no clear guidelines and stand in sharp contrast with cultures in which sexuality is deeply embedded and determined by moral culture. As philosopher Avishai Margalit put it: "Liberal morality does not recognize sexual morality as an independent moral domain. It recognizes the importance of sex in human life as well as its vulnerability to exploitation and domination. It recognizes sexuality as a sensitive domain in applying general moral principles. But it does not recognize sexuality as an autonomous moral domain with principles of its own, any more than it recognizes eating as a separate moral domain. Indeed, in the liberal view there is no more room for sexual morality than there is room for a morality of eating."[46] A clear consequence of this is a certain obliviousness to what legal philosopher Alan Wertheimer dubs "experiential harm," that is, the kind of harm that is inflicted on one's capacity to have an experience.[47] Dominant norms, Wertheimer suggests, are quite permissive with regard to sexual deception. One could add that they are quite permissive and even encouraging of breakups. Breaking up becomes morally benign or more simply irrelevant to the moral domain. Repeated breakups cause experiential harm either because they make one indifferent to the harm one inflicts on others or because it hurts the emotional integrity of people who are the object of breakups, affecting their capacity to believe they can reengage in similar experiences.

Alexander is a fifty-eight-year-old British accountant who was married at the age of twenty-nine and divorced at the age of thirty-three. He recounts his experience as follows:

ALEXANDER: I knew from the beginning we were not matched.
INTERVIEWER: You knew it from the beginning?
ALEXANDER: Yes. Actually, even before I got married. It was obvious we were incompatible, that we had different temperaments.
INTERVIEWER: Was it painful to divorce?
ALEXANDER: Actually, no. Maybe because I wanted it. The experience I was telling you about before, the woman I knew after my divorce, that was much more painful. I was in love, very much in love with her, but

after one year of going out together, she told me she wanted to break up
[silence]. Thinking about it, I think that tainted my entire life.

INTERVIEWER: In what way?

ALEXANDER: I think that experience was emotionally so difficult, so drench-
ing, that I closed down, something in me shut down, I could not ever open
up again to a woman in quite the same way. Maybe that is why I am still
single, more than twenty years after my divorce. I could not open up again.
Not since. You could say I was traumatized by that breakup. Actually never
realized it until now, that I am speaking to you.

In a similar and resonant vein, Cyril, a sixty-seven-year-old French man,
employed as a journalist, recounts his first experiences:

When I was young, two women left me; each one for her own reasons.
And each did that quite abruptly. I was in love with them and I think I
remained traumatized by this. I was never able to fall in love again. I did
not count on anyone anymore. I have very pleasant relationships with
women, but I have never fallen in love again in quite the same way. That's
why I find it so much more comfortable to have several relationships at
once. You are never quite vulnerable in the same way if you have several
relationships at once.

These examples illustrated how breakups affect the capacity to trust the
future, which in turn generates psychological and emotional structures to
close off and protect the self.

In the economic realm, exit has become the main mode of operation of
the market at its two opposite ends. On the side of production, firms off-
shore their operations, close plants, and lay off workers; and on the side of
consumption, large stores do not build a relationship based on personal
acquaintance and loyalty, and make exit a normal and routine option for
consumers looking for the best bargain. As Hirschman put it in *Exit, Voice
and Loyalty*, a deep assumption of economists is that the lapses or losses of
firms are *not* something to pay attention to: "As one firm loses out in the
competitive struggle, its market share is taken up and its factors are hired by
others, including newcomers; in the upshot, total resources may well be
better allocated."[48] The moral indifference to breakups seems to follow a
similar logic of blind efficiency. As they aim to maximize the individual
well-being, they are on the whole and are generally perceived as a way to

improve one's performance ("accumulating experience," "learning who one is," "choosing someone more compatible") and as a better way to allocate one's resources (choosing the right person). Both in the economic and sexual realms, the very notions of efficiency, costs, and utility break down the notion of contract. As Richard Sennett put it in his *Culture of the New Capitalism*:

> The head of a dynamic company recently asserted that no one owns their place in her organization, that past service in particular earns no employee a guaranteed place. [...] A peculiar trait of personality is needed to do so, one which discounts the experiences a human being has already had. This trait of personality resembles the consumer ever avid for new things, discarding old if perfectly serviceable goods, rather than the owner who jealousy guards what he or she already possesses.[49]

Breaking up is part and parcel of a culture in which people are quickly outdated, replaced by the reality or possibility of partners that correspond more narrowly to their emotional needs and lifestyle interests. The move from breakups to new relationships requires, as in the economic sphere, a certain forgetting of the past, the capacity and even necessity to update and renew oneself, learn new experiences, and face unknown horizons. This requires a personality able to adapt to a wide number of characters and persons; the capacity to adapt to insecurity, to change and build defensive strategies to protect the self. The rapid turnover of partners entails a capacity and desire to do short-term investments, not to waste one's time, to shift the line of production quickly, to make quick mental calculations about the worthiness of a relationship. As Sennett further puts it, it is a skill that is opposite of "possessiveness." Interestingly enough, possessiveness is an economic as well as a sexual term. One may even wonder if Joseph Schumpeter's phrase about capitalism "creative destruction"[50] is not as apt to describe economic self-destruction as it is to understand the emotional dynamic of negative choice.

Following Sennett, capitalism has two major effects particularly relevant to this study: one is the decrease of institutional loyalty and the other is the decrease of trust. The decrease of loyalty turns people into permanent self-entrepreneurs, who can only rely on themselves and their psychological resources to cope with uncertainty and adversity. What Sennett calls the process of delayering of corporations,[51] that is, getting rid of layers of a certain aspect of production and outsourcing it, has deep analogies with the realm of sexual-romantic relationships where self-entrepreneurship (figuring out on one's own how to behave smartly in a relationship, how to catch the man, how to "close the deal") is central in order to enter a relationship. Polyamory, for example, is a form of such entrepreneurial strategy, outsourcing to others one's different "selves" and "needs," a state of affairs endorsed by popular sexual therapist Esther Perel, who explains "infidelity" as the manifestation of an unexpressed self, outsourced to someone else other than to one's regular companion.[52] Because actors rely mostly on their entrepreneurial will to find a partner—assessing costs and risks, making relatively safe investments, securing one's worth, multiplying one's assets in entertaining several relationships—trust becomes difficult to come by.

This is consistent with Jennifer Silva's study of the young working class trying to enter adulthood. Faced with increasingly uncertain work prospects, young people's entry into traditional markers of adulthood such as marriage has become disorganized:

> As over a decade of scholarship has revealed, traditional markers of adulthood—leaving home, completing school, establishing financial independence, marrying, and having children—have become increasingly delayed, disorderly, reversible, or even forgone in the latter half of the twentieth century.[53]

Silva defines working-class lives of young adults as existing in a state of chaos, uncertainty, and insecurity. Although Silva does not indicate the ways in which her findings can be extended to other social classes, we may suggest this disorganization is present in the lives of most social classes, albeit in different degrees and shapes.

Trust and Uncertainty

While in the economic realm the contract created trust;[54] in the realm of intimate relationships it has undermined it. Economist Frank Knight has famously made a distinction between risk and uncertainty.[55] For Knight, risk is calculable; uncertainty is not.[56] Risks, for example, can be assessed statistically. Uncertainty, on the other hand, deals with what is fundamentally unknowable. The economic realm has created tools and instruments, such as derivatives, to reduce risk. To buy a derivative is to buy against market risk and uncertainty. But either romantic or sexual exchange, or both, has created emotional derivatives and demand the emotional attitude of the entrepreneur coping with uncertainty without insurance or financial tools to guarantee stability. In the face of emotional uncertainty, a number of emotional and economic strategies are possible: investing without certainty of returns, withdrawing the investment quickly when the returns seem uncertain, exiting when the demands are too high, developing insurance strategies in the form of defense mechanisms to protect oneself by being emotionally vigilant to the possibility of loss. All strategies point to a fundamental difficulty in building a social dynamic of trust.

In the aforementioned study of capitalism, Sennett distinguishes between formal and informal trust:

> Formal trust means one party entering into a contract, believing the other party will honor its terms. Informal trust is a matter of knowing on whom you can rely, especially when a group is under pressure: who will go to pieces, who will rise to the occasion.[57]

The old, pre-modern courtship system was able to produce both formal and informal trust, because the cost of defaulting on an engagement could be high (it was a blow to one's reputation) and because it engaged one's social networks as well. These social networks served as a sort of guarantee. David Haas and Forrest Deseran further define trust, based on Blau, as "a belief on the part of one person that another will fulfill his or her obligations and generally 'pull his (or her) weight' in their relationship to one another."[58] But trust as the belief one will fulfill his obligation has become seriously strained because uncertainty creates an emotional prisoner's dilemma: given the general desire of each to protect their sense of self-worth, given the sense of vulnerability in exposing oneself, trust that another will cooperate (that is, respond) can be given only if one *believes* the other will reciprocate. As Haas and Deseran further argue: "Trust is built up incrementally through a series of gradually increasing investments in the relationship, a series in which the partners can demonstrate their trustworthiness to each other."[59] Rational choice models of trust tend to assume that trust generally develops from iterative reciprocation: one person trusts and the other person's trust follows.[60] "Like Bayesian updating, each positive act increases the perceived probability of the other's continued trustworthiness and, over repeated interactions, additional positive information has less impact."[61] Incremental and iterative trust is likely to be considerably hampered by the difficulty in assessing other people's behavior and by the confusion or ambivalence that inhere in entering relationships because of the fear of the other's exit, which leads to strategies of self-defensiveness and self-protection. Indeed, Alvin Gouldner argues that social exchanges are possible because actors orient their action toward a general norm of reciprocity,[62] and expect others to reciprocate what they give. But in sexual exchanges where casualness prevails, the expectation of reciprocity is considerably undermined, precisely because the norm of freedom makes it difficult to establish whether, how much, and how one should reciprocate.

The freedom to exit the relationship at any point renders the future into a problem. Because the capacity to imagine the future and trust are closely intertwined, it becomes more difficult to generate trust. Studies show that trust increases considerably when in a prisoner's dilemma game people are expected to cooperate *after* the game.[63] In other words, the expectations about the future increase the tendency to cooperate and trust. Moreover, studies suggest that trust is not a rational game but rather demands that at least one of two players takes a risk.[64] In an influential paper, management theorists Roger Mayer, James Davis, and F. David Schoorman defined trust as the "willingness to be vulnerable to another," which suggests that trust best arises when the self is willing to be vulnerable.[65] If trust is defined by risk-taking, then the need to preserve self-worth makes the self more acutely aware of its vulnerability and thus less likely to take risks.[66] As Diego Gambetta puts it crisply, trust is the willingness to be vulnerable to loss, rather than the outcome of a rational process of deliberation of assessing future returns.[67] However, given the hegemonic importance of autonomy to frame selfhood, vulnerability can be interpreted as neediness, largely proscribed in contemporary emotional grammar.

Historically, the question of who took a risk was culturally scripted.[68] In pre-modern courtship, it was the man who played the cultural role of taking the risk, thus settling from the outset the question of who would make himself or herself emotionally vulnerable, which in turn enabled the start of a process of incremental trust building (that risk came with the prerogative of initiating). To be sure, taking an emotional risk was part and parcel of patriarchy, a prerogative that derived directly from men's power. With the disappearance of the ritualized courtship system organized in and by patriarchy, the question of who takes a risk is up for grabs and negotiated ad hoc rather than culturally scripted. Trust, according to Niklas Luhmann, has the main function of reducing social complexity.[69] That is, without trust, social life would become, in his words, "chaos and paralyzing fear"[70] and trust in that sense helps build predictable, orderly, and therefore less complex relationships. In contrast, contemporary relationships are disorganized and pervaded by fear, precisely because of the collapse of mechanisms for trust-building.

The lack or decrease of trust explains the demise of two cultural features of love: narrativity and idealization. Trust enables narrativity, the capacity to organize one's feelings and one's relationships into a plausible story line because it engages the future in one's feelings and actions. Lack of trust truncates narratives in blocking the plausibility of the next sequence and thus of the future. In a striking similar vein, Richard Sennett has documented a fundamental change in the structure of narratives in the workplace. After studying people who work in corporations, Sennett claims that members of older cohorts were more strategic and more focused while younger groups had more amorphous goals because their thinking was more short-term, present-oriented, "evoking possibility rather than progression."[71] The difficulty in involving the future in a plausible way resonates with changes from the idea of "career" to the idea of a succession of working "projects." While careers were defined as specific paths in which individuals needed to learn a definite set of skills in order to perform efficiently and climb the organizational ladder, projects are defined as unstructured arrays of paths, objectives, and risk-filled enterprises that demand individuals be flexible, autonomous, and creative.[72] Modern romantic-sexual pathways follow, as we have seen, the same structure: they become a series of "projects," tentative experiences, with no clear telos or built-in mechanism to move incrementally from one stage to another. This is why romantic stories increasingly have an ad hoc character.[73] They evolve without a conscious, purpose-oriented, or declared decision.[74]

Richard is a sixty-two-year-old American academic in a relationship for the last twenty-six years with a writer. He recounts his encounter with the man who became his lifelong partner.

> I was sleeping with lots of people at the time. I had four to five relationships going on at the same time. I slept with him too, and somehow we decided to take a trip. We crossed America; we didn't fight once during that trip. You know you can see who people are when you travel. We didn't fight and at the end of the trip I told myself: "Uhmmm...that could be it." It felt easy and comfortable. We just stayed on. It's been twenty-six years.

This gay man lived in a situation of sexual abundance and thus was more likely to view his partners as interchangeable. It was an actual shared experience that made him slide into a relationship rather than a conscious decision provoked by a clear emotion. He entered a relationship in a pragmatic way, through the capacity of the relationship to "flow," rather than through a conscious assessment of his own and his boyfriend's feelings. It is not scripted acts of willful directedness that move relationships "forward," but rather a non-narrative "flow" where sexual actors orient themselves pragmatically through various moments of well-being. This is in contrast with the narrative frame of love at first sight where sexual desire served as a peg to generate a clear temporal projection in the future and tightly knit emotional narrative.

A second significant impact of the lack of trust is to be found in the fact it hampers idealization, which was intrinsic to traditional ideals of romantic love. This is because idealizing another may be perceived as a threat to one's value, when one's self-value toward another is not secured and established. Therefore, whereas authors Sandra Murray, John Holmes, and Dale Griffin argue that "a sense of relationship security and well-being does indeed appear to necessitate a certain degree of illusion."[75] I would argue that it is the other way around: the capacity to have illusions depends on how secure a relationship feels, or at least it depends on the possibility of not being troubled by uncertainty and by the capacity to trust another. Forming "positive illusions" is crucial to the formation and maintenance of relationships, because such illusions have the effect of weathering out conflict, disappointment, lack of self-confidence, and defensive strategies of the self. Lack of trust, in contrast, is fed by what we may call "negative illusions," or the expectation that a relationship may end.

*

Falling in love, courting, choosing a mate, living with a mate have all been profoundly transformed by the institutionalization of freedom. Such freedom has even undermined the contractual freedom in which marriage and intimacy had been organized during the formation of modernity. This chapter has shown that the contract metaphor is inadequate to account for contemporary sexual and emotional freedom for a number of reasons: (1) It hides the fact that women and men enter sexual contracts in unequal ways; men are more emotionally detached and women are more vulnerable when they aim to transform such relationships into emotional relationships. (2) Emotions and sexual attraction are the sole legitimate basis of sexual bonds, and cannot properly be contractualized. (3) Sexual-emotional contracts can be revised in a unilateral way by one of the participants at any moment. (4) Entry in a contract can be obstructed by the need to maintain self-worth. (5) Emotional-sexual contracts can be exited without any (or little) penalty, thus making breakup a plausible and permanent threat to self-worth. (6) Because much of the content of intimate relationships cannot be contractualized, these relationships are entered and monitored with an expectation of their end, thus making actors adopt strategies of risk calculation and risk avoidance, thus leading to preemptive exit.

Richard Sennett has found that temporary workers, who may at first enjoy their nomadic character, quickly get tired and long for job security more than anything else. "They want someone to want them permanently; participating in a social structure comes to matter more than personal mobility."[76] Wanting to be wanted permanently and to participate in a social structure indeed becomes a longing of a society saturated with the freedom to move and exit. In such a society only the entrepreneur who knows how to exploit uncertainty, that is, what cannot be known in advance because it cannot be reduced to metrics, is the one who can use and profit from the market.[77] In economic life, risk-takers who face uncertainty are more likely to be the winners. The self-entrepreneurs of romantic life who succeed are either those who face little uncertainty (because they have numerous social and economic assets) or those who know to overcome their aversion to loss and uncertainty.

6

Divorce as a Negative Relationship

"No" is the most powerful word that you have in your vocabulary.
—Octavia Spencer[1]

Sa vulnerabilite à elle, personne ne s'en souciait jamais. Emilie remercie la thérapie, qui lui a appris à fermer sa porte, de temps à autre, c'est grace à ça qu'elle est encore dans la course (…) [E]lle n'a pas à se justifier, et encore moins à se culpabiliser.
—Virginie Despentes[2]

Her vulnerability, nobody cared about it. Emilie thanks therapy, which taught her how to close her door, from time to time, it is thanks to therapy that she remained in the race, (…) She does not have to justify herself, and even less to feel guilty.
—Author's Translation

In his *Relational Concepts in Psychoanalysis*, famous psychoanalyst Stephen Mitchell refers to Penelope's Loom to describe the activity of the psyche.

> Like Penelope in the seeming purposiveness of her daytime labors, we experience our daily lives as directional and linear; we are trying to get somewhere, to do things, to define ourselves in some fashion. Yet, like Penelope in her nighttime sabotage, we unconsciously counterbalance our efforts, complicate our intended goals, seek out and construct the very constraints and obstacles we struggle against.[3]

Mitchell's metaphor is both powerful and wrong, in at least two important respects. For one, Penelope *knows* exactly what she is doing when she "sabotages" her daily loom: she undoes it in order to delay her suitors because she is waiting for Odysseus's return and keeps the suitors at bay by claiming she cannot remarry until she has finished weaving a shroud for Odysseus's father, Laertes. To unravel her cloth by night is a conscious and cunning act:

she is protecting her loyalty to Odysseus and her autonomy against insistent suitors. Mitchell thus denies that we may be fully aware of the unraveling of the clothes we weave, that we may put others at bay consciously, through an act of full volition. Second, Mitchell presumes that we have "goals by day" that come undone in the night of our consciousness, thus making our psyche the only agent responsible for the unknitting of the clothes we knit, ignoring the social order's role in our shivering in the cold; unclad.

Mitchell's position is commonly held among psychologists who are by vocation and by profession oblivious to the institutional dual structure of modern selves—caught between the capitalist imperative to achieve autonomy and the romantic fantasy of durable and monogamous attachment. We may, in fact, purposefully and consciously undo our loom, and that purposiveness may be the effect of social forces we neither know nor control. While the previous chapters examined the non-formation of bonds through various mechanisms as frame confusion, ontological uncertainty, or lack of trust, in this chapter I examine the far more conscious and reflexive process of unloving in established relationships.

One of the most distinctive marks of twentieth-century modernity has been the transformation of the family through divorce whose possibility became a permanent potentiality of modern marriage. Divorce is a particularly interesting sociological phenomenon because it affects the central institution to have passed from the pre-modern to the modern world, namely the family. This institution ensures biological reproduction, channels sexuality, is crucial to social reproduction and social mobility, and helps achieve the accumulation and transfer of wealth. Divorce—as an act of non-choice that affects the crucial social institution of marriage—contains the key social and cultural forces of modernity analyzed throughout: the shift from reproductive to recreational sexuality; the transformation of economic patterns of wealth accumulation, away from the family to the consumer sphere; the role of consumer culture in constituting the self; the dissolution of bonds formed by ascription and their replacement by contractual forms based on choice. Divorce is the most salient and public category of non-choice, the most institutionalized form of unloving and it is, like other forms of non-choice, a direct effect of the social forces analyzed throughout the book.

At first blush, the negative relationship characterized by the quick and relatively effortless withdrawal (or its constant possibility) described in earlier chapters seems very different from divorce as the arduous and highly institutionalized undoing of a formal commitment. The unloving involved in divorce looks like a slow unweaving or a tear in a fabric while the former form of unloving looks like the incapacity or unwillingness to use any thread at all or to weave any cloth.

Divorce is an active choice to withdraw from an institutionalized relation and in that sense differs drastically from the "vaporous" forms of non-choice I have described in chapters 3, 4, and 5. Divorce (or separation) is almost always a conscious, protracted decision while non-choices described earlier often seem to occur because actors do not have clear wills and goal-directed desires. Divorce rarely takes the form of an abrupt breakup without justification (of the kind discussed in chapter 5): rather, it invokes reasons and occurs in a context that is both institutionalized and routinized. It involves legal institutions, incurs penalties, and is intensely argued over. In general, it implicates the material and legal world in ways that other forms of non-choice do not. However, while divorce and casual sexuality are at opposite ends of a spectrum of forms of withdrawal, I nonetheless claim in this final chapter that many of the forces that make people withdraw quickly are also present in the conscious and effortful act of non-choice known as divorce (or separation). This does not mean that the two acts of withdrawal are equivalent or even similar. Quick and penalty-free breakups and well-thought-out and costly withdrawals are different psychological events—one takes place in a context where rules of interaction are hazy while the other takes place in a highly institutionalized setting—but both are responses to the same tectonic changes that courtship, intimacy, sexuality, the family, and marriage have undergone. In that sense, we may say that the process of *forming* social bonds is subject to the same sociological pressure as *maintaining* them. Frame confusion, devaluation, defensive autonomy, threats to self-worth, and lack of trust are all present in the process of unloving whose manifestation and culmination is divorce.

The End of Love

Modern marriage is intimately related to romantic love as an emotional ideal (in 2013 a staggering 84 percent of gay people who had sought the formal bonds of marriage declared they did so for love).[4] The emotional ideal of love was formulated in "hot symbols" and tightly knit narrative structures that provided threads and lines to shape one's biography.[5] As Lauren Berlant has claimed:

[E]ven though the shapes desire takes can be infinite, one plot dominates scenes of proper fantasy and expectation. It is a plot in which the patterns of infantile desire develop into a love plot that will be sutured by the institutions of intimacy and the fantasy of familial continuity that links historical pasts to futures through kinship chains worked out in smooth ongoing relations. In the U.S., this plot has been legally and aesthetically privileged, although it has been widely adapted: and as a dream of what life should provide the desire for conventional love remains fairly strong across many fields of social difference.[6]

This fiction is an emotional fantasy, that is, a fantasy about the presence and permanence of specific emotions, about their mode of expression, about their intensity and durability, and about their content. Fantasy is constitutive of modern love and marriage, and stitches together emotions and the practices of production and reproduction of daily life. Unloving is a cognitive and emotional process in which this stitching together does not occur anymore, so that emotions of love and the reproduction of daily life no longer overlap. How does that unstitching occur? What must happen for the emotional script of the romantic fantasy to be disrupted and for new emotions to intrude in the process of maintaining bonds in daily life? In other words, what I call "unstitching" is the process by which a specific emotional experience and fantasy comes undone through the intrusion of events and facts that put into question and undermine the meaning of the relationship—real or imagined—one is engaged in. This unstitching occurs through an experience that seems to have the force of "reality," whether it is the "reality" of another person's personality, of an act of betrayal, or of irreconcilable differences. As I now show, what partners experience as the overwhelming flaws of an emotional bond contains economic, cultural, and social processes simmering below the surface of daily life. These processes include the transformation of sexuality into an autonomous ontological plane of reality; the role of the consumer sphere in shaping selfhood and identity; the performative defense of self-worth and autonomy; the fact that modes of evaluation have intensified and easily morph into devaluation accentuated by the fact that actors have developed clear emotional scripts about which emotions should be present in an interaction and how they should be expressed; all of the processes documented in this book exercise hidden and powerful pressures on established relationships. Unloving is the process by which actors unknowingly struggle with these pressures whose nature is at once normative, social, and economic.

Divorce and Women's Position in the Emotional Field

Sociologists have inquired about divorce as a discrete event—a termination of marriage—rather than as an emotional process of unloving (in which case divorces or separations are similar events). The main question that has interested sociologists is who divorces, why, and with what effects?[7] Standard causes for divorce include unemployment, alcoholism, financial difficulties, birth of children, unequal housework, infidelity, and women's entry in the workforce, with scholars stressing the overwhelming importance of women's greater employment rates and men's higher employment instability as contributing factors for the increase of the incidence of divorce.[8]

When divorce is approached as a culturally variable event, two striking facts appear: In the 1940s cited reasons for divorce were likely to be "objective," as alcoholism or neglect. From the 1970s onward, the reasons for divorce became "more abstract and affective,"[9] emotional and subjective: "growing apart," "becoming more distant," and "feeling unloved" became major grounds for divorce.[10] The 2014 American Relationships Survey, sponsored by Austin Institute for the Study of Culture and Family, found the following reasons for divorce invoked by the respondents: infidelity (37 percent), spouse unresponsive to needs (32 percent), growing tired of making a poor match work (30 percent), spouse's immaturity (30 percent), emotional abuse (29 percent), different financial priorities (24 percent), and alcohol (23 percent). The first five reasons are all emotional ones, thus suggesting the overwhelming importance of emotional processes inside marriage and as grounds for divorce.

To say it differently, in the words of sociologist Steven Ruggles: "[M]arriages in the past tended to be governed more by social norms and less by rational calculation to maximize individual happiness."[11] Indeed,

> the most common reasons for marital breakdown and divorce cited by men and women were a gradual growing apart and loss of closeness, not feeling loved and appreciated by one's spouse, sexual intimacy problems, and serious differences in lifestyle or values. Less frequently cited as reasons contributing to divorce were conflicts regarding children, substance abuse problems, and violence in the marriage.[12]

In another study of Australian divorce, the authors state that "71 per cent of all remaining men and women perceived affective issues as the main reason for marriage breakdown"—before abusive relationships (which includes violence or alcohol abuse) and external pressures (such as financial ones in Ilene Wolcott and Jody Hughes's work).[13] Clearly in the mid-1980s sexual and emotional problems were perceived as more acceptable or more compelling reasons for divorce than in previous decades. Emotions have become the centerpiece of marriage and of divorce, the very "thing" that makes or breaks relationships.

The second finding that must be put alongside this one is also striking: in the United States, Europe, and Australia, women are the main initiators of divorce.[14] This is consistent with the finding that women's employment increases chances of divorce. As Andrew Cherlin claims, "[A]lmost every well-known scholar who has addressed this topic [of divorce] in the twentieth-century has cited the importance of the increase in the employment of women."[15] The relative increase of women's economic power seems to be somehow connected to the fact that they initiate divorce for, more often than not, emotional reasons. In other words, access to economic independence enables emotions to become central. Michael Rosenfeld drives the point: "One paradox of gender, marriage, and the life course, is that young single women appear to desire marriage and commitment more than men do, yet married women appear to be less satisfied by their marital experiences than married men are."[16] Even when women stand to lose economically more than men in divorcing (despite the fact that women have more remunerated work than ever before, divorce makes a majority of them economically more vulnerable)[17] and even when they are less likely to have alternative opportunities—they are less likely to remarry—they are nonetheless more likely to initiate divorce, thus suggesting that opportunity theories explain divorce only to the extent that economic independence foregrounds specific emotions, which are in turn experienced as the reasons for divorce.

The findings evoked earlier—women are more likely to want commitment, to initiate divorce and to do so for emotional reasons—suggest that in the same way women *enter* sexual contracts differently from men, they also experience marriage and initiate divorce in a different way, precisely by using, invoking, and managing their emotionality. The paradox evoked by Michael Rosenfeld above is easily overcome if we suggest that women engage more willingly in an emotional terrain than men when entering relationships and break relationships more easily precisely in the same way, by raising emotional claims.[18]

Being fully aware that I will account only for a portion of the complex spectrum of reasons why marriages (or shared lives) end, we may say that women approach marriage on the basis of what we may call an emotional ontology, of what they perceive as a realm of "real" emotions, "real" emotional needs, and emotional norms prescribing how emotions should be felt, expressed, and exchanged. In the same way that men and women have different ways of approaching the sexual field, they also have different positions in and ways of approaching the emotional field. In the same way that sexuality has been constructed as a terrain for playing out masculine status, emotions and their management have played a crucial role in enacting feminine identity. If men are oriented to the accumulation of sexual capital, it is emotions that serve women as strategic ways to orient their actions and to display their social competence. This is true when they enter relationships, when they are inside a stable bond, and when they choose to end a relationship. Thus, while popular and even scientific literature has increasingly argued that men are from Mars and women from Venus, that men are rational problem-solvers while women are emotional and oriented to relationships, and going as far as explaining such differences by the structure of their brains,[19] new neuroscientific work converges with sociologists' claims that there is no or little "hard-wired" difference with regard to "an emotional brain." Women's self-definition as managers of the emotional realm has more to do with social roles and prescriptions than with biology. Indeed, women's position in the emotional field is related to their economic and social position as caretakers (of children, and of other men and women), a position that in turn makes them attuned to the management of relationships.[20]

Women have played a key role in redefining the vocation of marriage, from an economic to an emotional one,[21] and women have been prime managers of emotions in an institution increasingly defined as a purely emotional organization, held together by the emotions of its members and the achievement of the ideal of intimacy. Precisely because it became more emotional, marriage also became more uncertain, that is, less based on ascriptive clear gender roles distributed along the private/public distinction[22] and more based on the individual expression of emotions. The shift of marriage to an emotional institution in turn places women and men in different positions vis-à-vis such an emotional institution. In a study of a large statistically representative sample of 1,003 young adults, single and married, 80 percent of the women in the sample stated that they value more a husband's capacity to express his feelings deeply than his capacity to simply provide.[23] Emotional intimacy is for most women the chief goal and legitimating criterion of marriage. As such, emotional intimacy has been a force of dis-institutionalization, making marriage more likely to follow psychology than sociology, individual temperament rather than roles and norms. This is aptly summarized by sociologist of marriage Andrew Cherlin: "[P]ersonal choice and self-development loom large in people's construction of their marital careers."[24] Intimacy depends on the voluntary disclosure and expression of emotions of two people and thus seems to make marriage follow the curves and sinews of individual temperament. It is precisely for that reason that the discourse of therapy became crucial to the formation and monitoring of intimate bonds, as a technique to express and to manage emotions.

The Narrative Structure of Departing

Contrary to the forms of unloving described earlier in this book, divorce is a protracted decision that mobilizes a battery of justifications in order to make such a decision intelligible to the self and to one's environment. Because it takes the form of a conscious decision, it has a narrative structure, actors trying to explain, usually retrospectively, their own or another's decision. Unloving occurs through multiple events that are in turn perceived and connected together through narratives and reasons, what Luc Boltanski and Laurent Thevenot call "regimes of justification,"[25] invoking at once personal motives for doing or feeling something as well as norms that have a generalizable character. These regimes of justification contain what Michael Stoker calls "out of explanations" (i.e., motives of action) and "for the sake of" explanation (explaining an action by referring to the goal one wants to achieve).[26]

In stark contrast with the narrative of falling in love, the least common narrative of unloving is one of epiphany, of a revelation, or an understanding in which someone grasps and sees a new aspect of reality. Bertrand Russell provides an apt example, in reference to his first wife, Alyssa ("Alys") Pearsall Smith: "I went out bicycling one afternoon, and suddenly, as I was riding along a country road, I realized that I no longer loved Alys. I had had no idea until this moment that my love for her was lessening."[27] They had married in 1911 and were divorced in 1921 and Russell describes unloving as a sudden revelation. To take another example from my own sample, Daniel is a sixty-four-year-old Israeli literary critic who recalls:

> I remember crisply how [my decision to leave her] started. I was washing the dishes, and she came and said something, I don't remember what. At that moment, for the first time, I told myself, while washing the dishes: "I can't do this anymore." That was the end of it. As soon as I told myself these words, I couldn't stay anymore. I couldn't take it anymore.

The narrative of revelation can also take the form of a sudden event, as when falling in love with someone else or understanding something new about one's partner. Some respondents speak of "turning points," moments where something changes in their perception of their partner. The theme of (an emotional) "turning point" provoked by visible or invisible events has been central to many modern literary and cinematic works. For example, *Force Majeure*, the 2014 film directed by Swedish movie maker Ruben Ostlund, exposes the rift between a husband and wife, when after a snow avalanche the husband runs away from his wife and children to protect himself. The event marks a turning point, a new understanding by the wife of who her husband is, an understanding that creates a new rift between them (although the family ultimately remains intact).

The second form of narrative is one of accumulation: small events and daily conflicts tear progressively the fabric of intimacy. Avishai Margalit speaks of "erosion," a metaphor appropriate in the case where the nitty-gritty stuff of daily life corrodes the stitches holding together the fabric of daily life. Small events accumulate until what respondents describe as a point of no return, when they "can't anymore." In this narrative, people amass facts, actions, words, or gestures as evidence that "something is not working." Claire Bloom, the famous actress who was married to the writer Philip Roth, recounts as follows the announcement that he wanted a divorce:

"Why are you so angry with me?" I tried to be calm.

Philip went on to tell me, hardly pausing for breath, for two hours: My voice was so soft it made him feel alienated and I deliberately spoke to him that way. I behaved oddly in restaurants, looking at my watch and humming to myself. I panicked in the face of his illnesses and had no idea how to deal with them. When we checked into hospital for open-heart surgery I was unable to find a nurse, and he had to run up and down the corridor looking for one.[...]I made him attend the opera, which he detested.[...] And on, and on, and on.[28]

Here the complaint takes the form of repeated ways of being and behaving that annoy, irritate, or conflict with one's own.

This narrative takes the form of the "straw that broke the camel's back" or uses metaphors as the "drop of water that made the jug overflow" or "staying until you can't bear it anymore." It posits the self as coping with daily disagreements and conflicts whose accumulation becomes intolerable or which exceed in quantity the "good" aspects of a relationship. This narrative is often invoked when there are frequent disagreements or fights. This narrative is busy producing "evidence" that something was flawed either in the relationship, or in the partner, or in both.

In the third and perhaps most interesting narrative, some events, actions, or words function as "micro-traumatic" events, that is, they mark a rupture—small or large—with one's moral assumptions, and the subject retrospectively refers to this rupture as an event from which she or he cannot heal or recover. These traumatic events are experienced as breaches of trust, sexual or emotional, and mark wounds defined by the subject as irreparable, that cannot be healed or undone. They are often experienced as a deep assault on the self's worth and sense of dignity. Here is a first example from Irene, forty-five, a French teacher:

> I think that maybe the first time I stopped loving him, or loved him less at any rate, was when he was not able to take me to the emergency room when I felt very sick, because he would not cancel an appointment with an important client. During the years after, I found it very hard to forget. Whenever he wouldn't be with me at something that mattered to me, I felt abandoned and betrayed. I kept thinking of that moment, how lonely I felt in that hospital because my husband couldn't cancel an appointment with a client. So in hindsight, I was never able to forgive him. It is very strange to think that for twelve years—no, less, because it happened four years after we got married, so for eight years I lived with that. I never told him how hurt I was. I don't think he ever knew or guessed. But I never forgave him. I could never trust him in the same way again.

In this example, a single event marks a breach of trust never repaired. A micro-trauma serves as an interpretative frame for subsequent events. Here is Rebecca, an American-born forty-seven-year-old woman living in Israel:

> He was fifteen years older than me, and he had three children from two previous marriages. Four years into our relationship, I started wanting to have a child. But he didn't. He felt burned out, he had his own children and didn't want any more. He didn't mind me having a child on my own with a sperm bank or something like that, but he couldn't be again a full-time father, or take care of him. I had the child with the sperm bank, and maybe that's how fate avenges us; he started feeling a strong bond to him

[after the baby was born]. But I could not forgive him for not wanting from the start to do this with me, for not wanting our child, for letting me go to the sperm bank. I felt betrayed about something that really mattered to me. Even though in the end he was willing to act as a father to him, I could not forgive him for not wanting my child from the start.

In both stories, the trauma narrative is activated from within a core aspect of the self that feels "betrayed," "disappointed," or in some cases "assaulted."

The three forms of narratives—revelation, accumulation, trauma—constitute three emotional narrative structures through which actors retrospectively reconstruct and explain the process of disentangling themselves from an emotional bond in which they were engaged. The three narratives of decision-making are retrospective accounts of the ways in which the self disengaged from a relationship and for the reasons why and the ways in which the unconditional belonging that characterizes a "thick relationship" erodes, dissolves, and ends.[29] As I show now, these emotional narratives give a form to the social forces described in this book.

It should be clear, however, that the typology of divorce narratives provided does not exhaust the range of causes of divorce. Nor does it deny the fact that divorces are usually far more acrimonious and emotionally intense than breakups. Rather, I intend here to simply claim there is a continuity between the cultural forces at work at the beginning of relationships and those that insinuate themselves in established and in institutionalized relationships. The point then is that the formation and maintenance of intimate bonds are part of a general social ecosystem that burdens individuals and forces them to manage single-handedly several social constraints. These constraints are *sexuality as an autonomous field of action*; *(d)(e)valuation* as an ongoing activity, accentuated by the refinement of the consumer and psychological self; unconscious *goal conflict* between autonomy and dependence, and *threats to self-worth*. All of these are key motifs in the process of withdrawing from one's attachment and commitment, that is, of unloving.

Sexuality: The Great Separation

According to divorce statistics, sexuality is one of the chief causes of divorce, whether it is caused by infidelity[30] or by the fact that people stop having sex.

Judith Stacey's classic study of marriage suggests that the modern family provides two things at once: enduring care on the one hand and sexual desire on the other. Calling modern marriage a "one-size-fits-all" institution, she analyzes the tensions to which the monogamous and companionate marriage leads.[31] For Stacey, we have essentially sacrificed the endurance that domesticity needs for sexual desire. This analysis, however, does not examine the fine-grained emotional dynamic through which sexuality interferes and conflicts with domestic life.

As has been discussed in previous chapters, sexuality has become at once autonomous from the emotional realm and the site where the ontology of emotions is manifest, where the nature and intensity of intimate bonds is expressed. In becoming an autonomous plane of action, the repository of one's deepest and truest emotions, the site of pleasure, intimacy, and well-being, the sexual body has changed the perceived legitimacy of relationships that must conform to models of relatively continuous sexual interactions and pleasure.

Aurelie is a forty-five-year-old divorced French woman. She was married for twelve years:

INTERVIEWER: Is there a moment or an event where you understood you were not going to stay together anymore?

AURELIE: I think it happened around the time I was doing so many IVFs. My body became doctor's property. I think at this point he stopped seeing me as having a sexual body. Nor could I see my body as a sexual body. I badly wanted to have a child. We stopped having sex because it was the doctors who took possession of my body; he could not get it up when he saw me like that. It went on for two to three years. We spoke about why we weren't having sex anymore. He just couldn't do it after he saw my body like that. A doctor's property full of chemicals and needles. We stopped having sex for two years and I felt so hurt that we started having fights, which we never had before, and then we split. At that point it seemed the natural thing to do. Today I don't know why we did it. I mean, no, I know, I felt humiliated by the fact he did not desire me anymore. And once the sex stopped, it's like there was no *raison d'etre* to the relationship. But today, I think I look at things differently.

INTERVIEWER: How so?

AURELIE: Today I think people have all kinds of arrangements. Basically I even think that if you're going to live in the long term with someone, you need to have some arrangement. So maybe I shouldn't have been so upset by the fact he didn't desire me anymore.

In this story, once the body is medicalized, it stops being sexualized, and once it stops being sexualized, desire stops, which in turn has an effect on the woman's self-worth because she didn't feel desirable anymore (a reaction she can dwell on and revise later).[32] Indeed, if sexuality has become a fundamental plane for the experience of self-identity, uncertainty about sexual desirability seems to challenge the entire relationship because it challenges one's self-worth in it. This is because, as discussed in chapters 3 and 4, sexualization institutionalizes the separation of emotions and body and autonomizes the latter, thus splintering selfhood and creating two different, independent, and sometimes even competing forms of self-worth. This is true of relationships at their beginning but more surprisingly, this is also true when such relationships are established. Paula, a sixty-one-year-old French woman, recently separated from her husband of thirty-five years, and describes their recent separation as follows:

> It started, I think, when he took a subscription to the gym, a few years ago, maybe six or seven years ago? He started going to the gym. And also he started watching what he ate. He didn't go on a diet, but he watched what he ate. So he lost weight. He got thinner. And you know, it's amazing, from the moment he lost weight, his personality changed. He behaved, uuhmm— how shall I put it—more cocky, more sure of himself, I began to feel old and unattractive. He made me feel old and unattractive. I am two years older than him but had never felt my age before with him. After that, maybe one year later, he had his first affair. Since then he has had plenty of affairs, all with young women. It's like he became a teenager again. He says he never stopped loving me, but still he could not help having all these affairs. It was stronger than him. So I got fed up and left. We are now divorced.

In this story, the body of this married man undergoes a transformation: it becomes sexualized in virtue of becoming thinner and thus becomes an independent agent. The body acquires a new sexual agency, and subsequently searches for new sexual objects, young women—in conformity with the findings and claims of chapter 4. His bodily transformation generates a new form of subjectivity that affects his marriage, that is, it affects how his wife perceives him and herself, how he perceives himself, how she perceives him perceiving her, which in turn transforms the balance of sexual power between them. The newly sexualized body acts as if it had a will of its own and generates emotional withdrawal. In other words, as in the previous story with Aurelie, the body acts as an autonomous entity. Aurelie's body became devoid of sexuality and the body of Paula's husband acquired sexuality, in both cases as if outside the subject's volition and control. Their bodies act autonomously, so to speak, and in turn impact on the emotional bond.

Among the twenty-four divorced or separated people interviewed for this study, the overwhelming majority identified "stopping having sex" as either the sign or the cause of a deep change, followed by a breakup, suggesting that sexuality is a powerful way to organize the narrative of intimacy and the narrative of separation. Sexualization dissociates between personhood and the body at the beginning of relationships, but once institutionalized in an established relationship, it becomes the repository of emotions. A good sexuality reflects a good emotional bond, and vice versa, a bad sexuality is interpreted as a sign of poor emotional bonds. People grasp the reality of their relations and emotions through the reality of their sexuality and sexual desire. For example, the best-selling novel *Here I Am* by Jonathan Safran Foer recounts in minute psychological details the progressive process of unloving and its realization by the main protagonists. As told by the narrator, sexual desire plays a crucial role in the unweaving of the clothes the couple were weaving together. "[W]ith Julia's inability to express urgency, Jacob became even less sure that he was wanted, and more afraid of risking foolishness, which furthered the distance between Julia's hand and Jacob's body, which Jacob had no language to address."[33] Sexuality is the plane of experience where the self feels its worth (wanted or not), and where emotions gain an objective and tangible existence. Bernard, a forty-six-year-old French man who writes for TV series, explains why he separated from the woman he lived with for eleven years:

> I left my partner, D., because I couldn't give her an orgasm. I mean, she could but not with me. She could have an orgasm only by doing it to herself. I just could not make her climax. I felt really frustrated but I didn't understand how important it was to me until I met A., a woman who could climax with me. I realized how I felt guilty and inadequate with D. So I left her. I told her I just couldn't have sex with her anymore.

Bernard is here clearly referring to an ideal of sexual competence that was questioned by his companion's preference for self-pleasure. Sexual competence and sexual desirability are fundamental components of selfhood, whose absence immediately threaten the self. They are fundamental at the beginning of relationships and they continue to operate within relationships. Because bodies age, or become unresponsive to sexual excitement, or feel undesirable and sexually incompetent, sexuality can drive a wedge within the emotional bond itself, introducing an uncertainty about the nature of the self involved in the relationship.

Furthermore, the norm of monogamy has one powerful effect as it dictates that emotions and sexuality should be aligned, thus making it difficult to reconcile the frequently conflicting paths they take. Sandra, a forty-nine-year-old German academic has been married for a few years to another woman she has lived with for twenty-one years. She discusses the current crisis their marriage is facing:

> Recently she came with the claim that our sex life is not good; that it has never been good. Maybe it is true; we get along fantastically well on all levels—intellectual, spiritual, emotional—we laugh together, we understand each other but we don't have good sex. So in the last year she has decided to have a lover. She told me about it, and she looked for one, like on an Internet site, and she found one. She sleeps with her once a week, she tells me she does not need more, the other does not need more. She is happier this way. But it has been destructive. It has awakened in me all kinds of childhood demons. I pried on her private emails. That has made her furious. She felt violated. She has issues with violation. We are now in a difficult spot. We may split.

Here, as in some of the stories quoted above, sexuality—or lack of it—creates anxiety and uncertainty, making Sandra pry into her wife's privacy. Sexual outsourcing is at once a solution to a sexually unsatisfying relationship and a source of uncertainty as it puts strain on the expectation that sentiments and sexuality should be aligned. Thus the many ways in which people experience their sexual bodies as independent from their emotions creates alternative relational paths that sometimes compel them to experience conflicts and realign their emotions around their bodies.

Tara, the forty-eight-year-old Scandinavian professor of chemistry we already encountered in chapter 5, lived for many years with a man who was emotionally abusive but with whom sex was exciting. She separated from him, went through many years of loneliness and search, and finally met, in her words, a "wonderful man."

I've met the most wonderful, brilliant, verbal man. He so wants to be with me, be "serious." We talk 24/7. We challenge each other breathtakingly. I love him already, after just two weeks of acquaintance. But sexually— and I mean this in a broadened sense, not only in bed, but the full Eros aspect—I don't know. He seems to opt for absolute equality. A total inti- macy. No aggression. No tension. No distance. He wants to talk about every vibration in our interaction: "What happened there?" He's a therapist. [...] The feminist/therapeutic version of love and sex. I cringe. I asked him not to be scared of the dark, serious side of things, and he's processing this, but I fear he's been...castrating [sic]? His sexuality, his whole life he didn't dare to change. And I can't make my eroticism go back to what I now think tastes like baby-gruel as opposed to juicy grilled meat. There we stand.

This example echoes a literary topos of modernity[34] where sexuality becomes autonomous from other realms of action, valued for its own sake as a way for the self to "uncivilize" itself. For Tara, a wonderful relationship devoid of an exciting sexuality lacks some fundamental quality. Despite the fact this woman's boyfriend has "everything"—he's verbal, expressive, talkative, and caring—he is unfavorably evaluated by comparison to a past sexual experi- ence, more exciting and more intense. "Undomesticated" or raw sexuality is here an absolute reference point in her experience, because it reveals (and constitutes) the deepest and truest layer of her self, something she eventu- ally could not give up as she eventually separated from this "wonderful man," precisely for that reason (this was communicated to me by email). Whether she was having a relationship with an abusive man or a wonderful one, sexuality in both cases was autonomous and independent from the emotional realm; it was good with an abusive relationship, and unexciting with a wonderful man. Again, the body has an ontological status distinct from selfhood and from the emotional relationship. The autonomization of sexuality and the body can and does frequently conflict with emotional bonds, making emotional and sexual categories of experience compete with each other.

A second way in which sexuality initiates an emotional process of unlov- ing is due to the fact that sexual availability has considerably increased the perception of alternatives. Research conducted by Jeffry Simpson in 1987 with 120 young people showed that the perception of imagined alternatives has a significant impact on the stability of relationships; the more one has the perception of alternative relationships, the less stable the relationship is.[35] Indeed, an open sexual field almost by definition provides a mental map of alternative (and missed) sexual possibilities. Given the wide availability of either sexual bodies or more exciting sexualities, or both, and given the norm of monogamy, sexual energy geared outside the domestic unit is a looming threat over marriage. This is illustrated by Gil, a fifty-six-year-old Israeli man, who serves as the director of an NGO and has been divorced ten years prior to the interview:

GIL: My emotional divorce started long before I actually divorced. [*Silence*]
INTERVIEWER: What made you divorce? Do you mind telling me?
GIL: I think it started when I fell in love with a colleague of mine. That was a long time ago. I had been married for nine years I think. I had an affair with this woman. It was very intense. I could not keep it to myself so I told my wife. She took it surprisingly well. At first she was shocked, but she wanted to keep the marriage. Actually, she took it better than me. Because after I had this affair, I could never go back to loving my wife in the same way.
INTERVIEWER: Can you say why?
GIL: It's like I discovered a whole new world of passion I did not know existed before. I lusted [for] and desired this woman very strongly, and after that I could not stay in the marriage in the same way anymore. I loved my wife, but not in that way. Once I got to taste hot passion I couldn't go back to the lukewarm comfortable thing I had before. From there it was a steady slope downward.

In this narrative, an emotional event erupts. An alternative sexual relationship is on offer and opens up the mental and cognitive space of this man, in turn putting into question the taken-for-granted character of the emotionally low-key routine emotions of his marriage. As Adam Phillips put it: "There is always someone else who would love me more, understand me better, make me feel more sexually alive. This is the best justification we have for monogamy—and infidelity."[36] This is all the more the case that sexual actors direct their affective and sexual energy to a spectator, in public spaces and in the workplace. Sexual and affective energy is directed to anonymous others in a variety of social spaces and venues. In other words, sexual energy circulates widely and diffusely, within and outside the domestic sphere, putting bodies in a state of constant sexual availability that undermines the norm of sexual exclusivity still prevalent in close intimate bonds. The capitalist work sphere and the consumer sphere make sexuality into a spectacle and fragment it in directing it to an ongoing flow of possible onlookers and recipients, thus making such sexuality dispersed among numerous possible others. This is probably also the reason why the rate of divorce among people in their fifties has tripled in the last decade. This is not only because actors are encouraged to conceive of themselves as sexual beings at all or most ages of life but also because their sense of sexual possibility has increased. "In 1990, 1 in 10 persons who divorced was 50 or older. By 2011, according to the census's American Community Survey, more than 28 percent (more than 1 in 4) who said they divorced in the previous 12 months were 50 or older."[37]

Historian of marriage Stephanie Coontz attributes this "gray divorce revolution" to the fact that many are in second or third marriages (a fact that makes them statistically more prone to divorce) and that many are baby boomers—a generation more prone to divorce.[38] I would, however, venture the hypothesis that the rise of Internet dating sites explains this change as they make tangible the possibility of meeting alternative partners to members of an age group that traditionally had few possibilities to extend their social networks. The very possibility of relating to oneself as a sexual body after the age of fifty and having more alternatives for new sexual partners foregrounds the sexual self in an unprecedented way.

Finally, sexuality interferes with stable relationships because the capitalist work sphere has an impact on the sexual drive. Indeed, studies have showed that work-related stress diminishes sexual desire. A study commissioned by the French Institute Technologia (an Institute that works under the auspices of the Labor Ministry) suggests that stress and burnout from excessive work generate reactions of irritability and anhedonia (the difficulty in experiencing pleasure), responsible for diminished sexual desire.[39] According to this research, 70 percent of middle-rank managers claim that stress plays a negative role on their sexual life. In other words, the stress entailed by participation in ever-more demanding corporations and organizations undermines what consumer capitalism encourages: sexuality as a plane of experience that expresses the innermost core of the self and of intimate relationships. Another indirect indication that changes in the economic sphere—in the form of greater demands of performance and increased uncertainty about the future—may have an impact on sexual activity can be found in the *Relationships in America* survey:

> In their 1994 landmark study of human sexuality, Edward Laumann and colleagues reported that 1.3 percent of married men and 2.6 percent of

married women between the ages of 18 and 59 had not had sex within the past year. In contrast, twenty years later—in the *Relationships in America* survey—4.9 percent of married men and 6.5 percent of married women in the same age range report that it has been over a year since they have had sex with their spouse. Although the questions were asked in slightly different manners, it appears that there may have been an uptick in marital sexual inactivity in the past twenty years. The General Social Survey, which has consistently employed the same question since 1989 to determine sexual frequency, confirms this trend.[40]

The authors of the survey further hypothesize that "habituation" may be at fault. But habituation is hardly an explanation since habituation was no less likely to be a problem in the sexual lives of couples in previous decades than it is in the present one. I would surmise that changes in the work sphere—increased stress, longer working hours, and job uncertainty—may be responsible both for the preference for casual sex documented earlier in the book and for decreased sexual activity. Further (indirect) evidence for this can be found in other studies. The young women interviewed by Laura Hamilton and Elizabeth Armstrong reported that they engaged in casual sex because of a chronic lack of time, and because relationships require "too much time," and that they preferred investing this time in becoming full and competitive members of the market.[41] Time for these young women is viewed as a commodity, and is directed at getting ahead economically and socially, thus precisely suggesting that sexuality and time devoted to the workplace compete with each other for one's undivided attention and focus, in the context of both casual and established sexuality. Moreover, although she did not study the sexuality of married people per se, Alison Pugh's important study of middle- and working-class marriages, *The Tumbleweed Society*, confirms that job insecurity (e.g., uncertain schedules, frequent shifts from employment to unemployment, and the looming threat of losing one's job) challenges and undermines intimate bonds inside marriage.[42] In other words, different forms of work pressure (competitive markets and increasing demands of the work sphere) have a direct impact on the form and intensity of sexual activity. The upshot is that embedded in shared domestic life is the same contradiction that characterizes relationships at large: sexuality and emotions follow different routes and are splintered, yet emotions are validated only through sexuality. When sexuality diminishes, is outsourced, or is or absent it puts into question the very emotions that initiated the relationship in the first place. This contradiction is a source of uncertainty, conflict, and tension that compels partners to question and revise their emotional narrative. Unloving here is generated by the difficulty of aligning one's emotions with one's sexual body.

Consumer Objects: From Transitional to Exiting Objects

As documented in chapter 4, sexual and emotional subjects use consumer objects to shape their subjectivity, the public performance of their self and their intimacy. This world of objects and the tastes attendant on them can become a source of tension, conflict, and disagreement. Here's an example of Sunhil, aged forty-three, an English economist and researcher:

SUNHIL: After my divorce I dated a lot. Pffft. So many women. But it is very difficult to find the one. They look great at first, but then something always ends up posing a problem. There was this one woman I was crazy about; we lived together for three years. I really liked her; I was very serious about her and we almost got married. Actually it felt like we were married. But she had these weird eating habits; like no gluten, no sugar, no cabbage, no lentils, no banana, nothing basically. Trying to cook together was something. I mean, cooking was never as hellish. At first I respected her needs but then when I started asking her questions about why a certain kind of food was off limits, she would be upset. At some point, she went to a gastro because she was having reflux, and he said to her you have spent all your money on quacks, just quacks, you never got checked, never established a diagnosis, never established if you have gluten intolerance, you have diagnosed yourself. And spent countless money. I was with her at the doctor, and when he told her these things, I had this really weird creepy feeling. I suddenly stopped loving her, almost then and there. All my fights with her all came rushing to the same point.

INTERVIEWER: Why?

SUNHIL: Because it clarified to me she had no respect for science. I respect science. It clarified to me she believed in weird things. Like I lost my faith in her at that moment. It was like I could not take her seriously anymore. If she couldn't take doctors seriously, spend all that money on weird eating habits and quacks, I just couldn't respect her anymore.

This man uses a narrative of revelation (or turning point) to account for his estrangement from his former partner's consumption (of "quacks") and conscious non-consumption (of "gluten," etc.). It is her consumer taste that stops this man's love for her through a mechanism of evaluation ("her consumer tastes suggest she has no respect for science therefore I can no longer value her"). As a scientist, he views science as central to his own subjectivity. Because consumer objects and practices anchor intimacy in an objective world, differing consumer tastes breach their role of anchoring emotions in common activities. The narrator/male protagonist of Safran Foer's semi-autobiographical novel bears witness to the role objects and taste have in bringing closer or separating two people. Jacob muses about a brooch he wants to buy his wife: "Was it nice? It was risky. Did people wear brooches? Was it cornily figurative? Would it end up in the jewelry box, never to be seen again until it was bequeathed as an heirloom to one of the boy's brides so that she could put it in a jewelry box until it was one day passed down again? Was seven hundred fifty dollars an appropriate price for such a thing? It wasn't the money that concerned him, it was the risk of getting it wrong, the embarrassment of trying and failing—an extended limb is far easier to break than a bent one."[43] Here the brooch condenses the fine and subtle way in which objects contain and express relationships.

Taste plays a prevalent role in marriage not only in enabling to organize two subjectivities around a common world of objects and activities but also in being the focus of *how things are done*. In his fascinating study of couples, French sociologist Jean-Claude Kaufmann dubbed the term *agacements* or irritations.[44] In ample detail, Kaufmann documents what irritates couples in their daily lives. Inquiring about the sources of these irritations, Kaufmann finds—without properly theorizing that fact—that objects play a significant role in the production of irritations; one of his examples is the style of a table that irritated one of his interviewees' husband and made it the source of a conflict in the marriage.[45] Kaufmann is oblivious to the historical and cultural process that produces these irritations that can be understood as resulting from the consumer subjectivity that has been in the making for the last century, and especially since the second part of the twentieth century. Such subjectivity has become organized around tastes and self-expressiveness through and in objects. In other words, objects are both emotional meeting points and platforms for the engineering of emotional divergence. This is all the more the case that selves are increasingly compelled to define themselves through consumer tastes. In an article published in a blog of *Le Monde*, the author addresses the reasons why the furniture manufacturer Ikea is a source of tension and disputes between couples; this is because Ikea offers many possibilities to combine and recombine pieces of furniture. One consequence of such a large spectrum of consumer choices and combinations between them is that it encourages the formation of highly idiosyncratic tastes. As described in chapter 4, the dynamic of taste is a dynamic of subjectification: through the cultivation of tastes the self is made to experience its singularity. The more idiosyncratic the taste, the less tractable a taste is, and the more likely it is to be a source of strain. The Ikea catalog itself acknowledges this fact and tries to capitalize on it by advising to buy two sofas in order to accommodate differing tastes: "Tout est affaire de compromis. Vous aimez les canapés moelleux, il les préfère plus fermes. Avec deux canapés différents, vous pourriez bien vivre heureux pour toujours."[46] Not only choice of objects but also ways of handling and treating them entail irritations and tension.

Kaufmann speaks of "the toothpaste as a symbol," that is, the different ways in which people treat the toothpaste tube as a source of minor or major irritations (how people close it, where they put it, how they make it stand, how they extract the paste from it, etc.). In other words, commodities are an ongoing source of irritation both because subjects connect their sense of self to objects and because consumer practices are platforms where two subjects meet, interact, and forge bonds. Because commodities have become transitional objects around which people organize their emotions and relations,[47] they can also become points of repeated, daily tension in relationships, putting into question how and where people define themselves, creating a sense of "cumulative" strain at once centered on petty aspects of daily life and in the deep core of subjectivity. A sixty-year-old woman recalled one of the reasons her husband invoked for leaving her after twelve years of marriage (it was a third marriage for both): " [He said] we did not have the same activities, he liked camping and I liked museums." Thus, while the world of objects is traditionally taken for granted and sustains human action in a non-conspicuous way, consumer culture and consumer practices turn objects into active expressions of self and thus become foregrounded as "actants" that both constitute and mediate between two subjectivities and their relationships. "Actant" here is used in the sense it has in narratology, that is, as a structural component enabling the narrative to move forward (an actant is not necessarily a human and may well be an object).[48] It also has the sense given to this word by actor-network theory: as an entity—either a human, object, or idea—that has an impact on the course of action.[49] As actants, objects and modes of consumption can turn into sites of recriminations. David, a fifty-year-old Israeli attorney, said:

Yes, I think there was a moment where in fact I stopped loving her. But it was a slow process. It was a process made of many moments in which I felt we disagreed. I remember that my wife had a subscription to an expensive sports' club to which she never went. I said to her: "Cancel your subscription and buy a ticket each time you want to go. It will be cheaper." But she refused and got angry as usual, she said she wanted the subscription to have the option to go or not to go. Everything with her was about options. Now that we divorced, I understand that in fact she separated because she thought she would have all these options. But she doesn't. She is still alone with many options.

David and his wife understood consumption in different ways: she wanted to purchase a "right to use," while he wanted her to only purchase an actual use. An unused subscription became the symbol of ongoing acrimony and of their divorce. In the narrative he tells, her consumer subjectivity—wanting to have options—becomes the peg around which he hangs his unloving narrative, an actant in his unloving narrative.

The actantiality of consumer objects is all the more prevalent in intimate bonds that social actors experience their consumer self on the mode of permanent renewal, refinement, and change. In other words, consumer objects and practices make up the chief part of self-narratives, how selves perceive their change and progression, a process that, following the definition given in chapter 4, can be called a process of "refinement." Refining oneself can and does threaten both the "contract" initially agreed with someone and the perceived value of one's partner. Krista, a fifty-five-year-old German historian, related:

> I was married for thirteen years to my husband. It was a love marriage. We had two children. He was a curator, and I had a lot of interest in his work. We spoke about art, painting, architecture a lot. Then at some point, he stopped educating himself. I kept reading, learning new stuff, being interested in new stuff but he remained the same, he did not change, even now ten years after our divorce he did not change, he did not grow.

"Growing" presupposes a form of subjectivity that incessantly absorbs new objects and forms of knowledge integrated in cultural competence. But here cultural competence follows the logic of novelty and renewal that governs consumer culture. When individuals do not appropriate "refinement" or renewal in the same ways, this creates breaches in the evaluation partners

have of each other and changes the actancial character of consumer practices and objects as platforms for the encounter of two subjectivities. Once the
refinement of subjectivity through the cultivation of new tastes takes place,
withdrawal from a relationship occurs through the perception of separate
emotional and psychological worlds, when in fact these worlds are quite often
consumer worlds. Because consumer objects structure one's sense of self and
its unfolding through time, these objects can also undo the ways in which
emotions get organized. Consumer refinement acts as an agent of separateness and seems in turn to be an externalized and objectivized anchor for
one's sense of separateness.

Autonomy and Attachment: The Difficult Couple

In chapter 5, I analyzed extensively the tension between the ideal of autonomy
and attachment. This tension is interpreted by psychologists as inhering in
the human psyche. Yet, even if it is grounded in some universal property of
the self, this tension takes culturally variable forms. Indeed, in contemporary
capitalist society the tension between autonomy and attachment is widely
institutionalized in the division between the capitalist worksphere and the
family that itself overlaps with and reproduces the division of gender identities, autonomy marking masculinity and attachment marking femininity.
In the capitalist market, autonomy must be incessantly affirmed through
the display of self-reliance, creativity, and a sustained attention to one's
goals and interests, detached from those of others. On the other hand, attachment is institutionalized in a family that has taken on a primarily emotional
vocation.

An example of such male autonomy is provided by an article on the brave
new world of the single man trying to date women: "[His] past girlfriends
had complained about his lifestyle, which emphasized watching sports and
going to concerts and bars."[50] This man, the article recounts, is always eventually left by his partners. Autonomy entails an emotional style that becomes
a source of tension in married couples.

Marc is a sixty-three-year-old American CEO working in an Israeli high-
tech company:

My first wife and I divorced because she was bipolar. She had fits of
rage that were very scary. She would throw things at me, she would scream

at me, she would be nasty with me and with the children. It was a long and quite difficult divorce. It took me a while to realize what was happening. Then when we divorced it took me a while to want to be in a relationship again. There was a woman I had actually known a bit, during my marriage actually, I had a crush on her but didn't do anything. We were kind of in the same circles, but nothing happened for a while. Then all of a sudden, we started dating and I sort of fell in love with her. I quickly asked her to live with me and we lived together for, maybe seven, eight years? But we didn't make it. [*Silence*] At first, she was very sweet. But she needed me to tell her or show her all the time that I loved her. She would get offended if I did not respond to her SMS quickly enough, or forgot it was the anniversary of our first kiss, or if something else than her was getting my attention. She had all these expectations and I had no idea how to deal with them. It just got on my nerves. I guess I had no idea how to respond to these demands. I spoke to her less and less; I spent more time on my own, in my office or with friends. Eventually I stopped wanting to be with her. Which is a shame because at first I liked her so much. We actually had a good relationship for maybe three or four years. I don't know why it changed. I don't know what happened. It's really strange when you think of it how these things change without you noticing; it's like you go from one fight or disappointment to another and you don't notice it does something to you, that something in you is less happy or alive, because after a while you expect the fight. You brace up for it. Maybe she changed? Or I changed? At some point I couldn't deal with the feeling I disappointed her so often. I couldn't respond to her needs but I couldn't see [anymore] the disappointment and hurt in her eyes.

In this story, Marc and his companion enact "typical" male and female differences: his partner wanted an intensive relationality while he wanted a more bounded sense of self, differentiated from hers.[51] While in the work-sphere male power has been contested through policies of affirmative action and equal pay, in the private sphere contesting male power has taken the form of questioning men's performance of autonomy in relationships. Autonomy is defined as affirming one's self against perceived social obligations and duties. Marc's partner's intensive emotional style follows a highly scripted emotional ontology that makes her formulate scripts of the right emotion and expression of emotion. Marc experiences this model of intensive relationality as a set of obligations, a hindrance to his true or authentic self and a threat to his autonomy. As defined by philosopher Mark Piper, "[A]utonomy, in its most general formulation, refers to a property of self-government or self-determination such that an autonomous person is a person who is in some sense effective in governing herself according to a self-conception that captures her authentic or true self, and that autonomous actions refer to individual cases of such self-governing behavior."[52] The ideal of autonomy demands that one live one's life as an expression of what one cares most about.[53] For men social competence is manifest in the display of autonomy, while for women social competence is the performance of an ethics of care, manifest in intensive emotional exchanges. Autonomy and attachment are intractably diverging ideals of selfhood for the two genders because they express different forms of social competence.

A similar case is presented by Richard, a physicist working at an American university. He is freshly remarried and in his early fifties:

RICHARD: The second time is not easier than the first. We had fights then and we have fights now.
INTERVIEWER: Can you say what about?
RICHARD: Now or before?
INTERVIEWER: Before, for example.
RICHARD: She felt that I did not respect her needs; that if I wanted or did something different from what she wanted, then it meant somehow that I did not respect her needs. The more time passed, the more I needed to respect her needs: when she was pregnant, when she worked, when she was unemployed, when her mother died. It was always about her and her needs. And her criticisms that I was somewhat insufficient, or inadequate. It drove me crazy. I explained to her that the fact I had separate needs did not mean I had disrespect for her, that I couldn't be always attuned to her needs. But she didn't view it that way. It was quite difficult for me, because I liked being married and having a family, but it was always about her and her needs. So I got fed up and I left. I think we are both at peace with it.

Exit reaffirms Richard's threatened autonomy. Although my sample is not representative, it is interesting to observe that men seem to prefer exit to voice, leaving rather than engaging in elaborate emotional negotiations, because "voice"—expressing one's own needs—is culturally scripted as showing vulnerability and as threatening the boundaries of the self, and hence autonomy. It is here important to note that autonomy prescribes a set of social skills and a form of social competence crucial to masculine identity. Autonomy is not only a set of psychological traits, but a performance of competence and moral identity. Here is an example of the divergence of such two forms of moral competence. Arnaud, quoted in previous chapters, recounts his divorce as follows:

> ARNAUD: I divorced after I was diagnosed with stage 4 prostate cancer. For a change my wife was actually compassionate. She was so compassionate that I had a visceral reaction to her pity. She was, I don't know, full of solicitude to me, when before we fought all the time. Suddenly she became nice and compassionate, you know? I couldn't take it. All this pity just made me feel worse. I just wanted to be alone. I couldn't take so much compassion. I mean it's not like we had a great marriage before. We had been distant for a long time. But the cancer made everything move a lot faster. We divorced later.

Here clearly his ex-wife's solicitude—an expression of an ethics of care—threatens his sense of autonomy, to the point of preferring to face his disease on his own.

Autonomy and care are two equally intractable ideals of self. Naomi, a fifty-two-year-old Israeli political consultant and analyst, was married for eighteen years. Before her first child was born she says everything was fine, good even. Then when their first child was born, she understood that "it was not that anymore."

> INTERVIEWER: What did you understand?
> NAOMI: That he was not a partner in the whole thing. He worked, worked, worked. He was not with me at all in raising the children or making a home for us. He only knew to work. I understood he was not a partner. That I would be alone doing it.
> INTERVIEWER: That you would be alone.
> NAOMI: Umm, it is not a single feeling, you know, it is loneliness, anger, sadness, even betrayal, yes, betrayal in the friendship. We were friends beforehand, we did everything together, or if not, there was this sense that each one was free to be what he wanted, but with the children, it was forced on me, I had to take care of them, and I did it alone. He had the freedom to roam all over the world, but I was the one to stay at home. It felt like a betrayal.

Naomi illustrates the ways in which emotional intimacy appears as a form of moral legitimacy to conduct relationships. Naomi articulates an emotional normativity in which she wanted to share childcare with her husband, which undermines his claim to autonomy in the work sphere. The demands of corporations increasingly greedy of workers' time increases Naomi's husband's claim to autonomy, reducing his availability and his care. This in turn affected Naomi's own moral view that their relationships should take precedence. The conflict between them is thus about two moral views of the self, between autonomy achieved in the workplace and care achieved in the family, which in turn impact on each one's definition of self-worth.

Emotional Ontologies and Non-Binding Emotional Contracts

In a capitalist economy, needs tend to proliferate. In fact, consumer capitalism is made possible only *by* the expansion and proliferation of needs, real or false. We usually think of the proliferation of these needs as having a material character (purchasing technology or cars). Yet one of the most distinctive aspects of post-1960s capitalism has been the proliferation of psychological/emotional needs. Given that the consumer economy has inserted itself in the innermost crannies of subjectivity, a distinctive development of capitalism is the emotional commodity (what I have called an *emodity*),[54] the purchase of a service that changes and improves one's emotional makeup. This aspect of capitalism encourages women and men to think of their selves as a bundle of emotional attributes to be maximized. Relationships have been the main receptacle of emotional commodities, the site where we consume emotional goods in order not only to form them but also to maintain and improve them. Relationships follow what we may call an arc of needs that progressively gets flexed: the modern self conceives of itself as a work in progress, in need of improving itself and its performance, thrown in a movement forward of self-accomplishment and fulfillment of needs. Conversely, unsatisfied needs are the emotional ground for feeling emotional distance. "The original distance was closeness: the inability to overcome the shame of subterranean needs that no longer had a home aboveground."[55] The proliferation of needs in consumer culture means thus not only that they are many but also that they evolve in their intensity and focus and constitute the ground for selfhood. The proliferation of needs has been accomplished by the discourse and practice of therapy that provides techniques to formulate (mostly) emotional needs and make them objects of negotiation.

Therapy has been embraced by women for a number of reasons: Because they are providers of care, women have also been entrusted with the management of "psychic problems" in schools, marital counseling, and, more generally, personal relationships. Psychological techniques are ways to "care" by other means. Moreover, because women monitor themselves and their relationships far more closely than men, they are also the main clients/patients/consumers of therapy, using it precisely as a way to surveil themselves through the improvement of their psyche and their relationship skills. To that extent, therapy is an ambivalent social phenomenon: it helps control women's subjectivity by reminding them to monitor themselves and to care for others; but it also provides them with a social (and gender) competence defined as the ability to pay attention to one's and others' emotions and to shape emotionally expressive relationality. Women's emotional monitoring of their self and of relationships in marriage (or in a stable relationship) must thus be understood as an aspect of gender divisions and relationships.

Berenice, quoted in chapter 4, explains her divorce:

> BERENICE: You're asking me if there was one event that made me divorce, but I think for me it was a long process. It's not one single thing. It's a series of things. But still, I mean if I think of it, there was this one thing that put a definite distance between me and him. Many years back, before I started working at the theater, I wanted to rent a studio to do some art work. He worked and I didn't. I stayed home and raised the kids and when they got older I wanted to have a studio where I could do my art. We sort of could afford it, but it entailed some sacrifices, and he said no. He said it would be a too big expense. It is true that supporting a whole family with one salary is not easy. But even though I could see his point, I resented it. I felt betrayed. I felt he did not even try to see if we could make it work; this studio was important for my self-development and I felt he didn't care that I would develop. It was not a career move for me but I had an urge to paint or do art work. After that, I think I never went back to loving him the way I did before. Because he didn't help me pursue something that really mattered to me.

Berenice's emotional need has a tangible support: a studio. She conceives of herself as an entity that needs to develop through the cultivation of new tastes and activities, which in turn create new needs, emotional and material, thus changing the terms of the initial contract on which rested her marriage (the husband was the provider while she cared for the house and children). Her husband's refusal to rent a studio became for her an emotional event, a turning point she interpreted in the framework of an emotional ontology, a set of emotional needs that had for her a real existence. Because her then-husband did not participate in the transformation and development of her desires, needs, and tastes, their relationship became questioned and evaluated through a set of new emotions that his refusal generated.

The refinement of the will is the result of two powerful cultural forces in which women have been particularly solicited and active: consumption and therapy (therapy is an intangible emotional commodity). The inner dynamic of consumer culture and therapy converge in compelling the subject— women especially—to focus on their will and desire and to make their self into an aggregate of increasingly clearly spelled out preferences that express the inner emotional self and that therefore become increasingly intractable. Thus shared life rather than being the experience of a common emotional flow becomes a negotiation of diverging wills with different needs and desires. As Safran Foer's narrator puts it again: "Julia and Jacob's family life became characterized by process, endless negotiation, tiny adjustment."[56]

Therapeutic techniques instilled by a variety of psychological schools have been main cultural tools in the shaping of such negotiation and adjustment. Therapy has had three effects on intimacy: the first and perhaps most crucial effect of therapy is to have increased awareness and thresholds of self-worth, making anger a legitimate reaction to threats to self-worth and providing techniques to secure it in emotional interactions (being assertive, anxiety-free, or self-loving). Spearheaded by psychologists, marriage has observed an important change in the legitimacy of the expression of anger. As Francesca Cancian and Steven Gordon have argued, throughout the twentieth century, norms of love as self-fulfillment and expression of anger in marriage have gone hand in hand, suggesting that increased social expectations about love have been paradoxically accompanied with increased expressions of anger.[57] The second change is that therapeutic subjects become conscious of their emotions, both repressed and explicit, through a process of labeling ("I have been angry at my husband for a long time but was not aware of it"). Once clarified and made salient in one's consciousness, emotions become objects of interpersonal claims and negotiations ("finding ways to diminish one's anger").

Helena, a sixty-three-year-old therapist living in Boston, discusses her emotional distancing from her husband and her marriage crisis in this way:

> I think I started feeling it [emotional distancing] after I started my new therapy. I did many therapies before. But this one works much more powerfully. I am now much more aware of myself, it's like everything I tried to repress all these years is coming out now. This therapy manages to make me less depressed but I feel also more angry. Because I also started feeling all the needs I had and that had not been satisfied.

Helena resonates with Daniella, a forty-nine-year-old Israeli medical engineer:

> I always had the sense that he was not with me, that he would not in general support me and my way of understanding the world, he would not take my side of things in general. But we had a functioning marriage. I mean we had a family, friends; we took trips together. It all worked. But at some point I wanted to go to therapy, maybe five or six years ago, because I was having anxiety attacks, so I went to therapy, and slowly I realized that my relationship with him was a big source for my anxiety, that in fact I just did not feel supported by him. Externally I kept doing the same things. But I changed. I just couldn't accept anymore not to be supported the way I wanted to be supported. And at some point, I just made the decision, I am not sure when, maybe when my daughter left to Switzerland to learn cooking, I made the decision I was not going to stay. Because I felt this relationship was taking a heavy toll on me.

Therapy has here the direct effect of bringing to the surface "repressed" needs and emotions; it provides these with a label, and a frame to integrate these labeled emotions into a narrative that makes retrospective sense of the marriage difficulties. It solidifies and privileges one narrative and transforms a relationship based on non-reflexive emotional processes into reflexive and conscious ones, organizing the self around an inner emotional peg that becomes conscious, verbalized, and formulated in therapeutic sessions. Therapy then helps one to undergo a process of refinement of the self and its emotions, making women more aware of their needs and worth. As a sociologist of the family, Orly Benjamin, puts it: "The women's movement, and particularly its echoes within the therapeutic professions, introduced a turning point (…): Individual, family and couple counselling started supporting self-assertion, detachment from pleasing practices and self-development."[58] Both Helena and Daniella, as the result of their exposure to therapy, develop new thresholds of self-worth, which in turn challenge the implicit rules of their marriage. Therapy's goal is mostly to reinforce the self and in that respect it encourages what I would call a hyper-dignified vision of the self. A hyper-dignified vision of the self entails defensive strategies because it encourages a sustained attention to the wounds to the self. There follows an even clearer example of this process. Dana is a forty-six-year-old Israeli doctoral student:

INTERVIEWER: Can you tell me why you got divorced?

DANA: I wasn't happy. For many years I was not happy. We went to therapy. It wasn't easy to drag him there, but in the end we went. It helped a bit but I still felt unhappy so I decided to stay in therapy. I did a therapy for six years, and this therapy actually changed me and my perception of my marriage. It made me understand many things.

INTERVIEWER: How? Can you say how it changed you?

DANA: Sure. I think I was lacking in a clear sense of who I was. I very much depended on my husband to decide about our daily life. But it is not that I did not have opinions about things. I did. But I was afraid to voice them. I was afraid to have fights so I let him do what he wanted. He decided for everything. My therapist made me aware there was nothing wrong with having my own needs and opinions, but when I started voicing them, I realized he could not hear them, that I would have to remain the quiet, inexpressive woman I had been. So I guess when I changed, when I saw he could not cope with the new "me," that he wanted me to stay passive and voiceless, I went into inner immigration, I kind of stopped interacting meaningfully. I can't tell you when or how it happened. But it just happened. I think I was seething. I could love him when I was afraid of being myself; but when I stopped being afraid, the love I had for him had no real content anymore.

Here therapy leads to the formation of a new self in line with feminist views of selfhood. This new self is also achieved through an emotional ontology— becoming aware of her unconscious feelings as fear—which in turn changes the framing of the relationship, raises the threshold of her sense of worth, and provides her with the critical tools to re-evaluate her marriage. This woman acquires a sense of separateness by developing her will and wants, that, once objectified, demand to be "respected." This work of emotional redefinition substantially changes the will, thus illustrating the ways in which the refinement of the will that is at the heart of the market undermines the initial contract of the relationship.

Emotional Competence and Women's Position in the Relational Process

Sexuality, a sense of choice and alternative options, the refinement of a will through consumer tastes and therapy, the conflict between autonomy and attachment, the embattled need to secure a sense of self-worth through another—all generate a dynamic of unloving in settled and institutionalized relationships by creating new uncertainties. Sexualization, evaluation mediated by consumer tastes, the conflict between attachment and autonomy, and the need to secure self-worth are mediated by what I have called in this chapter "emotional ontologies." Women are more likely to use emotional ontologies in order to evaluate and criticize relationships because such ontologies are forms of social competence at the core of the ethics of care. To be sure, gender roles and identities create different positions in sexual and emotional fields, reflected in marriage. These positions in turn reflect the double position of women in capitalist society: as sexual actors ranked and consumed by the male gaze and as providers of care in charge of the emotional realm. Women are emotional and sexual agents. They oscillate between these two positions or use them both in their relationship to men.

Although my sample of divorced people is too small to help make generalizations, it is interesting to observe that divorced women are less likely than men to invoke narratives of revelation and more likely to invoke narratives of accumulation or trauma, both distinctly steeped in temporality, as they typically unfold in time, and both based on "reasons." These reasons in turn tend to be grounded in an emotional ontology, that is, in how they were made to feel. This is in line with research on divorce quoted at the beginning of this chapter.

Women use an emotional ontology in various ways: they pay close attention to their own emotions in an interaction; they pay attention to others' emotions in that interaction; they give names to fleeting and changing moods; they proffer standards of emotional expectations; they refer to emotional needs; they hold a highly scripted model of intimacy; and finally they are likely to redirect, monitor, and control the intensity and expression of emotions in an interaction, what Arlie Hochschild called "emotional labor."[59] Emotional ontology becomes the ground for raising claims, for displaying a specific form of competence, formulating expectations, and providing social scripts for interactions. Once emotions are named, monitored, and used in cultural models and ideals, they tend to become "hard facts" and entities. This is all the more the case that psychological frames tend to provide self-narratives and self-goals that give a frame and structure to emotions.

Women thus experience their emotions as an overwhelming ground of reality, self-identity, and social competence. Here are the examples of two women who belong to different generations but sound oddly similar in their invocation of emotional ontologies. Evelyne is a thirty-one-year-old French academic who separated from her companion of eight years:

> Why we separated? Not because there was anything wrong with him. He is a great guy. Everybody loves him actually. Every woman wants him. No wonder he is now with my best friend. He is just that kind of guy. But I didn't feel he understood me enough. He loved me and he admired me. But he didn't see me. He saw me as this mysterious, complex woman, and when I reacted in a way he didn't understand, he would say, "You're so interesting." But that's not what I needed from him. I needed from him to understand who I was. I didn't want to be a dark, mysterious woman. I just wanted to be understood.

Evelyne resonates with Helena, a sixty-three-year-old American woman, quoted above. When Helena described herself "in a marriage crisis after thirty-five years of being married," I asked her why:

> HELENA: Thomas [husband's name] loves me; he loves me in his own way; I even think he loves me very much. But I never feel deeply cared for or seen for who I am.
> INTERVIEWER: Can you give me an example?
> HELENA: Many many years ago, maybe twenty years ago, I gave a public speech, and after the speech, he was busy making remarks on how I made a tiny mistake about the date of an event I mentioned. I think I placed the event five years later or something like that. He didn't say a word about the talk. Just how I had made a mistake. You know, it stayed with me. Or I would buy myself some new clothes, and he would ask

immediately: "How much did it cost?" or he would buy me some mean-ingless present for my birthday, like things I don't need or don't like. I feel he doesn't see me. He does not know my taste; he does not know to respond to my deep needs.

Both Evelyne and Helena display a clear emotional ontology, a perception of and an orientation to emotional needs, such as "being seen" in a specific way, being understood and having their self validated. Such needs, it should be sure, are located in the recesses of one's subjectivity, are variable, and cannot be easily accessed by others. They can only be responded to after an elaborate work of verbalization and negotiation. These needs proceed of an ethics of care and thus have the imperious character of moral claims.

Some feminist philosophers have criticized the ethics of care for failing to instill autonomy in women, that is, for failing to instill the capacity to pur-sue their goals and to operate from within the boundaries of a self-defined sense of dignity. But when grounded in an emotional ontology, the ethics of care has the opposite effect. The ethics of care, combined with therapeutic techniques of self-knowledge and self-management, contains and even exacerbates dignity and authenticity through a sense of emotional compe-tence and thus ends up furthering women's sense of self and autonomy. Securing a sense of self-worth through emotions has become paramount to women's presentation and management of self in relationships. This is con-firmed by quantitative research:

> "[F]eeling unloved" was a frequently mentioned complaint among the women in both studies (67% of the women in the California Divorce Study and 75% of the women in the DMP study [Divorce Mediation Project]). Sensitivity to being belittled by one's spouse has apparently increased in the past 15 years. Whereas one third of the women in the California Divorce Study reported this complaint, 59% of the DMP women cited being belit-tled by their spouses.[60]

One of the most significant novelties of romantic love in modernity is that it is now mobilized to secure the subject's self-worth. The defense of self-worth then creates its own emotional normativity, that is, an inner reference point from which a relationship and an emotional interaction are evaluated. Psychological selves conduct and manage relationship from within the idio-syncratic core of the self—how an individual person is made to feel—and from a set of meta-emotional norms, norms about emotions (e.g., "it is not right you make me feel guilty;" "if I don't feel good about myself with you, then it is OK to leave"). This is, ironically, also the reason why emotional conflicts are often intractable. Individuals, especially women, develop their own idiosyncratic emotional normativity, learned through therapy and self-help culture in general. Such particularized emotions become the ground from which they conduct their interactions, evaluating such interactions as adequate to their emotions or not, sometimes dismissing them for the same reasons.

While I have questioned the role of the body and sexuality as ways to ground—enter and evaluate—relationships, emotions are a no less shaky basis for monitoring relationships. As philosopher Harry Frankfurt put it: "Facts about ourselves are not peculiarly solid and resistant to skeptical dissolution. Our natures are, indeed, elusively insubstantial—notoriously less stable and less inherent than the nature of other things."[61] Emotional ontologies do not properly acknowledge the difficulty of grounding relationships on the insubstantiality of emotions. Emotions are often left implicit in interactions because such interactions when unnamed enable them to flow and move smoothly. Attention to emotions is likely to make interactions more self-conscious,[62] to focus on one dimension of the interaction and to eliminate another. Naming emotions is thus a cultural act that transforms these emotions into quasi-hard facts and events that must in turn be newly transacted in a relationship. What William Reddy calls emotive—the expression of emotion shapes and changes the interaction where the emotion is expressed—becomes fixated in discourses where emotional claims have their own ground, legitimacy, and validity. To say: "I felt bad you did not pay attention to me" or " I do not feel loved the way I want to be loved" makes emotions into either events or facts, or both, which must be acknowledged, discussed, and transacted, drawing the self to change its most unconscious habits.

The French financial expert Christian Walter speaks of a "quantic theory of needs," where needs are not known prior to decision, are contradictory and therefore given to indeterminacy. In his view, it is the decision or choice that actually often reveals to the subject his or her own preferences. This theory suggests a different view of choice and decision-making, not as an inevitable component of the self and the psyche but as an emerging property of an interaction, as a dynamic process in which the subject shapes and discovers her preferences at the same time she formulates them. This is a far cry from the rational subject of economics or the psychological view according to which a subject discovers her needs and preferences whose validity is secured by the simple fact of feeling them. In fact, Walter claims, it is engagement that often makes the subject discover a preference she or he did not know she or he had. Similarly, we may suggest that needs are not fixed, but emerge through emotional ontologies—psychological discourses and narratives.

*

Perhaps the most significant claim of this chapter is that the unloving that precedes and brings about divorce is the result of the same social forces that shape non-committed negative relationships. Those social forces send people to inverted magnetic fields, fields that push people apart rather than bring people together.

All of the themes evoked above suggest that a large part of what we call "unloving" is the result of the ways in which the self is positioned in capitalist societies, which leave the self struggling to ascertain its worth on its own. Worth is established in four different arenas: through sexualization, through consumer objects and practices, through the capacity to affirm one's autonomy by exiting a relationship, and through emotional ontologies. Worth then is the very thing that is incessantly put into question by the ways in which love in domestic settings is played out. But it is also what is compulsively, incessantly performed both in entering and leaving relationships, making self-worth increasingly acquire a zero-sum structure. The self then experiences itself as deeply dependent on another for sexuality, desire, consumer identity, and emotional certainty—thus making the self experience intimacy and marriage as a set of constraints on one's freedom. The surprising upshot is that divorce becomes yet another path to freedom. One of the most wrenching experiences in most people's lives becomes ultimately yet another way of experiencing freedom. For example, the author of a newspaper article discusses writer Nicole Krauss's own account of her divorce from Jonathan Safran Foer:

> One of Krauss's major preoccupations since beginning *Forest Dark* is a question of freedom, her understanding of which has shifted radically over the last four years. The moment she realized she could get a divorce, she says, was "the moment I understood that, given a choice between teaching my children two things—one, it's important to stay bound to something you are committed to rather than hurt anyone else; two, giving them the example of what it is to live always toward your freedom and

your happiness and your larger sense of self—there was no question. Obviously the latter. Obviously that's what I wanted to show them."[63]

Here, divorce is no longer the wrenching experience that it is for many, but is rather the glamorous mark of freedom, the freedom that has been painstakingly crafted for us by the technological, therapeutic, and consumer institutions of modernity. We may wonder how glib that freedom is.

Conclusion

Negative Relations and the Butterfly Politics of Sex

Les gens n'aiment pas que l'on explique des choses qu'ils veulent garder "absolues." Moi, je trouve qu'il vaut mieux savoir. C'est très bizarre que l'on supporte si mal le réalisme. Dans le fond, la sociologie est très proche de ce qu'on appelle la sagesse. Elle apprend à se méfier des mystifications. Je préfère me débarrasser des faux enchantements pour pouvoir m'émerveiller des vrais "miracles." En sachant qu'ils sont précieux parce qu'ils sont fragiles.

—Pierre Bourdieu[1]

People don't like other people to explain to them the things they would like to maintain as absolute. As for me, I think it is better to know. It is very bizarre that we can bear so little realism. In the end, sociology is very close to what we call wisdom. It teaches to be cautious with mystifications. I prefer to get rid of false enchantments in order to be awed by true miracles. Knowing that they are precious because they are fragile.

—Author's Translation

I shall offer to the mind all its sorrows, all its mourning garments: this will not be a gentle prescription for healing, but cautery and the knife.

—Seneca[2]

In his controversial novel *Submission* (2015) Michel Houellebecq describes the near future where France will choose as its president an Islamist with a benevolent face. This collective shift is dramatized as a moral surrender in the person of François, an academic specializing in nineteenth-century literature. Throughout the novel, François faces the choice of converting to Islam or maintaining his morose and hedonist French secular identity. The first would entail a professional promotion, money, and access to multiple women who would serve him sexually and domestically in the legitimate frame of polygamy. The second would mean continuing a life punctuated by different episodes of casual or uncommitted sex and ongoing existential boredom. Ultimately, he is compelled to "submit" (convert to Islam) and it is the promise of the domestic and sexual services that will be provided by a submissive woman that ultimately convinces him to "surrender." This novel resonates and brings to a conclusion the preoccupation of two of Houellebecq's previous novels, *Whatever* (published in 1994 in French) and *Atomized* (published in 1998 in French). The first novel is the story of a man ("our hero") who ultimately commits suicide because he is unable to perform well in a sexual market increasingly governed by intense competitiveness. The second describes the post-1968 frantic search for authenticity through sex and its outcome in a new metaphysical void. Ultimately, the novel offers the vision of a humanity freed from the misery of sexuality through cloning. What these three novels have in common is their view of sexuality as central to contemporary societies, as a source of existential disarray and, ultimately, as a cause for political discontent and civilizational change. In the same way that Henry James, Balzac, or Zola examined in their novels the massive shift from pre-modern hierarchy and cosmos to a society governed by exchange and money, Houellebecq is the novelist who has examined the shift to a society governed by sexual freedom: consumption, social relationships, and politics are all somewhat imbued with a sexuality that dislocates "classic" social arrangements. More so, in Houellebecq's fictional universe the very future (and demise) of Western civilization lies in its (de)regulation of sexuality.

*

Casual sexuality and the sexualization of relationships may seem peripheral to the main problems of societies (only when framed as "economic" or "political" do problems seem to become "important") but they play a crucial role in the economy, demography, politics, and identity of all societies, and contemporary societies in particular. This is because, as phenomenological philosophers and feminist scholars have consistently claimed, the body is a crucial dimension of (social) existence.[3] Simone de Beauvoir put this point aptly in an entirely phenomenological vein:

> Our body is not first posited in the world the way a tree or a rock is. It lives in the world; it is our general way of having a world. It expresses our existence, which signifies not that it is an exterior accompaniment of our existence, but that our existence realizes itself in it.[4]

The body is the site where social existence accomplishes itself. The fact then that the sexualized body has become an essential unit of consumer capitalism, of intimacy, marriage, and even (ironically) of sexual relationships themselves, deserves the attention of sociologists, economists, philosophers, and policy makers. We follow here in the trail of Catherine MacKinnon's notion of what she calls "butterfly politics": that small microscopic changes can bring about large changes in the same way that according to chaos theory, the flapping of a butterfly's wings somewhere on earth can bring about massive weather changes somewhere else a few weeks later (known as the butterfly effect).[5] In a way, this book has described the butterfly politics of sex: seemingly fleeting moments and elusive phenomena both reflect and bring about large changes for the family and for the economy.

In his classical *Escape from Freedom*, Erich Fromm opposed positive to negative freedom: "Freedom, though it has brought him ['man'] independence and rationality, has made him isolated and, thereby, anxious and powerless."[6] Freedom for Fromm has a deep psychosocial effect; it produces anxiety that explains why some will prefer to give away their freedom to totalitarian regimes (or to misogynist ideologies, to family values, etc.). What Fromm did not and perhaps could not perceive,was that the anxiety of freedom was a direct effect of the injunction to self-realization and not its opposite. Far from standing opposed, positive and negative freedom can hardly be separated. What has made freedom into such a normatively troubled and ambiguous phenomenon was the fact that it was the ideological banner of political social movements, of a hedonic ethics of authenticity and, above all, as this book has stressed, of scopic capitalism—the intensive and ubiquitous form of exploitation of the sexual body through visual industries. Scopic capitalism has become the dominant frame organizing the images and stories that have made freedom into a concrete and lived reality for members of Western societies. This is why, I have argued, the normative ideal of freedom to realize one's projects and definition of the good life has morphed into negative relationships shaped by the consumer market and technology. The affinities between negative relationships and scopic capitalism have been the main thread running through this book. Let me draw this thread.

The first such affinity is to be found in the emergence of markets as sociological frames that organize encounters. Markets are social arenas where actors exchange something, and which are governed by supply and demand. Where in traditional marriage men and women were paired (more or less) horizontally (within their social group) and aimed to maximize property and wealth, in sexual markets men and women pair according to sexual capital, for a variety of purposes (economic, hedonic, emotional), often come from different social groups and backgrounds (cultural, religious, ethnic, or social), and often exchange asymmetrical attributes (e.g., beauty vs. social status). The second affinity between capitalism and negative relationships also derives from its market-form. Its prototypical unit is casual sex, an interaction between strangers who aim each at the satisfaction of a utility, thus mimicking the consumer interaction and its hedonic premises (consumer culture equally mirrors sexuality).

The third affinity stems from the fact that a sexuality governed by scopic capitalism generates different forms of economic and social value for men and women. Through the consumer market, women groom their bodies to produce value, at once economic and sexual, while men consume women's production of their sexual value as status markers in arenas of male competition.

A fourth affinity between negative relationships and capitalism concerns the uncertainty about the value of what is transacted. Uncertainty about one's own and others' value is pervasive, all the more that scopic capitalism makes the value of selves quickly obsolete. The demand for subjective value has increased (in the form of "self-esteem," "self-love," and "self-confidence") thus creating defensive strategies to perceived threats to one's value.

And finally, the fifth affinity is to be found in the difficulty in holding on to or forming emotional contracts because innovation, geographical mobility, investments in various lucrative fields, and flexibility in lines of production and workforce render corporations uncommitted entities. All of these form the hall-mark of what I have called negative relationships and point to the ways in which intimate relationships, sexuality, and the family reflect and appropriate characteristics of the market, of consumer practices, and of capitalist workplaces. Negative relationships have two properties: they are indeterminate (I cannot say in a final way what I want and who I am in them) and they are characterized by the fact they point to a breakdown in normal ways of doing things. Perhaps one of the most important claims of this book is that specific negative dynamics, shaped by social and economic forces, determine (if that is the right word) the non-formation of bonds and established bonds that dissolve. The evaporation of relationships and the breakdown of stable attachments are different psychological responses to a common matrix of cultural, economic, and social forces. Scopic capitalism has had a deep impact on sources of self-worth, on generating new sources of uncertainty, and on creating new forms of social hierarchy, disturbing what I would call traditional processes of recognition, how people feel worthwhile in the eyes of others, especially how women feel worthwhile in the eyes of the men who continue to control and organize their social lives. Organized under the aegis of neo-liberalism, scopic capitalism creates a selfhood in which economy and sex are seamlessly intertwined and mutually perform each other.

A new structure of feeling has emerged that crosses, pervades, and bridges the economic and sexual realms and generates a romantic and sexual self-hood that has a number of defining characteristics: flexibility (in the capacity to move between a multiplicity of partners and in the capacity to accumulate experiences and multitask); resilience to risk, failures, and rejections; and built-in disloyalty (like shareholders, lovers may leave to invest in a more profitable "enterprise"). Sexual agents, like economic agents, operate with an acute awareness of competition and develop skills of self-reliance as well as a pervasive sense of precariousness. Pervasive insecurity coexists with competitiveness and lack of trust. As a result, sexual agents develop techniques to defend their self-worth, alleviate anxiety, increase their (emotional) performance, and make investments in uncertain futures, all provided by the expanding market of self-help, psychology, and spirituality.

What this new situation means for sexuality and intimacy is ambiguous. There is no doubt that the ideal of freedom has fulfilled some or many of its promises, as women and men now move more freely in the sexual arena, approach domesticity on equal terms, and are more entitled to make sexual pleasure a dimension of the good life. There is no doubt too that in the realm of sexuality, sexual freedom has also entailed a greater equality between the sexes. Overall, sexual freedom has attenuated the binarity of gender roles in sexuality, the equation of desire with repression and prohibition. But freedom is too ample a term not to contain and maybe hide different logics. Because it has been harnessed to the goals and interests of scopic capitalism, freedom deepens inequalities, some of which preceded scopic capitalism (gender inequalities) and some of which have been created by it. Both old and new inequalities have enough negative effects to make freedom a pristine ideal with disquieting consequences.

The year 2018 had a strange Houellebecquian resonance and saw the rise of a new form of terrorism, neither religious nor political but sexual. Around the end of April 2018, a young man by the name of Alek Minassian killed ten or more people in the city of Toronto,[7] mostly women.

How much Minassian was mentally disturbed is unclear. What is uncontroversial however is the fact he subscribed to the violent ideology of incels, an online community of men united in their hatred for women because, in their view, men are entitled to sex and attention from women, yet are denied such sex and attention by women who prefer other men.

Tragically and ironically, the word *incel* had a very different beginning: It had been coined two decades earlier by a woman named Alana who, in reference to her own involuntary celibacy, wanted to create a supportive Internet community of people who had been unable to have sex or to be in a relationship.[8] The word was reinvented by misogynist incels who divide the world in two classes, Chads and Stacys, men and women, who are not only sexually attractive but also sexually attractive to each other.

We can (and should) express moral outrage at the phenomenon of incels. But it is far more productive and interesting to understand the social conditions that make possible such phenomena.

Sociologically, incels are relevant to this study to the extent that they are the most extreme and disturbing manifestation of the transformation of sexuality through the new social hierarchies generated by scopic capitalism. Incels perceive themselves as excluded from a social order where sexuality bestows status and is synonymous with the good life and with normative masculinity. Misogynist or not, incels are the (violent) manifestation of a new social order in which sexuality and intimacy are signs of social status and even social membership. To be deprived of sexuality and sexual intimacy is, as Houellebecq's novel *Whatever* showed some two decades ago, to be deprived of a social existence. While for some, sexuality is the arena for the exercise of freedom, for others it entails "involuntary" (and coerced) experiences of humiliation and exclusion. In that sense, incels are located at the tectonic fault line between traditional (violent) patriarchy and high-velocity forms of technological and scopic capitalism. Scopic capitalism creates new forms of social rankings and privileges, transforming and reinforcing old modes of domination of women, while using values of freedom, liberation, and emancipation.

Sexual hierarchies, like social or cultural hierarchies, are maintained through a process of "distinction." According to Pierre Bourdieu, "distinction" is the mental and structural process by which we distinguish ourselves from members of other groups, dismissing their tastes, for example, while affirming ours.[9] "Sexual distinction" is the mechanism at the heart of romantic identity and sexual status. Distinction is achieved through the process of rejecting others (and being rejected by them). Sexual distinction in that sense differs from class distinction: while the latter rests on the capacity to establish both value and value differences, the former struggles to properly establish the value of the sexual object. While class distinction is about cultural objects and consumer practices, sexual distinction is about people and affects directly their sense of worth. "Involuntary celibate" is a manifestation of such (negative) sexual distinction and more especially of the routine exercise of the freedom to reject others, which in turn creates groups for whom sexual rejection becomes a common social experience, entailing routine experiences of self-devaluation.

Being emotionally "unwanted" and sexually "undesired" is not a new form of social experience. Courtships in the past could end in breakups, with men and women feeling and experiencing unrequited love. Men and women could be and often were betrayed. As such, the experience of rejection is not new. But it takes today the character of a significant segment in the lives of many and has practically become an inevitable part of the sexual and romantic lives of many if not most. White supremacy, for example, is not only a reaction to immigration but also to transformations of relationships between the sexes.

The female counterparts to male incels are "the housewives of white supremacy,"[10] who reject both the sexual objectification of women and sexual freedom and reclaim traditional gender roles and family values. Their rejection of sexual freedom and equality plays an important, if less visible and less discussed, part in the phenomenon of white supremacy.[11] Indeed, scopic capitalism creates new forms of sexual inequalities between those endowed with sexual capital and those without, new forms of uncertainties, and new forms of devaluation, mostly of women, all of which cause ripple effects in the social bond. Because the sexualization of female identity has not been accompanied by a genuine redistribution of social and economic power and because it has in a way reinforced men's *sexual* power over women, it makes traditional patriarchy attractive. In using the idiom of freedom scopic capitalism has deepened the modes of domination of women, rendering freedom a social experience that generates unease and even generates reactive responses in the form of backlash to feminism. Freedom has both made more widespread and more legitimate experiences of uncertainty, devaluation, and worthlessness.

*

The kind of philosophical sociological analysis deployed in this book is not about hammering down some clear normative principles. Rather its aim is to look for the ambiguities and contradictions embedded in practices. These ambiguities are the most difficult aspects of our experience, which are often unspeakable and hard to make explicit; it is the task of sociology to uncover and discuss them with the help of philosophy. Commenting on Axel Honneth's work, the philosopher Joel Anderson exposes one of Honneth's essential ideas to analyze social phenomena around the *idea of a "semantischer Überschuss,"* a semantic excess, which is a "'surplus' of meaning and significance that goes beyond what we can now fully capture, appreciate and articulate. [...] It is within our inchoate feelings, and at the margins of traditions, and more generally in the encounter with the conflicted and the unresolved that the needed innovative resources for Critical Theory are to be found."[12]

Contemporary freedom produces such zones of ambiguity in the various forms of experiences of uncertainty described in this book. These experiences come to self-understanding through a deliberate work of clarification. It is such a work of clarification this book has hoped to achieve, by withholding the knee-jerk endorsement or condemnation of freedom, by refusing to use a psychological vocabulary of empowerment or trauma to clarify the nature of these experiences. This book has been an effort to counter the epistemic imperialism of psychology in the emotional realm. Sociology, no less than psychology, has much to contribute to the clarification of the baffling experiences that make up our private lives. In fact, sociology might be even better equipped than psychology in understanding the traps, impasses, and contradictions of modern subjectivity.

One question asked by idealist philosophy was how the subject was able to create unity from a variety of sensations and impressions that come from the outside world. The subject is that which forms a unity between disparate forces that enter consciousness. Hegel further developed this insight: In the process of aiming at unity, the self produces a set of oppositions, conflicts, contradictions, internal splitting, and dissociations, which he called "negations."[13] The self as a unity emerges from this work of negation in the capacity to negate negations. To quote Robert Pippin on Hegel: Consciousness is "always resolving its own conceptual activity; and in a way that means it can be said both to be self-affirming, issuing in judgments and imperatives, but also potentially 'self-negating,' aware that what it resolves to be the case might not be the case."[14]

In Hegel's view then, contradiction is productive and positive as it enables to generate a new entity. Contradiction is, for example, intrinsic to the process of recognition, and recognition manages to overcome the contradictions inherent in consciousness.

However, the sexual-economic subject documented in this book creates splits and negations, which are not "sublated" into a larger coherent whole and into a process of recognition. Its contradictions remain negativities, unresolved contradictions and splits. The internal splits are between sexuality and emotions, between masculine and feminine identities, the need for recognition and the need for autonomy, feminist equality and a selfhood regulated by a visuality that is produced by capitalist industries controlled by men. All these contradictions result from the subsumption of selfhood under a sexuality organized within and governed by the structures and procedures of scopic capitalism; and they often remain just that: contradictions that cannot be overcome or sublated, negations that turn into negativities.

In a social setting then, where the subject is busy managing such unresolvable contradictions, recognition—the process of overcoming intersubjective negation—cannot take place. This in a way is also Naomi Wolf's diagnosis in her now-classic study of beauty: "[E]motionally unstable relationships, high divorce rates, and a large population cast out into the sexual marketplace are good for business in a consumer economy. Beauty pornography is intent on making modern sex brutal and boring and only as deep as a mirror's mercury, anti-erotic for both men and women."[15]

The market—as an institution of freedom—throws the individual squarely into a consumer-technological path, which both rationalizes conduct and creates a nagging uncertainty about rules of interactions, about the nature of interactions, and about one's own and another's value. This uncertainty is in turn translated into further emotional commodities, provided by the infinite market of commodities supposed to help one achieve a more optimal self and relationships.

Some will ask, undoubtedly, whether this book perhaps overstates the case and confuses bleakness with healthy lucidity. After all, that romance has changed its form does not make it less present in our lives. And that freedom entails risks and uncertainty does not make it less worthwhile— nor does it alter the fact that most of us still live or long for stable couplehood. One may even invoke the reassuring statistics that one in three marriages today occurs through an Internet site,[16] which would seem to suggest that technology-cum-the market is far from being the ominous phenomenon that this book has described.

But these arguments make the discrete events of "marriage" or "couplehood" into the only relevant units of analysis and fail to understand how the very nature of the romantic and sexual *experience* before, during, and outside marriage has changed. Thus, this book is *not*—in no way—an anxious interrogation about the future of marriage or stable relationships and a plea against casual sex, although it can undoubtedly be read this way. In its flamboyant and jubilatory forms, casual sex is a source of self-affirmation and self-expression. My focus has not been for or against casual sex or for or against long-term commitments. I have described the various ways in which the appropriation of the sexual body by scopic capitalism transforms the self, the feeling of self-worth, and the rules for forming relationships. This new form of capitalism, so I argued, changes the ecology of intimate relationships, transforms the subjection of women, and creates a vast amount of experiences of rejection, hurt, disappointment—"unloving"—recycled through the vast economic and cultural machine of psychotherapy in all its forms. This is not its only effect but it is a very significant one.

Whether Marxist or functionalist, most approaches to society presume that society equips individuals with the tools to be competent members of it. The kind of critique advocated in this book parts company with such views and rejoins Freud's sociological critique in *Civilization and Its Discontents*. In that famous book, he argued that civilization had exacted too high a price from the individual in terms of demanding the repression of libidinal instincts and making guilt too central in the psychic economy of the modern subject.[17] *Civilization and Its Discontents* thus suggested that modernity was characterized by a lack of fit between the individual psychic structure and the social demands put on it. Freud thus offered an interesting type of critique: not one that started from a clear normative view but one that inquired about the fit between social and psychic structures. In a similar vein, I have argued that scopic capitalism exacts too high a psychic price from sexual and romantic actors and is at odds with the goals and ideals of contemporary actors. It is too high, because the inner life is too complex to be managed on one's own, mostly through self-scrutiny and through self-generated desires. It is too demanding because sexual markets are competitive and create inevitable exclusions and social experiences of sexual humiliation.

If introspection and the self are not reliable sources of commitment and clarity, freedom alone cannot generate sociality and exacts a very high psychic price from social actors. In order to generate social solidarity, what Honneth usefully calls social freedom, freedom needs rituals. Rituals create a common emotional focus that does not require introspection or the permanent self-generation and self-monitoring of desires. Yet these rituals of sociality have largely disappeared and been replaced by uncertainty, which in turn requires a massive psychological self-management, meaning a deep transformation of desire that is no longer defined in "heroic" terms or through its capacity to transcend the social order. Sex and love no longer represent the site where the self can oppose society. Sexuality and intimacy have become the arena par excellence where the economic self is performed, and can no longer be a source of creative tension between the individual and society. As Irving Howe put it:

> In every totalitarian society, there is and must be a deep clash between state and family, simply because the state demands complete loyalty from each person and comes to regard the family as a major competitor for that loyalty. [...] For both political and nonpolitical people, the family becomes the last refuge for humane values. Thereby the defense of the "conservative" institution of the family becomes under totalitarianism a profoundly subversive act.[18]

Howe referred to totalitarian societies but was oblivious to the surreptitious ways in which our own society—its economy and its politics—has also thoroughly penetrated the family, sexuality, and love that can no longer play the role of "last refuge for humane values." Sexuality and love are now the terrain par excellence to reproduce consumer capitalism and hone the skills of self-reliance and autonomy demanded and practiced everywhere. In his book *L'homme sans gravité* (2005), French psychoanalyst Charles Melman claims that contemporary societies have moved from desire to jouissance, where desire is regulated by scarcity and prohibition, while jouissance is about an unrestricted need to find an immediate satisfaction in objects that exist in abundance. Jouissance then is the true mode of desire of a consumer society, in which objects, affects, and sexual satisfaction displace the moral center of the self. But jouissance cannot properly find or constitute objects of interactions, love, and solidarity.

This book does not call for a return to family values, to community, or to a reduction of freedom. It does however take seriously feminist and religious critiques of sexual freedom and claims that freedom has let the tentacular power of scopic capitalism dominate our field of action and imagination, with the assistance of psychological industries to help manage the many emotional and psychic breaches it creates. If freedom is to mean anything, surely it must include the knowledge of the invisible forces that bind and blind us.

Endnotes

Epigraph

1. Quoted in Saphora Smith, "Marc Quinn: Evolving as an Artist and Social Chronicler," *New York Times*, August 13. 2015, accessed September 9, 2016. http://www.nytimes.com/2015/08/14/arts/marc-quinn-evolving-as-an-artist-and-social-chronicler.html?_r=0.
2. Understand that to be subversive is to move from the individual to the collective. See Adb Al Malik, "Césaire (Brazzaville via Oujda)," https://genius.com/Abd-al-malik-cesaire-brazzaville-via-oujda-lyrics, accessed February 13, 2018.
3. Quoted in Alison Flood, 2016. "Nobel Laureate Svetlana Alexievich Heads Longlist for UK's Top Nonfiction Award," *Guardian*, September 21, 2016, accessed February 13, 2018, https://www.theguardian.com/books/2016/sep/21/nobel-laureate-longlist-for-uks-top-nonfiction-award-baillie-gifford.

Chapter 1

1. George Orwell, "In Front of Your Nose," *The Collected Essays, Journalism and Letters of George Orwell* (1946; New York: Harcourt, Brace & World, 1968).
2. For extensive discussion on Plato's theory of forms, see Russell M. Dancy, *Plato's Introduction of Forms* (Cambridge: Cambridge University Press, 2004); Gail Fine, *Plato on Knowledge and Forms: Selected Essays* (Oxford: Oxford University Press, 2003).
3. This paragraph is taken from my article on unloving, "The Thrill Is Gone: Why Do We Fall Out of Love?" *Haaretz*, September 7, 2013, https://www.haaretz.com/.premium-why-do-we-fall-out-of-love-1.5329206, accessed February 13, 2018.
4. Émile Durkheim, *Suicide: A Study in Sociology*, trans. John A. Spaulding and George Simpson (1897; New York: Simon & Schuster, 1997).
5. Wendell Bell, "Anomie, Social Isolation, and the Class Structure," *Sociometry* 20, no. 2 (1957): 105–116; Émile Durkheim, 1997 [1897]. *Suicide: A Study in Sociology*, trans. John A. Spaulding and George Simpson (1897; New York: Simon & Schuster, 1997); Claude S. Fischer, "On Uban Alienations and Anomie: Powerlessness and Social Isolation," *American Sociological Review* 38, no. 3 (1973): 311–326; Robert D. Putnam, *Bowling Alone: The Collapse and Revival of American Community* (New York: Simon & Schuster, 2001); Frank Louis Rusciano, "'Surfing Alone': The Relationships among Internet Communities, Public Opinion, Anomie, and Civic Participation," *Studies in Sociology of Science* 5, no. 3 (2014): 1–8; Melvin Seeman, "On the Meaning of Alienation," *American Sociological Review* 24, no. 6 (1959), 783–791; Bryan Turner, "Social Capital, Inequality and Health: The Durkheimian Revival," *Social Theory and Health* 1, no. 1 (2003): 4–20.
6. Leslie Bell, *Hard to Get: Twenty-Something and the Paradox of Sexual Freedom* (Berkeley: University of California Press, 2013).

7. Pierre Bourdieu, *Distinction: A Social Critique of the Judgement of Taste*, trans. Richard Nice (Cambridge, MA: Harvard University Press, 1984); Mary Douglas and Baron Isherwood, *The World of Goods: Towards an Anthropology of Consumption*, vol. 6 (1979; London: Psychology Press, 2002); Mike Featherstone, *Consumer Culture and Postmodernism* (London: SAGE Publications, 2007); Eva Illouz, *Consuming the Romantic Utopia: Love and the Cultural Contradictions of Capitalism* (Berkeley: University of California Press, 1997); Eva Illouz, *Cold Intimacies: The Making of Emotional Capitalism* (Cambridge: Polity Press, 2007); Arlie Russell Hochschild, *The Managed Heart: Commercialization of Human Feeling* (Berkeley: University of California Press, 1992); Arlie Russell Hochschild, *The Commercialization of Intimate Life: Notes from Home and Work* (Berkeley: University of California Press, 2003); Axel Honneth, "Organized Self-realization Some Paradoxes of Individualization," *European Journal of Social Theory* 7, no. 4 (2004): 463–478; Micki McGee, *Self-help, Inc.: Makeover Culture in American Life* (New York: Oxford University Press, 2005); Ann Swidler, *Talk of Love: How Culture Matters* (Chicago: University of Chicago Press, 2003).

8. Milton Friedman, *Capitalism and Freedom* (1962; Chicago: University of Chicago Press, 2009); Friedrich August Hayek, *The Road to Serfdom: Text and Documents: The Definitive Edition*, ed. Bruce Caldwell (1944; New York: Routledge, 2014); Karl Polanyi, *The Great Transformation: The Political and Economic Origins of Our Time* (1944; Boston: Beacon Press, 1944).

9. As Beatrice Smedley remarks (personal communication) not all love stories in India (*Shakuntala* by Kalidasa, fourth–fifth century, or the Kama Sutra) and China (*The Carnal Prayer Mat* by Li Yu, seventeenth century) were informed by religious values, nor was *The Tale of Genji* by Murasaki Shikibu (eleventh-century Japan). Similarly, in the West a non-religious romantic tradition coexisted with the one shaped by Christianity: Sappho, Catullus, Ovid, Ronsard, and Petrarch found their sources in classical mythology.

10. Howard R. Bloch, *Medieval Misogyny and the Invention of Western Romantic Love* (Chicago: University of Chicago Press, 1992); Karen Lystra, *Searching the Heart: Women, Men, and Romantic Love in Nineteenth-century America* (New York: Oxford University Press, 1989); Steven Seidman, *Romantic Longings: Love in America, 1830–1980* (New York: Routledge, 1991); Irving Singer, *The Nature of Love*, vol. 3, *The Modern World* (Chicago: University of Chicago Press, 1989).

11. It was strangely omitted by Max Weber in his monumental study of the different cultural paths taken by the West and the East. See Max Weber, *The Religion of China: Confucianism and Taoism*, ed. and trans. Hans Gerth (1915; London: MacMillan Publishing Company, 1951).

12. Stephanie Coontz, *Marriage, A History: From Obedience to Intimacy, or How Love Conquered Marriage* (New York: Viking Press, 2006).

13. Ulrich Beck, Elisabeth Beck-Gernsheim, Mark Ritter, and Jane Wiebel, *The Normal Chaos of Love* (Cambridge: Polity Press, 1995); Ulrich Beck and Elisabeth Beck-Gernsheim, *Individualization: Institutionalized Individualism and Its Social and Political Consequences* (London: SAGE Publications, 2002); Stephanie Coontz, *Marriage, A History: From Obedience to Intimacy, or How Love Conquered Marriage* (New York: Viking Press, 2006); Helga Dittmar, *Consumer Culture, Identity and Well-being: The Search for the "Good Life" and the "Body Perfect"* (London: Psychology Press, 2007);

Anthony Giddens, *Modernity and Self Identity: Self and Society in Late-Modern Age* (Cambridge: Polity Press, 1991); Anthony Giddens, *The Transformation of Intimacy: Sexuality, Love, and Eroticism in Modern Societies* (Stanford, CA: Stanford University Press, 1992); Jason Hughes, "Emotional Intelligence: Elias, Foucault, and the Reflexive Emotional Self," *Foucault Studies* 8 (2010): 28–52; Alan Hunt, "The Civilizing Process and Emotional Life: The Intensification and Hollowing Out of Contemporary Emotions," in *Emotions Matter: A Relational Approach to Emotions*, ed. Alan Hunt, Kevin Walby, and Dale Spencer (Toronto: University of Toronto Press, 2012), 137–160; Mary Holmes, "The Emotionalization of Reflexivity," *Sociology* 44, no. 1 (2010): 139–154; Richard Sennett, *The Fall of Public Man* (Cambridge: Cambridge University Press, 1977); Lawrence D. Stone, *The Family, Sex and Marriage in England 1500–1800* (London: Penguin Books, 1982).

14. Stephanie Coontz, *Marriage, A History: From Obedience to Intimacy, or How Love Conquered Marriage* (New York: Viking Press, 2006).

15. Gerald Allan Cohen, *Self-ownership, Freedom, and Equality* (Cambridge: Cambridge University Press, 1995), 12.

16. Anthony Giddens, *Modernity and Self-Identity: Self and Society in Late-modern Age* (Cambridge: Polity Press, 1991); Anthony Giddens, *The Transformation of Intimacy: Sexuality, Love, and Eroticism in Modern Societies* (Stanford, CA: Stanford University Press, 1992).

17. Axel Honneth, *The Struggle for Recognition: The Moral Grammar of Social Conflicts*, trans. Joel Anderson (Cambridge: Polity Press, 1995).

18. Camille Paglia, *Sex, Art and American Culture* (New York: Vintage, 1992).

19. George G. Brenkert, "Freedom and Private Property in Marx," *Philosophy and Public Affairs* 2, no. 8 (1979): 122–147; Émile Durkheim, *The Elementary Forms of the Religious Life*, trans. Karen E. Fields (1912; New York: Simon & Schuster, 1995); Émile Durkheim, *Moral Education*, trans. Everett K. Wilson and Herman Schnurer (1925; New York: Free Press, 1961); Émile Durkheim, *Durkheim on Politics and the State*, ed. Anthony Giddens, trans. W. D. Halls (Stanford, CA: Stanford University Press, 1986); Émile Durkheim, *Suicide: A Study in Sociology*, trans. John A. Spaulding and George Simpson (1897; New York: Simon & Schuster, 1997); Anthony Giddens, *Capitalism and Modern Social Theory: An Analysis of the Writings of Marx, Durkheim and Max Weber* (Cambridge: Cambridge University Press, 1971); Karl Marx, *The Grundrisse*, ed. and trans. David McLellan (1939–1941; New York: Harper & Row, 1970); Karl Marx, "The Power of Money," in *Karl Marx and Friedrich Engels: Collected Works*, vol. 3 (1844; New York: International Publishers, 1975); Karl Marx, "Speech on the Question of Free Trade," in *Karl Marx and Friedrich Engels: Collected Works*, vol. 6 (1848; New York: International Publishers, 1976); Karl Marx and Friedrich Engels, "The German Ideology," in *Karl Marx and Friedrich Engels: Collected Works*, vol. 5 (1932; New York: International Publishers, 1975); Karl Marx and Friedrich Engels, "Manifesto of the Communist Party," in *Karl Marx and Friedrich Engels: Collected Works*, vol. 6 (1848; New York: International Publishers, 1976); Georg Simmel, *Freedom and the Individual*, in *On Individuality and Social Forms: Selected Writings*, ed. and with an introduction by Donald N. Levine (Chicago: University of Chicago Press, 1971), 217–226; Georg Simmel, "The

Stranger," in *On Individuality and Social Forms: Selected Writings*, ed. and with an introduction by Donald N Levine (Chicago: University of Chicago Press, 1971), 143–149; Max Weber, *Die Verhältnisse der Landarbeiter im ostelbischen Deutschland*, vol. 55 (Leipzig: Duncker & Humblot, 1892); Max Weber, *The Protestant Ethic and the Spirit of Capitalism*, trans. T. Parsons, A. Giddens, with an introduction by A. Giddens (1904–1905; London: Routledge, 1992); Max Weber, *Max Weber: The Theory of Social and Economic Organization*, trans. A. M. Henderson and T. Parsons, ed. and with an introduction by T. Parsons (1947; New York: The Free Press, 1964).

20. Axel Honneth, *Freedom's Right: The Social Foundations of Democratic Life*, trans. Joseph Ganahl (New York: Columbia University Press, 2014).

21. Wendy Brown, *States of Injury: Power and Freedom in Late Modernity* (Princeton, NJ: Princeton University Press, 1995), 5.

22. David Bloor, *Knowledge and Social Imagery* (London: Routledge & Kegan Paul, 1976).

23. Richard Posner, *Sex and Reason* (Cambridge, MA: Harvard University Press, 1994).

24. See Robin West, "Sex, Reason, and a Taste for the Absurd" (Georgetown Public Law and Legal Theory Research Paper No. 11–76, 1993).

25. Lila Abu-Lughod, "Do Muslim Women Really Need Saving? Anthropological Reflections on Cultural Relativism and Its Others," American Anthropologist 104, no. 3 (2002): 783–790, esp. 785; Saba Mahmood, *Politics of Piety: The Islamic Revival and the Feminist Subject* (Princeton, NJ: Princeton University Press, 2011).

26. Michel Foucault, *Discipline and Punish: The Birth of the Prison*, trans. Alan Sheridan (1975; New York: Pantheon Books, 1977).

27. Michel Foucault, *Security, Territory, Population: Lectures at the Collège de France 1977–1978*, ed. Arnold I. Davidson, trans. Graham Burchell (New York: Palgrave Macmillan, 2007); Michel Foucault, *The Government of Self and Others: Lectures at the Collège de France 1982–1983*, ed. Arnold I. Davidson, trans. Graham Burchell (New York: Palgrave Macmillan, 2010).

28. Nikolas Rose, *Inventing Our Selves: Psychology, Power, and Personhood* (Cambridge: Cambridge University Press, 1998); Nikolas Rose, *Powers of Freedom: Reframing Political Thought* (Cambridge: Cambridge University Press, 1999).

29. Deborah L. Tolman, *Dilemmas of Desire: Teenage Girls Talk about Sexuality* (Cambridge, MA: Harvard University Press, 2002), 5–6.

30. Quoted in Wendy Brown, *States of Injury: Power and Freedom in Late Modernity* (Princeton, NJ: Princeton University Press), 20.

31. See in particular David M. Halperin and Trevor Hoppe, who document the expansion of sexual rights in the United States in their work *The War on Sex*. As they document, while there has been progress in marriage equality, reproductive rights, and access to birth control, there remain many areas that are socially controlled by government such as sex offender registries, criminalization of HIV, and punitive measures against sex work. See David M. Halperin and Trevor Hoppe, eds., *The War on Sex* (Durham, NC: Duke University Press, 2017).

32. For an elaborated discussion on this issue, see Dana Kaplan, "Recreational Sexuality, Food, and New Age Spirituality: A Cultural Sociology of Middle-Class Distinctions" (PhD diss., Hebrew University, 2014); Dana Kaplan, "Sexual Liberation and the Creative Class in Israel," in *Introducing the New Sexuality Studies*, ed.

S. Seidman, N. Fisher, and C. Meeks (2011; London: Routledge, 2016), 363–370; Volker Woltersdorff, "Paradoxes of Precarious Sexualities: Sexual Subcultures under Neo-liberalism," *Cultural Studies* 25, no. 2 (2011): 164–182.

33. Modern homosexuality constitutes the historical accomplishment of sexual freedom its moral embodiment because, in contrast to Greek homosexuality, it does not organize and naturalize inequality (it is not about the display of power of a man over a slave or a young man).

34. Camille Paglia, *Sex, Art, and American Culture: Essays* (1992; New York: Vintage, 2011, ii).

35. Ibid.

36. Jeffrey Weeks, *Invented Moralities: Sexual Values in an Age of Uncertainty* (New York: Columbia University Press, 1995).

37. Ibid., 29. The claim, however, is relevant to the Western world, less so to societies like that of China.

38. This is, by the way, no less true of homosexual encounters than it is of heterosexual ones.

39. Beckert, Jens. *Imagined Futures: Fictional Expectations in the Economy.* In *Theory and Society* 42(2), 219–240.

40. Leo Tolstoy, *War and Peace*, trans. George Gibian (1896; New York: W. W. Norton & Company, 1966), 24.

41. James Duesenberry, "Comment on 'An Economic Analysis of Fertility,'" in Mark Granovetter, *Demographic and Economic Change in Developed Countries*, ed. Universities National Bureau Committee for Economic Research (Princeton, NJ: Princeton University Press, 1985), 233; Mark Granovetter, "Economic Action and Social Structure: The Problem of Embeddedness," *American Journal of Sociology* 91, no. 3 (1985): 458–510.

42. Sven Hillenkamp, Das Ende der Liebe: Gefühle im Zeitalter unendlicher Freiheit. (Stuttgart: Klett-Cotta, 2010); Anthony Giddens, *Modernity and Self-identity: Self and Society in the Late Modern Age* (1991; Stanford, CA: Stanford University Press, 2009); Ian Greener, "Towards a History of Choice in UK Health Policy," *Sociology of Health and Illness* 31, no. 3 (2009): 309–324; Renata Salecl, "Society of Choice," *Differences* 20, no. 1 (2009): 157–180; Renata Salecl, "Self in Times of Tyranny of Choice," *FKW//Zeitschrift für Geschlechterforschung und visuelle Kultur*, no. 50 (2010): 10–23; Renata Salecl, *The Tyranny of Choice* (London: Profile Books, 2011).

43. Stephenie Meyer, "Frequently Asked Questions: Breaking Dawn," accessed September 11, 2016, http://stepheniemeyer.com/the-books/breaking-dawn/frequently-asked-questions-breaking-dawn/.

44. Renata Salecl, "Society of Choice," *Differences* 20, no. 1 (2009): 157–180; Renata Salecl, "Self in Times of Tyranny of Choice," *FKW//Zeitschrift für Geschlechterforschung und visuelle Kultur*, no. 50 (2010); Renata Salecl, *The Tyranny of Choice* (London: Profile Books, 2011).

45. Durkheim, *Suicide*.

46. Günther Anders, "The Pathology of Freedom: An Essay on Non-identification," trans. Katharine Wolfe, *Deleuze Studies* 3, no. 2 (2009): 278–310. See also Eric S. Nelson, "Against Liberty: Adorno, Levinas and the Pathologies of Freedom," *Theoria* 59, no. 131 (2012): 64–83.

47. See Manuel Castells, "The Net and the Self: Working Notes for a Critical Theory of the Informational Society," *Critique of Anthropology* 16, no. 1 (1996): 9–38.

48. Eva Illouz, *Why Love Hurts* (Cambridge: Polity Press, 2012).

49. See Wolfgang Streeck, "How to Study Contemporary Capitalism?" *European Journal of Sociology/Archives Européennes de Sociologie* 53, no. 1 (2012): 1–28.

50. See, for example, Peter Brooks and Horst Zank, "Loss Averse Behavior," *Journal of Risk and Uncertainty* 31, no. 3 (2005): 301–325; Matthew Rabin, "Psychology and Economics," *Journal of Economic Literature* 36, no. 1 (1998): 11–46; Colin F. Camerer, "Prospect Theory in the Wild: Evidence from the Field," in *Choices, Values, and Frames*, ed. Daniel Kahneman and Amos Tversky (Cambridge: Cambridge University Press, 2000), 288–300.

51. "I Don't," *The Economist*, September 1, 2016, http://www.economist.com/news/asia/21706321-most-japanese-want-be-married-are-finding-it-hard-i-dont.

52. Fraser, Nancy. 2016. "Contradictions of Capitalism and Care, *New Left Review*, June–July, pp. 99–117.

53. As Daniel Bachman and Akrur Barua describe based on US Census Bureau reports: "Between 1960 and 2014, the median age of first marriage rose to 29.3 years for men and 27.0 years for women from 22.8 years and 20.3 years, respectively.1 During this time, the share of single-person households in total households more than doubled to 27.7 percent and the average number of people per household fell to 2.54 from 3.33." "Between 1999 and 2014, the number of single-person households went up to about 34.2 million from 26.6 million, an average annual rise of 1.7 percent. Growth in total households during the same period was lower (1.1 percent), leading to a more than 2 percentage point rise in the share of single-person households in total households." "The projections show that single-person households are set to reach about 41.4 million by 2030, an average annual rise of 1.1 percent over 2015–2030." US Census Bureau, "Families and Living Arrangements: Marital Status," October 21, 2015, https://www.census.gov/hhes/families/data/marital.html; US Census Bureau, "Families and Living Arrangements: Households," October 21, 2015. Ibid. Daniel Bachman and Akrur Barua "Single-person Households: Another Look at the Changing American Family." (n.p.: Deloitte University Press, 2015), http://dupress.deloitte.com/dup-us-en/economy/behind-the-numbers/single-person-households-and-changing-american-family.html, accessed September 11, 2016.

54. W. Bradford Wilcox "The Evolution of Divorce," *National Affairs* (Fall 2009), accessed September 11, 2016, http://nationalaffairs.com/publications/detail/the-evolution-of-divorce.

55. As Claire Cain Miller shows based on "Survey of Income and Program Participation." It is important to note that Miller also shows that since the peak in the 1970s and early 1980s, the divorce rate has been declining for people who married since the 1990s. Claire Cain Miller, "The Divorce Surge Is Over, but the Myth Lives On," *New York Times*, December 4, 2014, accessed September 11, 2016, http://www.nytimes.com/2014/12/02/upshot/the-divorce-surge-is-over-but-the-myth-lives-on.html.

56. Charlotte Lytton, "I Me Wed: Why Are More Women Choosing to Marry Themselves?" *The Telegraph* (London), September 28, 2017 http://www.telegraph.co.uk/women/life/women-choosing-marry/, accessed February 13, 2018.

57. G. Oscar Anderson, *Loneliness among Older Adults: A National Survey of Adults 45+*. Washington, DC: AARP Research, September 2010, https://doi.org/10.26419/res.00064.001.

58. Julianne Holt-Lunstad, "So Lonely I Could Die," *American Psychological Association*, August 5, 2017, https://www.apa.org/news/press/releases/2017/08/lonely-die.aspx.

59. Jane E. Brody, "The Surprising Effects of Loneliness on Health," *New York Times*, December 11, 2017, accessed February 13, 2018, https://www.nytimes.com/2017/12/11/well/mind/how-loneliness-affects-our-health.html?_r=0.

60. Anna Goldfarb, "How to Maintain Friendships," *New York Times*, January 18, 2018, https://www.nytimes.com/2018/01/18/smarter-living/how-to-maintain-friends.html, accessed February 13, 2018.

61. Julian, Kate. 2018. "Why Are Young People Having So Little Sex?" in *Atlantic* 2018 December, https://www.theatlantic.com/magazine/archive/2018/12/the-sex-recession/573949/.

62. Some of the people were interviewed in cafes and were found through snowball procedure. Others were acquaintances who shared with me their experiences. All names have been anonymized. When details about an interviewee were potentially revealing of his or her identity, I deliberately changed them to ensure maximum anonymity (for example if someone occupied a unique professional position, I deliberately changed that position while maintaining a roughly similar educational and economic background). I interviewed a majority of heterosexual men and women but occasionally refer to homosexuals when I thought they reflect quite well processes at work in heterosexual couples as well. The sample included twenty-four divorcees, thirty-four married people, and thirty-four people in casual relationships or without relationships. It included forty-seven women and forty-five men. Because of the sensitive nature of the interviews, I quickly abandoned my recording device and interview protocol and instead used informal conversations to elicit accounts that were written down from memory immediately after my encounters. This method was most definitely less obtrusive and is in line with ethnographic mode of analysis. Occasionally, I wrote down by hand the main points of the conversation while it was happening. These conversations lasted anywhere from thirty minutes to one and a half hours.

63. Lauren Berlant, "Slow Death (Sovereignty, Obesity, Lateral Agency)," *Critical Inquiry* 33, no. 4 (2007): 754–780.

Chapter 2

1. Anthony Trollope, *An Old Man's Love* (1884; Oxford: Oxford University Press, 1951), 33.

2. See Charles Horton Cooley, *Human Nature and the Social Order* (1902; Pisataway, NJ: Transaction Publishers, 1992), 184; David D. Franks and Viktor Gecas,

"Autonomy and Conformity in Cooley's Self-theory: The Looking-glass Self and Beyond," *Symbolic Interaction* 15, no. 1 (1992): 49–68; George. H. Mead, "Cooley's Contribution to American Social Thought," *American Sociological Review* 35, no. 5 (1930): 693–706; George H. Mead, *Mind, Self and Society* (Chicago: University of Chicago Press, 1934); J. Sidney Shrauger and Thomas J. Schoeneman, "Symbolic Interactionist View of Self-concept: Through the Looking Glass Darkly," *Psychological bulletin* 86, no. 3 (1979): 549–573; Dianne M. Tice, "Self-concept Change and Self-presentation: The Looking Glass Self Is Also a Magnifying Glass," *Journal of Personality and Social Psychology* 63, no. 3 (1992): 435–451.

3. Durkheim, *Suicide.*

4. The end of the nineteenth century saw the emergence of a new social type, the hedonist single man who became abundantly described in literature by Gustave Flaubert, Charles Baudelaire, Marcel Proust, or later Stefan Zweig and Irene Nemirovsky. This was a new social and literary character who was characterized by his lack of desire to enter matrimony, thus shunning what was still for many a privileged way to financial and social mobility.

5. Durkheim, *Suicide*, 234; Émile Durkheim, *Le suicide: Étude de sociologie* (Paris: F. Alcan, 1897), 304–305.

6. Si ses jouissances [de l'homme marie] sont définies, elles sont assurées, et cette certitude consolide son assiette mentale. Tout autre est la situation du célibataire. Comme il peut légitimement s'attacher à ce qui lui plaît, il aspire à tout et rien ne le contente. Ce mal de l'infini, que l'anomie apporte partout avec elle, peut tout aussi bien atteindre cette partie de notre conscience que toute autre; il prend très souvent une forme sexuelle que Musset a décrite (1). Du moment qu'on n'est arrêté par rien, on ne saurait s'arrêter soi-même. Au delà des plaisirs dont on a fait l'expérience, on en imagine et on en veut d'autres; s'il arrive qu'on ait à peu près parcouru tout le cercle du possible, on rêve à l'impossible; on a soif de ce qui n'est pas (2). Comment la sensibilité ne s'exaspérerait-elle pas dans cette poursuite qui ne peut pas aboutir? Pour qu'elle en vienne à ce point, il n'est même pas nécessaire qu'on ait multiplié à l'infini les expériences amoureuses et vécu en Don Juan. L'existence médiocre du célibataire vulgaire suffit pour cela. Ce sont sans cesse des espérances nouvelles qui s'éveillent et qui sont déçues, laissant derrière elles une impression de fatigue et de désenchantement. Comment, d'ailleurs, le désir pourrait-il se fixer, puisqu'il n'est pas sûr de pouvoir garder ce qui l'attire; car l'anomie est double. De même que le sujet ne se donne pas définitivement, il ne possède rien à titre définitif. L'incertitude de l'avenir, jointe à sa propre indétermination, le condamne donc à une perpétuelle mobilité. De tout cela résulte un état de trouble, d'agitation et de mécontentement qui accroît nécessairement les chances de suicide."

7. Véronique Mottier, *Sexuality: A Very Short Introduction* (New York: Oxford University Press, 2008), 5.

8. See William. E. Mann, "Augustine on Evil and Original Sin," in *The Cambridge Companion to Augustine*, ed. Eleonore Stump and Norman Kretzmann (Cambridge: Cambridge University Press, 2001), 40–48; Marjorie Hewitt Suchocki, *The Fall to Violence: Original Sin in Relational Theology* (New York: Continuum, 1994).

9. See John Giles Milhaven, "Thomas Aquinas on Sexual Pleasure," *The Journal of Religious Ethics* 5, no. 2 (1977): 157–181.

10. For Augustine's later thirteenth-century companion theologian Thomas Aquinas, sex should be engaged in only for the sake of reproduction, and not for pleasure. Aquinas allowed married people to have sex, but only reluctantly conceded that pleasurable sexuality could be tolerated as long as it took place within the frame of marriage.

11. See Jack Goody, *The Development of the Family and Marriage in Europe* (Cambridge: Cambridge University Press, 1983); Philip Lyndon Reynolds, *Marriage in the Western Church: The Christianization of Marriage during the Patristic and Early Medieval Periods*, vol. 24 (Leiden: Brill, 1994).

12. Faramerz Dabhoiwala, "Lust and Liberty," *Past & Present* 207, no. 1 (2010): 89–179, esp. 90.

13. Richard Godbeer, *Sexual Revolution in Early America* (Baltimore: Johns Hopkins University Press, 2002), 10–11.

14. Ibid., 3.

15. Faramerz Dabhoiwala, "Lust and Liberty," *Past & Present* 207, no. 1 (2010): 89–179, esp. 90.

16. For a review of history of Western sexual mores, see Richard A. Posner, *Sex and Reason* (Cambridge, MA: Harvard University Press, 1994), 37–65.

17. Immanuel Kant, "Duties to the Body and Crimes against Nature," in D. P. Verene, *Sexual Love and Western Morality* (1972; Boston: Jones and Bartlett, 1995), 110.

18. Ibid.

19. See Ann Heilmann, "Mona Caird (1854–1932): Wild Woman, New Woman, and Early Radical Feminist Critic of Marriage and Motherhood," *Women's History Review* 5, no. 1 (1996): 67–95; Joanne E. Passet, *Sex Radicals and the Quest for Women's Equality*, vol. 112 (Urbana and Chicago: University of Illinois Press, 2003).

20. For more on love, courtship, and sex in medieval France, see E. Jane Burns, *Courtly Love Undressed: Reading through Clothes in Medieval French Culture* (Philadelphia: University of Pennsylvania Press, 2005); Laurie A. Finke, "Sexuality in Medieval French Literature: 'Séparés, on est ensemble,'" in *Handbook of Medieval Sexuality*, ed. Vern L. Bullough and James A. Brundage (New York/London: Taylor & Francis, 1996), 345–368; Simon Gaunt, *Love and Death in Medieval French and Occitan Courtly Literature: Martyrs to Love* (Oxford University Press on Demand, 2006); Robert W. Hanning, "Love and Power in the Twelfth Century, with Special Reference to Chrétien de Troyes and Marie de France," in *The Olde Daunce: Love, Friendship, Sex, and Marriage in the Medieval World*, ed. Robert R. Edwards and Stephen Spector (Albany: SUNY Press, 1991), 87–103.

21. Famous examples of medieval love as those of Dante and Petrarch suggest that a man could love a woman and vow a poetic cult to her long after her death, as if courtship was a ritual for the sheer solipsistic expression of love, rather than for the actual interaction with another, enacting a quasi-religious prayer-like emotion.

22. As Catherine Bates describes: "'Courting' lent itself to the art of love-making because wooing a member of the opposite sex came to be regarded as a highly

complex, tactical, and strategic rhetorical procedure. Partners were perceived as two remote and distanced individuals between whom communication was presented as difficult and highly pressurized. Norbert Elias considers this transformation of emotional and amorous behavior a direct consequence of the wholesale 'civilizing process' which, from the Middle Ages, was the product of centralized power as autocratic rulers maintained their monopoly by minimizing spontaneous displays of violence or emotion among their subjects. Individuals were encouraged to sublimate their desires, lastingly transforming the imperatives of 'civilized' social behavior into self-constraints." See Catherine Bates, *The Rhetoric of Courtship in Elizabethan Language and Literature* (Cambridge: Cambridge University Press, 1992), 11.

23. For more on the history of courtship, see ibid.; Catherine Bates, *Courtship and Courtliness* (PhD diss., University of Oxford, 1989); Ilona Bell, *Elizabethan Women and the Poetry of Courtship* (New York: Cambridge University Press, 1998); Ellen K. Rothman, *Hands and Hearts: A History of Courtship in America* (New York: Basic Books, 1984).

24. Niklas Luhmann, *Love as Passion: The Codification of Intimacy* (Cambridge, MA: Harvard University Press, 1986), 77.

25. For a review of this trend in America, see John D'Emilio and Estelle B. Freedman, *Intimate Matters: A History of Sexuality in America* (Chicago: University of Chicago Press, 1998).

26. This is why Don Juan—the seventeenth-century transgressor of religious morality worthy of Divine punishment—is a seducer of women. It is because betraying moral rules of courtship was equivalent to betraying society and morality writ large.

27. Lawrence Stone, *Uncertain Unions: Marriage in England, 1660–1753* (Oxford: Oxford University Press, 1992), 8).

28. Anthony Giddens, *Modernity and Self-identity: Self and Society in the Late Modern Age* (Stanford, CA: Stanford University Press, 1991).

29. See Niklas Luhmann, *Love as Passion: The Codification of Intimacy* (Cambridge, MA: Harvard University Press, 1986), 147–148; and Niklas Luhmann, *Social Systems* (Stanford, CA: Stanford University Press, 1995).

30. Niklas Luhmann, *Love: A Sketch* (Cambridge: Polity Press, 2010), 10.

31. Denise Haunani Solomon and Leanne K. Knobloch. "Relationship Uncertainty, Partner Interference, and Intimacy within Dating Relationships," *Journal of Social and Personal Relationships* 18, no. 6 (2001): 804–820, esp. 805.

32. *The Blackwell Encyclopedia of Sociology*, ed. George Ritzer, s.v. "Uncertainty" (Hoboken, NJ: Blackwell, 2007), http://www.blackwellreference.com/public/tocnode?id=g9781405124331_chunk_g978140512433127_ss1-1#citation, accessed June 21, 2017.

33. See Anthony Fletcher, "Manhood, the Male Body, Courtship and the Household in Early Modern England," *History* 84, no. 275 (1999): 419–436; Marie H. Loughlin, *Hymeneutics: Interpreting Virginity on the Early Modern Stage* (Lewisburg, PA: Bucknell University Press, 1997); Kim M. Phillips and Barry Reay, *Sex before Sexuality: A Premodern History* (Cambridge: Polity Press, 2011); Ulrike Strasser,

State of Virginity: Gender, Religion, and Politics in an Early Modern Catholic State (Ann Arbor: University of Michigan Press, 2004).

34. Adele Schopenhauer quoted in Diethe Carol, *Towards Emancipation: German Women Writers of the Nineteenth Century* (New York/Oxford: Berghahn Books, 1998), 55. Victoria Gairin depicts the episode in "Comment devient-on-misogyne," in *Le Point Hors-série* 21 (2016): S. 23.

35. Richard Godbeer, *Sexual Revolution in Early America* (Baltimore: Johns Hopkins University Press, 2002), 3.

36. Thomas E. Buckley, ed. *"If You Love That Lady Don't Marry Her"*: *The Courtship Letters of Sally McDowell and John Miller, 1854–1856* (Columbia: University of Missouri Press, 2000, 6), emphasis added.

37. George Herbert Palmer was an American scholar and author who translated many classics such as *The Odyssey* (1884); Alice Freeman was an American educator who advocated college education for women and was the president of Wellesley College.

38. Quoted in M. A. DeWolfe Howe, "An Academic Courtship: Letters of Alice Freeman Palmer and George Herbert Palmer," *The New England Quarterly* 14, no. 1 (March 1941): 153–155, emphasis added.

39. Quoted from John Mullan, *Courtship, Love and Marriage in Jane Austen's Novels: Discovering Literature*, Romantics and Victorians, British Library, May 15, 2017, http://www.bl.uk/romantics-and-victorians/articles/courtship-love-and-marriage-in-jane-austens-novels#, accessed June 21, 2017.

40. Marilyn Ferris Motz, "'Thou Art My Last Love': The Courtship and Remarriage of a Rural Texas Couple in 1892," *The Southwestern Historical Quarterly* 93, no. 4 (1990): 457–474, esp. 457.

41. John R. Gillis, *For Better, for Worse: British Marriages, 1600 to the Present* (New York: Oxford University Press, 1985), 33.

42. Ibid.

43. Ibid.

44. Ibid., 33–34.

45. Richard Bulcroft, Kris Bulcroft, Karen Bradley, and Carl Simpson, "The Management and Production of Risk in Romantic Relationships: A Postmodern Paradox," *Journal of Family History* 25, no. 1 (2000): 63–92, esp. 69.

46. James H. S. Bossard, "Residential Propinquity as a Factor in Marriage Selection," *American Journal of Sociology* 38, no. 2 (1932): 219–224.

47. Gustave Flaubert, *Madame Bovary*, trans. *Margaret Mauldon* (1856; Oxford: Oxford University Press, 2004), 23–24.

48. Ibid., 24.

49. Richard Bulcroft et al., "The Management and Production of Risk in Romantic Relationships: A Postmodern Paradox," *Journal of Family History* 25, no. 1 (2000): 63–92, esp. 69. See also John R. Gillis, *For Better, for Worse: British Marriages, 1600 to the Present* (New York: Oxford University Press, 1985).

50. Quoted in Carol Berkin, *Civil War Wives* (New York: Vintage, 2009), 58.

51. Quoted in Robert K. Nelson, "'The Forgetfulness of Sex': Devotion and Desire in the Courtship Letters of Angelina Grimke and Theodore Dwight Weld," *Journal of Social History* 37, no. 3 (2004): 663–679, esp. 670.

52. Quoted in ibid., 671, emphasis added.

53. McDowell and Miller. *"If You Love That Lady Don't Marry Her,"* 15, emphasis added.

54. Darlene Clark Hine and Earnestine L. Jenkins, eds., *A Question of Manhood: A Reader in U.S. Black Men's History and Masculinity*, vol. 2: *The 19th Century: From Emancipation to Jim Crow* (Bloomington: Indiana University Press, 2001), 234.

55. Anthony Trollope, *The Claverings* (1867; 2008), 120.

56. Émile Durkheim, *Elementary Forms of the Religious Life* (1912; New York: Free Press, 1995)..

57. Ibid. See also Douglas A. Marshall, "Behavior, Belonging and Belief: A Theory of Ritual Practice," *Sociological Theory* 20, no. 3 (November 2002): 360–380.

58. Joel Robbins, "Ritual Communication and Linguistic Ideology: A Reading and Partial Reformulation of Rappaport's Theory of Ritual," in *Current Anthropology* 42, no. 5 (December 2001): 591–614, esp. 592.

59. Ibid.

60. "Conversations with History: Harry Kreisler with Michael Walzer," Institute of International Studies at the University of California, Berkeley (November 12, 2013), accessed June 21, 2017, http://conversations.berkeley.edu/content/michael-walzer.

61. Niklas Luhmann, *Social Systems* (Stanford, CA: Stanford University Press), 1995; Niklas Luhmann, *Die Gesellschaft der Gesellschaft* (Frankfurt: Suhrkamp, 1997).

62. Åsa Boholm, "The Cultural Nature of Risk: Can There Be an Anthropology of Uncertainty," *Ethnos* 68, no. 2 (2003): 159–178; Niklas Luhmann, *Trust and Power* (New York: John Wiley & Sons, 1979).

63. Véronique Mottier, *Sexuality: A Very Short Introduction* (New York: Oxford University Press, 2008, 1).

64. For a brilliant analysis of the relationship between different political regimes and sex, see Dagmar Herzog, *Sex after Fascism: Memory and Morality in Twentieth-century Germany* (Princeton, NJ: Princeton University Press, 2007).

65. Michel Foucault, *The History of Sexuality: An Introduction*, vol. 1, trans. Robert Hurley (1976; New York: Vintage, 1990); James O'Higgins and Michel Foucault. "II. Sexual Choice, Sexual Act: An Interview with Michel Foucault," *Salmagundi* 58/59 (1982): 10–24. For a discussion dealing with Foucault's view on freedom (and truth), see Charles Taylor, "Foucault on Freedom and Truth," *Political Theory* 12, no. 2 (1984): 152–183.

66. Faramerz Dabhoiwala, "Lust and Liberty," *Past & Present*, no. 207 (May 2010): 89–179, esp. 92.

67. Samuel D. Warren and Louis D. Brandeis, "The Right to Privacy," *Harvard Law Review* 4, no. 5 (December 1, 1890): 5; 193–220.

68. Mary Beth Oliver and Janet Shibley Hyde, "Gender Differences in Sexuality: A Meta-analysis," *Psychological Bulletin* 114, no. 1 (1993): 29–51; Véronique Mottier, *Sexuality: A Very Short Introduction* (New York: Oxford University Press, 2008), 187.

69. Lisa Wade, *American Hookup: The New Culture of Sex on Campus* (New York: W. W. Norton & Company, 2017), 57.

70. For review, see Mari Jo Buhle, *Feminism and Its Discontents: A Century of Struggle with Psychoanalysis* (Cambridge, MA: Harvard University Press, 2009); Thea

Cacchioni, "The Medicalization of Sexual Deviance, Reproduction, and Functioning," in *Handbook of the Sociology of Sexualities*, ed. John DeLamater and Rebecca F. Plante (New York: Springer International Publishing, 2015), 435–452; Eva Illouz, *Saving the Modern Soul: Therapy, Emotions, and the Culture of Self-help* (Berkeley: University of California Press, 2008); Janice M. Irvine, *Disorders of Desire: Sexuality and Gender in Modern American Sexology* (Philadelphia: Temple University Press, 2005); Jeffrey Weeks, *Sexuality and Its Discontents: Meanings, Myths, and Modern Sexualities* (New York: Routledge, 2002).

71. T. J. Jackson Lears, *No Place of Grace: Antimodernism and the Transformation of American Culture, 1880–1920* (Chicago/London: University of Chicago Press, 1981); Lawrence Birken, *Consuming Desire* (Ithaca: Cornell University Press), 1988.

72. David Allyn, *Make Love, Not War: The Sexual Revolution: An Unfettered History* (London: Routledge, 2016); Attwood Feona and Clarissa Smith, "More Sex! Better Sex! Sex Is Fucking Brilliant! Sex, Sex, Sex, SEX," in *Routledge Handbook of Leisure Studies*, ed. Tony Blackshaw (London: Routledge, 2013), 325–336. See also Jay A. Mancini and Dennis K. Orthner, "Recreational Sexuality Preferences among Middle-class Husbands and Wives," *Journal of Sex Research* 14, no. 2 (1978): 96–106; Edward O. Laumann, John H. Gagnon, Robert T. Michael, and Stuart Michaels, *The Social Organization of Sexuality: Sexual Practices in the United States* (Chicago: University of Chicago Press, 1994).

73. Charles I. Glicksberg, *The Sexual Revolution in Modern American Literature* (The Hague: Martinus Nijhoff, 1971); Charles I. Glicksberg, "The Sexual Revolution and the Modern Drama," in *The Sexual Revolution in Modern English Literature* (The Hague: Springer Science+Business Media, 1973), 43–70.

74. For an analysis of the sexual revolution in Europe, see "Pleasure and Rebellion 1965 to 1980" in Dagmar Herzog, *Sexuality in Europe: A Twentieth-century History*, vol. 45 (Cambridge: Cambridge University Press, 2011).

75. John Levi Martin, "Structuring the Sexual Revolution," *Theory and Society* 25, no. 1 (February 1996): 105–151.

76. See Richard Dyer, *Heavenly Bodies: Film Stars and Society* (London: Psychology Press, 2004).

77. See Elizabeth Goren, "America's Love Affair with Technology: The Transformation of Sexuality and the Self over the Twentieth Century," *Psychoanalytic Psychology* 20, no. 3 (2003): 487–508; Brian McNair, *Striptease Culture: Sex, Media and the Democratization of Desire* (London: Psychology Press, 2002).

78. See Heather Addison, "Hollywood, Consumer Culture and the Rise of 'Body Shaping,'" in *Hollywood Goes Shopping*, ed. David Desser and Garth Jowett (Minneapolis: University of Minnesota Press, 2000), 3–33; Mike Featherstone, "The Body in Consumer Culture," *Theory, Culture & Society* 1, no. 2 (1982): 18–33; Valerie Steele, *Fashion and Eroticism: Ideals of Feminine Beauty from the Victorian Era to the Jazz Age* (New York: Oxford University Press, 1985); Elizabeth Wilson, *Adorned in Dreams: Fashion and Modernity* (1985; London: IB Tauris, 2003).

79. See Peter Biskind, *Easy Riders Raging Bulls: How the Sex-Drugs-and Rock 'n' Roll Generation Saved Hollywood* (New York: Simon & Schuster, 1999); Thomas Doherty,

Pre-Code Hollywood: Sex, Immorality, and Insurrection in American Cinema, 1930–1934 (New York: Columbia University Press, 1999); Juliann Sivulka, *Soap, Sex, and Cigarettes: A Cultural History of American Advertising* (Boston: Cengage Learning, 2011).

80. Quoted in Esteban Buch, *La musique fait l'amour: Une enquête sur la bande-son de la vie sexuelle* (submitted for publication), 7.

81. See Eva Illouz, ed., *Emotions as Commodities* (London: Routledge, 2018).

82. Wolfgang Streeck, "Citizens as Customers: Considerations on the New Politics of Consumption," *New Left Review* 76 (2012): 27–47, esp. 33.

83. See Stuart Hall, *The Hard Road to Renewal: Thatcherism and the Crisis of the Left* (London: Verso, 1988). See also Thomas Frank, *The Conquest of Cool: Business Culture, Counterculture, and the Rise of Hip Consumerism* (Chicago: University of Chicago Press, 1997).

84. Susie Bright, *Full Exposure: Opening Up to Sexual Creativity and Erotic Expression* (New York: HarperCollins, 2009), 52–53.

85. Ibid., 6, emphasis added.

86. Véronique Mottier, *Sexuality: A Very Short Introduction*, vol. 187 (New York: Oxford University Press, 2008), 44.

87. Stephen Garton, *Histories of Sexuality: Antiquity to Sexual Revolution* (New York: Routledge, 2004), 210.

88. Kate Millett, *Sexual Politics* (New York: Doubleday Publishers, 1970).

89. Quoted in Micaela Di Leonardo and Roger Lancaster, "Gender, Sexuality, Political Economy," *New Politics* 6, no. 1 (1996): 29–43, esp. 35.

90. Quoted in Dagmar Herzog, "What Incredible Yearnings Human Beings Have," *Contemporary European History* 22, no. 2 (May 2013): 303–317. Originally located in Kurt Starke [in conversation with Uta Kolano], "…ein romantisches Ideal," in Uta Kolano, *Nackter Osten* (Frankfurt and Oder: Frankfurter Oder Editionen, 1995), 103–104.

91. Robert Sherwin and Sherry Corbett, "Campus Sexual Norms and Dating Relationships: A Trend Analysis," *Journal of Sex Research* 21, no. 3 (1985): 258–274, esp. 265.

92. Paula England, Emily Fitzgibbons Shafer, and Alison C. K. Fogarty, "Hooking Up and Forming Romantic Relationships on Today's College Campuses" in *The Gendered Society Reader*, 3rd ed., ed. Michael S. Kimmel and Amy Aronson (New York: Oxford University Press, 2008), 531–593.

93. Vanessa Friedman, "Pinups in the Post-Weinstein World," *New York Times*, November 27, 2017, https://www.nytimes.com/2017/11/27/style/victorias-secret-fashion-show-love-advent-weinstein.html?emc=eta1&_r=0.

94. Ibid.

95. See Gill Rosalind and Angela MacRobbie for excellent discussions in Rosalind Gill, *Gender and the Media* (Hoboken, NJ: Wiley, 2015); and Angela McRobbie, *The Aftermath of Feminism: Gender, Culture and Social Change* (London: SAGE Publications, 2009).

96. For the use of this type of logic in romantic dating sites, see Eva Illouz, "Romantic Webs," in *Cold Intimacies: The Making of Emotional Capitalism* (Cambridge: Polity Press, 2007), 74–114.

97. Rosalind Gill, *Gender and the Media* (Hoboken, NJ: Wiley, 2015); Catharine A. MacKinnon, *Feminism Unmodified: Discourses on Life and Law* (Cambridge, MA: Harvard University Press, 1987); Naomi Wolf, *The Beauty Myth: How Images of Beauty Are Used against Women* (New York: Random House, 2013).

98. See Barbara A. Brown, Thomas I. Emerson, Gail Falk, and Ann E. Freedman, "The Equal Rights Amendment: A Constitutional Basis for Equal Rights for Women," *The Yale Law Journal* 80, no. 5 (1971): 871–985; Nicola Lacey, "Feminist Legal Theories and the Rights of Women," in *Gender and Human Rights: Collected Courses of the Academy of European Law (XII/2)*, ed. Karen Knop (Oxford University Press, 2004), 13–56; Diane Richardson, "Constructing Sexual Citizenship: Theorizing Sexual Rights," *Critical Social Policy* 20, no. 1 (2000): 105–135.

99. See Ester Boserup, *Woman's Role in Economic Development* (Routledge: Abingdon-on-Thames, 2007); Derek H. C. Chen, "Gender Equality and Economic Development: The Role for Information and Communication Technologies," World Bank Policy Research Working Paper 3285 (Washington, DC, 2004); Matthias Doepke, Michèle Tertilt, and Alessandra Voena, "The Economics and Politics of Women's Rights," *Annual Review of Economics* 4, no. 1 (2012): 339–372; Esther Duflo, "Women Empowerment and Economic Development," *Journal of Economic Literature* 50, no. 4 (2012): 1051–1079; Ronald F. Inglehart, "Changing Values among Western Publics from 1970 to 2006," *West European Politics* 31, nos. 1–2 (2008): 130–146.

100. See Robert G. Dunn, "Identity, Commodification, and Consumer Culture," in *Identity and Social Change*, ed. Joseph E. Davis (New York: Routledge, 2000), 109–134; Yiannis Gabriel and Tim Lang, *The Unmanageable Consumer* (London: SAGE Publications, 2015); Margaret K. Hogg and Paul C. N. Michell, "Identity, Self and Consumption: A Conceptual Framework," *Journal of Marketing Management* 12, no. 7 (1996): 629–644; Alan Tomlinson, ed., *Consumption, Identity and Style: Marketing, Meanings, and the Packaging of Pleasure* (New York: Routledge, 2006).

101. Axel Honneth, *Freedom's Right: The Social Foundations of Democratic Life*, trans. Joseph Ganahl (New York: Columbia University Press, 2014).

102. Peter Brown, "Rome: Sex and Freedom," review of *From Shame to Sin: The Christian Transformation of Sexual Morality in Late Antiquity*, by Kyle Harper, *The New York Review of Books*, December 9, 2013, http://www.nybooks.com/articles/2013/12/19/rome-sex-freedom/, accessed September 9, 2016.

103. Hauzel Kamkhenthang, *The Paite: A Transborder Tribe of India and Burma* (New Delhi: Mittal Publications, 1988), 161.

104. Marshall Sahlins, *What Kinship Is—and Is Not* (Chicago: University of Chicago Press, 2013), 2.

105. Enric Porqueres i Gené and Jérôme Wilgaux, "Incest, Embodiment, Genes and Kinship," *European Kinship in the Age of Biotechnology*, ed. Jeanette Edwards and Carles Salazar (New York, Oxford: Berghahn, 2009), 112–127, esp. 122, emphasis added.

106. Ibid., 123.

107. Martin King Whyte, *Dating, Mating, and Marriage* (Berlin: Aldine de Gruyter, 1990), 22–24), quoted in Barry Reay, "Promiscuous Intimacies: Rethinking the History of American Casual Sex," *Journal of Historical Sociology* 27, no. 1 (2014): 1–24, esp. 5.

108. Manning et al. (116) argue that since the age at marriage in the United States is at a historic high point (27.6 years for men and 25.9 years for women), emerging adults have more time to experience a range of premarital relationships. In a survey conducted in 1992, which included 8,450 males and females aged 14–22, it was found that young age at first coitus was associated with increased odds that females and males had had two or more partners in the previous three months, and being married lowered the odds. In addition, it was found that 31.1 percent of the twenty-one-year-old females and 45 percent of the twenty-one-year-old males had already had six or more previous sexual partners (John S. Santelli, Nancy D. Brener, Richard Lowry, Amita Bhatt, and Laurie S. Zabin, "Multiple Sexual Partners among US Adolescents and Young Adults," *Family Planning Perspectives* 30, no. 6 (1998): 271–275, esp. 271). In the classic study of Lauman it was found that 20.9 percent of the men and 8.2 percent of the women who were born between the years of 1963 and 1974 had had more than five sexual partners before their formal marriage (Edward O. Laumann, *The Social Organization of Sexuality: Sexual Practices in the United States* (Chicago: University of Chicago Press, 1994), 208; Wendy D. Manning, Jessica A. Cohen, and Pamela J. Smock, "The Role of Romantic Partners, Family, and Peer Networks in Dating Couples' Views about Cohabitation," *Journal of Adolescent Research* 26, no. 1 (2011): 115–149.

109. For more on the processes of justification, see Luc Boltanski and Laurent Thévenot *On Justification: Economies of Worth* (Princeton, NJ: Princeton University Press, 2006).

110. Ibid., 348.

111. Gayle Rubin, *Deviations: A Gayle Rubin Reader* (Durham, NC: Duke University Press, 2011), 154.

Chapter 3

1. *The Misunderstanding*, 2013 [1926], London: Vintage Books: p. 17.

2. See Drucilla Cornell, *At the Heart of Freedom: Feminism, Sex, and Equality* (Princeton, NJ: Princeton University Press, 1998); Naomi B. McCormick, *Sexual Salvation: Affirming Women's Sexual Rights and Pleasures* (Santa Barbara: Greenwood Publishing Group, 1994); Diane Richardson, "Constructing Sexual Citizenship: Theorizing Sexual Rights," *Critical Social Policy* 20, no. 1 (2000): 105–135; Steven Seidman, "From the Polluted Homosexual to the Normal Gay: Changing Patterns of Sexual Regulation in America," in *Thinking Straight: The Power, the Promise, and the Paradox of Heterosexuality*, ed. Chrys Ingraham (London: Psychology Press, 2005), 39–61.

3. For a descriptive overview of different definitions of sexual health that stresses the importance of sexual life to the physical and mental health of individuals, see Weston M. Edwards and Eli Coleman, "Defining Sexual Health: A Descriptive Overview," *Archives of Sexual Behavior* 33, no. 3 (2004): 189–195.

4. See, for example, Ruth Colker, "Feminism, Sexuality and Authenticity," in *At the Boundaries of Law (RLE Feminist Theory): Feminism and Legal Theory*, ed. Martha

Albertson Fineman and Nancy Sweet Thomadsen (New York: Routledge, 2013), 135–148; Fiona Handyside, "Authenticity, Confession and Female Sexuality: From Bridget to Bitchy," *Psychology & Sexuality* 3, no. 1 (2012): 41–53.

5. See Friedrich Engels and Lewis Henry Morgan, *The Origin of the Family, Private Property and the State* (1884; Moscow: Foreign Languages Publishing House, 1978); Christopher Freeman and Luc Soete, *The Economics of Industrial Innovation* (London: Psychology Press, 1997).

6. Gilles Deleuze, "Postscript on the Societies of Control," *October* 59 (Winter 1992): 3–7, esp. 6.

7. Ibid., 6. See also Nicholas Thoburn, *Deleuze, Marx and Politics* (London: Routledge, 2003, 96.

8. See chapter 4.

9. See Richard Godbeer, *Sexual Revolution in Early America* (Baltimore: John Hopkins University Press, 2002).

10. Erica Jong, *Fear of Flying* (New York: Signet, 1973).

11. See Justin R. Garcia et al., "Sexual Hookup Culture: A Review," *Review of General Psychology* 16, no. 2 (2012): 161; Lisa Wade, *American Hookup: The New Culture of Sex on Campus* (New York: W.W. Norton & Company, 2017); Jocelyn J. Wentland and Elke Reissing, "Casual Sexual Relationships: Identifying Definitions for One Night Stands, Booty Calls, Fuck Buddies, and Friends with Benefits," *The Canadian Journal of Human Sexuality* 23, no. 3 (2014): 167–177; Angela D. Weaver, Kelly L. MacKeigan, and Hugh A. MacDonald, "Experiences and Perceptions of Young Adults in Friends with Benefits Relationships: A Qualitative Study," *The Canadian Journal of Human Sexuality* 20, nos. 1/2 (2011): 41–53.

12. Barry Reay, "Promiscuous Intimacies: Rethinking the History of American Casual Sex," *Journal of Historical Sociology* 27, no. 1 (2014): 1–24, esp. 13.

13. Nancy Jo Sales, "Tinder and the Dawn of the 'Dating Apocalypse,'" *Vanity Fair* (September 2015), http://www.vanityfair.com/culture/2015/08/tinder-hook-up-culture-end-of-dating, accessed April 27, 2017.

14. See Kathleen A. Bogle, "The Shift from Dating to Hooking Up in College: What Scholars Have Missed" *Sociology Compass* 1, no. 2 (2007): 775–778; Kathleen A. Bogle, *Hooking Up: Sex, Dating, and Relationships on Campus* (New York: New York University Press, 2008); Christopher R. Browning and Matisa Olinger-Wilbon, "Neighborhood Structure, Social Organization, and Number of Short-Term Sexual Partnerships," *Journal of Marriage and Family* 65, no. 3 (2003): 730–774; Paula England and Jonathan Bearak, "The Sexual Double Standard and Gender Differences in Attitudes toward Casual Sex Among US University Students," *Demographic Research* 30 (2014): 1327–1338; Edward O. Laumann, *The Social Organization of Sexuality: Sexual Practices in the United States* (Chicago: University of Chicago Press, 1994); Edward O. Laumann, Anthony Paik, and Raymond C. Rosen, "Sexual Dysfunction in the United States: Prevalence and Predictors," *Jama* 281, no. 6 (1999): 537–544.

15. Leslie C. Bell, *Hard to Get: Twenty-something Women and the Paradox of Sexual Freedom* (Berkeley: University of California Press, 2013), 4.

16. The popular TV series *Crazy Ex-girlfriend* even presented a parody song on this situation in season 1, episode 4 "Sex with a Stranger," https://www.youtube.com/watch?v=iH3FPrI_Cuw, accessed April 27, 2017.

17. Lisa Wade, *American Hookup: The New Culture of Sex on Campus* (New York: W. W. Norton & Company, 2017), 33.

18. As early as 1903, Georg Simmel wrote about the ways in which the excessive stimuli and the lack of familiarity with other people,characterize the city and create indifference and alienation toward the social environment See Georg Simmel, *The Metropolis and Mental Life* (1903; London: Routledge, 1997). London

19. Daniel Mendelsohn, *Elusive Embrace: Desire and the Riddle of Identity* (New York: Vintage, 2012), 87–88.

20. Natalie Kitroeff, "In Hookups, Inequality Still Reigns" *New York Times*, November 11, 2013, http://mobile.nytimes.com/blogs/well/2013/11/11/women-find-orgasms-elusive-in-hookups/, accessed April 27, 2017.

21. Wade, *American Hookup*, 167.

22. Quoted in Barry Reay, "Promiscuous Intimacies: Rethinking the History of American Casual Sex," *Journal of Historical Sociology* 27, no. 1 (2014): 1–24, esp. 12.

23. "Have You Ever Had Sex with a Complete Stranger, and If So, What's Your Story?" *Quora*, https://www.quora.com/Have-you-ever-had-sex-with-a-complete-stranger-Whats-your-story, accessed April 27, 2017.

24. See Kath Albury, "Porn and Sex Education, Porn as Sex Education," *Porn Studies* 1, nos. 1–2 (2014): 172–181; Nicola M. Döring, "The Internet's Impact on Sexuality: A Critical Review of 15 Years of Research," *Computers in Human Behavior* 25, no. 5 (2009): 1089–1101; Panteá Farvid and Virginia Braun, "The 'Sassy Woman' and the 'Performing Man': Heterosexual Casual Sex Advice and the (Re)constitution of Gendered Subjectivities," *Feminist Media Studies* 14, no. 1 (2014): 118–134; Alain Giami and Patrick de Colomby, "Sexology as a Profession in France," *Archives of Sexual Behavior* 32, no. 4 (2003): 371–379; Julia Hirst, "Developing Sexual Competence? Exploring Strategies for the Provision of Effective Sexualities and Relationships Education," *Sex Education* 8, no. 4 (2008): 399–413; Brian McNair, 2002; Ross Morrow, "The Sexological Construction of Sexual Dysfunction," *The Australian and New Zealand Journal of Sociology* 30, no. 1 (1994): 20–35.

25. Monique Mulholland, "When Porno Meets Hetero: SEXPO, Heteronormativity and the Pornification of the Mainstream," *Australian Feminist Studies* 26, no. 67 (2011): 119–135; Monique Mulholland, *Young People and Pornography: Negotiating Pornification* (New York: Springer, 2013); Brian McNair, *Striptease Culture: Sex, Media and the Democratization of Desire* (London: Psychology Press, 2002).

26. Luc Boltanski, *The Foetal Condition: A Sociology of Engendering and Abortion* (Hoboken, NJ: Wiley, 2013), 28–29.

27. See Barbara Critchlow Leigh, "Reasons for Having and Avoiding Sex: Gender, Sexual Orientation, and Relationship to Sexual Behavior," *Journal of Sex Research* 26, no. 2 (1989): 199–209; Cindy M. Meston and David M. Buss, "Why Humans Have Sex," *Archives of Sexual Behavior* 36, no. 4 (2007): 477–507.

28. In gay casual sex on the other hand, people interact in clear, non-confused cultural frames; have similar expectations; perceive each other as having symmetrical power and gender identities; and for that reason homosexual casual sex is more likely to generate jubilation rather than anxiety.

29. Lena Dunham, *Not That Kind of Girl: A Young Woman Tells You What She's "Learned"* (New York: Random House, 2014).

30. Quoted in Elizabeth Bernstein, *Temporarily Yours: Intimacy, Authenticity, and the Commerce of Sex* (Chicago: University of Chicago Press, 2007), 11–12.

31. See Virginie Despentes, *King Kong Theory* for a position that is not far from this one. *King Kong Theory* (Paris: Grasset, 2006).

32. Russell D. Clark, "The Impact of AIDS on Gender Differences in Willingness to Engage in Casual Sex," *Journal of Applied Social Psychology* 20, no. 9 (1990): 771–782; Catherine M. Grello, Deborah P. Welsh, and Melinda S. Harper, "No Strings Attached: The Nature of Casual Sex in College Students," *Journal of Sex Research* 43, no. 3 (2006): 255–267, esp. 255; Edward S. Herold and Dawn-Marie K. Mewhinney, "Gender Differences in Casual Sex and AIDS Prevention: A Survey of Dating Bars," *Journal of Sex Research* 30, no. 1 (1993): 36–42; Eleanor Maticka-Tyndale, Edward S. Herold, and Dawn Mewhinney, "Casual Sex on Spring Break: Intentions and Behaviors of Canadian Students," *Journal of Sex Research* 35, no. 3 (1998): 254–264; Jennifer L. Petersen and Janet Shibley Hyde, "A Meta-analytic Review of Research on Gender Differences in Sexuality, 1993–2007," *Psychological Bulletin* 136, no. 1 (2010): 21–38.

33. Robert William Connell, *The Men and the Boys* (Berkeley: University of California Press, 2000), 120, quoted in Rachel O'Neill, *Seduction Men, Masculinity, and Mediated Intimacy* (Cambridge: Polity Press, 2018), 83.

34. O'Neill, *Seduction Men,* 3–45

35. See study in ibid.

36. *Real Women One Night Stands,* http://www.refinery29.com/one-night-stand, accessed April 21, 2017.

37. Laura Hamilton and Elizabeth A. Armstrong, "Gendered Sexuality in Young Adulthood: Double Binds and Flawed Options," *Gender & Society* 23, no. 5 (2009): 589–616. As they put it incisively: 'Privileged young Americans, both men and women, are now expected to defer family formation until the mid-twenties or even early-thirties to focus on education and career investment—what we call the self-development imperative (Arnett 2004; Rosenfeld 2007). This imperative makes committed relationships less feasible as the sole contexts for premarital sexuality. Like marriage, relationships can be "greedy," siphoning time and energy away from self-development (Gerstel and Sarkisian 2006; Glenn and Marquardt 2001). In contrast, hookups offer sexual pleasure without derailing investment in human capital and are increasingly viewed as part of life-stage appropriate sexual experimentation. Self-protection—both physical and emotional—is central to this logic, suggesting the rise of a strategic approach to sex and relationships (Brooks 2002; Illouz 2005). This approach is reflected in the development of erotic marketplaces offering short-term sexual partners, particularly on college campuses' (Collins 2004).

38. Jerel P. Calzo, Epstein Marina, Andrew P. Smiler, L. Monique Ward, "'Anything from Making Out to Having Sex': Men's Negotiations of Hooking Up and Friends with Benefits Scripts," *Journal of Sex Research* 46, no. 5 (2009): 414–424.

39. See Melanie A. Beres and Panteá Farvid, "Sexual Ethics and Young Women's Accounts of Heterosexual Casual Sex," *Sexualities* 13, no 3 (2010): 377–393; Lisa Duggan and Nan D. Hunter, *Sex Wars: Sexual Dissent and Political Culture* (Abingdon-on-Thames: Taylor & Francis, 2006); Elisa Glick, "Sex Positive: Feminism, Queer Theory, and the Politics of Transgression," *Feminist Review* 64, no. 1 (2000): 19–45; Marcelle Karp and Debbie Stoller, eds., *The BUST Guide to the New Girl Order* (New York: Penguin Books, 1999), especially part 3: "Sex and the Thinking Girl," 75–124; Angela McRobbie, "Top Girls? Young Women and the Post-Feminist Sexual Contract," *Cultural Studies* 21, nos. 4–5 (2007): 718–737; Lynne Segal, *Straight Sex: Rethinking the Politics of Pleasure* (Berkeley: University of California Press, 1994); Kate Taylor "Sex on Campus: She Can Play That Game, Too," *New York Times*, July 12, 2013, http://www.nytimes.com/2013/07/14/fashion/sex-on-campus-she-can-play-that-game-too.html?pagewanted=1&_r=1, accessed April 21, 2017.

40. Eva Illouz, *Why Love Hurts: A Sociological Explanation* (Cambridge: Polity Press, 2012).

41. François Berthomé, Julien Bonhomme, and Grégory Delaplace, "Preface: Cultivating Uncertainty," *HAU: Journal of Ethnographic Theory* 2, no. 2 (2012): 129–137, esp. 129.

42. Elizabeth Cooper and David Pratten, eds., *Ethnographies of Uncertainty in Africa* (New York: Springer, 2014), 1.

43. Erving Goffman, *Frame Analysis: An Essay on the Organization of Experience* (Cambridge, MA: Harvard University Press, 1974).

44. "Was It a Date?" *New Yorker Videos*, http://video.newyorker.com/watch/shorts-murmurs-was-it-a-date, May 1, 2016, accessed April 21, 2017.

45. Sarah Dunn, *The Big Love* (Boston: Little, Brown and Company, 2004), 102–104.

46. Kathryn Bogle, *Hooking Up: Sex, Dating, and Relationships on Campus* (New York: NYU Press, 2008), 39.

47. Madeleine Holden, "Dating with Tinder: Your Definitive Guide to Getting All the Tinder Matches," https://uk.askmen.com/dating/curtsmith/dating-with-tinder.html, accessed April 21, 2017, emphasis added.

48. Elaine M. Eshbaugh and Gary Gute, "Hookups and Sexual Regret among College Women," *The Journal of Social Psychology* 148, no. 1 (2008): 77–90.

49. Elizabeth L. Paul, Brian McManus, and Allison Hayes, "'Hookups': Characteristics and Correlates of College Students' Spontaneous and Anonymous Sexual Experiences," *Journal of Sex Research* 37, no. 1 (2000): 76–88; Elizabeth L. Paul and Kristen A. Hayes, "The Casualties of 'Casual' Sex: A Qualitative Exploration of the Phenomenology of College Students' Hookups," *Journal of Social and Personal Relationships* 19, no. 5 (2002): 639–661; N. J. Roese, G. L. Pennington, J. Coleman, M. Janicki, N. P. Li, and D. Kenrick, "Sex Differences in Regret: All for Love or Some for Lust?" *Personality and Social Psychology Bulletin* 32 (2006): 770–780.

50. Elaine M. Eshbaugh and Gary Gute, "Hookups and Sexual Regret among College Women," *The Journal of Social Psychology*148, no. 1 (2008): 77–90, esp. 78.

51. In a review of the difference between the sexuality of men and women Letitia Peplau describes: "Like heterosexual women, lesbians tend to have less permissive attitudes toward casual sex and sex outside a primary relationship than do gay or heterosexual men. Also like heterosexual women, lesbians have sex fantasies that are more likely to be personal and romantic than the fantasies of gay or heterosexual men. [...] Gay men in committed relationships are more likely than lesbians or heterosexuals to have sex with partners outside their primary relationship." See Letitia Anne Peplau, "Human Sexuality: How Do Men and Women Differ?" *Current Directions in Psychological Science* 12, no. 2 (2003): 37–40, esp. 38.

52. C. M. Grello, D. P. Welsh, M. S. Harper, and J. W. Dickson, "Dating and Sexual Relationship Trajectories and Adolescent Functioning," *Adolescent & Family Health* 3, no. 3 (2003): 103–112.

53. D. P. Welsh, C. M. Grello, and M. S. Harper, "When Love Hurts: Depression and Adolescent Romantic Relationships," in *Adolescent Romantic Relations and Sexual Behavior: Theory, Research, and Practical Implications*, ed. P. Florsheim (Mahwah, NJ: Lawrence Erlbaum Associates, 2003), 185–212, esp. 197.

54. Elizabeth L. Paul, Brian McManus, and Allison Hayes, "'Hookups': Characteristics and Correlates of College Students' Spontaneous and Anonymous Sexual Experiences," *Journal of Sex Research* 37, no. 1 (2000): 76–88.

55. Ibid., 85.

56. For example, Amy L. Gentzler and Kathryn A. Kerns, "Associations between Insecure Attachment and Sexual Experiences," *Personal Relationships* 11, no. 2 (2004): 249–265; Elizabeth L. Paul, Brian McManus, and Allison Hayes, "'Hookups': Characteristics and Correlates of College Students' Spontaneous and Anonymous Sexual Experiences," *Journal of Sex Research* 37, no. 1 (2000): 76–88; Anthony Walsh, "Self-esteem and Sexual Behavior: Exploring Gender Differences," *Sex Roles* 25, no. 7 (1991): 441–450.

57. Hamilton and Armstrong, "Gendered Sexuality in Young Adulthood," 593.

58. See Michele Hoffnung, "Wanting It All: Career, Marriage, and Motherhood during College-Educated Women's 20s," *Sex Roles* 50, nos. 9–10 (2004): 711–723; Eva Illouz, *Cold Intimacies: The Making of Emotional Capitalism* (Cambridge: Polity Press, 2007); Heather AK Jacques and H. Lorraine Radtke, "Constrained by Choice: Young Women Negotiate the Discourses of Marriage and Motherhood," *Feminism and Psychology* 22, no. 4 (2012): 443–461; Allan G. Johnson, *The Gender Knot: Unraveling Our Patriarchal Legacy* (Philadelphia: Temple University Press, 2005); Dennis K. Mumby, "Organizing Men: Power, Discourse, and the Social Construction of Masculinity(s) in the Workplace," *Communication Theory* 8, no. 2 (1998): 164–183; Ann Shola Orloff, "Gender and the Social Rights of Citizenship: The Comparative Analysis of Gender Relations and Welfare States," *American Sociological Review* (1993): 303–328.

59. Gaëlle Ferrant, Luca Maria Pesando, and Keiko Nowacka, "Unpaid Care Work: The Missing Link in the Analysis of Gender Gaps in Labour Outcomes," *Issues Paper,*

OECD Development Centre (December 2014); Nancy Folbre, "Measuring Care: Gender, Empowerment, and the Care Economy," *Journal of Human Development* 7, no. 2 (2006): 183–199; Michele Hoffnung, "Wanting It All: Career, Marriage, and Motherhood during College-Educated Women's 20s," *Sex Roles* 50, no. 9–10 (2004): 711–723; Heather AK Jacques and H. Lorraine Radtke, "Constrained by Choice: Young Women Negotiate the Discourses of Marriage and Motherhood," *Feminism & Psychology* 22, no. 4 (2012): 443–461; Julia McQuillan et al., "The Importance of Motherhood among Women in the Contemporary United States," *Gender & Society* 22, no. 4 (2008): 477–496; Madonna Harrington Meyer, ed., *Care Work: Gender, Labor, and the Welfare State* (London: Routledge, 2002); Fiona Robinson, "Beyond Labour Rights: The Ethics of Care and Women's Work in the Global Economy," *International Feminist Journal of Politics* 8, no. 3 (2006): 321–342; Liana C. Sayer, "Gender, Time and Inequality: Trends in Women's and Men's Paid Work, Unpaid Work and Free Time," *Social Forces* 84, no. 1 (2005): 285–303; Linda Thompson and Alexis J. Walker, "Gender in Families: Women and Men in Marriage, Work, and Parenthood," *Journal of Marriage and the Family* (1989): 845–871.

60. Lisa Wade presents a similar argument based on her research on the hookup culture in colleges. See Wade, *American Hookup*.

61. Nancy Jo Sales, https://archive.vanityfair.com/article/2015/9/tinder-is-the-night, September 2015.

62. This is the summary of the American Psychological Association (APA) Task Force on the Sexualization of Girls, "Report of the APA Task Force on the Sexualization of Girls" (2010), 1, http://www.apa.org/pi/women/programs/girls/report-full.pdf, accessed April 21, 2017.

63. The APA's definition constitutes a basis for contemporary discussion on sexualization. For example, see Linda Hatch, "The American Psychological Association Task Force on the Sexualization of Girls: A Review, Update and Commentary," *Sexual Addiction & Compulsivity* 18, no. 4 (2011): 195–211; Linda Smolak, Sarah K. Murnen, and Taryn A. Myers, "Sexualizing the Self: What College Women and Men Think About and Do to Be 'Sexy,'" *Psychology of Women Quarterly* 38, no. 3 (2014): 379–397.

64. See Gerald Dworkin, *The Theory and Practice of Autonomy* (Cambridge: Cambridge University Press, 1988); Jerome B. Schneewind, *The Invention of Autonomy: A History of Modern Moral Philosophy* (Cambridge: Cambridge University Press, 1998). See also chapter 2.

65. Marcel Mauss and Wilfred Douglas Halls, *The Gift: The Form and Reason for Exchange in Archaic Societies* (1925; New York: W. W. Norton & Company, 2000).

66. For a review of Bourdieu's gift theory, see Ilana F. Silber, "Bourdieu's Gift to Gift Theory: An Unacknowledged Trajectory," *Sociological Theory* 27, no. 2 (2009): 173–190.

67. *The Blackwell Encyclopedia of Sociology*, s.v. "Uncertainty." See also in this matter Niklas Luhmann, *Risk: A Sociological Theory* (New York: Aldine de Gruyter, 1993).

68. Gaëlle Ferrant, Luca Maria Pesando, and Keiko Nowacka (December 2014); Nancy Folbre, "Measuring Care: Gender, Empowerment, and the Care Economy," *Journal of Human Development* 7, no. 2 (2006): 183–199; Madonna Harrington Meyer,

eds., *Care Work: Gender, Labor, and the Welfare State* (London: Routledge, 2002); Fiona Robinson "Beyond Labour Rights: The Ethics of Care and Women's Work in the Global Economy," *International Feminist Journal of Politics* 8, no. 3 (2006): 321–342; Liana C. Sayer, "Gender, Time and Inequality: Trends in Women's and Men's Paid Work, Unpaid Work and Free Time," *Social Forces* 84, no. 1 (2005): 285–303.

69. See chapters 4 and 6.

70. SiaLv82, "Keeping His Options Open," March 13, 2016, http://www.loveshack.org/forums/breaking-up-reconciliation-coping/breaks-breaking-up/573363-keeping-his-options-open, accessed April 27, 2017.

71. Pierre Bourdieu, *Marriage Strategies as Strategies of Social Reproduction* (Baltimore: Johns Hopkins University Press, 1976); Pierre Bourdieu, *Outline of a Theory of Practice*, vol. 16 (Cambridge: Cambridge University Press, 1977); Pierre Lamaison, "From Rules to Strategies: An Interview with Pierre Bourdieu," *Cultural Anthropology* 1, no. 1 (1986): 110–120; Ann Swidler, "Culture in Action: Symbols and Strategies," *American Sociological Review* (1986): 273–286; Ann Swidler, *Talk of Love: How Culture Matters* (2001; Chicago: University of Chicago Press, 2013).

72. Zygmunt Bauman, *Liquid Modernity* (2000; Hoboken, NJ: Wiley, 2013); Zygmunt Bauman, *Liquid Love: On the Frailty of Human Bonds* (2003; Hoboken, NJ: Wiley, 2013); Zygmunt Bauman, *Liquid Life* (Cambridge: Polity Press, 2005).

73. Venn, "On the Verge of Killing Myself," February 26, 2016, http://www.loveshack.org/forums/breaking-up-reconciliation-coping/breaks-breaking-up/571318-verge-killing-myself, accessed April 27, 2017.

74. Theodor W. Adorno, *Negative Dialectics*, vol. 1 (London: A&C Black, 1973).

75. Georg Wilhelm Friedrich Hegel, *Phenomenology of Spirit* (1807; Delhi: Motilal Banarsidass Publishers, 1998).

76. Alexandre Kojève, *Introduction to the Reading of Hegel* (Ithaca, NY: Cornell University Press, 1980), 38.

77. See Jacques Lacan, "The Subversion of the Subject and the Dialectic of Desire in the Freudian Unconscious," in *Hegel and Contemporary Continental Philosophy*, ed. Dennis King Keenan (Albany: SUNY Press, 2004), 205–235.

78. Sarah Bakewell, *At the Existentialist Café: Freedom, Being and Apricot Cocktails* (London: Chatto and Windus, 2016), 153.

79. Martin Heidegger, *Being and Time* (1927; Albany: SUNY Press, 2010).

80. Bakewell, *At the Existentialist Café*, 69. Bakewell also describes how Heidegger sums it up: *Das Nur-noch-vorhandensein eines Zuhandenen* (The being-just-present-at-hand-and-no-more of something ready to hand). See ibid.

81. In fact, given that "positive relationships" were based on moral strictures and social inequality, they are morally more negative than negative relations themselves.

82. Ulrich Beck and Elisabeth Gernsheim-Beck, *The Normal Chaos of Love* (Cambridge: Polity Press, 1995).

83. While Foucault would insist that such injunctions enable the deployment of an apparatus of surveillance through self-governing, Anthony Giddens and Ulrich Beck and Elizabeth Gernsheim-Beck viewed these changes as auguring of a

democratization of relationships. See Beck and Gernsheim-Beck, *The Normal Chaos of Love*; Michel Foucault, *Discipline and Punish: The Birth of the Prison*, trans. Alan Sheridan (1975; New York: Pantheon Books, 1977). See also Johanna Oksala, *Foucault on Freedom* (Cambridge: Cambridge University Press, 2005); Anthony Giddens, *The Transformation of Intimacy: Sexuality, Love and Eroticism in Modern Societies* (Hoboken, NJ: Wiley, 2013).

84. See the excellent Rosalind Gill, *Gender and the Media* (Cambridge: Polity Press, 2007).

85. Quoted in Ivan Krastev, *After Europe* (Philadelphia: University of Pennsylvania Press, 2017), 24.

86. Harry Kreisler, "The Individual, Charisma, and the Leninist Extinction," *Conversations with History*, quoted in Ivan Kratsev, "The Return of Majoritarian Politics" in *The Great Regression*, ed. Heinrich Geiselberger (Wiley: Hoboken, NJ, 2017), 69.

Chapter 4

1. Franz Kafka, *Letters to Milena*, 1920–1923 (New York: Schocken Books, 1990, 49).

2. Stanley Cavell, *Must We Mean What We Say?* (New York: Scribner, 1969), 201.

3. https://www.bbc.com/news/entertainment-arts-41593384.

4. There are too many studies stressing the intertwining of sexuality and violence to be quoted here. One can refer to the Catharine MacKinnon classic *Only Words* (Cambridge, MA: Harvard University Press, 1993).

5. Adam I. Green, "Toward a Sociology of Collective Sexual Life," in *Sexual Fields: Toward a Sociology of Collective Sexual Life*, ed. Adam I. Green (Chicago: University of Chicago Press), 1–24, esp. 15.

6. Michel Foucault, *Histoire de la Sexualite*, vols. 1–3 (Paris: Editions Gallimard, 1976–1984).

7. T. J. Jackson Lears, *No Place of Grace: Antimodernism and the Transformation of American Culture, 1880–1920* (Chicago: University of Chicago Press, 1981); Naomi Wolf, *The Beauty Myth: How Images of Beauty Are Used against Women* (New York: Random House, 2013).

8. Lauren Berlant and Michael Warner, "Sex in Public," *Critical Inquiry* 24, no. 2 (1998): 547–566; Lauren Gail Berlant, ed., *Intimacy* (Chicago: University of Chicago Press, 2000); Lauren Gail Berlant, *Cruel Optimism* (Durham, NC: Duke University Press, 2011).

9. Michael J. Sandel, *What Money Can't Buy: The Moral Limits of Markets* (New York: Macmillan, 2012).

10. Karl Marx, "Part 1: Commodities and Money; Chapter 1: Commodities; Section 3: The Form of Value or Exchange-Value," in *Capital: A Critique of Political Economy. The Process of Capitalist Production*, vol. 1 (1867; New York: Cosimo Classics, 2007, 54–80. See also Arun Bose, "Marx on Value, Capital, and Exploitation," *History of Political Economy* 3, no. 2 (1971): 298–334.

11. Michèle Lamont, "Toward a Comparative Sociology of Valuation and Evaluation," *Annual Review of Sociology* 38 (2012): 201–221; Luc Boltanski and Eve Chiapello,

"The New Spirit of Capitalism," *International Journal of Politics, Culture, and Society* 18, nos. 3–4 (2005): 161–188.

12. Think of George Soros's expressing lack of trust in the British pound in September 1992 causing it to lose its value; see Steve Schaefer, "Forbes Flashback: How George Soros Broke the British Pound and Why Hedge Funds Probably Can't Crack The Euro," *Forbes*, https://www.forbes.com/sites/steveschaefer/2015/07/07/forbes-flash-back-george-soros-british-pound-euro-ecb/#668029186131, accessed December 12, 2017.

13. See Axel Honneth's notion of normative paradoxes in Martin Hartmann and Axel Honneth, "Paradoxes of Capitalism," *Constellations* 13, no. 1 (2006): 41–58; Axel Honneth, "Organized Self-realization: Some Paradoxes of Individualization," *European Journal of Social Theory* 7, no. 4 (2004): 463–478; Axel Honneth, "Work and Recognition: A Redefinition," *The Philosophy of Recognition: Historical and Contemporary Perspectives* (2010): 223–239.

14. Roy F. Baumeister and Kathleen D. Vohs, "Sexual Economics: Sex as Female Resource for Social Exchange in Heterosexual Interactions," *Personality and Social Psychology Review* 8, no. 4 (2004): 339–363; Paola Tabet, Sexualité des Femmes et échange économico-sexuel (Paris: L'Harmattan [Bibliothèque du féminisme], 2004); Paola Tabet, "Through the Looking-glass: Sexual-Economic Exchange," *Chic, chèque, choc: Transactions autour des corps et stratégies amoureuses contemporaines*, ed. Françoise Omokaro and Fenneke Reysoo (Geneva: Graduate Institute Publications, 2012), 39.

15. Baumeister and Vohs, "Sexual Economics"; Denise Brennan, *What's Love Got to Do with It?: Transnational Desires and Sex Tourism in the Dominican Republic* (Durham, NC: Duke University Press, 2004); Carol E. Kaufman and Stavros E. Stavrou, "'Bus Fare Please': The Economics of Sex and Gifts among Young People in Urban South Africa," *Culture, Health & Sexuality* 6, no. 5 (2004): 377–391.

16. See Mark Regnerus, *Cheap Sex: The Transformation of Men, Marriage, and Monogamy* (New York: Oxford University Press, 2017).

17. Carole Pateman, "What's Wrong with Prostitution?" *Women's Studies Quarterly* 27, nos. 1/2, Teaching about Violence against Women (Spring–Summer 1999): 53–64, esp. 53.

18. Kathy Peiss, *Hope in a Jar: The Making of America's Beauty Culture* (Philadelphia: University of Pennsylvania Press, 2011); Naomi Wolf, *The Beauty Myth: How Images of Beauty Are Used against Women* (New York: Random House, 2013).

19. Ashley Mears, *Pricing Beauty: The Making of a Fashion Model* (Berkeley: University of California Press, 2011).

20. Alison Hearn, "Structuring Feeling: Web 2.0, Online Ranking and Rating, and the Digital 'Reputation' Economy," *Ephemera: Theory and Politics in Organisation* 10, nos. 3/4 (2010): 421–438, esp. 424. See also Warren Sussman, *Culture as History: The Transformation of American Society in the 20th Century* (New York: Pantheon, 1984).

21. Feona Attwood, "Sexed Up: Theorizing the Sexualization of Culture," in *Sexualities* 9, no. 1 (February 2006): 77–94, esp. 82.

22. Walter Benjamin, *The Arcades Project*, ed. Rolf Tiedemann, trans. Howard Eiland and Kevin McLaughlin (Cambridge, MA: Harvard University Press, 1999), 339.

23. Colin Campbell, *The Romantic Ethic and the Spirit of Modern Consumerism* (New York: Blackwell, 1987); Eva Illouz, "Emotions, Imagination and Consumption: A New Research Agenda," *Journal of Consumer Culture* 9, no. 3 (2009): 377–413.

24. Rosalind Gill, *Gender and the Media* (Cambridge: Polity Press, 2007).

25. Pierre Bourdieu, *Language and Symbolic Power* (Cambridge, MA: Harvard University Press, 1991).

26. Guy Debord, *Society of the Spectacle* (1967; Berlin: Bread and Circuses Publishing, 2012).

27. For example: "[Q]ueer identities and visibility are themselves enabled through the reconfiguration of identity as stylised, self-fashioning and malleable in consumer culture. So strong are the resonances between queer and consumer capitalism's life-stylism that Hennessy argues queer theory itself must be understood as participating in the aestheticisation of everyday life." See Lisa Adkins, "Sexuality and the Economy: Historicisation vs. Deconstruction," *Australian Feminist Studies* 17, no. 37 (2002): 33; see also Beverley Skeggs, *Formations of Class and Gender: Becoming Respectable* (London: SAGE Publications, 1997).

28. Feona Attwood, "'Tits and Ass and Porn and Fighting': Male Heterosexuality in Magazines for Men," *International Journal of Cultural Studies* 8, no. 1 (2005): 83–100; Samantha Holland and Feona Attwood, *Keeping Fit in Six Inch Heels: The Mainstreaming of Pole Dancing* (London: IB Tauris, 2009); Feona Attwood, ed., *Mainstreaming Sex: The Sexualization of Western Culture* (London: IB Tauris, 2014).

29. Nicholas Mirzoeff, *An Introduction to Visual Culture* (London: Psychology Press, 1999).

30. See Robert R. Williams, *Hegel's Ethics of Recognition* (Berkeley: University of California Press), 1997.

31. See Holland and Attwood, *Keeping Fit in Six Inch Heels*; Annabelle Mooney, "Boys Will Be Boys: Men's Magazines and the Normalisation of Pornography," *Feminist Media Studies* 8, no. 3 (2008): 247–265; Laramie D. Taylor, "All for Him: Articles about Sex in American Lad Magazines," *Sex Roles* 52, no. 3 (2005): 153–163.

32. "Wannabe Sugarbaby," http://spoilmedaddy.blogspot.co.il/search?updated-min= 2004-01-01T00:00:00–05:00&updated-max=2005-01-01T00:00:00–05:00&max-results=17, accessed 12 December 2017.

33. Lisa Adkins, "Sexuality and the Economy: Historicisation vs. Deconstruction," *Australian Feminist Studies* 17, no. 37 (2002):31–4.1.

34. Daniel Mendelsohn, *The Elusive Embrace: Desire and the Riddle of Identity* (1999: New York: Vintage, 2012), 103.

35. Roy F. Baumeister and Kathleen D. Vohs, "Sexual Economics."

36. Catherine Hakim, "Erotic Capital," *European Sociological Review* 26, no. 5 (2010): 499–518.

37. Michael Hardt and Antonio Negri, *Multitude: War and Democracy in the Age of Empire* (London: Hamish Hamilton, 2005); Rosalind Gill and Andy Pratt, "In the Social Factory? Immaterial Labour, Precariousness and Cultural Work," *Theory, Culture & Society* 25, nos. 7–8 (2008): 1–30.

38. Mears, *Pricing Beauty*, 75.

39. Hearn, "Structuring Feeling," 427.

40. Laura Marsh, "Being Charlie," review of *The Naughty Nineties: The Triumph of the American Libido*, by David Friend, *The New York Review of Books*, April 5, 2018, http://www.nybooks.com/articles/2018/04/05/naughty-nineties-being-charlie/?utm_medium=email&utm_campaign=NYR%20Hamlet%20slavery%20 1990s&utm_content=NYR%20Hamlet%20slavery%201990s+CID_721fe596a7310f 9afb4b7318b9d925f5&utm_source=Newsletter, accessed DATE.

41. This is the situation in the media corporations (at the end of 2017). The two executive chairmen, the CEO and the president of the American multinational mass media corporation 21st Century Fox, are all males; the president of the American film studio, production company, and film distributor Columbia Pictures Industries, Inc. (owned today by Sony Corporation), is also a male; the chairman and CEO of the American media company Metro-Goldwyn-Mayer Studios Inc., of the American film studio Paramount Pictures Corporation, and of the American multinational mass media and entertainment conglomerate Time Warner Inc. are also males. The vice chairman and CEO of the American multinational media conglomerate NBCUniversal are also males. This is the situation in the fashion corporations (at the end of 2017): the CEO and managing director of the European multinational luxury goods conglomerate LVMH are males; the chairman and CEO of the international luxury group Kering is also a male; the chairman of the luxury goods holding company the Compagnie Financière Richemont SA is also a male; the CEO of the company that operates in the fashion and fragrance sectors Puig is also a male; the president and CEO of the parent company of multinational fashion brand OTB are also males. Similarly, Jessica Assaf described in 2015 that the CEOs of L'Oreal, Revlon, Estée Lauder, OPI Nail Polish, and MAC Cosmetics are all men. The same trend characterized the advertisement industry. Ali Hanan describes in an article in the *Guardian*: "In 2008, just 3.6% of the world's creative directors were female. Since then it has tripled to 11%; in London, my research shows, the figure is about 14%—still shockingly low. Unsurprisingly, according to research, 91% of female consumers feel advertisers don't understand them. Seven in 10 women go further to say they feel 'alienated' by advertising. Men overwhelmingly dominate creative departments and their output....I know this firsthand, having worked as a creative director in the industry for 15 years. Over that time female representation in creative departments has barely changed: I can count the female executive creative directors I know on my fingers." In the same tone, Avi Dan described in an article published at *Forbes* at 2016 that in the advertisement companies located in New York's Madison Avenue "there isn't even one single woman CEO in any of the six holding companies, those ad conglomerates that control 75% of ad spending. And, only one woman, Tamara Ingram from JWT, runs one of the 15 global networks." See Jessica Assaf, "Why Do Men Run the Beauty Industry?" *Beauty Lies Truth*, February 9, 2015), http://www.beautyliestruth.com/blog/2015/2/why-do-men-run-the-beauty-industry, accessed December 12, 2017; Ali Hanan, "Five Facts That Show How the Advertising Industry Fails Women," *Guardian*, February 3, 2016, https://www.theguardian.com/women-in-leadership/2016/feb/03/how-advertising-industry-fails-women, accessed December 12, 2017; Avi Dan, "Why Aren't Women Starting Their Own Ad Agencies?" June 1, 2016, https://www.forbes.com/sites/

avidan/2016/06/01/why-arent-women-starting-their-own-ad-agencies/ #17b684981b98, accessed December 12, 2017.

42. Maureen Dowd, "Bringing Down Our Monsters," *New York Times*, December 16, 2017, https://www.nytimes.com/2017/12/16/opinion/sunday/sexual-harassment-salma-hayek.html, accessed December 16, 2017.

43. As for the production, the CEO and COO of MindGeek, which owns and operates many of the most popular pornographic websites, are both males. In the largest pornography site on the Internet, Pornhub (owned by MindGeek), the vice president of operations, vice president of product, lead developer, and the community coordinator are all males.

44. Heather A. Rupp and Kim Wallen, "Sex Differences in Response to Visual Sexual Stimuli: A Review," *Archives of Sexual Behavior* 37, no. 2 (2008): 206–218, esp. 206.

45. To demonstrate, according to the statistics portal Statista, the worldwide yearly revenue of the Viagra sold by the American pharmaceutical corporation Pfizer was more than $1.5 billion each year in the last decade when in 2012 it was more than $2 billion. The business consulting firm Grand View Research Inc. reports that the global erectile dysfunction drugs market is expected to reach $3.2 billion by 2022. See Grand View Research, "Erectile Dysfunction Drugs Market Worth $3.2 Billion by 2022," July 2016, https://www.grandviewresearch.com/press-release/global-erectile-dysfunction-drugs-market, accessed December 12, 2017); Statista, "Worldwide Revenue of Pfizer's Viagra from 2003 to 2017 (in million U.S. dollars), https://www.statista.com/statistics/264827/pfizers-worldwide-viagra-revenue-since-2003/, accessed May 23, 2018.

46. Emily Badger wrote an article in *The Washington Post* that estimates the economic size of these activities. Badger describes that "Urban's researchers estimate that, in 2007, the entire illegal sex economy in Atlanta—including brothels, escort services and dubious massage parlors—was valued at $290 million. In Miami, it was $205 million (that's more than twice the size of the market there for illegal drugs). In Washington, it was $103 million." Emily Badger, "We Now Know More about the Economics of Prostitution Than Ever," *Washington Post*, March 12, 2014, https://www.washingtonpost.com/news/wonk/wp/2014/03/12/we-now-know-more-about-the-economics-of-prostitution-than-ever/?utm_term=.22c20bb8e508, accessed December 12, 2017.

47. Ori Schwarz, "On Friendship, Boobs and the Logic of the Catalogue: Online Self-Portraits as a Means for the Exchange of Capital," *Convergence* 16, no. 2 (2010): 163–183.

48. Jessica Ringrose, Lura Harvey, Rosalind Gill, and Sonia Livingstone, "Teen Girls, Sexual Double Standards and Sexting," *Feminist Theory* 14, no. 3 (2013): 305–323.

49. See Bryant Kelly, "YouTube and L'Oreal Paris Are Launching a Beauty Vlogger School," *Instyle*, April 21, 2016, http://www.instyle.com/beauty/youtube-and-loreal-paris-are-launching-beauty-vlogger-school, accessed February 1, 2018; Eva Wiseman, "Lights, Camera, Lipstick: Beauty Vloggers Are Changing the Face of the Make-up Industry," *Guardian*, July 20, 2014, https://www.theguardian.com/fashion/2014/jul/20/beauty-bloggers-changing-makeup-industry, accessed February 1, 2018; "L'Oreal Finds a New Way of Working with Top Beauty Vloggers," *thinkwithgoogle*, February 2015, https://www.thinkwithgoogle.com/intl/en-gb/advertising-channels/video/loreal-finds-a-new-way-of-working-with-top-beauty-vloggers/, accessed February 1, 2018.

50. Companies will pay hundreds of dollars for a single photo featuring their product, and thousands for a brand campaign featuring multiple posts over a period of time. See, for example, Ross Logan, "Instagram Model: I Make More Money from Posting a Single Selfie than Doing Four Days' Work," *The Mirror* (UK), October 4, 2015, https://www.mirror.co.uk/news/world-news/instagram-model-make-more-money-6569672, accessed February 26, 2018.

51. Quoted from http://www.sugardaddysite.org/, accessed December 12, 2017.

52. Indeed, some sites auction sugar babies, letting sugar daddies compete for the most attractive bodies. For example, this is how the site WhatsYourPrice.com is described in a site that characterized different sugar daddies sites: "On WhatsYourPrice.com, generous and successful men bid to date attractive women.... The process is simple. A woman decides her price and places a bid on the site. Generous men can start the bidding process and the highest bidder gets to take the girl on a date. Only the winning bidder has to pay the amount." See "WhatsYourPrice Review," http://www.sugardaddysite.org/whats-your-price.html, accessed February 26, 2018.

53. Ann Ferguson, Rosemary Hennessy, and Mechthild Nagel, "Feminist Perspectives on Class and Work," *Stanford Encyclopedia of Philosophy*, 2004; Catherine Hoskyns, and Shirin M. Rai, "Recasting the Global Political Economy: Counting Women's Unpaid Work," *New Political Economy* 12, no. 3 (2007): 297–317; Ann Shola Orloff, "Gender and the Social Rights of Citizenship: The Comparative Analysis of Gender Relations and Welfare States," *American Sociological Review* (1993): 303–328; Carole Pateman, *The Sexual Contract* (1988; Hoboken, NJ: Wiley, 2014); Marilyn Waring and Gloria Steinem, *If Women Counted: A New Feminist Economics* (San Francisco: Harper & Row, 1988); Lise Vogel, *Marxism and the Oppression of Women: Toward a Unitary Theory* (Leiden: Brill 2013).

54. Pateman, *Sexual Contract*, 17.

55. See Axel Honneth, "Invisibility: On the Epistemology of 'Recognition,'" *Supplements of the Aristotelian Society* 75, no. 1 (2001): 111–126; Axel Honneth, *Unsichtbarkeit. Stationen einer Theorie der Intersubjektivität* (Frankfurt: Suhrkamp Verlag, 2003). See also James Jardine, "Stein and Honneth on Empathy and Emotional Recognition," *Human Studies* 38, no. 4 (2015): 567–589.

56. Luc Boltanski and Laurent Thévenot, "Finding One's Way in Social Space: A Study Based on Games," *Social Science Information* 22, nos. 4–5 (1983): 631–680; Luc Boltanski and Laurent Thévenot, "The Reality of Moral Expectations: A Sociology of Situated Judgement," *Philosophical Explorations* 3, no. 3 (2000): 208–231; Annick Bourguignon and Eve Chiapello, "The Role of Criticism in the Dynamics of Performance Evaluation Systems," *Critical Perspectives on Accounting* 16, no. 6 (2005): 665–700; Peter Dahler-Larsen, *The Evaluation Society* (Stanford, CA: Stanford University Press, 2011); Michèle Lamont, "Toward a Comparative Sociology of Valuation and Evaluation," *Annual Review of Sociology* 38 (2012); Peter Wagner, "After Justification: Repertoires of Evaluation and the Sociology of Modernity," *European Journal of Social Theory* 2, no. 3 (1999): 341–357.

57. See, for example, Simon Thorpe, Denis Fize, and Catherine Marlot, "Speed of Processing in the Human Visual System," *Nature* 381, no. 6582 (1996): 520–522; Holle Kirchner and Simon J. Thorpe, "Ultra-rapid Object Detection with Saccadic Eye

Movements: Visual Processing Speed Revisited," *Vision Research* 46, no. 11 (2006): 1762–1776; Thorpe, Fize, and Marlot, ibid.

58. Juliet A. Conlin, "Getting Around: Making Fast and Frugal Navigation Decisions," *Progress in Brain Research* 174 (2009): 109–117; Pierre Jacob and Marc Jeannerod, *Ways of Seeing: The Scope and Limits of Visual Cognition* (Oxford: Oxford University Press, 2003); Daniel Kahneman, *Thinking, Fast and Slow* (New York: Macmillan, 2011).

59. Jessica Ringrose, Lura Harvey, Rosalind Gill, and Sonia Livingstone, "Teen Girls, Sexual Double Standards and Sexting," *Feminist Theory* 14, no. 3 (2013): 305–323.

60. Matt Hill, Leon Mann, and Alexander J. Wearing, "The Effects of Attitude, Subjective Norm and Self-Efficacy on Intention to Benchmark: A Comparison between Managers with Experience and No Experience in Benchmarking," *Journal of Organizational Behavior* 17, no. 4 (1996): 313–327, esp. 314. The authors refer to Carol Jean McNair and Kathleen H. J. Leibfried, *Benchmarking: A Tool for Continuous Improvement* (New York: John Wiley & Sons, 1992).

61. Rhiannon Williams, "How Tinder Ranks Its Users with a Secret 'Desirability Score,'" *Telegraph* (UK), January 12, 2016), http://www.telegraph.co.uk/technology/news/12094539/How-Tinder-ranks-its-users-with-a-secret-desirability-score.html, accessed December 12, 2017.

62. Alexandra Schwartz, "What Teen-Age Girls See When They Look in the Mirror," *The New Yorker*, May 7, 2017, https://www.newyorker.com/culture/photo-booth/what-teen-age-girls-see-when-they-look-in-the-mirror, accessed December 12, 2017.

63. Beth L. Bailey, *From Front Porch to Back Seat: Courtship in Twentieth-century America* (Baltimore: Johns Hopkins University Press, 1989); Eva Illouz, *Consuming the Romantic Utopia: Love and the Cultural Contradictions of Capitalism* (Berkeley: University of California Press, 1997); Steven Mintz and Susan Kellogg, *Domestic Revolutions: A Social History of American Family Life* (New York: Simon & Schuster, 1989).

64. Bailey, *From Front Porch to Back Seat*; John D'emilio and Estelle B. Freedman, *Intimate Matters: A History of Sexuality in America* (Chicago: University of Chicago Press, 1988); Paula S. Fass, *The Damned and the Beautiful: American Youth in the 1920s*, book 567 (New York: Oxford University Press, 1979); Illouz, *Consuming the Romantic Utopia*.

65. Jason Hayes, "The Six Pizzas of Your Failed Relationship," *The New Yorker*, March 7, 2017, https://www.newyorker.com/humor/daily-shouts/the-six-pizzas-of-your-failed-relationship, accessed December 12, 2017.

66. Brooke Lea Foster, "When You Know It's Love: A Vision Out of Your Dreams," *New York Times*, May 9, 2017, https://www.nytimes.com/2017/05/09/fashion/weddings/when-you-know-its-love-paul-rust-lesley-arfin-dreams.html?emc=edit_tnt_20170509&nlid=47676527&tntemail0=y&_r=0, accessed December 12, 2017, emphasis added.

67. Donald W. Winnicott, "Transitional Objects and Transitional Phenomena: A Study of the First Not-Me," *International Journal of Psycho-Analysis* 34 (1953): 89–97.

68. Quoted in Micaela Di Leonardo, "White Ethnicities, Identity Politics, and Baby Bear's Chair," *Social Text* 41 (1994): 165–191, esp. 178; Alice Echols, *Daring to Be Bad: Radical Feminism in America, 1967–1975* (Minneapolis: University of Minnesota Press, 1989), 6.

69. Eva Illouz, *Why Love Hurts* (Cambridge: Polity Press, 2012).

70. Mark Regnerus, *Cheap Sex* (New York: Oxford University Press, 2017).

71. Ibid., 11.

72. Randi Gunther, "Stop Spinning Your Wheels: Here's How to Finally Find the Love of Your Life," *Catch Him and Keep Him.com*, October 28, 2017, https://www.dont-payfull.com/at/catchhimandkeephim.com/newsletter/date-works-1299332, accessed December 12, 2017, emphasis added.

73. Linda Smolak and Sarah K. Murnen, "The Sexualization of Girls and Women as a Primary Antecedent of Self-Objectification," in *Self-objectification in Women: Causes, Consequences, and Counteractions*, ed. Rachel M. Calogero, Stacey Ed Tantleff-Dunn, and J. Thompson (Washington, DC: *American Psychological Association*, 2011), 53–75, esp. 54.

74. See for a useful discussion and critique of the pornification thesis, Clarissa Smith, "Pornographication: A Discourse for All Seasons," *International Journal of Media & Cultural Politics* 6, no. 1 (2010): 103–108. For an indictment of pornification see, for example, Ariel Levy, *Female Chauvinist Pigs: Women and the Rise of Raunch Culture* (New York: Free Press, 2005).

75. Sendhil Mulllainathan, "The Hidden Taxes on Women," *International New York Times*, March 3–4, 2018, 15.

76. Francine D. Blau, *Gender, Inequality, and Wages*, ed. Anne C. Gielen and Klaus F. Zimmermann (New York: Oxford University Press, 2016); Herminia Ibarra, Nancy M. Carter, and Christine Silva, "Why Men Still Get More Promotions Than Women," *Harvard Business Review* 88, no. 9 (2010): 80–85; Cecilia L. Ridgeway, *Framed by Gender: How Gender Inequality Persists in the Modern World* (New York: Oxford University Press, 2011). For data on the OECD: OECDGender Wage Gap (indicator), 2017, doi: 10.1787/7cee77aa-en https://data.oecd.org/earnwage/gender-wage-gap.htm, accessed November 23, 2017; on USA: International Labour Organization, Gender Inequality and Women in the US Labor Force, http://www.ilo.org/washington/areas/gender-equality-in-the-workplace/WCMS_159496/lang--en/index.htm, accessed November 23, 2017.

77. The men interviewed by Rachel O'Neill in her study of seduction workshops recognize that women give less importance to the looks of men than the men for whom women's physical appearance is necessary to attraction. See Rachel O'Neill, *Seduction Men, Masculinity, and Mediated Intimacy* (Cambridge: Polity Press, 2018).

78. Illouz, *Why Love Hurts*, 77.

79. Calogero, Tantleff-Dunn, and Thompson, *Self-objectification in Women*, 53–54.

80. Avishai Margalit, *The Decent Society* (Cambridge, MA: Harvard University Press, 1998), 100–112; Martha C. Nussbaum, "Objectification," *Philosophy & Public Affairs* 24, no. 4 (1995): 249–291. See also in this matter Lynn Morris and Jamie Goldenberg, "Women, Objects, and Animals: Differentiating Between Sex- and Beauty-based

Objectification Femme, Objets et animaux: différencier l'objectivation basée sur le sexe et la beauté," *Revue Internationale de Psychologie* (2015): 15–38; Steve Loughnan and Maria Giuseppina Pacilli, "Seeing (and Treating) Others as Sexual Objects: Toward a More Complete Mapping of Sexual Objectification," *TPM: Testing, Psychometrics, Methodology in Applied Psychology* 21, no. 3 (2014): 309–325.

81. Barbara L. Fredrickson and Tomi-Ann Roberts, "Objectification Theory: Toward Understanding Women's Lived Experiences and Mental Health Risks," *Psychology of Women Quarterly* 21, no. 2 (1997): 173–206; Bonnie Moradi and Yu-Ping Huang, "Objectification Theory and Psychology of Women: A Decade of Advances and Future Directions," *Psychology of Women Quarterly* 32, no. 4 (2008): 377–398; Dawn M. Szymanski, Lauren B. Moffitt, and Erika R. Carr, "Sexual Objectification of Women: Advances to Theory and Research 1ψ7" *The Counseling Psychologist* 39, no. 1 (2011): 6–38. For research on this matter see Rachel M. Calogero, "A Test of Objectification Theory: The Effect of the Male Gaze on Appearance Concerns in College Women," *Psychology of Women Quarterly* 28, no. 1 (2004): 16–21; Sarah J. Gervais, Theresa K. Vescio, and Jill Allen, "When What You See Is What You Get: The Consequences of the Objectifying Gaze for Women and Men," *Psychology of Women Quarterly* 35, no. 1 (2011): 5–17; Brit Harper and Marika Tiggemann, "The Effect of Thin Ideal Media Images on Women's Self-objectification, Mood, and Body Image," *Sex Roles* 58, no. 9–10 (2008): 649–657; Sarah J. Gervais, Arianne M. Holland, and Michael D. Dodd, "My Eyes Are Up Here: The Nature of the Objectifying Gaze toward Women," *Sex Roles* 69, nos. 11–12 (2013): 557–570.

82. See David Harvey for an analysis of the Marxist distinction between production and realization of value in *The Enigma of Capital: And the Crises of Capitalism* (New York: Oxford University Press, 2010).

83. Vicki Ritts, Miles L. Patterson, and Mark E. Tubbs, "Expectations, Impressions, and Judgments of Physically Attractive Students: A Review," *Review of Educational Research* 62, no. 4 (1992): 413–426.

84. Adelle Waldman, *The Love Affairs of Nathaniel P.: A Novel* (London: Macmillan, 2014), 39, emphasis added.

85. Rosemary Henessy, *Profit and Pleasure: Sexual Identities in Late Capitalism* (Abingdon-on-Thames: Routledge, 2000).

86. For a contemporary discussion on beauty and neoliberalism, see Ana Elias, Rosalind Gill, and Christina Scharff, eds., *Aesthetic Labour: Rethinking Beauty Politics in Neoliberalism* (London: Palgrave Macmillan, 2017).

87. Two out of the endless row of such examples are Donald Trump with Melania Trump or his Secretary of the Treasury Steven Mnuchin with Louise Linton.

88. See Mears, *Pricing Beauty*.

89. A few numbers that demonstrate the size of the cosmetic and the fashion industries: According to the statistics portal, Statista, the US beauty and personal care market generated approximately $84 billion in revenue in 2016. In addition, the portal describes that in 2016 "L'Oreal was the top ranked global beauty manufacturer with a revenue that amounted to about 28.6 billion U.S. dollars." Lydia Ramsey stated in 2015 that cosmetics such as face wash, lipstick, makeup, and nail polish constituted a $60 billion market in the US. Chloe Sorvino described in 2017 that "Forbes

estimates that there are at least 40 prominent beauty startups today founded by women, making the $445 billion (sales) industry one of the most prevalent places for women to self-start their way to big-time success." First name McKinsey stated at the end of 2016 that "[f]ashion is one of the past decade's rare economic success stories. Over that period, the industry has grown at 5.5 percent annually, according to the McKinsey Global Fashion Index, to now be worth an estimated $2.4 trillion. In fact, not only does it touch everyone, but it would be the world's seventh-largest economy if ranked alongside individual countries' GDP." Statista states that revenue of the "fashion" segment in the US is "expected to show an annual growth rate (CAGR 2017–2022) of 8.8% resulting in a market volume of US$123,403m in 2022." See "Statistics & Facts on the U.S. Cosmetics and Makeup Industry," https://www.statista.com/topics/1008/cosmetics-industry/ Statista, accessed December 12, 2017; "Revenue of the Leading 20 Beauty Manufacturers Worldwide in 2016 (in Billion U.S. dollars)," https://www.statista.com/statistics/243871/revenue-of-the-leading-10-beauty-manufacturers-worldwide/, accessed December 12, 2017; Lydia Ramsey, "A $60 Billion Industry Is Shockingly Unregulated," October 11, 2015. http://www.businessinsider.com/cosmetic–industry–is–shockingly–unregulated–2015–10, accessed December 12, 2017; Chloe Sorvino, "Why the $445 Billion Beauty Industry Is a Gold Mine for Self-Made Women," May 18, 2017, https://www.forbes.com/sites/chloesorvino/2017/05/18/self-made-women-wealth-beauty-gold-mine/#1936d672a3a5, accessed December 12, 2017; McKinsey & Company, "The State of Fashion 2017," December 2016; "The State of Fashion 2017," December 2016, https://www.mckinsey.com/industries/retail/our-insights/the-state-of-fashion, accessed December 12, 2017; "Fashion," December 12, 2017, https://www.statista.com/outlook/244/109/fashion/united-states#, accessed December 12, 2017.

90. See, for example, Rachel M. Calogero and J. Kevin Thompson, "Potential Implications of the Objectification of Women's Bodies for Women's Sexual Satisfaction," *Body Image* 6, no. 2 (2009): 145–148; Ellen E. Fitzsimmons-Craft et al., "Explaining the Relation between Thin Ideal Internalization and Body Dissatisfaction among College Women: The Roles of Social Comparison and Body Surveillance," *Body Image* 9, no. 1 (2012): 43–49; Brit Harper and Marika Tiggemann, "The Effect of Thin Ideal Media Images on Women's Self-objectification, Mood, and Body Image," *Sex Roles* 58, nos. 9–10 (2008): 649–657; Peter Strelan, Sarah J. Mehaffey, and Marika Tiggemann, "Brief Report: Self-objectification and Esteem in Young Women: The Mediating Role of Reasons for Exercise," *Sex Roles* 48, no. 1 (2003): 89–95.

91. Conversely, in a meta-analytic review of the research linking self-proclaimed feminist beliefs and opinions about one's body, Sarah Murnen and Linda Smolak found that across twenty-six studies, having feminist attitudes was associated with greater body satisfaction. See Sarah K. Murnen, and Linda Smolak, "Are Feminist Women Protected from Body Image Problems? A Meta-analytic Review of Relevant Research," *Sex Roles* 60, nos. 3–4 (2009): 186.

92. Glosswitch, "Why Is It So Hard for Women to Accept Their Bodies?" *New Statesman America*, December 3, 2015, http://www.newstatesman.com/politics/feminism/2015/12/why-it-so-hard-women-accept-their-bodies, accessed December 12, 2017.

93. Angela MacRobbie, "Notes on the Perfect: Competitive Femininity in Neoliberal Times," *Australian Feminist Studies* 30, no. 83 (2015): 3–20.

94. P. Bernard, S. Gervais, J. Allen, S. Campomizzi, and O. Klein, "Integrating Sexual Objectification with Object versus Person Recognition: The Sexualized Body-inversion Hypothesis," *Psychological Science* 23, no. 5 (2012): 469–471.

95. Rosalind Gill, "From Sexual Objectification to Sexual Subjectification: The Resexualisation of Women's Bodies in the Media," *Feminist Media Studies* 3, no. 1 (2003): 100–106.

96. Kathy Martinez-Prather and Donna M. Vandiver, "Sexting among Teenagers in the United States: A Retrospective Analysis of Identifying Motivating Factors, Potential Targets, and the Role of a Capable Guardian," *International Journal of Cyber Criminology* 8, no. 1 (2014): 21–35, esp. 21.

97. Lee Murray, Thomas Crofts, Alyce McGovern, and Sanja Milivojevici, *Sexting and Young People*, Report to the Criminology Research Advisory Council Grant: CRG 53/11–12, November 2015, 5, http://www.criminologyresearchcouncil.gov.au/reports/1516/53-1112-FinalReport.pdf, accessed February 27, 2018.

98. Richard Posner, "Sale of Body Parts—Posner," *The Becker-Posner Blog*, October 21, 2012, http://www.becker-posner-blog.com/2012/10/sale-of-body-partsposner.html, accessed December 12, 2017.

99. Pateman, "What's Wrong with Prostitution?" 3–64, esp. 60.

100. In his article Hans Jonas, "Toward a Philosophy of Technology," *Hastings Center Report* 9, no. 1 (1979): 34–43.

101. Ibid., 35.

102. Jessica Benjamin, *Like Subjects, Love Objects: Essays on Recognition and Sexual Difference* (New Haven: Yale University Press, 1998); Jessica Benjamin, "Recognition and Destruction," *Relational Perspectives in Psychoanalysis* (1992); Nancy Fraser, "Rethinking Recognition," *New Left Review* 3 (2000): 107; Nancy Fraser and Axel Honneth, *Redistribution or Recognition?: A Political-philosophical Exchange.* (London and New York: Verso Books, 2003); Nancy Fraser, "Rethinking the Public Sphere: A Contribution to the Critique of Actually Existing Democracy," *Social Text* 25/26 (1990): 56–80; Axel Honneth, *The Struggle for Recognition: The Moral Grammar of Social Conflicts* (Cambridge: MIT Press, 1996).

103. Axel Honneth, with Judith Butler, Raymond Geuss, and Jonathan Lear, *Reification: A New Look at an Old Idea*, ed. Martin Jay, The Berkeley Tanner Lectures (New York: Oxford University Press, 2008).

104. Ibid., 58.

105. Pierre Bourdieu, *Distinction: A Social Critique of the Judgement of Taste* (Cambridge, MA: Harvard University Press, 1984); Jukka Gronow, *The Sociology of Taste* (Abingdon-on-Thames: Routledge, 2002); Sarah Thornton, *Club Cultures: Music, Media, and Subcultural Capital* (Middletown, CT: Wesleyan University Press, 1996).

106. Bourdieu, *Distinction*, 91, 175.

107. Eva Illouz, "Emotions, Imagination and Consumption: A New Research Agenda," *Journal of Consumer Culture* 9, no. 3 (2009): 377–413, esp. 401.

108. Leo Bersani and Adam Phillips, *Intimacies* (Chicago: University of Chicago Press, 2008), 94.

109. Jens Beckert and Patrik Aspers, eds., *The Worth of Goods* (New York: Oxford University Press), 6.

110. Christopher K. Hsee and Jiao Zhang, "Distinction Bias: Misprediction and Mischoice Due to Joint Evaluation," *Journal of Personality and Social Psychology* 86, no. 5 (2004): 680.

111. S.A.M. I Am, "True Life Dating Stories," http://www.explode.com/rr/lifesucks-dating.shtml, accessed December 12, 2017.

112. Mears, *Pricing Beauty*, 10.

113. Sheena S. Iyengar and Mark R. Lepper, "When Choice Is Demotivating: Can One Desire Too Much of a Good Thing?" *Journal of Personality and Social Psychology* 79, no. 6 (2000): 995–1006.

114. David Harvey, *Marx, Capital, and the Madness of Economic Reason* (New York: Oxford University Press, 2017).

115. Karl Marx, "Part 3: The Law of the Tendency of the Rate of Profit to Fall," in *Capital: A Critique of Political Economy*, vol 3, Penguin Classics (1863–1883; London: Penguin Books, 1993), 279–306, 317–376. See also Ben Fine and Laurence Harris, "The Law of the Tendency of the Rate of Profit to Fall," *Rereading Capital* (London: Macmillan Education, 1979), 58–75.

116. David Harvey, *Seventeen Contradictions and the End of Capitalism* (New York: Oxford University Press, 2014), 234.

117. Adam Arvidsson, "The Potential of Consumer Publics," *Ephemera* 13, no. 2 (2013): 367–391; Adam Arvidsson, "The Ethical Economy of Customer Coproduction," *Journal of Macromarketing* 28, no. 4 (2008): 326–338.

118. Milton Friedman, *Capitalism and Freedom* (Chicago: University of Chicago 2009); Friedrich August Hayek, "The Use of Knowledge in Society," *The American Economic Review* 35, no. 4 (1945): 519–530. For a review see David Harvey, *A Brief History of Neoliberalism* (Oxford: Oxford University Press, 2007); Thomas I. Palley, "From Keynesianism to Neoliberalism: Shifting Paradigms in Economics," in *Neoliberalism: A Critical Reader*, ed. Alfredo Saad-Filho and Deborah Johnston (Chicago: University of Chicago Press, 2005), 20–29.

119. See writing on the economy of attention Daniel Kahneman, *Attention and Effort* (Englewood Cliffs, NJ: Prentice Hall, 1973); Warren Thorngate, "The Economy of Attention and the Development of Psychology," *Canadian Psychology/Psychologie Canadienne* 31, no. 3 (1990): 262–271.

120. American Psychological Association, Task Force on the Sexualization of Girls "Report of the APA Task Force on the Sexualization of Girls," 2007, http://www.apa.org/pi/women/programs/girls/report-full.pdf, accessed February 26, 2018.

121. Ine Vanwesenbeeck, "The Risks and Rights of Sexualization: An Appreciative Commentary on Lerum and Dworkin's 'Bad Girls Rule,'" *Journal of Sex Research* 46, no. 4 (2009): 268–270, esp. 269.

122. For a very useful and enlightening discussion, see Gill, "From Sexual Objectification to Sexual Subjectification."

123. Rosalind Gill, "Empowerment/sexism: Figuring Female Sexual Agency in Contemporary Advertising," *Feminism & Psychology* 18, no. 1 (2008): 35–60.

124. See Gill, "From Sexual Objectification to Sexual Subjectification."

125. Max Horkheimer and Theodor W. Adorno, *Dialectic of Enlightenment*, ed. Noeri Gunzelin (1944; Stanford, CA: Stanford University Press, 2002).

126. Ann Swidler, "Culture in Action: Symbols and Strategies," *American Sociological Review* (1986): 273–286.

127. Martin Heidegger, *Basic Writings*, ed. David Farrell Krell, trans. William Lovitt (New York: Harper & Row, 1977), 295–301.

128. See Bakewell, *At the Existentialist Café*, 183.

129. A letter from 19.12. 1922, quoted in Maria Popova, "How Virginia Woolf and Vita Sackville-West Fell in Love," *Brain Pickings*, accessed December 12, 2017, https://www.brainpickings.org/2016/07/28/virginia-woolf-vita-sackville-west/.

130. "Ma vision de l'amour n'a pas changé, mais ma vision du monde, oui. C'est super agréable d'être lesbienne. Je me sens moins concernée par la féminité, par l'approbation des hommes, par tous ces trucs qu'on s'impose pour eux. Et je me sens aussi moins préoccupée par mon âge: c'est plus dur de vieillir quand on est hétéro. La séduction existe entre filles, mais elle est plus cool, on n'est pas déchue à 40 ans," in Virginie Despentes, "Punk un jour, punk toujours," *Elle Québec*, January 2011.

131. "The Oppression of Women in the Western World," *Shannon Prusak's Stories Revealed*, https://shannonprusak.wordpress.com/the-oppression-of-women-in-the-western-world/.

Chapter 5

1. *The Claverings*.

2. From *Sie Liebten Sich Beide*, trans. A. S. Kline, in *All Poetry*, https://allpoetry.com/Sie-Liebten-Sich-Beide, accessed March 5, 2018. (The poem strictu sensu has no title; it is part of the cycle Die Heimkehr from "Book of Songs." Dt.: Buch der Lieder: Die Heimkehr, Gedicht 33.)

3. For more on their relationship, see Robert Schumann, Clara Schumann, and Gerd Nauhaus, *The Marriage Diaries of Robert and Clara Schumann: From Their Wedding Day through the Russia Trip* (Boston: Northeastern University, 1993); John Worthen, *Robert Schumann: Life and Death of a Musician* (New Haven: Yale University Press, 2007).

4. Georg Wilhelm Friedrich Hegel, *The Philosophy of Right* (1820; Indianapolis: Hackett Publishing, 2015), 143.

5. Axel Honneth, *Freedom's Right: The Social Foundations of Democratic Life* (New York: Columbia University Press, 2014).

6. See chapter 2.

7. Axel Honneth, *The Struggle for Recognition: The Moral Grammar of Social Conflicts* (Cambridge: MIT Press, 1996); Honneth, *Freedom's Right*; Christopher Zurn, *Axel Honneth: A Critical Theory of the Social* (Hoboken, NJ: Wiley, 2015), esp. chapter 6 "Social Freedom and Recognition," 155–205.

8. James Leonard Park, *Loving in Freedom*, https://s3.amazonaws.com/aws-website-james-leonardpark---freelibrary-3puxk/CY-L-FRE.html, accessed December 31, 2017.

9. Pateman, *The Sexual Contract* 39.

10. Ibid., 15.

11. See Alberto Abadie and Sebastien Gay, "The Impact of Presumed Consent Legislation on Cadaveric Organ Donation: A Cross-country Study," *Journal of Health Economics* 25, no. 4 (2006): 599–620; Morris R. Cohen, "The Basis of Contract," *Harvard Law Review* 46, no. 4 (1933): 553–592; Ruth R. Faden and Tom L. Beauchamp, *A History and Theory of Informed Consent* (Oxford: Oxford University Press, 1986); Roscoe Pound, "The Role of the Will in Law," *Harvard Law Review* 68, no. 1 (1954): 1–19.

12. As described in the *Guardian*, Sir Nicholas Wall, the most senior family law judge in England and Wales, stated at 2012 that "'No fault' divorces should become the standard means for couples to separate rather than proving that one side is responsible for the breakdown." See Owen Bowcott, "No-fault Divorces 'Should Be Standard,'" March 27, 2012, theguardian.com https://www.theguardian.com/law/2012/mar/27/no-fault-divorces-standard-judge, accessed December 31, 2017

13. Anthony Giddens, *The Transformation of Intimacy: Sexuality, Love and Eroticism in Modern Societies* (Stanford, CA: Stanford University Press, 1992), 58.

14. Neil Gross and Solon Simmons, "Intimacy as a Double-edged Phenomenon? An Empirical Test of Giddens," *Social Forces* 81, no. 2 (2002): 531–555, esp. 536.

15. See Pateman, *The Sexual Contract*, "Contracting In," 1–18.

16. Andrew Dilts, "From 'Entrepreneur of the Self' to 'Care of the Self': Neoliberal Governmentality and Foucault's Ethics," *Western Political Science Association 2010 Annual Meeting Paper*, https://ssrn.com/abstract=1580709, accessed March 7, 2018; Michel Feher, "Self-Appreciation; Or, the Aspirations of Human Capital," *Public Culture* 21, no. 1 (2009): 21–41; Patricia Mccafferty, "Forging a 'Neoliberal Pedagogy': The 'Enterprising Education' Agenda in Schools," *Critical Social Policy* 30, no. 4 (2010): 541–563.

17. Mandy Len Catron, "*To Stay in Love, Sign on the Dotted Line*," *New York Times*, June 23, 2017, https://www.nytimes.com/2017/06/23/style/modern-love-to-stay-in-love-sign-on-the-dotted-line-36-questions.html?emc=edit_tnt_20170623&eml_thmb=1&nlid=47676527&tntemail0=y, accessed December 31, 2017, emphasis added.

18. Pateman, *The Sexual Contract*, 1–2.

19. See William H. Sewell Jr., "Geertz, Cultural Systems, and History: From Synchrony to Transformation," in *The Fate of "Culture": Geertz and Beyond*, ed. Sherry B. Ortner (Berkeley: University of California Press, 1999), 47.

20. Laura Sessions Stepp, "*A New Kind of Date Rape*," *Cosmopolitan*, October 12, 2007, http://web.archive.org/web/20071012024801/http://www.cosmopolitan.com/sex-love/sex/new-kind-of-date-rape, accessed December 31, 2017, emphasis added.

21. I wish to thank deeply Elizabeth Armstrong for having drawn, in private communication, my attention to the notion of situationship.

22. See Aidan Neal, "9 Signs You're in a Situationship?" August 6, 2014, http://aidanneal.com/2014/08/06/9-signs-youre-situationship/, accessed December 31, 2017.

23. Rachel O'Neill, *Seduction: Men, Masculinity, and Mediated Intimacy* (Cambridge: Polity, 2018). See also Rachel O'Neill, "The Work of Seduction: Intimacy and Subjectivity in the London 'Seduction Community,'" *Sociological Research Online* 20, no. 4 (2015): 1–14, esp. 10.

24. eHarmony Staff, "Deciding Factors: Eight Solid Reasons to Break Up," September 26, 2013, https://www.eharmony.com/dating-advice/relationships/eight-solid-reasons-to-break-up/,accessed December 31, 2017, emphasis added.

25. Denise Haunani Solomon and Leanne K. Knobloch, "Relationship Uncertainty, Partner Interference, and Intimacy within Dating Relationships," *Journal of Social and Personal Relationships* 18, no. 6 (2001): 804–820, esp. 805.

26. Alice Boyes, "51 Signs of an Unhealthy Relationship," February 10, 2015, https://www.psychologytoday.com/blog/in-practice/201502/51-signs-unhealthy-relationship, accessed December 31, 2017, emphasis added.

27. Rori Raye, "Stop Wondering if He's Going to Call…Because He'll Be Clamoring for Your Time and Attention," https://www.catchhimandkeephim.com/m/email/nl/roriraye/did-he-pursue-you-and-then-get-distant.html?s=57508&e=1&cid=UZZZCD&lid=1&sbid=SdYj, accessed December 31, 2017, emphasis added.

28. Ann Swidler, *Talk of Love: How Culture Matters* (Chicago: University of Chicago Press, 2001), 107. See also Ann Swidler, "Culture in Action: Symbols and Strategies," *American Sociological Review* (1986): 273–286, esp. 280.

29. Karin Knorr Cetina, "What Is a Financial Market?: Global Markets as Microinstitutional and Post-Traditional Social Forms," in *The Oxford Handbook of the Sociology of Finance*, ed. Karin Knorr Cetina and Alex Preda (Oxford: Oxford University Press, 2012), 115–133, esp. 122.

30. Terje Aven, "Risk Assessment and Risk Management: Review of Recent Advances on Their Foundation," *European Journal of Operational Research* 253, no. 1 (2016): 1–13; Terje Aven and Yolande Hiriart, "Robust Optimization in Relation to a Basic Safety Investment Model with Imprecise Probabilities," *Safety Science* 55 (2013): 188–194; James Lam, *Enterprise Risk Management: From Incentives to Controls* (Hoboken, NJ: Wiley, 2014); José A. Scheinkman, *Speculation, Trading, and Bubbles* (New York: Columbia University, 2014).

31. Tali Kleiman and Ran R. Hassin, "Non-conscious Goal Conflicts," *Journal of Experimental Social Psychology* 47, no. 3 (2011): 521–532, esp. 521.

32. Ibid., 522.

33. Goal12, "I Feel Lost." loveshack.org, April 3, 2016, http://www.loveshack.org/forums/breaking-up-reconciliation-coping/breaks-breaking-up/575980-i-feel-lost, accessed December 31, 2017 emphasis added.

34. Quoted in Ivan Krastev, *After Europe* (Philadelphia: University of Pennsylvania Press, 2017), 51.

35. Valeriya Safronova, "Exes Explain Ghosting, the Ultimate Silent Treatment," June 26 2015, http://www.nytimes.com/2015/06/26/fashion/exes-explain-ghosting-the-ultimate-silent-treatment.html?WT.mc_id=2015-JULY-OTB-INTL_AUD_DEV-0629–0802&WT.mc_ev=click&ad-keywords=IntlAudDev&_r=0, accessed December 31, 2017. (The *Times's* original wording mentions Casper instead of Cole, possibly

confusing Cole him with the ghost Casper in the 1995 fantasy-comedy of the same name.)

36. Luc Boltanski and Laurent Thévenot, *On Justification: Economies of Worth* (Princeton, NJ: Princeton University Press, 2006).

37. Volkmar Sigusch, "Lean Sexuality: On Cultural Transformations of Sexuality and Gender in Recent Decades," *Sexuality & Culture* 5, no. 2 (2001): 23–56.

38. Hellen Chen, "Hellen Chen's Love Seminar: The Missing Manual that Will Make Your Relationship Last," 2013, https://youtu.be/ezEeaBs84w0. See also "Over 85% of Dating Ends up in Breakups—Upcoming New Book on Relationships Sheds Light," October 28, 2013, http://www.prweb.com/releases/finding_right_date/lasting_marriages/prweb11278931.htm, accessed December 31, 2017.

39. Albert O. Hirschman, *Exit, Voice, and Loyalty: Responses to Decline in Firms, Organizations, and States* (Cambridge, MA: Harvard University Press, 1970).

40. Deborah Davis, Phillip R. Shaver, and Michael L. Vernon, "Physical, Emotional, and Behavioral Reactions to Breaking Up: The Roles of Gender, Age, Emotional Involvement, and Attachment Style," *Personality and Social Psychology Bulletin* 29, no. 7 (2003): 871–884, esp. 871.

41. Augustine J. Kposowa, "Marital Status and Suicide in the National Longitudinal Mortality Study," *Journal of Epidemiology & Community Health* 54, no. 4 (2000): 254–261, esp. 254.

42. Marianne Wyder, Patrick Ward, and Diego De Leo, "Separation as a Suicide Risk Factor," *Journal of Affective Disorders* 116, no. 3 (2009): 208–213.

43. Erica B. Slotter, Wendi L. Gardner, and Eli J. Finkel, "Who Am I without You? The Influence of Romantic Breakup on the Self-concept," *Personality and Social Psychology Bulletin* 36, no. 2 (2010): 147–160.

44. Robin West, "The Harms of Consensual Sex," November 11, 2011, http://unityand-struggle.org/wp-content/uploads/2016/04/West_The-harms-of-consensual-sex.pdf, accessed December 31, 2017.

45. Mike Hardcastle, "Am I in Love?" http://teenadvice.about.com/u/sty/datinglove/breakup_stories/He-d-Tell-Me-I-was-a-Horrible-Person.htm, accessed July 2015.

46. Avishai Margalit, *On Betrayal* (Cambridge, MA: Harvard University Press, 2017), 7. Given the prevalence of veganism as a new form of morality, Margalit obviously chose the wrong analogy but his point remains valid.

47. Alan Wertheimer, *Consent to Sexual Relations* (Cambridge: Cambridge University Press, 2010).

48. Hirschman, *Exit, Voice, and Loyalty*, 2.

49. Richard Sennett, *The Culture of the New Capitalism* (New Haven: Yale University Press, 2006), 4–5.

50. Joseph A. Schumpeter, *Capitalism, Socialism and Democracy* (London: Routledge, 1942; 2013) specifically chapter 7, "The Process of Creative Destruction," 81–86.

51. Sennett, *The Culture of the New Capitalism*, 48.

52. Esther Perel, *The State of Affairs: Rethinking Infidelity* (New York: HarperCollins, 2017).

53. Jennifer M. Silva, *Coming Up Short: Working Class Adulthood in an Age of Uncertainty* (Oxford: Oxford University Press, 2013), 6.

54. Uriel Procaccia, *Russian Culture, Property Rights, and the Market Economy* (Cambridge: Cambridge University Press, 2007).

55. Frank H. Knight, *Risk, Uncertainty and Profit* (1921; North Chelmsford: Courier Corporation, 2012).

56. Ibid., 19.

57. Sennett, *The Culture of the New Capitalism*, 66.

58. David F. Haas and Forrest A. Deseran, "Trust and Symbolic Exchange," *Social Psychology Quarterly* (1981): 3–13, esp. 4; Peter Michael Blau, *Exchange and Power in Social Life* (New York: John Wiley & Sons, 1964).

59. Haas and Deseran, "Trust and Symbolic Exchange," 3.

60. Joyce Berg, John Dickhaut, and Kevin McCabe, "Trust, Reciprocity, and Social History," *Games and Economic Behavior* 10, no. 1 (1995): 122–142; Ernst Fehr and Simon Gachter, "How Effective Are Trust- and Reciprocity-based Incentives?" *Economics, Values and Organizations* (1998): 337–363; Elinor Ostrom, "A Behavioral Approach to the Rational Choice Theory of Collective Action: Presidential Address, American Political Science Association, 1997," *American Political Science Review* 92, no. 1 (1998): 1–22; Elinor Ostrom and James Walker, eds., *Trust and Reciprocity: Interdisciplinary Lessons for Experimental Research* (New York: Russell Sage Foundation, 2003).

61. J. Mark Weber, Deepak Malhotra, and J. Keith Murnighan, "Normal Acts of Irrational Trust: Motivated Attributions and the Trust Development Process," *Research in Organizational Behavior* 26 (2004): 75–101, esp. 78.

62. Alvin W. Gouldner, "The Norm of Reciprocity: A Preliminary Statement," *American Sociological Review* (1960): 161–178.

63. John Duffy and Jack Ochs found higher levels of cooperation in repeated prisoner's dilemma games, compared to treatments in which subjects are randomly rematched after each round. Dal Bó found that "the shadow of the future" (the threat of future retaliations) reduces opportunistic behavior in prisoners' dilemma games. Jim Engle-Warnick and Robert Slonim found that in indefinite trust games the strategy of the player will include the construction of repeated-game equilibria. See Pedro Dal Bó, "Cooperation under the Shadow of the Future: Experimental Evidence from Infinitely Repeated Games," *American Economic Review* 95, no. 5 (December 2005): 1591–1604; John Duffy and Jack Ochs, "Cooperative Behavior and the Frequency of Social Interaction," *Games and Economic Behavior* 66, no. 2 (2009): 785–812; Jim Engle-Warnick and Robert L. Slonim, "Inferring Repeated-game Strategies from Actions: Evidence from Trust Game Experiments," *Economic Theory* 28, no. 3 (2006): 603–632.

64. As Denise Rousseau et al. argue in a cross-discipline article that deals with trust, "Risk creates an opportunity for trust, which leads to risk taking. Moreover, risk taking buttresses a sense of trust when the expected behavior materialize." See Denise M. Rousseau et al., "Not So Different After All: A Cross-discipline View of Trust," *Academy of Management Review* 23, no. 3 (1998): 393–404, esp. 395.

65. Roger C. Mayer, James H. Davis, and F. David Schoorman, "An Integrative Model of Organizational Trust," *Academy of Management Review* 20, no. 3 (1995): 709–734, esp. 726.

66. See Weber, Malhotra, and Murnighan, "Normal Acts of Irrational Trust," 75–101.

67. Diego Gambetta, "Can We Trust Trust?" *Trust: Making and Breaking Cooperative Relations* 13 (2000): 213–237.

68. Weber and Murnighan, "Normal Acts of Irrational Trust," 75–101.

69. Niklas Luhmann, *Trust and Power* (New York: John Wiley & Sons, 1979), especially chapter 4, "Trust as a Reduction of Complexity," 24–31.

70. Ibid., 5.

71. Sennett, *The Culture of the New Capitalism*, 79.

72. Eva Illouz and Edgar Cabanas, *Happycratie Comment l'industrie du bonheur a pris le contrôle de nos vies* (Paris: Premier Parallèle Editeur, 2018).

73. Stefano Bory, *Il Tempo Sommerso. Strategie Identitarie Nei Giovani Adulti Del Mezzogiorno* (Naples : Liguori, 2008).

74. For a literary example, consider the best-selling novel *The Love Affairs of Nathaniel*, which describes a new narrative of love and self. A young man has a relationship with a smart, generous, kind, accomplished woman. But he leaves her, and the narrative lets us understand that he leaves her precisely because he becomes increasingly impressed with her personality, which makes him feel not "good enough" and "inadequate." He then goes on to find another woman who seems to pop up in his life almost haphazardly, about whom he says at first that she is not his type, but as time passes, they seem to get along, and she moves in with him. It is not really an act of emotional will engineered from within the strictures and structures of courtship and sentiment that makes him stay with her, but rather the result of an emotional flow that is inchoate, that does not start out of a clear structure that channels emotions, gives them a shape, or a purpose. Both decide to move in because they "feel good with each other," and not because they experience a romantic revelation, or imbue their interaction with a purpose. See Adelle Waldman, *The Love Affairs of Nathaniel P.: A Novel* (New York: Macmillan, 2014).

75. Sandra L. Murray, John G. Holmes, and Dale W. Griffin, "The Self-fulfilling Nature of Positive Illusions in Romantic Relationships: Love Is Not Blind, But Prescient," *Journal of Personality and Social Psychology* 71, no. 6 (1996): 1155–1180, esp. 1157.

76. Sennett, *The Culture of the New Capitalism*, 77.

77. See David Stark, *The Sense of Dissonance: Accounts of Worth in Economic Life* (Princeton, NJ: Princeton University Press, 2011).

Chapter 6

1. Emma Gray, "Octavia Spencer Reveals the Role She Was 'Destined to Play,'" *Huffington Post*, July 2, 2017, https://www.huffingtonpost.com/entry/octavia-spencer-reveals-the-role-she-was-destined-to-play_us_58996e44e4b0c1284f27ea2d, accessed May 8, 2018.

2. *Vernon Subutex*, Tome 1 (Paris: Grasset,) 63.

3. Stephen A. Mitchell, *Relational Concepts in Psychoanalysis* (Cambridge, MA: Harvard University Press, 1988), 273.

4. Andrew Cherlin ("Marriage Has Become a Trophy," *The Atlantic*, March 20, 2018, https://www.theatlantic.com/family/archive/2018/03/incredible-everlasting-institution-marriage/555320/?utm_source=newsletter&utm_medium=email&utm_campaign=atlantic-daily-newsletter&utm_content=20180320&silverid=MzY5MzUwNzM2Njc2S0, accessed May 8, 2018.

5. Anthony Giddens, *The Transformation of Intimacy: Sexuality, Love and Eroticism in Modern Societies* (Hoboken: Wiley, 2013).

6. Lauren Berlant, *Desire/Love* (Brooklyn, NY: Punctum Books, 2012), 44.

7. See, for example, Paul R. Amato, "The Consequences of Divorce for Adults and Children," *Journal of Marriage and Family* 62, no. 4 (2000): 1269–1287; Paul R. Amato and Denise Previti, "People's Reasons for Divorcing: Gender, Social Class, the Life Course, and Adjustment," *Journal of Family Issues* 24, no. 5 (2003): 602–626; Paul R. Amato and Brett Beattie, "Does the Unemployment Rate Affect the Divorce Rate? An Analysis of State Data 1960–2005," *Social Science Research* 40, no. 3 (2011): 705–715; Anne-Marie Ambert, *Divorce: Facts, Causes, and Consequences.* (Ottawa: Vanier Institute of the Family, 2005); Lynn Prince Cooke, "'Doing' Gender in Context: Household Bargaining and Risk of Divorce in Germany and the United States," *American Journal of Sociology* 112, no. 2 (2006): 442–472; Paul M. De Graaf and Matthijs Kalmijn, "Change and Stability in the Social Determinants of Divorce: A Comparison of Marriage Cohorts in the Netherlands," *European Sociological Review* 22, no. 5 (2006): 561–572; Tamar Fischer, "Parental Divorce and Children's Socio-economic Success: Conditional Effects of Parental Resources Prior to Divorce, and Gender of the Child," *Sociology* 41, no. 3 (2007): 475–495; Matthijs Kalmijn and Anne-Rigt Poortman, "His or Her Divorce? The Gendered Nature of Divorce and Its Determinants," *European Sociological Review* 22, no. 2 (2006): 201–214; Ludwig F. Lowenstein, "Causes and Associated Features of Divorce as Seen by Recent Research," *Journal of Divorce & Remarriage* 42, nos. 3–4 (2005): 153–171; Michael Wagner and Bernd Weiss, "On the Variation of Divorce Risks in Europe: Findings from a Meta-analysis of European Longitudinal Studies," *European Sociological Review* 22, no. 5 (2006): 483–500; Yoram Weiss, "The Formation and Dissolution of Families: Why Marry? Who Marries Whom? And What Happens upon Divorce," *Handbook of Population and Family Economics* 1 (1997): 81–123.

8. Selected studied that found these causes include those of Amato and Previti, "People's Reasons for Divorcing"; Amato and Beattie, "Does the Unemployment Rate Affect the Divorce Rate?"; Ambert, *Divorce*; De Graaf and Kalmijn, "Change and Stability in the Social Determinants of Divorce"; Kalmijn and Poortman, "His or Her Divorce?"; Ludwig F. Lowenstein, 2005; and Wagner and Weiss, "On the Variation of Divorce Risks in Europe.

9. Lynn Gigy and Joan B. Kelly, "Reasons for Divorce: Perspectives of Divorcing Men and Women," *Journal of Divorce & Remarriage* 18, nos. 1–2 (1993): 169–188, esp. 170.

10. Paul M. De Graaf and Matthijs Kalmijn, "Divorce Motives in a Period of Rising Divorce: Evidence from a Dutch Life-history Survey," *Journal of Family Issues* 27, no. 4 (2006): 483–505; Gigy and Kelly, "Reasons for Divorce"; John Mordechai

Gottman, *What Predicts Divorce?: The Relationship between Marital Processes and Marital Outcomes* (London: Psychology Press, 2014); Ilene Wolcott and Jody Hughes, "Towards Understanding the Reasons for Divorce," (working paper, Australian Institute of Family Studies, 1999).

11. Steven Ruggles, "The Rise of Divorce and Separation in the United States, 1880–1990," *Demography* 34, no. 4 (1997): 455–466, esp. 455.

12. Gigy and Kelly, "Reasons for Divorce," 173.

13. Wolcott and Hughes, "Towards Understanding the Reasons for Divorce," 11–12.

14. Michael J. Rosenfeld, "Who Wants the Breakup? Gender and Breakup in Heterosexual Couples" in *Social Networks and the Life Course*, ed. Duane Alwin, Diane Felmlee, and Derek Kreager (New York: Springer, 2017), 221–243, esp. 221.

15. Andrew J. Cherlin, *Marriage, Divorce, Remarriage*, rev. and enl. ed. (Cambridge, MA: Harvard University Press, 1992), 51.

16. Rosenfeld, "Who Wants the Breakup?" 239.

17. Karen C. Holden and Pamela J. Smock, "The Economic Costs of Marital Dissolution: Why Do Women Bear a Disproportionate Cost?" *Annual Review of Sociology* 17, no. 1 (1991): 51–78.

18. See chapter 5.

19. See Ruben C. Gur and Raquel E. Gur, "Complementarity of Sex Differences in Brain and Behavior: From Laterality to Multimodal Neuroimaging," in *Journal of Neuroscience Research* 95 (2017): 189–199.

20. See Greer Litton Fox and Velma McBride Murry, "Gender and Families: Feminist Perspectives and Family Research," *Journal of Marriage and Family* 62, no. 4 (2000): 1160–1172; Arlie Hochschild, *The Second Shift: Working Families and the Revolution at Home* (1989; New York: Penguin Books, 2012); Joan B. Landes, "The Public and the Private Sphere: A Feminist Reconsideration," in *Feminists Read Habermas: Gendering the Subject of Discourse.,*ed. Johanna Meehan (London: Routledge, 2013), 107–132; Linda Thompson and Alexis J. Walker, "Gender in Families: Women and Men in Marriage, Work, and Parenthood," *Journal of Marriage and the Family* (1989): 845–871.

21. Francesca Cancian, *Love in America: Gender and Self-Development* (Cambridge: Cambridge University Press, 1990).

22. See Julia Brannen and Jean Collard, *Marriages in Trouble: The Process of Seeking Help* (London: Taylor & Francis, 1982); Jean Duncombe and Dennis Marsden, "Love and Intimacy: The Gender Division of Emotion and 'Emotion Work': A Neglected Aspect of Sociological Discussion of Heterosexual Relationships," *Sociology* 27, no. 2 (1993): 221–241; Rebecca J. Erickson, "Why Emotion Work Matters: Sex, Gender, and the Division of Household Labor," *Journal of Marriage and Family* 67, no. 2 (2005): 337–351; Penny Mansfield and Jean Collard, *The Beginning of the Rest of Your Life?* (London: Macmillan, 1988).

23. See Barbara Dafoe Whitehead and David Popenoe, "Who Wants to Marry a Soul Mate?" in *The State of Our Unions: The Social Health of Marriage in America* (New Brunswick, NJ: Rutgers University, 2001), 6–16, https://www.stateofourunions.org/past_issues.php.

24. Andrew J. Cherlin, "The Deinstitutionalization of American Marriage," *Journal of Marriage and Family* 66, no. 4 (2004): 848–861, esp. 853.

25. Luc Boltanski and Laurent Thevenot, *On Justification: Economies of Worth* (Princeton: Princeton University Press, 2006).

26. Quoted in Avishai Margalit, *On Betrayal* (Cambridge, MA: Harvard University Press, 2017), 109.

27. Quoted in ibid., 97.

28. Claire Bloom, *Leaving a Doll's House* (New York: Little, Brown and Company, 1996), 201.

29. See Margalit, *On Betrayal*, 56.

30. Paul R. Amato and Denise Previti, "People's Reasons for Divorcing; Denise Previti and Paul R. Amato, "Is Infidelity a Cause or a Consequence of Poor Marital Quality?" *Journal of Social and Personal Relationships* 21, no. 2 (2004): 217–223; Shelby B. Scott et al., "Reasons for Divorce and Recollections of Premarital Intervention: Implications for Improving Relationship Education," *Couple and Family Psychology: Research and Practice* 2, no. 2 (2013): 131–145.

31. Judith Stacey, *Brave New Families: Stories of Domestic Upheaval in Late-twentieth-century America* (Berkeley: University of California Press, 1990).

32. So widespread and deep is the assumption that sexuality defines the core of couplehood that a scientific study financed by a Science Foundation defines its goal as follows: "It's a story that's all too familiar for many couples: they may still love each other, but their sexual desire dwindles over time. But according to new research funded by BSF there's hope for couples wishing to rekindle the flames of passion." See "A New BSF-Supported Study Brings Promising News for Couples Looking to Put the Spark Back in Their Sex Lives," United States-Israel Binational Science Foundation, http://www.bsf.org.il/bsfpublic/DefaultPage1.aspx?PageId=6144&innerTextID=6144, accessed April 27, 2017.

33. Jonathan Safran Foer, *Here I Am* (New York: Penguin Books, 2016), 46.

34. See, for example, Joseph Kessel, *Belle de Jour* (1928); D. H. Lawrence, *Lady Chatterley's Lover* (1928); and Tennessee Williams, *A Streetcar Named Desire* (1947).

35. Jeffry A. Simpson, "The Dissolution of Romantic Relationships: Factors Involved in Relationship Stability and Emotional Distress," *Journal of Personality and Social Psychology* 53, no. 4 (1987): 683–692.

36. Adam Phillips, *Monogamy* (1996; London: Faber & Faber, 2017), 69.

37. Sam Roberts, "Divorce after 50 Grows More Common," *New York Times*, September 20, 2013, http://www.nytimes.com/2013/09/22/fashion/weddings/divorce-after-50-grows-more-common.html, accessed May 10, 2018.

38. Ibid.

39. Agnès Martineau-Arbes, Magali Giné, Prisca Grosdemouge, Rémi Bernad, "Le Syndrome d'epuisement, Une maladie professionnelle," May 2014, http://www.rpbo.fr/wp-content/uploads/2017/04/Rapport-TechnologiaBurnOut.pdf, accessed May 10, 2018.

40. David Gordon et al., "How Common Are Sexually 'Inactive' Marriages?" *Relationships in America Survey 2014*, The Austin Institute for the Study of Family and Culture, http://

relationshipsinamerica.com/relationships-and-sex/how-common-are-sexually-inactive-marriages, accessed May10, 2018.

41. Laura Hamilton and Elizabeth A. Armstrong, "Gendered Sexuality in Young Adulthood: Double Binds and Flawed Options," *Gender & Society* 23, no. 5 (2009): 589–616.

42. See Alison J. Pugh, *The Tumbleweed Society: Working and Caring in an Age of Insecurity* (New York: Oxford University Press, 2015).

43. Safran Foer, *Here I Am*, 50.

44. Jean-Claude Kaufmann, *Agacements: Les petites guerres du couple* (Paris: Armand Colin, 2007).

45. Ibid., 26.

46. "Comment Ikea se transforme en cauchemar pour les couples," *Le Monde*, September 21, 2015, http://bigbrowser.blog.lemonde.fr/2015/09/21/comment-ikea-se-transforme-en-cauchemar-pour-les-couples/, accessed May 10, 2018.

47. See chapter 4.

48. Algirdas Julien Greimas, *Structural Semantics: An Attempt at a Method* (1966; Lincoln: University of Nebraska Press, 1983).

49. Bruno Latour, *Changer de société. Refaire de la sociologie* (Paris: La Découverte, 2006).

50. Dan Slater, "A Million First Dates," *The Atlantic*, January–February 2013, https://www.theatlantic.com/magazine/archive/2013/01/a-million-first-dates/309195/?utm_source=promotional-email&utm_medium=email&utm_campaign=familynewsletter-everyone&utm_content=20182004&silverID=MzY5MzUwNzM2Njc2S0 [Accessed 10 May 2018].

51. Carol Gilligan, *In a Different Voice: Psychological Theory and Women's Development* (Cambridge, MA: Harvard University Press, 1982).

52. Mark Piper, "Achieving Autonomy," *Social Theory and Practice* 42, no. 4 (October 2016): 767–779, esp. 768.

53. Joel Anderson, "Regimes of Autonomy," *Ethical Theory and Moral Practice* 17, no. 3 (June 2014): 355–368.

54. Eva Illouz, ed., *Emotions as Commodities: Capitalism, Consumption and Authenticity* (Abingdon-on-Thames: Routledge, 2018).

55. Safran Foer, *Here I Am*, 50.

56. Ibid., 60.

57. Francesca M. Cancian and Steven L. Gordon, "Changing Emotion Norms in Marriage: Love and Anger in US Women's Magazines since 1900," *Gender & Society* 2, no. 3 (1988): 308–342.

58. Orly Benjamin, "Therapeutic Discourse, Power and Change: Emotion and Negotiation in Marital Conversations," *Sociology* 32, no. 4 (1998): 771–793, esp. 772.

59. Arlie Hochschild, *The Managed Heart: Commercialization of Human Feeling* (Berkeley: University of California Press, 1983).

60. Lynn Gigy and Joan B. Kelly, "Reasons for Divorce," 184.

61. Harry G. Frankfurt, *On Bullshit* (Princeton, NJ: Princeton University Press, 2009), 66–67.

62. Keith Payne "Conscious or What? Relationship between Implicit Bias and Conscious Experiences, " *(Un)Consciousness: A Functional Perspective* (August 25–27, 2015), Israel Institute for Advanced Studies, The Hebrew University of Jerusalem.

63. Keziah Weir, "Nicole Krauss Talks Divorce, Freedom, and New Beginnings," *Elle*, October 2017, https://www.elle.com/culture/books/a12119575/nicole-krauss-profile-october-2017/.

Conclusion

1. Entretien avec Catherine Portevin et Jean-Philippe Pisanias, "Pierre Bourdieu- Les aventuriers de l'île enchantée," *Télérama* n°2536,19/08/98. http://www.homme-moderne.org/societe/socio/bourdieu/Btele985.html (Retrieved 27 May 2018).

2. Seneca, *Letter to Helvia* (around the year 49 CE), *On the Shortness of Life* (*Translated by C. D. N. Costa*), 1997, Penguin Book, p. 35.

3. See George Lakoff and Mark Johnson, *Philosophy in the Flesh: The Embodied Mind and Its Challenge to Western Thought* (New York: Basic Books, 1999); Janet Price and Margrit Shildrick, eds. *Feminist Theory and the Body: A Reader* (Abingdon-on-Thames: Routledge, 2017); Hilary Putnam, *The Threefold Cord: Mind, Body and World* (New York: Columbia University Press, 2000); Susan Wendell, *The Rejected Body: Feminist Philosophical Reflections on Disability* (Abingdon-on-Thames: Routledge, 2013); Richard M. Zaner, *The Context of Self: A Phenomenological Inquiry Using Medicine as a Clue* (Athens: Ohio University Press, 1981).

4. Simone de Beauvoir, *La phénoménologie de la perception* de Maurice Merleau-Ponty, Paris: Les temps modernes 1, no. 2 : 363–67 ("A Review of *The Phenomenology of Perception* by Maurice Merleau-Ponty," trans. Marybeth Timmermann in *Simone de Beauvoir: Philosophical Writings*, ed. M. A. Simons (Champaign: University of Illinois Press, 2004), 161.

5. Catharine A. MacKinnon, *Butterfly Politics* (Cambridge, MA: Harvard University Press, 2017).

6. Erich Fromm, *Escape from Freedom* (1941; New York: Henry Holt and Company, 1994), x.

7. Niraj Chokshi, "What Is an Incel? A Term Used by the Toronto Van Attack Suspect, Explained," *New York Times*, April 24, 2018, https://www.nytimes.com/2018/04/24/world/canada/incel-reddit-meaning-rebellion.html, accessed May 27, 2018.

8. Ashifa Kassam, "Woman behind 'Incel' Says Angry Men Hijacked Her Word 'as a Weapon of War,'" *Guardian*, April 26, 2018, https://www.theguardian.com/world/2018/apr/25/woman-who-invented-incel-movement-interview-toronto-attack, accessed May 27, 2018.

9. Pierre Bourdieu, *Distinction: A Social Critique of the Judgement of Taste* (Cambridge, MA: Harvard University Press, 1984).

10. Annie Kelly, "The Housewives of White Supremacy," *New York Times*, June 1, 2018, https://www.nytimes.com/2018/06/01/opinion/sunday/tradwives-women-alt-right.html?emc=edit_th_180602&nl=todaysheadlines&nlid=476765270602.

11. Many of the white men who voted for Trump and support him to the present day surely respond to the type of masculinity he embodies.

12. Joel Anderson, "Situating Axel Honneth in the Frankfurt School Tradition," in *Axel Honneth: Critical Essays: With a reply by Axel Honneth*, ed. Danielle Petherbridge (Leiden: Brill, 2011), 31–58, esp. 50.

13. See Terry Pinkard, *Hegel's Phenomenology: The Sociality of Reason* (Cambridge: Cambridge University Press, 1996), 66, 394; Robert B. Pippin, *Hegel on Self-Consciousness: Desire and Death in the Phenomenology of Spirit* (Princeton, NJ: Princeton University Press, 2011), 21–39.

14. Pippin, *Hegel on Self-Consciousness* 25–26.

15. Naomi Wolf, *The Beauty Myth: How Images of Beauty Are Used against Women* (1990; London: Vintage: 2013), 144.

16. Sharon Jayson, "Study: More Than a Third of New Marriages Start Online," *USA Today*, June 3, 2013, https://www.usatoday.com/story/news/nation/2013/06/03/online-dating-marriage/2377961/, accessed May 27, 2018.

17. See Sigmund Freud, *Civilization and Its Discontents*, ed. J. Riviere (London: Hogarth Press, 1930), https://bradleymurray.ca/freud-civilization-and-its-discontents-pdf/, accessed May 27, 2018.

18. Irving Howe, quoted by Judith Shulevitz in "Kate Millett: 'Sexual Politics' Family Values," *The New York Review of Books*, September 29, 2017.

Bibliography

The bibliography covers scientific, literary, and statistical works, but not Internet sources such as blogs, forums, or articles, and the works from which the mottos are taken. These sources are acknowledged in the notes.

Abadie, Alberto, and Sebastien Gay. "The Impact of Presumed Consent Legislation on Cadaveric Organ Donation. A Cross-Country Study." *Journal of Health Economics* 25, no. 4 (2006): 599–620.

Abu-Lughod, Lila. "Do Muslim Women Really Need Saving? Anthropological Reflections on Cultural Relativism and Its Others." *American Anthropologist* 104, no. 3 (2002): 783–790.

Addison, Heather. "Hollywood, Consumer Culture and the Rise of 'Body Shaping.'" In *Hollywood Goes Shopping*, edited by David Desser and Garth S. Jowett, 3–33. Minneapolis: University of Minnesota Press, 2000.

Adkins, Lisa, "Sexuality and the Economy. Historicisation vs. Deconstruction." *Australian Feminist Studies* 17, no. 37 (2002): 31–41.

Adorno, Theodor W. *Negative Dialectics*. Great Britain: Routledge, 1990.

Albury, Kath. "Porn and Sex Education, Porn as Sex Education." In *Porn Studies* 1, nos. 1/2 (2014): 172–181.

Allyn, David. *Make Love, Not War: The Sexual Revolution: An Unfettered History* New York: Routledge, 2016.

Amato, Paul R. "The Consequences of Divorce for Adults and Children." In *Journal of Marriage and Family* 62, no. 4 (2000): 1269–1287.

——, and Brett Beattie. "Does the Unemployment Rate Affect the Divorce Rate? An Analysis of State Data 1960–2005." In *Social Science Research* 40, no. 3 (2011): 705–715.

——, and Denise Previti. "People's Reasons for Divorcing: Gender, Social Class, the Life Course, and Adjustment." *Journal of Family Issues* 24, no. 5 (2003): 602–626.

Ambert, Anne-Marie. *Divorce. Facts, Causes, and Consequences* (Ottawa: Vanier Institute of the Family, 2005).

American Psychological Association Task Force on the Sexualization of Girls. *Report of the APA Task Force on the Sexualization of Girls*, 2007, http://www.apa.org/pi/women/programs/girls/report-full.pdf,

Anders, Günther. "Pathologie de la liberté. Essai sur la non-identification" In *Recherches Philosophiques* 6 (1936/37): 32–57.

Anderson, Joel. "Regimes of Autonomy." In *Ethical Theory and Moral Practice* 17, no. 3 (2014): 355–368.

——. "Situating Axel Honneth in the Frankfurt School Tradition" In *Axel Honneth: Critical Essays: With a Reply by Axel Honneth*. Edited by Danielle Petherbridge. Leiden: Brill 2011, 31–58.

Arvidsson, Adam. "The Ethical Economy of Customer Coproduction." In *Journal of Macromarketing* 28, no. 4 (2008): 326–338.

——. "The Potential of Consumer Publics." In *Ephemera* 13, no. 2 (2013): 367–391.

Attwood, Feona. "Sexed Up. Theorizing the Sexualization of Culture." In *Sexualities* 9, no. 1 (2006): 77–94.

——. "'Tits and Ass and Porn and Fighting:' Male Heterosexuality in Magazines for Men." In *International Journal of Cultural Studies* 8, no. 1 (2005): 83–100.

——, and Clarissa Smith. "Leisure Sex. More Sex! Better Sex! Sex Is Fucking Brilliant! Sex, Sex, Sex, SEX." In *Routledge Handbook of Leisure Studies*. Edited by Tony Blackshaw. New York 2013, 325–336.

Austen, Jane. *Kloster Northanger*. Edited by Ursula Grawe and Christian Grawe. 1818. Reprint, Stuttgart: Reclam, 2008.

Aven, Terje. "Risk Assessment and Risk Management: Review of Recent Advances on Their Foundation." In *European Journal of Operational Research* 253, no. 1 (2016): 1–13.

——, and Yolande Hiriart. "Robust Optimization in Relation to a Basic Safety Investment Model with Imprecise Probabilities." *Safety Science* 55 (2013): 188–194.

Bailey, Beth L. *From Front Porch to Back Seat: Courtship in Twentieth-Century America*. Baltimore: Johns Hopkins University Press, 1989.

Bakewell, Sarah. *At the Existentialist Café: Freedom, Being, and Apricot Cocktails with Jean-Paul Sartre, Simone de Beauvoir, Albert Camus, Martin Heidegger, Maurice Merleau-Ponty and Others*. Translated by Rita Seuss. New York: Other Press, 2016.

Bates, Catherine. *Courtship and Courtliness: Studies in Elizabethan Courtly Language and Literature*. PhD diss., Oxford University, 1989.

——. *The Rhetoric of Courtship in Elizabethan Language and Literature*. Cambridge, Cambridge University Press, 1992.

Bauman, Zygmunt. *Flüchtige Moderne*. Translated by Reinhard Kreissl. Frankfurt: Suhrkamp Verlag, 2003.

——. *Liquid Life*. Cambridge: Malden, 2005.

——. *Liquid Love: On the Frailty of Human Bonds*. Cambridge: Malden, 2003.

Baumeister, Roy F., and Kathleen D. Vohs. "Sexual Economics: Sex as Female Resource for Social Exchange in Heterosexual Interactions." In *Personality and Social Psychology Review* 8, no. 4 (2004): 339–363.

Beauvoir, Simone de. *La phénoménologie de la perception* de Maurice Merleau-Ponty, Paris: Les temps modernes 1, no. 2: 363–367 ("A Review of *The Phenomenology of Perception* by Maurice Merleau-Ponty"). Translated by Marybeth Timmermann. In *Simone de Beauvoir: Philosophical Writings*. Edited by M. A. Simons, 159–164. Champaign: University of Illinois Press, 2004.

Beck, Ulrich, and Elisabeth Beck-Gernsheim. *Individualization: Institutionalized Individualism and Its Social and Political Consequences*. London: SAGE Publications, 2002.

Beck, Ulrich, Elisabeth Beck-Gernsheim. *The Chaos of Love*. Translated by Mark Ritter and Jane Wiebel. Cambridge: Polity Press, 1995.

Beckert, Jens, and Patrik Apsers, eds. *The Worth of Goods: Valuation and Pricing in the Economy*. New York: Oxford University Press, 2011.

Bell, Ilona. *Elizabethan Women and the Poetry of Courtship*. Cambridge: Cambridge University Press, 1998.

Bell, Leslie C. *Hard to Get: Twenty-Something Women and the Paradox of Sexual Freedom*. Berkeley: University of California Press, 2013.

Bell, Wendell. "Anomie, Social Isolation, and the Class Structure." In *Sociometry* 20, no. 2 (1957): 105–116.

Benjamin, Jessica, *Like Subjects, Love Objects: Essays on Recognition and Sexual Difference.* New Haven: Yale University Press, 1998.

——. "Recognition and Destruction: An Outline of Intersubjectivity." In *Relational Perspectives in Psychoanalysis.* Edited by Neil J. Skolnick and Susan C. Warshaw, 43–60. New York: Routledge, 1992.

Benjamin, Orly. "Therapeutic Discourse, Power and Change: Emotion and Negotiation in Marital Conversations." *Sociology* 32, no. 4 (1998): 771–793.

Benjamin, Walter. *Das Passagenwerk.* Edited by Rolf Tiedemann. Frankfurt: Suhrkamp Verlag, 1983.

Beres, Melanie A., and Panteá Farvid. "Sexual Ethics and Young Women's Accounts of Heterosexual Casual Sex." In *Sexualities* 13, no. 3 (2010): 377–393.

Berg, Joyce, John Dickhaut, and Kevin McCabe. "Trust, Reciprocity, and Social History." In *Games and Economic Behavior* 10, no. 1 (1995): 122–142.

Berkin, Carol. *Civil War Wives: The Lives and Times of Angelina Grimké Weld, Varina Howell Davis, and Julia Dent Grant.* New York: Vintage, 2009.

Berlant, Lauren Gail, ed. *Intimacy.* Chicago: University of Chicago Press, 2000.

——, *Cruel Optimism.* Durham, NC: Duke University Press, 2011.

——, *Desire/Love.* Brooklyn, NY: Punctum Books, 2012.

——, "Slow Death (Sovereignty, Obesity, Lateral Agency)." In *Critical Inquiry* 33, no. 4 (2007): 754–780.

——, and Michael Warner. "Sex in Public." In *Critical Inquiry* 24, no. 2 (1998): 547–566.

Bernard, Philippe, Sarah J. Gervais, Jill Allen, Sophie Campomizzi, and Olivier Klein. "Integrating Sexual Objectification with Object versus Person Recognition: The Sexualized-Body-Inversion Hypothesis." In *Psychological Science* 23, no. 5 (2012): 469–471.

Bernstein, Elizabeth. *Temporarily Yours: Intimacy, Authenticity, and the Commerce of Sex.* Chicago: University of Chicago Press, 2007.

Bersani, Leo, and Adam Phillips. *Intimacies.* Chicago: University of Chicago Press, 2008.

Berthomé, François, Julien Bonhomme, and Grégory Delaplace. "Preface: Cultivating Uncertainty." *HAU. Journal of Ethnographic Theory* 2, no. 2 (2012): 129–137.

Birken, Lawrence. *Consuming Desire: Sexual Science and the Emergence of a Culture of Abundance 1871–1914.* Ithaca, NY: Cornell University Press, 1988.

Biskind, Peter. *Easy Riders, Raging Bulls. Wie die Sex-and-Drugs-and-Rock'n'Roll-Generation Hollywood rettete.* Edited by Fritz Schneider. Munich: Heyne, 2004.

Blau, Francine D. *Gender, Inequality, and Wages.* New York: Oxford University Press, 2016.

Blau, Peter M. *Exchange and Power in Social Life.* New York: John Wiley and Sons, 1964.

Bloch, Howard R. *Medieval Misogyny and the Invention of Western Romantic Love* Chicago: University of Chicago Press, 1992.

Bloom, Claire. *Leaving a Doll's House: A Memoir.* New York: Little, Brown and Company, 1996.

Bloor, David. *Knowledge and Social Imagery.* London: Routledge and Kegan Paul, 1976.

Bogle, Kathleen A. *Hooking Up: Sex, Dating, and Relationships on Campus.* New York: New York University Press, 2008.

——. "The Shift from Dating to Hooking Up in College: What Scholars Have Missed." *Sociology Compass* 1, no. 2 (2007): 775–778.

Boholm, Åsa. "The Cultural Nature of Risk: Can There Be an Anthropology of Uncertainty?" *Ethnos* 68, no. 2 (2003): 159–178.

Boltanski, Luc. *The Foetal Condition: A Sociology of Engendering and Abortion*. Translated by Catherine Porter. Cambridge: Polity Press, 2013.

——, and Ève Chiapello. "The New Spirit of Capitalism." In *International Journal of Politics, Culture, and Society* 18, nos. 3/4 (2005): 161–188.

Boltanski, Luc, and Laurent Thévenot. "Finding One's Way in Social Space: A Study Based on Games." In *Social Science Information* 22, nos. 4/5 (1983): 631–680.

——. "The Reality of Moral Expectations: A Sociology of Situated Judgement." In *Philosophical Explorations* 3, no. 3 (2000): 208–231.

——. *On Justification: Economies of Worth*. Translated by Catherine Porter. Princeton, NJ: Princeton University Press , 2006.

Bory, Stefano. *Il Tempo Sommerso: Strategie Identitarie Nei Giovani Adulti Del Mezzogiorno*, Naples: Liguori, 2008.

Bose, Arun. "Marx on Value, Capital, and Exploitation." In *History of Political Economy* 3, no. 2 (1971): 298–334.

Boserup, Ester. *Women's Role in Economic Development*. Translated by Suse Bouché. 1988. Reprint: Abingdon, Earthscan Publications, 2015.

Bossard, James H. S. "Residential Propinquity as a Factor in Marriage Selection." In *American Journal of Sociology* 38, no. 2 (1932): 219–224.

Bourdieu, Pierre. *Distinction : A Social Critique of the Judgement of Taste*. Translated by Richard Nice and Tony Bennett. 1984. Reprint, Abingdon, Routledge, 2015.

——. *Outline of a Theory of Practice*. Translated by Richard Nice. 1977. Reprint, Cambridge: Cambridge University Press, 2003.

——. "Heiratsstrategien im System der Reproduktionsstrategien." In *Junggesellenball: Studien zum Niedergang der bäuerlichen Gesellschaft*. Translated by Eva Kessler and Daniela Böhmer, 163–203. 1972. Reprint, Konstanz: UVK, 2008.

——. *Language and Symbolic Power*. Translated by Hella Beister. 1982. Reprint, Cambridge: Polity Press , 1991.

Bourguignon, Annick, and Eve Chiapello. "The Role of Criticism in the Dynamics of Performance Evaluation Systems." In *Critical Perspectives on Accounting* 16, no. 6 (2005): 665–700.

Brannen, Julia, and Jean Collard. *Marriages in Trouble: The Process of Seeking Help*. London: Taylor and Frances, 1982.

Brenkert, George G. "Freedom and Private Property in Marx." In *Philosophy and Public Affairs* 2, no. 8 (1979): 122–147.

Brennan, Denise. *What's Love Got to Do with It? Transnational Desires and Sex Tourism in the Dominican Republic*. Durham, NC: Duke University Press, 2004.

Bright, Susie. *Full Exposure: Opening Up to Sexual Creativity and Erotic Expression*. New York: HarperCollins, 2009.

Brooks, Peter, and Horst Zank. "Loss Averse Behavior." In *Journal of Risk and Uncertainty* 31, no. 3 (2005): 301–325.

Brown, Barbara A., Thomas I. Emerson, Gail Falk, and Ann E. Freedman. "The Equal Rights Amendment: A Constitutional Basis for Equal Rights for Women." *The Yale Law Journal* 80, no. 5 (1971): 871–985.

Brown, Peter. "Rome: Sex and Freedom." Review of *From Shame to Sin*, by Kyle Harper. *The New York Review of Books* (December 9, 2013). http://www.nybooks.com/articles/2013/12/19/rome-sex-freedom/.

Brown, Wendy. *States of Injury: Power and Freedom in Late Modernity*. Princeton, NJ: Princeton University Press, 1995.

Browning, Christopher R., and Matisa Olinger-Wilbon. "Neighborhood Structure, Social Organization, and Number of Short-Term Sexual Partnerships." In *Journal of Marriage and Family* 65, no. 3 (2003): 730–774.

Buch, Esteban. *La musique fait l'amour. Une enquête sur la bande-son de la vie sexuelle.* Forthcoming.

Buckley, Thomas E., ed. *"If You Love That Lady Don't Marry Her." The Courtship Letters of Sally McDowell and John Miller, 1854–1856*. Columbia: University of Missour Press, 2000.

Buhle, Mari Jo. *Feminism and Its Discontents: A Century of Struggle with Psychoanalysis.* Cambridge: Harvard University Press, 2009.

Bulcroft, Richard, Kris Bulcroft, Karen Bradley, and Carl Simpson. "The Management and Production of Risk in Romantic Relationships: A Postmodern Paradox." In *Journal of Family History* 25, no. 1 (2000): 63–92.

Burns, E. Jane, *Courtly Love Undressed: Reading through Clothes in Medieval French Culture*. Philadelphia: University of Pennsylvania Press, 2005.

Cacchioni, Thea, "The Medicalization of Sexual Deviance, Reproduction, and Functioning." In *Handbook of the Sociology of Sexualities*. Edited by John DeLamater and Rebecca F. Plante, 435–452. Switzerland: Springer, 2015.

Calogero, Rachel M., "A Test of Objectification Theory: The Effect of the Male Gaze on Appearance Concerns in College Women." In *Psychology of Women Quarterly* 28, no. 1 (2004): 16–21.

——, and J. Kevin Thompson. "Potential Implications of the Objectification of Women's Bodies for Women's Sexual Satisfaction." In *Body Image* 6, no. 2 (2009): 145–148.

Campbell, Colin. *The Romantic Ethic and the Spirit of Modern Consumerism*. New York: Blackwell, 1987.

Camerer, Colin F. "Prospect Theory in the Wild" Evidence from the Field." In *Choices, Values, and Frames*. Edited by Daniel Kahneman and Amos Tversky, 288–300. Cambridge: Cambridge University Press, 2000.

Cancian, Francesca. *Love in America: Gender and Self-Development*. Cambridge: Cambridge University Press, 1990.

——, and Steven L. Gordon. "Changing Emotion Norms in Marriage: Love and Anger in US Women's Magazines since 1900." *Gender and Society* 2, no. 3 (1988): 308–342.

Castells, Manuel. "The Net and the Self: Working Notes for a Critical Theory of the Informational Society." In *Critique of Anthropology* 16, no. 1 (1996): 9–38.

Chen, Derek H. C. "Gender Equality and Economic Development: The Role for Information and Communication Technologies." World Bank Policy Research Working Paper 3285. Washington, DC, 2004.

Chen, Hellen. *Hellen Chen's Love Seminar: The Missing Love Manual that Makes Your Relationship Last*. 2013. https://youtu.be/ezEeaBs84w0.

Cherlin, Andrew J. "The Deinstitutionalization of American Marriage." In *Journal of Marriage and Family* 66, no. 4 (2004): 848–861.

——. *Marriage, Divorce, Remarriage*. Revised and enlarged edition. Cambridge: Harvard University Press, 1992.

Clark, Russell D. "The Impact of AIDS on Gender Differences in Willingness to Engage in Casual Sex." *Journal of Applied Social Psychology* 20, no. 9 (1990): 771–782.

Cohen, G. A. *Self-Ownership, Freedom, and Equality*. Cambridge: Cambridge University Press, 1995.

Cohen, Morris R. "The Basis of Contract." In *Harvard Law Review* 46, no. 4 (1933): 553–592.

Colker, Ruth. "Feminism, Sexuality and Authenticity." In *At the Boundaries of Law: Feminism and Legal Theory*. Edited by Martha Albertson Fineman and Nancy Sweet Thomadsen, 135–148. New York: Routledge, 2013.

Conlin, Juliet A. "Getting Around: Making Fast and Frugal Navigation Decisions." *Progress in Brain Research* 174 (2009): 109–117.

Cooke, Lynn Prince. "'Doing' Gender in Context: Household Bargaining and Risk of Divorce in Germany and the United States." In *American Journal of Sociology* 112, no. 2 (2006): 442–472.

Cooley, Charles Horton. *Human Nature and the Social Order*. 1902. Reprint, Piscataway, NJ: Transaction Publishers, 1992.

Coontz, Stephanie. *Marriage, a History: How Love Conquered Marriage*. New York: Penguin, 2006.

Cooper, Elizabeth, and David Pratten, eds. *Ethnographies of Uncertainty in Africa*. New York: Springer, 2014.

Cornell, Drucilla. *At the Heart of Freedom: Feminism, Sex, and Equality*. Princeton, NJ: Princeton University Press, 1998.

Dabhoiwala, Faramerz. "Lust and Liberty" In *Past and Present* 207, no. 1 (2010): 89–179.

Dahler-Larsen, Peter. *The Evaluation Society*. Stanford, CA: Stanford University Press, 2011.

Dal Bó, Pedro, "Cooperation under the Shadow of the Future: Experimental Evidence from Infinitely Repeated Games." *American Economic Review* 95, no. 5 (2005): 1591–1604.

Dancy, Russell M. *Plato's Introduction of Forms*. Cambridge: Cambridge University Press, 2004.

Davis, Deborah, Phillip R. Shaver, and Michael L. Vernon. "Physical, Emotional, and Behavioral Reactions to Breaking Up: The Roles of Gender, Age, Emotional Involvement, and Attachment Style." *Personality and Social Psychology Bulletin* 29, no. 7 (2003): 871–884.

Debord, Guy. *Society of the Spectacle*. Translated by Ken Knapp. 1967. Reprint, London: Rebel Press, 2005.

De Graaf, Paul M., and Matthijs Kalmijn. "Divorce Motives in a Period of Rising Divorce: Evidence from a Dutch Life-History Survey." In *Journal of Family Issues* 27, no. 4 (2006): 483–505.

——. "Change and Stability in the Social Determinants of Divorce: A Comparison of Marriage Cohorts in the Netherlands." *European Sociological Review* 22, no. 5 (2006): 561–572.

Deleuze, Gilles. "Postscripts on Control Societies." In *Negotiations 1972–1990*. Translated by Martin Joughin, 177–182. New York: Columbia University Press, 1995.

D'Emilio, John, and Estelle B. Freedman. *Intimate Matters: A History of Sexuality in America*. Chicago: University of Chicago Press, 1998.

Despentes, Virginie. *King Kong Theorie*. Translated by Kerstin Krolak. Berlin: Berliner Taschenbuchverlag, 2007.

Diethe, Carol. *Towards Emancipation. German Women Writers of the Nineteenth Century*. New York: Oxford, 1998.

Di Leonardo, Micaela. "White Ethnicities, Identity Politics, and Baby Bear's Chair." *Social Text*, no. 41 (1994): 165–191.

——, and Roger Lancaster. "Gender, Sexuality, Political Economy." In *New Politics* 6, no. 1 (1996): 29–43.

Dilts, Andrew. "From 'Entrepreneur of the Self' to 'Care of the Self': Neoliberal Governmentality and Foucault's Ethics." *Western Political Science Association 2010 Annual Meeting Paper*. https://papers.ssrn.com/sol3/papers.cfm?abstract_id=1580709.

Dittmar, Helga. *Consumer Culture, Identity and Well-being: The Search for the "Good Life" and the "Body Perfect."* New York: Psychology Press, 2007.

Doepke, Matthias, Michele Tertilt, and Alessandra Voena. "The Economics and Politics of Women's Rights." In *Annual Review of Economics* 4 (2012): 339–372.

Doherty, Thomas. *Pre-Code Hollywood: Sex, Immorality, and Insurrection in American Cinema, 1930–1934*. New York: Columbia University Press, 1999.

Döring, Nicola M. "The Internet's Impact on Sexuality: A Critical Review of 15 Years of Research." In *Computers in Human Behavior* 25, no. 5 (2009): 1089–1101.

Douglas, Mary, and Baron Isherwood. *The World of Goods: Towards an Anthropology of Consumption*. 1979. Reprint, London: Psychology Press, 2002.

Duffy, John, and Jack Ochs. "Cooperative Behavior and the Frequency of Social Interaction." *Games and Economic Behavior* 66, no. 2 (2009): 785–812.

Duflo, Esther. "Women Empowerment and Economic Development." In *Journal of Economic Literature* 50, no. 4 (2012): 1051–1079.

Duggan, Lisa, and Nan D. Hunter. *Sex Wars: Sexual Dissent and Political Culture*. Abingdon-on-Thames: Taylor and Frances, 2006.

Duncombe, Jean, and Dennis Marsden. "Love and Intimacy: The Gender Division of Emotion and 'Emotion Work': A Neglected Aspect of Sociological Discussion of Heterosexual Relationships." *Sociology* 27, no. 2 (1993): 221–241.

Dunham, Lena. *Not That Kind of Girl: A Young Woman Tells You What She's "Learned."* New York: Random House, 2015.

Dunn, Robert G. "Identity, Commodification, and Consumer Culture." In *Identity and Social Change*. Edited by Joseph E. Davis, 109–134. New York: Routledge, 2000.

Dunn, Sarah. *The Big Love*. New York: Little Brown and Company, 2004.

Durkheim, Emile. *Suicide: A Study in Sociology*. Translated by John A. Spaulding and George Simpson. 1951. Reprint, New York: The Free Press, 1979.

——. *The Elementary Forms of Religious Life*. Translated by Carol Cosman. Oxford: Oxford University Press, 2001.

——. *Moral Education*. Translated by Librarie Felix Alcan. 1925. New York: The Free Press, 1961.

Dworkin, Gerald. *The Theory and Practice of Autonomy*. Cambridge: Cambridge University Press, 1988.

Dyer, Richard. *Heavenly Bodies: Film Stars and Society*. New York: Psychology Press, 2004.

Echols, Alice. *Daring to Be Bad: Radical Feminism in America, 1967–1975*. Minneapolis: University of Minnesota Press, 1989.

Edwards, Weston M., and Eli Coleman. "Defining Sexual Health: A Descriptive Overview." *Archives of Sexual Behavior* 33, no. 3 (2004): 189–195.

Elias, Ana Sofia, Rosalind Gill, and Christina Scharff, eds. *Aesthetic Labour: Rethinking Beauty Politics in Neoliberalism*. London: Palgrave Macmillan, 2017.

Engels, Friedrich. *The Origin of the Family, Private Property, and the State, in the Light of the Researches of Lewis H. Morgan*. New York: International Publishers Co., 1972, 25–173.

England, Paula, and Jonathan Bearak. "The Sexual Double Standard and Gender Differences in Attitudes toward Casual Sex among US University Students." *Demographic Research* 30, no. 46 (2014): 1327–1338.

England, Paula, Emily Fitzgibbons Shafer, and Alison C. K. Fogarty. "Hooking Up and Forming Romantic Relationships on Today's College Campuses." In *The Gendered Society Reader*. 3rd ed. Edited by Michael S. Kimmel and Amy Aronson, 531–593. New York Oxford University Press, 2008.

Engle-Warnick, Jim, and Robert L. Slonim. "Inferring Repeated-Game Strategies from Actions: Evidence from Trust Game Experiments." *Economic Theory* 28, no. 3 (2006): 603–632.

Epstein, Marina, Jerel P. Calzo, Andrew P. Smiler, and L. Monique Ward. "'Anything from Making Out to Having Sex': Men's Negotiations of Hooking Up and Friends with Benefits Scripts." *Journal of Sex Research* 46, no. 5 (2009): 414–424.

Erickson, Rebecca J. "Why Emotion Work Matters: Sex, Gender, and the Division of Household Labor." *Journal of Marriage and Family* 67, no. 2 (2005): 337–351.

Eshbaugh, Elaine M., and Gary Gute. "Hookups and Sexual Regret among College Women." *The Journal of Social Psychology* 148, no. 1 (2008): 77–90.

Faden, Ruth R., and Tom L. Beauchamp. *A History and Theory of Informed Consent*. New York: Oxford University Press, 1986.

Farvid, Panteá, and Virginia Braun. "The 'Sassy Woman' and the 'Performing Man.' Heterosexual Casual Sex Advice and the (Re)constitution of Gendered Subjectivities." *Feminist Media Studies* 14, no. 1 (2014): 118–134.

Fass, Paula S. *The Damned and the Beautiful: American Youth in the 1920s*. Book 567. New York: Oxford University Press, 1979.

Featherstone, Mike. "The Body in Consumer Culture." In *The American Body in Context: An Anthology*. Edited by Jessica R. Johnston. 1982. Reprint, Wilmington: Rowman and Littlefield, 2001, 79–102.

——. *Consumer Culture and Postmodernism*. London: Sage Publications Ltd, 2007.

Feher, Michel. "Self-Appreciation; Or, the Aspirations of Human Capital." In *Public Culture* 21, no. 1 (2009): 21–41.

Fehr, Ernst, and Simon Gächter. "How Effective Are Trust- and Reciprocity-Based Incentives?" In *Economics, Values and Organizations*. Edited by Avner Ben-Ner and Louis Putterman, 337–363. Cambridge: Cambridge University Press, 1998.

Ferguson, Ann, Rosemary Hennessy, and Mechthild Nagel. "Feminist Perspectives on Class and Work." In *The Stanford Encyclopedia of Philosophy*. Edited by Edward N. Zalta. 2004, Reprint, 2018, https://plato.stanford.edu/archives/spr2018/entries/feminism-class/.

Ferrant, Gaëlle, Luca Maria Pesando, and Keiko Nowacka. "Unpaid Care Work: The Missing Link in the Analysis of Gender Gaps in Labour Outcomes." Issues Paper. OECD Development Centre. December 2014.

Fine, Ben, and Laurence Harris. "The Law of the Tendency of the Rate of Profit to Fall." In *Rereading Capital*. London: Macmillan Education UK, 1979, 58–75.

Fine, Gail. *Plato on Knowledge and Forms: Selected Essays*. Oxford: Oxford University Press, 2003.

Finke, Laurie A. "Sexuality in Medieval French Literature. 'Séparés, on est ensemble'" In *Handbook of Medieval Sexuality*. Edited by Vern L. Bullough and James A. Brundage. New York/London: Taylor and Francis, 1996), 345–368.

Fischer, Claude S. "On Urban Alienations and Anomie: Powerlessness and Social Isolation." *American Sociological Review* 38, no. 3 (1973): 311–326.

Fischer, Tamar. "Parental Divorce and Children's Socio-economic Success: Conditional Effects of Parental Resources Prior to Divorce, and Gender of the Child." In *Sociology* 41, no. 3 (2007): 475–495.

Fitzsimmons-Craft, Ellen E. "Explaining the Relation between Thin Ideal Internalization and Body Dissatisfaction among College Women: The Roles of Social Comparison and Body Surveillance." *Body Image* 9, no. 1 (2012): 43–49.

Flaubert, Gustave. *Madame Bovary*. Translated by Eleanor Marx-Aveling. 1856. Reprint, London: Macmillan, 2017.

Fletcher, Anthony. "Manhood, the Male Body, Courtship and the Household in Early Modern England." *History* 84, no. 275 (1999): 419–436.

Folbre, Nancy. "Measuring Care: Gender, Empowerment, and the Care Economy." In *Journal of Human Development* 7, no. 2 (2006): 183–199.

Foucault, Michel. *The Government of Self and Others: Lectures at the Collège de France 1982–1983*. Translated by Graham Burchell. New York: Picador, 2010.

———. *Security, Territory, Population: Lectures at the Collège de France 1977–1978*. Translated by Graham Burchell. New York: Picador, 2007.

———. *The History of Sexuality*. Volume 1: *An Introduction*. 1978; Volume 2: *The Use of Pleasure*. 1985; Volume 3: *The Care of the Self* 1986, Translated by Ulrich Raulff and Walter Seitter. Reprint, New York: Vintage Press, 1990.

———. "Sexuelle Wahl, sexueller Akt." Translated by Hans-Dieter Gondek. In *Dits et Ecrits: Schriften in vier Bänden*, book 4. 1980–1988. 1982. Reprint, Frankfurt: Suhrkamp Verlag, 2005, 382–402.

———. *Discipline and Punish: The Birth of the Prison*. Translated by Alan Sheridan. 1977. Reprint, New York: Vintage Books, 1995.

Fox, Greer Litton, and Velma McBride Murry. "Gender and Families: Feminist Perspectives and Family Research." *Journal of Marriage and Family* 62, no. 4 (2000): 1160–1172.

Frank, Thomas. *The Conquest of Cool: Business Culture, Counterculture, and the Rise of Hip Consumerism*. Chicago: University of Chicago Press, 1997.

Frankfurt, Harry G. *Bullshit*. Translated by Michael Bischoff. Frankfurt: Publisher, 2006.

Franks, David D., and Viktor Gecas. "Autonomy and Conformity in Cooley's Self-Theory: The Looking-Glass Self and Beyond." *Symbolic Interaction* 15, no. 1 (1992): 49–68.

Fraser, Nancy. "Rethinking the Public Sphere: A Contribution to the Critique of Actually Existing Democracy." In *Social Text*, no. 25/26 (1990): 56–80.

———. "Rethinking Recognition." *New Left Review*, no. 3 (2000): 107–118.

———, and Axel Honneth. *Redistribution or Recognition?: A Political-Philosophical Exchange* . Translated by Joel Golb, James Ingram, and Christiane Wilke. London: Verso, 2018.

Fredrickson, Barbara L., and Tomi-Ann Roberts, "Objectification Theory: Toward Understanding Women's Lived Experiences and Mental Health Risks." In *Psychology of Women Quarterly* 21, no 2 (1997): 173–206.

Freeman, Chris, and Luc Soete. *The Economics of Industrial Innovation*. London: Psychology Press, 1997.

Freud, Sigmund. *Das Unbehagen in der Kultur.* Edited by Lothar Bayer and Kerstin Krone-Bayer. 1930. Reprint, Stuttgart: Reclam Verlag, 2010, http://gutenberg.spiegel. de/buch/das-unbehagen-in-der-kultur-922/1.

Friedman, Milton. *Capitalism and Freedom.* 1962. Reprint, Chicago: Chicago University Press, 2002.

Fromm, Erich. *The Fear of Freedom.* 1941. London, Routledge, 2010.

Gabriel, Yiannis, and Tim Lang. *The Unmanageable Consumer.* 1995. London: Sage Publications Ltd., 2015.

Gambetta, Diego. "Can We Trust Trust?" In *Trust: Making and Breaking Cooperative Relations.* Oxford: Blackwell Publishing, 2000, 213–237.

Garcia, Justin R., Chris Reiber, Sean G. Massey, and Ann M. Merriwether. "Sexual Hookup Culture: A Review." In *Review of General Psychology* 16, no. 2 (2012): 161–176.

Garton, Stephen. *Histories of Sexuality: Antiquity to Sexual Revolution.* New York: Routledge, 2004.

Gaunt, Simon. *Love and Death in Medieval French and Occitan Courtly Literature: Martyrs to Love.* Oxford University Press on Demand, 2006.

Gentzler, Amy L., and Kathryn A. Kerns. "Associations between Insecure Attachment and Sexual Experiences." *Personal Relationships* 11, no. 2 (2004): 249–265.

Gervais, Sarah J., Arianne M. Holland, and Michael D. Dodd. "My Eyes Are Up Here: The Nature of the Objectifying Gaze toward Women." In *Sex Roles* 69, nos. 11/12 (2013): 557–570.

Gervais, Sarah, Theresa K. Vescio, and Jill Allen. "When What You See Is What You Get: The Consequences of the Objectifying Gaze for Women and Men." In *Psychology of Women Quarterly* 35, no. 1 (2011): 5–17.

Giami, Alain, and Patrick de Colomby. "Sexology as a Profession in France." In *Archives of Sexual Behavior* 32, no. 4 (2003): 371–379.

Giddens, Anthony. *Capitalism and Modern Social Theory: An Analysis of the Writings of Marx, Durkheim and Max Weber.* Cambridge: Cambridge University Press, 1971.

——, ed. *Durkheim on Politics and the State.* Translated by W. D. Halls. Stanford: Stanford University Press, 1986.

——. *Modernity and Self-Identity: Self and Society in Late Modern Age.* Cambridge: Polity Press, 1991.

——. *The Transformation of Intimacy: Sexuality, Love, and Eroticism in Modern Societies.* Cambridge: Polity Press, 1992.

Gigy, Lynn, and Joan B. Kelly. "Reasons for Divorce: Perspectives of Divorcing Men and Women." In *Journal of Divorce and Remarriage* 18, nos. 1/2 (1993): 169–188.

Gill, Rosalind. "From Sexual Objectification to Sexual Subjectification: The Resexualisation of Women's Bodies in the Media." In *Feminist Media Studies* 3, no. 1 (2003): 100–106.

——. "Empowerment/Sexism: Figuring Female Sexual Agency in Contemporary Advertising." In *Feminism and Psychology* 18, no. 1 (2008): 35–60.

——. *Gender and the Media.* Cambridge: Malden, 2007.

——, and Andy Pratt. "In the Social Factory? Immaterial Labour, Precariousness and Cultural Work." In *Theory, Culture and Society* 25, nos. 7/8 (2008): 1–30.

Gilligan, Carol. *In a Different Voice: Psychological Theory and Women's Development.* 1982. Reprint, Cambridge: Harvard University Press, 2003.

Gillis, John R. *For Better, for Worse: British Marriages, 1600 to the Present.* New York: Oxford University Press, 1985.

Glick, Elisa. "Sex Positive: Feminism, Queer Theory, and the Politics of Transgression." In *Feminist Review* 64, no. 1 (2000): 19–45.

Glicksberg, Charles I."The Sexual Revolution and the Modern Drama." In *The Sexual Revolution in Modern English Literature*. The Hague: Springer Science+Business Media, 1973, 43–70.

——. *The Sexual Revolution in Modern American Literature*. The Hague: Martinus Nijhoff, 1971.

Godbeer, Richard. *Sexual Revolution in Early America*. Baltimore: Johns Hopkins University Press, 2002.

Goffman, Erving. *Frame Analysis: An Essay on the Organization of Experience*. 1974. Reprint: Boston: Northeastern University Press, 2010.

Goody, Jack. *The Development of the Family and Marriage in Europe*. Cambridge: Cambridge University Press, 1983.

Gordon, David, Austin Porter, Mark Regnerus, Jane Ryngaert, and Larissa Sarangaya. *Relationships in America Survey 2014*. The Austin Institute for the Study of Family and Culture. "How Common Are Sexually 'Inactive' Marriages?" http://relationshipsina-merica.com/relationships-and-sex/how-common-are-sexually-inactive-marriages.

Goren, Elizabeth. "America's Love Affair with Technology: The Transformation of Sexuality and the Self over the 20th Century." In *Psychoanalytic Psychology* 20, no. 3 (2003): 487–508.

Gottman, John Mordechai. *What Predicts Divorce? The Relationship between Marital Processes and Marital Outcomes*. New York: Hove, 2014.

Gouldner, Alvin W. "The Norm of Reciprocity: A Preliminary Statement." *American Sociological Review* 25, no. 2 (1960): 161–178.

Granovetter, Mark. "Economic Action and Social Structure: The Problem of Embeddedness." *American Journal of Sociology* 91, no. 3 (1985): 481–510.

Green, Adam Isaiah. "Toward a Sociology of Collective Sexual Life." In *Sexual Fields: Toward a Sociology of Collective Sexual Life*. Chicago: University of Chicago Press, 1–24.

Greener, Ian. "Towards a History of Choice in UK Health Policy." In *Sociology of Health and Illness* 31, no. 3 (2009): 309–324.

Greimas, Algirdas Julien. *Structural Semantics: An Attempt at a Method*. Translated by Daniele McDowell, Ronald Schleifer, and Alan Velie. Lincoln: University of Nebraska Press, 1983.

Grello, Catherine M., Deborah P. Welsh, and Melinda S. Harper. "No Strings Attached: The Nature of Casual Sex in College Students." *Journal of Sex Research* 43, no. 3 (2006): 255–267.

Grello, Catherine M., Deborah P. Welsh, Melinda S. Harper, and Joseph W. Dickson. "Dating and Sexual Relationship Trajectories and Adolescent Functioning." In *Adolescent and Family Health* 3, no. 3 (2003): 103–112.

Gronow, Jukka. *The Sociology of Taste*. Abingdon-on-Thames: Routledge, 2002.

Gross, Neil, and Solon Simmons. "Intimacy as a Double-Edged Phenomenon? An Empirical Test of Giddens." In *Social Forces* 81, no. 2 (2002): 531–555.

Gur, Ruben C., and Raquel E. Gur. "Complementarity of Sex Differences in Brain and Behavior: From Laterality to Multimodal Neuroimaging." In *Journal of Neuroscience Research* 95, nos. 1/2 (2017): 189–199.

Haas, David F., and Forrest A. Deseran. "Trust and Symbolic Exchange." *Social Psychology Quarterly* 44, no. 1 (1981): 3–13.

Hakim, Catherine. "Erotic Capital." *European Sociological Review*. 26, no. 5 (2010): 499–518.

Hall, Stuart. *The Hard Road to Renewal: Thatcherism and the Crisis of the Left*. London: Verso, 1988.

Halperin, David M., and Trevor Hoppe, eds. *The War on Sex*. Durham, NC: Duke University Press, 2017.

Hamilton, Laura, and Elizabeth A. Armstrong. "Gendered Sexuality in Young Adulthood: Double Binds and Flawed Options." *Gender and Society* 23, no. 5 (2009): 589–616.

Handyside, Fiona. "Authenticity, Confession and Female Sexuality: From Bridget to Bitchy." In *Psychology and Sexuality* 3, no. 1 (2012): 41–53.

Hanning, Robert W. "Love and Power in the Twelfth Century, with Special Reference to Chrétien de Troyes and Marie de France." In *The Olde Daunce: Love, Friendship, Sex, and Marriage in the Medieval World*. Edited by Robert R. Edwards und Stephen Spector. Albany: SUNY Press, 1991, 87–103.

Hardt, Michael, and Antonio Negri. *Multitude: War and Democracy in the Age of Empire*. New York: Penguin Books, 2004.

Harper, Brit, and Marika Tiggemann. "The Effect of Thin Ideal Media Images on Women's Self-Objectification, Mood, and Body Image." In *Sex Roles* 58, nos. 9/10 (2008): 649–657.

Hartmann, Martin, and Axel Honneth. "Paradoxien des Kapitalismus: Ein Untersuchungsprogramm." In *Berliner Debatte Initial* 15, no. 1 (2004): 4–17.

Harvey, David. *A Brief History of Neoliberalism*. Oxford: Oxford University Press, 2005.

——. *The Enigma of Capital and the Crises of Capital*. London: Profile Books, 2011.

——. *Marx, Capital, and the Madness of Economic Reason*. Oxford: Oxford University Press, 2017.

——. *Seventeen Contradictions and the End of Capitalism*. London: Profile Books, 2015.

Hatch, Linda. "The American Psychological Association Task Force on the Sexualization of Girls: A Review, Update and Commentary." In *Sexual Addiction and Compulsivity* 18, no. 4 (2011): 195–211.

Hayek, Friedrich August. *The Road to Serfdom*. Edited by Bruce Caldwell. 1944. Reprint, London: University of Chicago Press, 2007.

——. "The Use of Knowledge in Society." *The American Economic Review* 35, no. 4 (1945): 519–530.

Hearn, Alison. "Structuring Feeling: Web 2.0, Online Ranking and Rating, and the Digital 'Reputation' Economy." *Ephemera. Theory and Politics in Organization* 10, nos. 3/4 (2010): 421–438.

Hegel, Georg Wilhelm Friedrich. *Elements of the Philosophy of Right*. Vol. 7. 1820. Translated by H. B. Nisbet. Cambridge: Cambridge University Press, 1991.

Heidegger, Martin. "The Question Concerning Technology." In *Basic Writings*. Edited by David Farrell Krell. Harper and Row, 1977, 307–242.

Heilmann, Ann, "Mona Caird (1854–1932): "Wild Woman, New Woman, and Early Radical Feminist Critic of Marriage and Motherhood." *Women's History Review* 5, no. 1 (1996): 67–95.

Hennessy, Rosemary. *Profit and Pleasure: Sexual Identities in Late Capitalism*, Abingdon-on-Thames: Routledge, 2000.

Herold, Edward S., and Dawn-Marie K. Mewhinney. "Gender Differences in Casual Sex and AIDS Preventio: A Survey of Dating Bars." *Journal of Sex Research* 30, no. 1 (1993): 36–42.

Herzog, Dagmar. *Sex after Fascism: Memory and Morality in Twentieth-Century Germany.* Princeton, NJ: Princeton University Press, 2005.

———. *Sexuality in Europe: A Twentieth-Century History.* Cambridge: Cambridge University Press, 2011.

———. "What Incredible Yearnings Human Beings Have." In *Contemporary European History* 22, no. 2 (2013): 303–317.

Hill, Matt, Leon Mann, and Alexander J. Wearing. "The Effects of Attitude, Subjective Norm and Self-Efficacy on Intention to Benchmark: A Comparison between Managers with Experience and No Experience in Benchmarking." *Journal of Organizational Behavior* 17, no. 4 (1996): 313–327.

Hillenkamp, Sven. *Das Ende der Liebe: Gefühle im Zeitalter unendlicher Freiheit.* Stuttgart: Klett-Cotta, 2009.

Hine, Darlene Clark, and Earnestine L. Jenkins, eds. *A Question of Manhood: A Reader in U.S. Black Men's History and Masculinity.* Volume 2: *The 19th Century: From Emancipation to Jim Crow.* Bloomington: Indiana University Press, 2001.

Hirschman, Albert O. *Exit, Voice and Loyalty: Responses to Decline in Firms, Organizations and States.* Cambridge: Harvard University Press, 1970.

Hirst, Julia. "Developing Sexual Competence? Exploring Strategies for the Provision of Effective Sexualities and Relationships Education." *Sex Education* 8, no. 4 (2008): 399–413.

Hochschild, Arlie Russell. *The Commercialization of Intimate Life: Notes from Home and Work.* Berkeley: University of California Press, 2003.

———. *The Managed Heart: Commercialization of Human Feeling.* 1983. Reprint, Berkeley: University of California Press, 2012.

———, with Anne Machung. *The Second Shift: Working Families and the Revolution at Home.* 1989. Reprint, New York: Penguin Books, 2015.

Hoffnung, Michele. "Wanting It All: Career, Marriage, and Motherhood during College-Educated Women's 20s." *Sex Roles* 50, nos. 9/10 (2004): 711–723.

Hogg, Margaret K., and Paul C. N. Michell. "Identity, Self and Consumption: A Conceptual Framework." *Journal of Marketing Management* 12, no. 7 (1996): 629–644.

Holden, Karen C., and Pamela J. Smock. "The Economic Costs of Marital Dissolution: Why Do Women Bear a Disproportionate Cost?" *Annual Review of Sociology* 17, no. 1 (1991): 51–78.

Holland, Samantha, and Feona Attwoo. "Keeping Fit in Six Inch Heels: The Mainstreaming of Pole Dancing." In *Mainstreaming Sex: The Sexualization of Western Culture.* Edited by Feona Attwood. London: IB Tauris, 2009, 165–181.

Holmes, Mary. "The Emotionalization of Reflexivity." In *Sociology* 44, no. 1 (2010): 139–154.

Honneth, Axel. "Arbeit und Anerkennung: Versuch einer Neubestimmung." *Deutsche Zeitschrift für Philosophie* 56, no. 3 (2008): 327–341.

———. "Invisibility: On the Epistemology of 'Recognition.'" In *Supplements of the Aristotelian Society* 75, no. 1 (2001): 111–126.

———. *The Struggle for Recognition: The Moral Grammer of Social Conflicts.* Translated by Joel Anderson. Cambridge: Polity Press, 1995.

———. *Suffering from Indeterminacy: An Attempt at a Reactualization of Hegel's Philosophy of Right.* Assen: Van Gorcum, 2000.

——. "Organisierte Selbstverwirklichung: Paradoxien der Individualisierung." In *Befreiung aus der Mündigkeit: Paradoxien des gegenwärtigen Kapitalismus*, ed. Honneth. Frankfurt: Campus Verglag, 2002, 141–158.

——. *Freedom's Right: The Social Foundations of Democratic Life.* Translated by Joseph Ganahl. New York: Columbia University Press, 2014.

——. *Unsichtbarkeit: Stationen einer Theorie der Intersubjektivität.* Frankfurt: Suhrkamp Verlag, 2003.

——. *Verdinglichung: Eine anerkennungstheoretische Studie.* Frankfurt: Suhrkamp Verlag, 2005.

Horkheimer, Max, and Theodor W. Adorno. *Dialectic of Enlightenment: Philosophical Fragments.* Translated by Edmund Jephcott. Stanford: Stanford University Press, 2007.

Hoskyns, Catherine, and Shirin M. Rai. "Recasting the Global Political Economy: Counting Women's Unpaid Work," *New Political Economy* 12, no. 3 (2007): 297–317.

Howe, M. A. DeWolfe. "An Academic Courtship: Letters of Alice Freeman Palmer and George Herbert Palmer." *The New England Quarterly* 14, no. 1 (1941): 153–155.

Hsee, Christopher K., and Jiao Zhang. "Distinction Bias: Misprediction and Mischoice Due to Joint Evaluation." *Journal of Personality and Social Psychology* 86, no. 5 (2004): 680–695.

Hughes, Jason. "Emotional Intelligence: Elias, Foucault, and the Reflexive Emotional Self." *Foucault Studies* no. 8 (February 2010): 28–52.

Hunt, Alan. "The Civilizing Process and Emotional Life: The Intensification and Hollowing Out of Contemporary Emotions." In *Emotions Matter: A Relational Approach to Emotions.* Edited by Dale Spencer, Kevin Walby, and Alan Hunt. Toronto: University of Toronto Press, 2012, 137–160.

Ibarra, Herminia, Nancy M. Carter, and Christine Silva. "Why Men Still Get More Promotions Than Women." *Harvard Business Review* 88, no. 9 (2010): 80–85.

Illouz, Eva. "Emotions, Imagination and Consumption: A New Research Agenda." *Journal of Consumer Culture* 9, no. 3 (2009): 377–413.

——. *Saving the Modern Soul: Therapy, Emotions, and the Culture of Self-Help.* Berkeley: University of California Press, 2008.

——. *Cold Intimacies: The Making of Emotional Capitalism.* Cambridge: Polity Press, 2007

——. *Consuming the Romantic Utopia: Love and the Cultural Contradictions of Capitalism.* Berkeley: University of California Press, 1997.

——, ed. *Emotions as Commodities: Capitalism, Consumption and Authenticity.* New York: Routledge, 2018.

——. *Why Love Hurts: A Sociological Explanation.* Cambridge: Polity Press, 2012.

——, and Edgar Cabanas. *Happycratie: Comment l'industrie du bonheur a pris le contrôle de nos vies.* Paris: Premier Parallèle, 2018.

Inglehart, Ronald F. "Changing Values among Western Publics from 1970 to 2006." *West European Politics* 31, nos. 1/2 (2008): 130–146.

Irvine, Janice M. *Disorders of Desire: Sexuality and Gender in Modern American Sexology.* Philadelphia: Temple University Press, 2005.

Iyengar, Sheena S., and Mark R. Lepper. "When Choice Is Demotivating: Can One Desire Too Much of a Good Thing?" *Journal of Personality and Social Psychology* 79, no. 6 (2000): 995–1006.

Jacob, Pierre, and Marc Jeannerod. *Ways of Seeing: The Scope and Limits of Visual Cognition.* Oxford: Oxford University Press, 2003.

Jacques, Heather A. K., and H. Lorraine Radtke. "Constrained by Choice: Young Women Negotiate the Discourses of Marriage and Motherhood." In *Feminism and Psychology* 22, no. 4 (2012): 443–461.

Jardine, James. "Stein and Honneth on Empathy and Emotional Recognition." *Human Studies* 38, no. 4 (2015): 567–589.

Johnson, Allan G. *The Gender Knot: Unraveling Our Patriarchal Legacy.* Philadelphia: Temple University Press, 2005.

Jonas, Hans. "Toward a Philosophy of Technology." *Hastings Center Report* 9, no. 1 (1979): 34–43.

Jong, Erica. *Angst vorm Fliegen.* Translated by Kai Molvig. 1973. Reprint, Berlin 2014.

Kahneman, Daniel. *Attention and Effort.* Englewood Cliffs, NJ: Prentice Hall, 1973.

——. *Thinking, Fast and Slow.* New York: Farrar, Straus and Giroux, 2011.

Kalmijn, Matthijs, and Anne-Rigt Poortman. "His or Her Divorce? The Gendered Nature of Divorce and Its Determinants." In *European Sociological Review* 22, no. 2 (2006): 201–214.

Kamkhenthang, Hauzel. *The Paite: A Transborder Tribe of India and Burma.* New Delhi: Mittal Publications, 1988.

Kant, Immanuel. *Kants gesammelte Schriften.* Akademie-Ausgabe 27. *Vorlesungen über Moralphilosophie.* First half published Berlin: De Gruyter, 1974.

Kaplan, Dana. "Recreational Sexuality, Food, and New Age Spirituality: A Cultural Sociology of Middle-Class Distinctions." PhD dissertation, Hebrew University, 2014.

——. "Sexual Liberation and the Creative Class in Israel." In *Introducing the New Sexuality Studies*, 3rd ed. Edited by Steven Seidman, Nancy Fisher, and Chet Meeks. London: Routledge, 2016.

Karp, Marcelle, and Debbie Stoller, eds. *The BUST Guide to the New Girl Order.* New York, Penguin Books, 1999.

Kaufman, Carol E., and Stavros E. Stavrou. " 'Bus Fare Please': The Economics of Sex and Gifts among Young People in Urban South Africa." *Culture, Health and Sexuality* 6, no. 5 (2004): 377–391.

Kaufmann, Jean-Claude, *Gripes: The Little Quarrels of Couples.* Translated by Helen Morrison. Cambridge: Polity Press, 2009.

Kirchner, Holle, and Simon J. Thorpe. "Ultra-Rapid Object Detection with Saccadic Eye Movements: Visual Processing Speed Revisited." *Vision Research* 46, no. 11 (2006): 1762–1776.

Kleiman, Tali, and Ran R. Hassin. "Non-Conscious Goal Conflicts." *Journal of Experimental Social Psychology* 47, no. 3 (2011): 521–532.

Knight, Frank H. *Risk, Uncertainty and Profit.* 1921. Reprint, North Chelmsford Courier Corporation, 2012.

Knorr Cetina, Karin. "What Is a Financial Market? Global Markets as Microinstitutional and Post-Traditional Social Forms." In *The Oxford Handbook of the Sociology of Finance.* Edited by Karin Knorr Cetina and Alex Preda. Oxford: Oxford University Press, 2012, 115–133.

Kojève, Alexandre. *Introduction to the Reading of Hegel: Lectures on the Phenomenology of Spirit.* Translated by James H. Nichols, Jr. 1947. New York: Basic Books, 1969.

Kposowa, Augustine J. "Marital Status and Suicide in the National Longitudinal Mortality Study." *Journal of Epidemiology and Community Health* 54, no. 4 (2000): 254–261.

Krastev, Ivan. "Majoritarian Futures" In *The Great Regression.* Edited by Heinrich Geiselberger. Cambridge: Polity Press, 2017. 117–134.

——. *After Europe*. Philadelphia: University of Pennsylvania Press, 2017.

Lacan, Jacques. "The Subversion of the Subject and the Dialectic of Desire in the Freudian Unconscious." In *Écrits: A Selection*. London: W. W. Norton and Company, 2002, 281–312.

Lacey, Nicola. "Feminist Legal Theories and the Rights of Women." In *Gender and Human Rights: Collected Courses of the Academy of European Law (XII/2)*. Edited by Karen Knop. Oxford: Oxford University Press, 2004, 13–56.

Lakoff, George, and Mark Johnson. *Philosophy in the Flesh: The Embodied Mind and Its Challenge to Western Thought*. New York: Basic Books, 1999.

Lam, James. *Enterprise Risk Management: From Incentives to Controls*. Hoboken, NJ: Wiley, 2014.

Lamaison, Pierre, "From Rules to Strategies: An Interview with Pierre Bourdieu." *Cultural Anthropology* 1, no. 1 (1986): 110–120.

Lamont, Michèle. "Toward a Comparative Sociology of Valuation and Evaluation." *Annual Review of Sociology* 38 (2012).

Landes, Joan B. "The Public and the Private Sphere: A Feminist Reconsideration." In *Feminists Read Habermas: Gendering the Subject of Discourse*. Edited by Johanna Meehan. Abingdon-on-Thames: Routledge, 2013, 107–132.

Laumann, Edward O., John H. Gagnon, Robert T. Michael, and Stuart Michaels. *The Social Organization of Sexuality: Sexual Practices in the United States*. Chicago: University of Chicago Press, 1994.

——, Anthony Paik, and Raymond C. Rosen. "Sexual Dysfunction in the United States: Prevalence and Predictors." *JAMA* 281, no. 6 (1999): 537–544.

Lears, T. J. Jackson. *No Place of Grace: Antimodernism and the Transformation of American Culture, 1880–1920*. Chicago: University of Chicago Press, 1981.

Lee, Murray, Thomas Crofts, Alyce McGovern, and Sanja Milivojevic. *Sexting and Young People*. Report to the Criminology Research Advisory Council. November 2015. http://www.criminologyresearchcouncil.gov.au/reports/1516/53-1112-FinalReport.pdf.

Leigh, Barbara Critchlow. "Reasons for Having and Avoiding Sex: Gender, Sexual Orientation, and Relationship to Sexual Behavior." In *Journal of Sex Research* 26, no. 2 (1989): 199–209.

Levy, Ariel. *Female Chauvinist Pigs: Women and the Rise of Raunch Culture*. New York: Free Press, 2005.

Loughlin, Marie H. *Hymeneutics: Interpreting Virginity on the Early Modern Stage*. Lewisburg, PA: Bucknell University Press, 1997.

Loughnan, Steve, and Maria Giuseppina Pacill., "Seeing (and Treating) Others as Sexual Objects: Toward a More Complete Mapping of Sexual Objectification." *TPM: Testing, Psychometrics, Methodology in Applied Psychology* 21, no. 3 (2014): 309–325.

Lowenstein, Ludwig F. "Causes and Associated Features of Divorce as Seen by Recent Research." *Journal of Divorce and Remarriage* 42, nos. 3/4 (2005): 153–171.

Luhmann, Niklas. *Die Gesellschaft der Gesellschaft*. Frankfurt: Suhrkamp Verlag, 1997.

——. *Love: A Sketch*. Translated by Kathleen Cross. Cambridge: Polity Press, 2010.

——. *Love as Passion: The Codification of Intimacy*. Translated by Jeremy Gaines. Cambridge: Harvard University Press, 1987.

——. *Macht*. 1975. Konstanz, Munich: UVK, 2012.

——. *Soziale Systeme: Grundriß einer allgemeinen Theorie*. Frankfurt: Suhrkamp Verlag, 1984.

——. *Vertrauen: Ein Mechanismus der Reduktion sozialer Komplexität.* 1968. Konstanz, München: UVK, 2014.

Lystra, Karen. *Searching the Heart: Women, Men, and Romantic Love in Nineteenth-Century America.* New York: Oxford University Press, 1989.

MacKinnon, Catharine A. *Butterfly Politics.* Cambridge: Harvard Univesity Press, 2017.

——. *Feminism Unmodified: Discourses on Life and Law.* Cambridge: Harvard University Press, 1987.

——. *Only Words.* Cambridge: Harvard University Press, 1993.

Mahmood, Saba. *Politics of Piety: The Islamic Revival and the Feminist Subject* Princeton, NJ: Princeton University Press, 2011.

Mancini, Jay A., and Dennis K. Orthner. "Recreational Sexuality Preferences among Middle-Class Husbands and Wives." *Journal of Sex Research* 14, no. 2 (1978): 96–106.

Mann, William E., "Augustine on Evil and Original Sin." In *The Cambridge Companion to Augustine.* Edited by Eleonore Stump and Norman Kretzmann. Cambridge: Cambridge University Press, 2001, 40–48.

Manning, Wendy D., Jessica A. Cohen, and Pamela J. Smock. "The Role of Romantic Partners, Family, and Peer Networks in Dating Couples' Views about Cohabitation." *Journal of Adolescent Research* 26, no. 1 (2011): 115–149.

Mansfield, Penny, and Jean Collard. *The Beginning of the Rest of Your Life?* London: Macmillan, 1988.

Margalit, Avishai. *On Betrayal.* Cambridge: Harvard University Press, 2017.

——. *The Decent Society.* Translated by Naomi Goldblum. 1996. Reprint, Cambridge: Harvard University Press, 1998.

Marshall, Douglas A. "Behavior, Belonging and Belief: A Theory of Ritual Practice." *Sociological Theory* 20, no. 3 (2002): 360–380.

Martin, John Levi. "Structuring the Sexual Revolution." *Theory and Society* 25, no. 1 (1996): 105–151.

Martineau-Arbes, Agnès, Magali Giné, Prisca Grosdemouge, and Rémi Bernad. "Le Syndrome d'épuisement, une maladie professionnelle." May 2014. http://www.techno-logia.fr/blog/wp-content/uploads/2014/04/BurnOutVersiondef.pdf..

Martinez-Prather, Kathy, and Donna M. Vandiver, "Sexting among Teenagers in the United States: A Retrospective Analysis of Identifying Motivating Factors, Potential Targets, and the Role of a Capable Guardian." *International Journal of Cyber Criminology* 8, no. 1 (2014): 21–35.

Marx, Karl. *Capital: A Critique of Political Economy,* Vol. 1, 1976.] Reprint: New York: Penguin Classics, 1990.

——. *Capital: A Critique of Political Economy* Vol. 3, 1981. Reprint: New York; Penguin Classics, 1991.

——. *Grundrisse der Kritik der politischen Ökonomie.* Frankfurt: Europäische Verlags-Anstalt. 1967. http://catalog.hathitrust.org/api/volumes/oclc/6570978.html.

——. *Economic and Philosophic Manuscripts of 1844.* Third manuscript, "Money." Translated by Martin Milligan. Floyd, VA: Wilder Publications, 2014.

——. "Rede über die Frage des Freihandels." ["On the Question of Free Trade"] MEW 4. 1848. Reprint, Berlin: Dietz Verlag, 1990, 444–458.

——, and Friedrich Engels. "The German Ideology." In *Collected Works of Karl Marx and Friedrich Engels,* 1845–1847: Volume 05. 1932. Reprint, London: Lawrence and Wishart, 1976, 9–530.

——, and Friedrich Engels. "Manifest der Kommunistischen Partei." ["The Manifesto of the Communist Party"] MEW 4. 1848. Reprint, Berlin: Dietz Verlag: 1990, 459–493.

Maticka-Tyndale, Eleanor, Edward S. Herold, and Dawn Mewhinney. "Casual Sex on Spring Break: Intentions and Behaviors of Canadian Students." In *Journal of Sex Research* 35, no. 3 (1998): 254–264.

Mauss, Marcel. *The Gift: Forms and Functions of Exchange in Archaic Societies.* Translated by W. D. Halls. London: Routledge, 1990.

Mayer, Roger C., James H. Davis, and F. David Schoorman. "An Integrative Model of Organizational Trust." *The Academy of Management Review* 20, no. 3 (1995): 709–734.

Mccafferty, Patricia. "Forging a 'Neoliberal Pedagogy': The 'Enterprising Education' Agenda in Schools." *Critical Social Policy* 30, no. 4 (2010): 541–563.

McCormick, Naomi B. *Sexual Salvation: Affirming Women's Sexual Rights and Pleasures.* Westport: Greenwood Publishing Group, 1994.

McGee, Micki. *Self-Help, Inc.: Makeover Culture in American Life.* New York: Oxford University Press, 2005.

McNair, Brian. *Striptease Culture: Sex, Media and the Democratization of Desire.* London: Psychology Press, 2002.

McQuillan, Julia, Arthur L. Greil, Karina M. Shreffler, and Veronica Tichenor. "The Importance of Motherhood among Women in the Contemporary United States." *Gender and* Society 22, no. 4 (2008): 477–496.

McRobbie, Angela. *The Aftermath of Feminism: Gender, Culture and Social Change.* London: SAGE Publications, 2009.

——. "Notes on the Perfect: Competitive Femininity in Neoliberal Times." *Australian Feminist Studies* 30, no. 83 (2015): 3–20.

——. "Top Girls? Young Women and the Post-Feminist Sexual Contract." *Cultural Studies* 21, nos. 4/5 (2007): 718–737.

Mead, George H. "Cooley's Contribution to American Social Thought." *American Sociological Review* 35, no. 5 (1930): 693–706.

——. *Geist, Identität und Gesellschaft aus der Sicht des Sozialbehaviorismus.* Translated by Ulf Pacher. 1934. Reprint, Frankfurt, 1988.

Mears, Ashley. *Pricing Beauty: The Making of a Fashion Model.* Berkeley: University of California Press, 2011.

Mendelsohn, Daniel. *The Elusive Embrace: Desire and the Riddle of Identity.* New York: Vintage, 1999.

Meston, Cindy M., and David M. Buss. "Why Humans Have Sex." *Archives of Sexual Behavior* 36, no. 4 (2007): 477–507.

Meyer, Madonna Harrington, ed. *Care Work: Gender, Labor, and the Welfare State.* London: Routledge, 2002.

Millett, Kate. *Sexual Politics.* 1969. Reprint, New York: Columbia University Press, 2016.

Milhaven, John Giles. "Thomas Aquinas on Sexual Pleasure." *The Journal of Religious Ethics* 5, no. 2 (1977): 157–181.

Mintz, Steven, and Susan Kellogg. *Domestic Revolutions: A Social History of American Family Life.* New York: Simon and Schuster, 1989.

Mirzoeff, Nicholas. *An Introduction to Visual Culture.* London: Psychology Press, 1999.

Mitchell, Stephen A., *Relational Concepts in Psychoanalysis: An Integration.* Cambridge: Harvard University Press, 1988.

Mooney, Annabelle. "Boys Will Be Boys: Men's Magazines and the Normalisation of Pornography." *Feminist Media Studies* 8, no. 3 (2008): 247–265.

Moradi, Bonnie, and Yu-Ping Huang. "Objectification Theory and Psychology of Women: A Decade of Advances and Future Directions." *Psychology of Women Quarterly* 32, no. 4 (2008): 377–398.

Morris, Kasey Lynn, and Jamie Goldenberg. "Women, Objects, and Animals: Differentiating between Sex- and Beauty-Based Objectification." *Revue Internationale de Psychologie Sociale* 28, no. 1 (2015): 15–38.

Morrow, Ross. "The Sexological Construction of Sexual Dysfunction." *The Australian and New Zealand Journal of Sociology* 30, no. 1 (1994): 20–35.

Mottier, Véronique. *Sexuality: A Very Short Introduction.* New York: Oxford University Press, 2008.

Motz, Marilyn Ferris. "'Thou Art My Last Love': The Courtship and Remarriage of a Rural Texas Couple in 1892." *The Southwestern Historical Quarterly* 93, no. 4 (1990): 457–474.

Mulholland, Monique. "When Porno Meets Hetero: SEXPO, Heteronormativity and the Pornification of the Mainstream." *Australian Feminist Studies* 26, no. 67 (2011): 119–135.

———. *Young People and Pornography: Negotiating Pornification.* New York: Springer, 2013.

Mumby, Dennis K. "Organizing Men: Power, Discourse, and the Social Construction of Masculinity(s) in the Workplace." *Communication Theory* 8, no. 2 (1998): 164–183.

Murnen, Sarah K., and Linda Smolak. "Are Feminist Women Protected from Body Image Problems? A Meta-analytic Review of Relevant Research." *Sex Roles* 60, nos. 3/4 (2009): 186–197.

Murray, Sandra L., John G. Holmes, and Dale W. Griffin. "The Self-Fulfilling Nature of Positive Illusions in Romantic Relationships: Love Is Not Blind, but Prescient." *Journal of Personality and Social Psychology* 71, no. 6 (1996): 1155–1180.

Nelson, Eric S. "Against Liberty: Adorno, Levinas and the Pathologies of Freedom." *Theoria* 59, no. 131 (2012): 64–83.

Nelson, Robert K. "'The Forgetfulness of Sex': Devotion and Desire in the Courtship Letters of Angelina Grimke and Theodore Dwight Weld." In *Journal of Social History* 37, no. 3 (2004): 663–679.

Nussbaum, Martha C. "Objectification." In *Sex and Social Justice.* New York: Oxford University Press, 1999. 213-239.

Oksala, Johanna. *Foucault on Freedom.* Cambridge: Cambridge University Press, 2005.

Oliver, Mary Beth, and Janet Shibley Hyde. "Gender Differences in Sexuality: A Meta-Analysis." *Psychological Bulletin* 114, no. 1 (1993): 29–51.

O'Neill, Rachel. *Seduction: Men, Masculinity, and Mediated Intimacy.* Cambridge: Polity Press, 2018.

———. "The Work of Seduction: Intimacy and Subjectivity in the London 'Seduction Community.'" *Sociological Research Online* 20, no. 4 (2015): 1–14.

Orloff, Ann Shola. "Gender and the Social Rights of Citizenship: The Comparative Analysis of Gender Relations and Welfare States." *American Sociological Review* 58, no. 3 (1993): 303–328.

Ostrom, Elinor. "A Behavioral Approach to the Rational Choice Theory of Collective Action: Presidential Address, American Political Science Association, 1997." *American Political Science Review* 92, no. 1 (1998): 1–22.

——, and James Walker, eds. *Trust and Reciprocity: Interdisciplinary Lessons for Experimental Research*. New York: Russel Sage Foundation, 2003.

Paglia, Camille. *Sex, Art, and American Culture: Essays*. New York: Vintage Books, 1990.

Palley, Thomas I. "From Keynesianism to Neoliberalism: Shifting Paradigms in Economics." In *Neoliberalism: A Critical Reader*. Edited by Alfredo Saad-Filho and Deborah Johnston. Chicago: University of Chicago Press, 2005, 20–29.

Passet, Joanne E. *Sex Radicals and the Quest for Women's Equality*. Urbana and Chicago: University of Illinois Press, 2003.

Pateman, Carole. *The Sexual Contract*. Stanford: Stanford University Press, 1988.

—— "What's Wrong with Prostitution?" *Women's Studies Quarterly* 27, nos. 1/2 (1999): 53–64.

Paul, Elizabeth L., and Kristen A. Hayes. "The Casualties of 'Casual' Sex: A Qualitative Exploration of the Phenomenology of College Students' Hookups." *Journal of Social and Personal Relationships* 19, no. 5 (2002): 639–661.

——, Brian McManus, and Allison Hayes. "'Hookups': Characteristics and Correlates of College Students' Spontaneous and Anonymous Sexual Experiences." *Journal of Sex Research* 37, no. 1 (2000): 76–88.

Payne, Keith. "Conscious or What? Relationship between Implicit Bias and Conscious Experiences (25 August 2015). Conference Lecture, *(Un)Consciousness: A Functional Perspective* (25.-27.8. 2015). Israel Institute for Advanced Studies. Hebrew University Jerusalem.

Peiss, Kathy. *Hope in a Jar: The Making of America's Beauty Culture*. Philadelphia: University of Pennsylvania Press, 2011.

Peplau, Letitia Anne. "Human Sexuality: How Do Men and Women Differ?" *Current Directions in Psychological Science* 12, no. 2 (2003): 37–40.

Petersen, Jennifer L., and Janet Shibley Hyde. "A Meta-Analytic Review of Research on Gender Differences in Sexuality, 1993–2007." *Psychological Bulletin* 136, no. 1 (2010): 21–38.

Phillips, Adam. *Monogamy*. New York: Vintage Books, 1996.

Phillips, Kim M., and Barry Reay. *Sex before Sexuality: A Premodern History*. Cambridge: Polity Press, 2011.

Pinkard, Terry. *Hegel's Phenomenology: The Sociality of Reason*. Cambridge: Cambridge University Press, 1996.

Piper, Mark. "Achieving Autonomy." *Social Theory and Practice* 42, no. 4 (2016): 767–779.

Pippin, Robert B. *Hegel on Self-Consciousness: Desire and Death in the* Phenomenology of Spirit. Princeton, NJ: Princeton University Press, 2011.

Polanyi, Karl. *The Great Transformation: The Political and Economic Origins of Our Time*. 1944. Reprint, Boston, Beacon Press, 2014.

Porqueres i Gené, Enric, and Jérôme Wilgaux. "Incest, Embodiment, Genes and Kinship." In *European Kinship in the Age of Biotechnology*. Edited by Jeanette Edwards and Carles Salazar, 112–127. New York, Oxford: Berghahn, 2009.

Posner, Richard A. *Sex and Reason*. Cambridge: Harvard University Press, 1992.

Pound, Roscoe "The Role of the Will in Law." *Harvard Law Review* 68, no. 1 (1954): 1–19.

Previti, Denise, and Paul R. Amato. "Is Infidelity a Cause or a Consequence of Poor Marital Quality?" *Journal of Social and Personal Relationships* 21, no. 2 (2004): 217–223.

Price, Janet, and Margrit Shildrick, eds. *Feminist Theory and the Body: A Reader* Abingdon-on-Thames: Routledge, 2017.

Procaccia, Uriel. *Russian Culture, Property Rights, and the Market Economy*. Cambridge: Cambridge University Press, 2007.

Pugh, Alison J. *The Tumbleweed Society: Working and Caring in an Age of Insecurity*. New York: Oxford University Press, 2015.

Putnam, Hilary. *The Threefold Cord: Mind, Body and World*. New York: Columbia University Press, 2000.

Putnam, Robert D. *Bowling Alone: The Collapse and Revival of American Community*. New York: Simon and Schuster, 2001.

Rabin, Matthew. "Psychology and Economics." *Journal of Economic Literature* 36, no. 1 (1998): 11–46.

Reay, Barry. "Promiscuous Intimacies: Rethinking the History of American Casual Sex." *Journal of Historical Sociology* 27, no. 1 (2014): 1–24.

Regnerus, Mark. *Cheap Sex: The Transformation of Men, Marriage, and Monogamy*. New York: Oxford University Press, 2017.

Reynolds, Philip Lyndon. *Marriage in the Western Church: The Christianization of Marriage during the Patristic and Early Medieval Periods*. Leiden: Brill, 1994.

Richardson, Diane. "Constructing Sexual Citizenship: Theorizing Sexual Rights." *Critical Social Policy* 20, no. 1 (2000): 105–135.

Ridgeway, Cecilia L. *Framed by Gender: How Gender Inequality Persists in the Modern World*. New York: Oxford University Press, 2011.

Ringrose, Jessica, Laura Harvey, Rosalind Gill, and Sonia Livingstone. "Teen Girls, Sexual Double Standards and Sexting." *Feminist Theory* 14, no. 3 (2013): 305–323.

Ritts, Vicki, Miles L. Patterson, and Mark E. Tubbs. "Expectations, Impressions, and Judgments of Physically Attractive Students: A Review." *Review of Educational Research* 62, no. 4 (1992): 413–426.

Robbins, Joel. "Ritual Communication and Linguistic Ideology: A Reading and Partial Reformulation of Rappaports Theory of Ritual." *Current Anthropology* 42, no. 5 (2001): 591–614.

Robinson, Fiona. "Beyond Labour Rights: The Ethics of Care and Women's Work in the Global Economy." *International Feminist Journal of Politics* 8, no. 3 (2006): 321–342.

Rose, Nikolas. *Inventing Our Selves: Psychology, Power, and Personhood*. Cambridge: Cambridge University Press, 1998.

——. *Powers of Freedom: Reframing Political Thought*. Cambridge: Cambridge University Press, 1999.

Rosenfeld, Michael J. "Who Wants the Breakup? Gender and Breakup in Heterosexual Couples." In *Social Networks and the Life Course: Integrating the Development of Human Lives and Social Relational Networks*. Edited by Duane F. Alwin, Diane H. Felmlee, and Derek A. Kreager, 221–243. Cham: Springer, 2018.

Rothman, Ellen K. *Hands and Hearts: A History of Courtship in America*. New York: Basic Books, 1984.

Rousseau, Denise M., Sim B. Sitkin, Ronald S. Burt, and Colin Camerer. "Not So Different after All: A Cross-Discipline View of Trust." *The Academy of Management Review* 23, no. 3 (1998): 393–404.

Rubin, Gayle S. *Deviations: A Gayle Rubin Reader*. Durham, NC: Duke University Press, 2011.

Ruggles, Steven. "The Rise of Divorce and Separation in the United States, 1880–1990." *Demograph* 34, no. 4 (1997): 455–466.

Rupp, Heather A., and Kim Wallen. "Sex Differences in Response to Visual Sexual Stimuli: A Review." *Archives of Sexual Behavior* 37, no. 2 (2008): 206–218.

Rusciano, Frank Louis. " 'Surfing Alone': The Relationships among Internet Communities, Public Opinion, Anomie, and Civic Participation." *Studies in Sociology of Science* 5, no. 3 (2014): 1–8.

Sahlins, Marshall. *What Kinship Is—and Is Not*. Chicago: University of Chicago Press, 2013.

Salecl, Renata. *The Tyranny of Choice*. London: Profile Books, 2010.

——. "Self in Times of Tyranny of Choice." *FKW//Zeitschrift für Geschlechterforschung und visuelle Kultur*, no. 50 (2010): 10–23.

——. "Society of Choice." *differences* 20, no. 1 (2009): 157–180.

Sandel, Michael J. *What Money Can't Buy: The Moral Limits of Markets*. New York: Farrar, Straus and Giroux, 2012.

Santelli, John S., Nancy D. Brener, Richard Lowry, Amita Bhatt, and Laurie S. Zabin. "Multiple Sexual Partners among US Adolescents and Young Adults." *Family Planning Perspectives* 30, no. 6 (1998): 271–275.

Sayer, Liana C. "Gender, Time and Inequality: Trends in Women's and Men's Paid Work, Unpaid Work and Free Time." *Social Forces* 84, no. 1 (2005): 285–303.

Scheinkman, José A., with Kenneth J. Arrow, Patrick Bolton, Sanford J. Grossman, and Joseph E. Stiglitz. *Speculation, Trading, and Bubbles*. New York: Columbia University Press, 2014.

Schneewind, Jerome B. *The Invention of Autonomy: A History of Modern Moral Philosophy*. Cambridge: Cambridge University Press, 1998.

Schumann, Robert, Clara Schumann, and Gerd Nauhaus. *The Marriage Diaries of Robert and Clara Schumann: From Their Wedding Day to the Russia Trip*. Translated by Peter Oswald. London: Robson Books, 1993.

Schumpeter, Joseph A. *Capitalism, Socialism, and Democracy*. 1942. Reprint, New York: Harper Perennial, 2008.

Schwarz, Ori. "On Friendship, Boobs and the Logic of the Catalogue: Online Self-Portraits as a Means for the Exchange of Capital." *Convergence* 16, no. 2 (2010): 163–183.

Scott, Shelby B., Galena K. Rhoades, Scott M. Stanley, Elizabeth S. Allen, and Howard J. Markman. "Reasons for Divorce and Recollections of Premarital Intervention: Implications for Improving Relationship Education." *Couple and Family Psychology: Research and Practice* 2, no. 2 (2013): 131–145.

Segal, Lynne. *Straight Sex: Rethinking the Politics of Pleasure*. Berkeley: University of California Press, 1994.

Seeman, Melvin. "On the Meaning of Alienation." *American Sociological Review* 24, no. 6 (1959): 783–791.

Seidman, Steven. "From the Polluted Homosexual to the Normal Gay: Changing Patterns of Sexual Regulation in America." In *Thinking Straight: The Power, the Promise, and the Paradox of Heterosexuality*. Edited by Chrys Ingraham, 39–61. London: Psychology Press, 2005.

——. *Romantic Longings: Love in America, 1830–1980*. New York: Routledge, 1991.

Sennett, Richard. *The Culture of the New Capitalism*. New Haven: Yale University Press, 2006.

——. *The Fall of Public Man*. 1974. Reprint, New York: W.W. Norton and Company, 2017.

Sewell, William H., Jr., "Geertz, Cultural Systems, and History: From Synchrony to Transformation." In *The Fate of "Culture": Geertz and Beyond*. Edited by Sherry B. Ortner, 35–55. Berkeley: University of California Press, 1999.

Sherwin, Robert, and Sherry Corbett. "Campus Sexual Norms and Dating Relationships: A Trend Analysis." *Journal of Sex Research* 21, no. 3 (1985): 258–274.

Shrauger, J. Sidney, and Thomas J. Schoeneman. "Symbolic Interactionist View of Self-Concept: Through the Looking Glass Darkly." *Psychological Bulletin* 86, no. 3 (1979): 549–573.

Sigusch, Volkmar. "Lean Sexuality: On Cultural Transformations of Sexuality and Gender in Recent Decades." *Sexuality and Culture* 5, no. 2 (2001): 23–56.

Silber, Ilana F. "Bourdieu's Gift to Gift Theory: An Unacknowledged Trajectory." *Sociological Theory* 27, no. 2 (2009): 173–190.

Silva, Jennifer M. *Coming Up Short: Working Class Adulthood in an Age of Uncertainty*. Oxford: Oxford University Press, 2013.

Simmel, Georg. "Der Individualismus der modernen Zeit." *Postume Veröffentlichungen: Schulpädagogik*. Gesamtausgabe, vol. 20. Frankfurt: Suhrkamp Verlag, 2004, 249–258.

——. "Die Großstädte und das Geistesleben." In *Aufsätze und Abhandlungen 1901–1908*, volume 1. Gesamtausgabe, vol. 7. Frankfurt: Suhrkamp Verlag, 1995, S. 116–131.

——. "The Stranger." *The Sociology of Georg Simmel*. Translated by Kurt H. Wolff. New York: The Free Press, 1950, 402–408.

Simpson, Jeffry A. "The Dissolution of Romantic Relationships: Factors Involved in Relationship Stability and Emotional Distress." *Journal of Personality and Social Psychology* 53, no. 4 (1987): 683–692.

Singer, Irving. *The Nature of Love*. Vol. 3, *The Modern World*. Chicago: University of Chicago Press, 1989.

Sivulka, Juliann. *Soap, Sex, and Cigarettes: A Cultural History of American Advertising*. Boston: Cengage, 2011.

Skeggs. Beverley. *Formations of Class and Gender: Becoming Respectable*. London; SAGE Publications, 1997.

Slotter, Erica B., Wendi L. Gardner, and Eli J. Finkel. "Who Am I Without You? The Influence of Romantic Breakup on the Self-Concept." *Personality and Social Psychology Bulletin* 36, no. 2 (2010): 147–160.

Smith, Clarissa. "Pornographication: A Discourse for All Seasons." In *International Journal of Media and Cultural Politics* 6, no. 1 (2010): 103–108.

Smolak, Linda, and Sarah K. Murnen. "The Sexualization of Girls and Women as a Primary Antecedent of Self-Objectification." *Self-Objectification in Women: Causes, Consequences, and Counteractions*. Edited by Rachel M. Calogero, Stacey Tantleff-Dunn, and J. Kevin Thompson. Washington, DC: American Psychological Association, 2011, 53–75.

——, Sarah K. Murnen, and Taryn A. Myers. "Sexualizing the Self: What College Women and Men Think about and Do to Be 'Sexy'" In *Psychology of Women Quarterly* 38, no. 3 (2014): 379–397.

Solomon, Denise Haunani, and Leanne K. Knobloch. "Relationship Uncertainty, Partner Interference, and Intimacy within Dating Relationships." *Journal of Social and Personal Relationships* 18, no. 6 (2001): 804–820.

Stacey, Judith. *Brave New Families: Stories of Domestic Upheaval in Late-Twentieth-Century America*. Berkeley: University of California Press, 1990.

Stark, David. *The Sense of Dissonance: Accounts of Worth in Economic Life.* Princeton, NJ: Princeton University Press, 2011.

Steele, Valerie. *Fashion and Eroticism: Ideals of Feminine Beauty from the Victorian Era to the Jazz Age.* New York: Oxford University Press, 1985.

Stone, Lawrence D. *The Family, Sex and Marriage in England 1500–1800.* London: Penguin Books, 1982.

——. *Uncertain Unions: Marriage in England, 1660–1753.* Oxford: Oxford University Press, 1992.

Strasser, Ulrike. *State of Virginity: Gender, Religion, and Politics in an Early Modern Catholic State.* Ann Arbor: University of Michigan Press, 2004.

Streeck, Wolfgang. "Bürger als Kunden: Überlegungen zur neuen Politik des Konsums." In *Kapitalismus und Ungleichheit: Die neuen Verwerfungen.* Edited by Heinz Bude and Philipp Staab. Frankfurt: Campus Verlag, 2016, 261–284.

——. "How to Study Contemporary Capitalism?" *European Journal of Sociology/ Europäisches Archiv für Soziologie* 53, no. 1 (2012): 1–28.

Strelan, Peter, Sarah J. Mehaffey, and Marika Tiggemann. "Brief Report: Self-Objectification and Esteem in Young Women: The Mediating Role of Reasons for Exercise." *Sex Roles* 48, no. 1 (2003): 89–95.

Suchocki, Marjorie Hewitt. *The Fall to Violence: Original Sin in Relational Theology.* New York: Continuum, 1994.

Susman, Warren. *Culture as History: The Transformation of American Society in the 20th Century.* New York: Pantheon, 1984.

Swidler, Ann. "Culture in Action: Symbols and Strategies." *American Sociological Review* 51, no. 2 (1986): 273–286.

——. *Talk of Love: How Culture Matters.* Chicago: University of Chicago Press, 2001.

Szymanski, Dawn M., Lauren B. Moffitt, and Erika R. Carr. "Sexual Objectification of Women: Advances to Theory and Research 1ψ7." *The Counseling Psychologist* 39, no. 1 (2011): 6–38.

Tabet, Paola. *La Grande Arnaque: Sexualité des femmes et échange économico-sexuel.* Paris: L'Harmattan, 2004.

——. "Through the Looking-Glass: Sexual-Economic Exchange." In *Chic, chèque, choc: Transactions autour des corps et stratégies amoureuses contemporaines.* Edited by Françoise Grange Omokaro and Fenneke Reysoo. Genève: Graduate Institute Publications, 2016, 39–51.

Taylor, Charles. "Foucault über Freiheit und Wahrheit." In *Negative Freiheit? Zur Kritik des neuzeitlichen Individualismus.* Translated by Hermann Kocyba. Frankfurt: Suhrkamp Verlag, 1995, 188–234.

Taylor, Laramie D. "All for Him: Articles about Sex in American Lad Magazines." *Sex Roles* 52, no. 3 (2005): 153–163.

Thoburn, Nicholas. *Deleuze, Marx and Politics.* London, New York: Routledge, 2003.

Thompson, Linda, and Alexis J. Walker. "Gender in Families. Women and Men in Marriage, Work, and Parenthood," *Journal of Marriage and Family* 51, no. 4 (1989), 845–871.

Thorngate, Warren, "The Economy of Attention and the Development of Psychology," *Canadian Psychology/Psychologie Canadienne* 31, no. 3 (1990), 262–271.

Thornton, Sarah, *Club Cultures. Music, Media, and Subcultural Capital,* Cambridge 1995.

Thorpe, Simon, Denis Fize und Catherine Marlot, "Speed of Processing in the Human Visual System," *Nature* 381, no. 6582 (1996), 520–522.

Tice, Dianne M., "Self-Concept Change and Self-Presentation: The Looking Glass Self Is Also a Magnifying Glass." *Journal of Personality and Social Psychology* 63, no. 3 (1992): 435–451.

Tolman, Deborah L. *Dilemmas of Desire: Teenage Girls Talk about Sexuality*. Cambridge: Harvard University Press, 2002.

Tolstoy, Leo. *War and Peace*, Vol. 1. Translated by Louise and Aylmer Maude. 1896. Reprint, New York: Knopf, 1992.

Tomlinson, Alan, ed. *Consumption, Identity and Style: Marketing, Meanings, and the Packaging of Pleasure*. New York: Routledge, 2006.

Trollope, Anthony. *The Claverings*. 1867. Reprint, New York: Oxford University Press, 1998.

——. *An Old Man's Love*. 1884. Reprint, Oxford: Oxford University Press, 1951.

Turner, Bryan. "Social Capital, Inequality and Health: The Durkheimian Revival." *Social Theory and Health* 1, no. 1 (2003): 4–20.

Vanwesenbeeck, Ine. "The Risks and Rights of Sexualization: An Appreciative Commentary on Lerum and Dworkin's 'Bad Girls Rule.'" *Journal of Sex Research* 46, no. 4 (2009): 268–270.

Vogel, Lise. *Marxism and the Oppression of Women: Toward a Unitary Theory*. 1983. Reprint, Chicago: Haymarket Books, 2014.

Wade, Lisa. *American Hookup: The New Culture of Sex on Campus*. New York: W.W. Norton and Company, 2017.

Wagner, Michael, and Bernd Weiss. "On the Variation of Divorce Risks in Europe: Findings from a Meta-Analysis of European Longitudinal Studies." In *European Sociological Review* 22, no. 5 (2006): 483–500.

Wagner, Peter. "After Justification: Repertoires of Evaluation and the Sociology of Modernity." *European Journal of Social Theory* 2, no. 3 (1999): 341–357.

Waldman, Adelle. *Love Affairs of Nathaniel P.* New York: Picador, 2014.

Walsh, Anthony. "Self-Esteem and Sexual Behavior: Exploring Gender Differences." *Sex Roles* 25, no. 7 (1991): 441–450.

Waring, Marilyn, and Gloria Steinem. *If Women Counted: A New Feminist Economics*. San Francisco: Harper and Row, 1988.

Warren, Samuel D., and Louis D. Brandeis. "The Right to Privacy." *Harvard Law Review* 4, no. 5 (1890): 193–220.

Weaver, Angela D., Kelly L. MacKeigan, and Hugh A. MacDonald. "Experiences and Perceptions of Young Adults in Friends with Benefits Relationships: A Qualitative Study." *The Canadian Journal of Human Sexuality* 20, nos. 1/2 (2011): 41–53.

Weber, J. Mark, Deepak Malhotra, and J. Keith Murnighan. "Normal Acts of Irrational Trust: Motivated Attributions and the Trust Development Process." In *Research in Organizational Behavior* 26 (2004): 75–101.

Weber, Max. *Die Lage der Landarbeiter im ostelbischen Deutschland*. Gesamtausgabe vol. 1, no. 3, 2 Halbbde. 1892. Reprint, Tübingen, Mohr Siebeck, 1984.

——. *The Protestant Ethic and the Spirit of Capitalism: And Other Writings*. Translated by Peter Baehr and Gordon C. Wells. New York: Penguin Books, 2002.

——. *Die Wirtschaftsethik der Weltreligionen: Konfuzianismus und Taoismus. Regulations 1915-1920*. Gesamtausgabe, vol. 1, no. 19. Tübingen:Mohr Siebeck, 1991.

——. *Economy and Society*. Edited by Guenther Roth and Claus Wittich. Berkeley: University of California Press, 2013.

Weeks, Jeffrey. *Invented Moralities: Sexual Values in an Age of Uncertainty*. New York: Columbia University Press, 1995.

——. *Sexuality and Its Discontents: Meanings, Myths, and Modern Sexualities.* 1985. New York: Routledge, 2002.

Weiss, Yoram. "The Formation and Dissolution of Families: Why Marry? Who Marries Whom? And What Happens Upon Divorce." *Handbook of Population and Family Economics* 1A. Oxford: North Holland (1997): 81–123.

Welsh, Deborah P., Catherine M. Grello, and Melinda S. Harper. "When Love Hurts: Depression and Adolescent Romantic Relationships." In *Adolescent Romantic Relations and Sexual Behavior: Theory, Research, and Practical Implications.* Edited by Paul Florsheim, 185–212. Mahwah, NJ: Lawrence Erlbaum Associates, 2003.

Wendell, Susan. *The Rejected Body: Feminist Philosophical Reflections on Disability.* Abingdon-on-Thames: Routledge, 2013.

Wentland, Jocelyn J., and Elke Reissing. "Casual Sexual Relationships: Identifying Definitions for One Night Stands, Booty Calls, Fuck Buddies, and Friends with Benefits." *The Canadian Journal of Human Sexuality* 23, no. 3 (2014): 167–177.

Wertheimer, Alan. *Consent to Sexual Relations.* Cambridge: Cambridge University Press, 2010.

West, Robin. "The Harms of Consensual Sex." November 2011, 11. http://unityandstruggle. org/wp-content/uploads/2016/04/West_The-harms-of-consensual-sex.pdf.

——. "Sex, Reason, and a Taste for the Absurd." Georgetown Public Law and Legal Theory Research Paper No. 11–76. 1993. https://scholarship.law.georgetown.edu/cgi/viewcontent.cgi?referer=https://www.google.com/andhttpsredir=1andarticle=1658andcontext=facpub.

Whitehead, Barbara Dafoe, and David Popenoe. "Who Wants to Marry a Soul Mate?" In *The State of Our Unions: The Social Health of Marriage in America.* New Brunswick, NJ: Rutgers University, 2001, 6–16, https://www.stateofourunions.org/past_issues.php.

Williams, Robert R. *Hegel's Ethics of Recognition* Berkeley: University of California Press, 1997.

Wilson, Elizabeth. *Adorned in Dreams: Fashion and Modernity.* 1985. Reprint: London; New York : I.B. Tauris and Co. Ltd., 2016.

Winnicott, Donald W. "Transitional Objects and Transitional Phenomena." *Through Paediatrics to Psycho-Analysis: Collected Papers.* 1992. Reprint, Abingdon: Routledge, 2014. 229–242, 307.

Wolcott, Ilene, and Jody Hughes. "Towards Understanding the Reasons for Divorce." *Australian Institute of Family Studies.* Working Paper 20 (1999).

Wolf, Naomi. *The Beauty Myth: How Images of Beauty Are Used Against.* 1991. Reprint: New York, Harper Perennial, 2002.

Woltersdorff, Volker. "Paradoxes of Precarious Sexualities: Sexual Subcultures under Neo-Liberalism." *Cultural Studies* 25, no. 2 (2011): 164–182.

Worthen, John. *Robert Schumann: Life and Death of a Musician.* New Haven: Yale University Press, 2007.

Wyder, Marianne, Patrick Ward, and Diego De Leo. "Separation as a Suicide Risk Factor." *Journal of Affective Disorders* 116, no. 3 (2009): 208–213.

Zaner, Richard M. *The Context of Self: A Phenomenological Inquiry Using Medicine as a Clue.* Athens: Ohio University Press, 1981.

Zinn, Jens. "Uncertainty." Edited by George Ritzer. *Blackwell Encyclopedia of Sociology.* 2007. https://doi.org/10.1002/9781405165518.wbeosu001.

Zurn, Christopher F. *Axel Honneth: A Critical Theory of the Social.* Hoboken, NJ: Wiley, 2015.

Index